Challenging the State

CHALLENGING THE STATE

Churches as Political Actors

in South Africa,

1980–1994

Tristan Anne Borer

University of Notre Dame Press

Notre Dame, Indiana

The author and publisher are grateful to the following for
permission to publish:

Portions of chapter 1, reprinted from *Journal of Church and
State* 35 (Spring 1993): 299-334; used by permission.

Chapter 3, a version of which appeared in *Disruptive
Religion: The Force of Faith in Social Movement Activism* (1996),
edited by Christian Smith, used by permission of Routledge.

Library of Congress Cataloging-in-Publication Data

Borer, Tristan Anne, 1965–
Challenging the state : churches as political actors in South
Africa, 1980-1994 / Tristan Anne Borer.
p.   cm. — (A title from the Helen Kellogg Institute for
International Studies.)
Includes bibliographical references (p.   ) and index.
ISBN 0-268-00829-9 (pbk.)
1. Christianity and politics—South Africa—History—20th century.
2. South Africa—Church history—20th century.   3. South Africa—
Politics and government—1978-1989.   4. South Africa—Politics and
government—1989-1994.   I. Title.   II. Series.
BR1450.B67   1998
261.7'0968'09048—dc21   98-18608
                                                               CIP

For Peter Walshe,
mentor and friend

Contents

Acknowledgments

THIS BOOK WOULD not have been written without the support of many people, both in the United States and in South Africa. For their gifts of time, advice, commitment, and encouragement, I am honored to thank the following people.

This book owes the most—in terms of subject, theory, and style—to Peter Walshe, who was unfailing in his advice, time, and patience. Peter has inspired and challenged me in myriad ways, and I dedicate this book to him. I also thank Scott Mainwaring for his guidance and suggestions, not only on this project but throughout graduate school. For reading this manuscript and providing critical comments, I thank my colleagues W. John Coats Jr. and Marion Doro. Kurt Mills was extraordinarily patient in his computer assistance. Jackie Smith's support and encouragement made the countless triumphs and tribulations which accompany the writing of a book infinitely more bearable. Rebecca De-Boer at the University of Notre Dame Press provided insightful comments, and was a helpful and supportive editor. For keeping me grounded and reminding me to keep the academic world in perspective, I thank Matthew Holden Zimmer.

In the span of four years I undertook three separate trips to South Africa. At the risk of inadvertently overlooking some deserving individuals, I wish to acknowledge a deep and heartfelt gratitude to several people. I thank all who made room in their hectic schedules to answer my questions, offer advice and opinions, and sometimes to tell their own personal stories. A list of interviewees is provided in the bibliography. I thank all of them for their time, patience, and encouragement. In addition, a few people went above and beyond the call of professional duty, by giving me access to personal archives and by granting me numerous interviews. I especially want to thank Father Bernard Connor, O.P., and Wolfram Kistner for inviting me to their homes and allowing me to photocopy anything I wished from their personal papers. I would like to thank Father Albert Nolan, O.P., for being readily available for multiple interviews and conversations at the Institute for Contextual Theology. Ian Linden made time for conversational updates during each of three summers, and I appreciate his insights into the changing South African situation.

On a more personal level, I have made friendships in South Africa that will last a lifetime. Many people opened their homes to me, allowing me a glimpse into the lives of ordinary South Africans in their attempts to cope with the difficult political context of South Africa in the early 1990s. Their personal stories added a rich human dimension to the more theoretical work I was undertaking there. I especially need to thank the following people: for their love and support, and for being my South African family, I thank Jean and André Vermaerke; for giving me my first job in South Africa, and for introducing me to the religious community there, I thank Sister Natalie Kuhn, O.P.; for their deep and lasting friendships, and for sharing their personal stories of the struggle, I thank Andrew and Aline Johnson, Ismail Lagardien, and Johnny Pitswane; and for their generous hospitality, I thank Jenny and Pat McKenzie, and John and Jill Fresen.

At the University of Notre Dame, I acknowledge with thanks the Kellogg Institute for International Studies for giving me a Summer Seed Grant as well as a Dissertation Writing Grant. Also, I thank the University's Zahm Research Travel Fund for facilitating my field research by giving me a travel grant. Finally, I thank the Institute for the Study of World Politics in Washington, D.C., for its Dissertation Research Fellowship.

Some of the ideas in this book have been previously published elsewhere. Portions of what is now chapter 1 appeared as "Challenging the State: Churches as Political Actors in South Africa," *Journal of Church and State* 35 (Spring, 1993): 299–334. What is now substantially chapter 3 appeared originally as "Church Leadership, State Repression, and the 'Spiral of Involvement' in the South African Anti-Apartheid Movement, 1983–1990," in *Disruptive Religion: The Force of Faith in Social Movement Activism,* edited by Christian Smith (New York: Routledge, 1996), pp. 125–143. I thank the publishers for permission to use these articles.

My most personal thanks go to those closest to me during this entire process: my parents, Joan and Don Borer.

Preface

THREE BODIES OF literature are addressed in this book. The first is the literature on political movements for social change. That religious institutions, including churches and ecumenical organizations, often play a crucial role in political upheavals is well known. On reflection, most people would acknowledge that movements from the United States' black civil rights movement to the Polish Solidarity Movement had important religious elements to them. And yet, this "common sense" acceptance of the role of religion has frequently been ignored, or at least understudied, in academic accounts of political upheaval.[1] Specifically, what is lacking are studies that address concrete questions about exactly how religious organizations contribute to political movements for change, how these organizations are themselves changed in the process, and what the consequences of this interaction are. This book addresses these questions for one particular movement—the South African anti-apartheid movement—at one historic moment, in order to provide a broader understanding of the contribution of religion to social and political change. It analyzes how and why two religious organizations, the South African Council of Churches and the Southern African Catholic Bishops' Conference, initiated and intensified their commitment to directly challenge the apartheid regime, and the consequences of that change for both institutions.

The second body of literature consists of much recent work analyzing the specific reasons for the changing political context of 1980s South Africa. Two characteristics of the political situation set the 1980s apart from any preceding time in South African history. The first was the intensity of state repression, in the aftermath of the popular uprising against a reform program that was deemed inadequate and insincere. In its attempts to quell the rising protests, the South African police, and eventually the armed forces, employed a systematic campaign of repression that was unprecedented in its degree of violence and terror. The second distinguishing characteristic was the intensity of opposition to the government, both international and domestic, with the diffusion of protest throughout all aspects of everyday life. The explosion of grass-roots organizations laid the foundation for a nationwide liberation movement of tremendous strength. This process resulted in a spiral of violence which the regime was never quite able to contain, leaving South Africa teetering on the brink of civil war by the end of the decade. The situation was only defused through the unbanning of liberation movements, the release of political prisoners, and the regime's consenting to enter into negotiations with those popularly considered to be legitimate political leaders.

As apartheid drew to a close, and in the aftermath of its demise, scholars began trying to explain how this seemingly unlikely series of events—the unbannings, prisoner releases, and negotiations—came to pass. They tend to point to two groups of factors: international events and the spiraling domestic crisis. Those who focus on international factors concentrate primarily on the impact of the international sanctions movement,[2] and on the demise of the Soviet Union and its effect on post–cold war, third-world politics.[3] For those studies that look to domestic factors for explaining apartheid's collapse, a curious phenomenon exists: rarely, if ever, do these works mention, let alone focus on, the role of religious institutions and religious leaders in their analysis.[4] Instead, an array of actors, from trade unions and civic organizations to more militant youth groups, as well as the role of the military and police and the uprisings against them, are pointed to as explanatory factors.[5] Despite this lack of attention, religious organizations, specifically the SACC and SACBC, but others as well, *did* play a role in apartheid's demise.

The above two areas of inquiry do not treat religious organizations as primary units of analysis. When (if at all) churches and other religious institutions are discussed, they are seen as explanatory factors, or independent variables, that in some way help explain other political phenomena. However, there is a body of literature, broadly known as "Religion and Politics," in which religious ideas and institutions are the primary units of analysis. The framework developed here for explaining the South African case falls squarely within this area of study.

Scholars in the field of religion and politics are concerned with the changing relationships between religious organizations and society as a whole. Church leaders constantly make choices in assessing the proper relationship between religion and politics. This is especially true when some segments of the population call upon the churches to act as forces for social change, as was the case with Latin American churches under military dictatorships or South African churches under apartheid. In such instances, church leaders must strike a balance between a range of concerns. Strictly sacramental or liturgical issues must be balanced against pressure to become actively involved in the socioeconomic and political questions of the day. Even when church leaders have decided that fulfilling the gospel imperative requires them to address political issues, they are still faced with choices about types of action, from simply denouncing injustice, to providing shelter for those suffering from human rights abuses, to adopting the highest level of commitment—engaging in acts of civil disobedience in their challenge to a particular regime. When religion is placed at the center of inquiry, several questions emerge: What factors determine and guide the interaction of religious organizations with the political world? Why do some organizations become more highly politicized than others? Why is political action seen as legitimate use of church authority in some cases but not in others? What are the consequences of this politicization, both for political outcomes in society in general, and for the organizations themselves?

These questions were first tackled by scholars interested in the interaction of religion and politics in Latin America, and their studies have done much to advance our understanding of the complexity of answers.[6] The intellectual debt that new case studies, such as this South African study, owe to these early investigations is obvious. The present framework for understanding the South African case draws on these existing Latin American analyses of why churches change, and specifically, how they come to challenge authoritarian regimes. In retrospect, however, these cases appear to leave some questions unanswered, such as the role of institutional characteristics and the interaction of ideas and institutions. An examination of such factors can only further advance our understanding of the conditions under which churches become overtly political actors.

The current framework contributes to the literature on religion and politics in several ways: by extending the scope of analysis, by furnishing a new case study, and by providing a parsimonious explanation of church change. Many of the major works in this field have two things in common: they concentrate on one denomination, the Roman Catholic Church, and they are case studies of Latin American countries (either single or comparative studies). This South African study broadens the comparative analysis, both in terms of denominations and area. While there are reasons for a uni-denominational focus, including the numerical majority of Catholics in Latin America, the overall understanding of how churches change, and why there are degrees of change, is increased by expanding the number and types of cases.

The multi-denominational approach makes clear that any understanding of how churches come to adopt specific self-identities must take organizational characteristics into account. Studies in organizational theory indicate that different organizations have different capacities for implementing new ideas, and this holds true for South African church organizations. What is clear is that institutional structures, the decision-making processes, and international linkages of the SACC and the SACBC facilitated the emergence and maintenance of new ideas in the former case, while inhibiting them in the latter. Studies that concentrate solely on one religious institution fail to reveal the crucial intermediary step between ideas and actions; that is, how new religious ideas work through and become embedded in ecclesial organizations. The importance of institutional mediation is most clear when different types of organizations are compared.

The South African case also contributes to the comparative literature on religion and politics by furnishing an additional case by which to test the hypotheses that have been developed through Latin American studies. The similarities that exist between some of these countries and South Africa are striking and create a theoretical situation ripe for comparison. Both areas were faced with distinctly similar religious and political contexts. The churches in both South Africa and several Latin American countries, such as Brazil and Chile, were faced with authoritarian regimes which increasingly turned to the use of force to maintain illegitimate power. And in both areas, church elites were being pressured by radical Christians to take notice of new religious ideas, often originating from the grass roots, which challenged them to confront the governments of these states. The South African case, then, lends itself as testing ground for many of the hypotheses about the role of religion in repressive political situations that have been advanced as a result of studies on Latin America. Interestingly, the most rigorous theoretical analyses of the interaction of religion and politics in South African have been conducted *not* by political scientists but by theologians.[7]

Scholars studying the changing relationship between churches and politics in Latin America have proposed various frameworks and factors for understanding and explaining outcomes, with the result that we are faced with a myriad of explanations and variables when trying to apply these studies to new cases. In previously existing studies, scholars employ varying levels of analysis, from the elite level of church hierarchy to a primary concentration on the "popular church."[8] Additionally, several variables are used to explain the dynamics of church change. For example, in his study on Chile, Brian Smith employs four variables to explain the evolving relationship between the Catholic Church and the state: graduated binding force and specificity of church norms; hierarchical authority flows across a layered administrative organization; diversified nature of church membership; and resource transactions among center and periphery units.[9] From a different perspective, in his effort to explain the emergence of liberation theology as a social movement in Latin America, Christian Smith turns to social movement literature, employing variables borrowed from the theoretical model known as Political Process, including political opportunity structure, organizational strength, and insurgent consciousness. Again from a different perspective, in their edited volume on the causes and consequences of the Latin American "progressive church," Mainwaring and Wilde look at more general "conditioning factors."[10] These include factors which emerged from within the Catholic Church itself, such as European reform movements, the second Vatican Council, and the subsequent Medellín meeting of Latin American bishops. Additionally, they examine factors which arose outside institutional church structures, such as the broad political context. Political factors noted as important to the rise of radical Catholicism include the Cuban revolution, the perceived failures of the Alliance for Progress, and the rise of military dictatorships in various Latin American countries. The major framework underpinning their analysis is summed up as "the interaction between Church change and political repression."[11] Clearly, this approach influenced the framework developed in this study. However, it neglects the issue of institutional mediation, and the process by which church changes were translated into policy outcomes. Likewise, in his study of the transformation within the Brazilian Catholic Church, Mainwaring focuses on two types of factors: changes in Brazilian society and politics, and changes in the international Catholic Church.[12] Again, Mainwaring's study was influential in analyzing South Africa, while at the same time the South African case contributes other factors, such as how ideas and values become institutionalized in some religious organizations and not in others. In addition, while international linkages are seen as important in this book, the rise of new religious ideas on a domestic level—influenced by and yet independent of international changes—are also addressed. In summary, one contribution of this study is its attempt to synthesize and bridge two sets of explanations of why churches change. The first focuses on issues that are external to church organizations, including the changing political context. The second includes factors internal to these institutions, including the rise of new religious ideas and organizational-specific factors, such as the decision-making processes and the degree of overlapping leaderships.

The framework developed here indicates that churches become overtly political actors under the influence of a specific set of circumstances, when three distinct factors coalesce to produce a highly politicized outcome. At a bare minimum, three factors influence the adoption of an explicitly political "model of the church": a changing political context characterized by simultaneously increasing repression and increasingly militant opposition; a changing religious context whereby the rise of a new universe of religious discourse forms the basis of new agendas for organizations, allowing issues that were formerly not considered legitimate for theological debate to now become so; and the character of the institutional contexts of political debates. The interrelation of all three factors influences how easily church organizations will be able to reconstitute their self-identities, and how well entrenched this reorientation will become. The first two factors (changing religious and political contexts) primarily explain *the direction of* change—that is, how and why church organizations become overtly political actors; while the third factor (institutional context) explains *degree of* change—that is, why some organizations become more highly politicized than others.

This study is based on three types of data. The vast bulk of material includes documents, correspondence, periodicals, and other material from South African archives and libraries not generally available in the United States. A second source of information was semi-structured interviews conducted in South Africa with theologians, religious leaders, and lay people representing both "official" and opposition thinking within the SACC, the SACBC, and the ICT. A final data source involves secondary material. Besides the literature in the field of religion and politics on why churches change, this study draws heavily on the existing literature on the relationship between religion and politics in South Africa. This South African literature is quite extensive and includes several general analyses of the historical relationship between the churches and the political situation,[13] as well as works which treat the struggle against apartheid by the SACC and SACBC specifically.[14] Other texts are generally theologically oriented and treat such issues as the rise of Black Theology.[15] Some deal with specific debates within the churches, such as the issues of violence, counterviolence, and the support of the liberation movements.[16] There is also a growing literature examining the role of the South African churches in the 1980s. While some works are impressionistic, others are excellent analyses of the issues with which the churches grappled, the tremendous conflict this engendered within the churches, and the changing relationship between some churches and the state.[17] Finally, several tributes, biographies and autobiographies have added a rich human depth to this literature.[18]

List of Acronyms

AAC	All-African Convention (held in 1935)
ANC	African National Congress
AZAPO	Azanian People's Organization
BCM	Black Consciousness Movement
BPC	Black People's Convention
BPSG	Black Priests' Solidarity Group
CALS	Center for Applied Legal Studies (of the University of Witwatersrand, Johannesburg)
CCSA	Christian Council of South Africa (the precursor to the SACC)
CELAM	Latin American Bishops' Conference (Consejo Episcopal Latinoamericano in Bogotá, Colombia)
CIIR	Catholic Institute for International Relations, London
CLSA	Christian League of South Africa
CNBB	National Council of Brazilian Bishops (Conferência Nacional dos Bispos do Brasil)
CODESA	Convention for a Democratic South Africa
COSATU	Congress of South African Trade Unions
CP	Conservative Party
DRC	Dutch Reformed Church (usually used in reference to the NGK)
ECC	End Conscription Campaign
EMPSA	Ecumenical Monitoring Programme in South Africa
FRELIMO	Front for the Liberation of Mozambique
GNU	Government of National Unity
ICT	Institute for Contextual Theology, Johannesburg
IEC	Independent Electoral Commission
IFP	Inkatha Freedom Party
IMBISA	Inter-Territorial Meeting of Bishops of Southern Africa
ISAL	Church and Society in Latin America (Iglesia y Sociedad en América Latina)
MDM	Mass Democratic Movement
MK	Shorthand for Umkhonto we Sizwe (Spear of the Nation)
MPLA	Popular Movement for the Liberation of Angola
NCCR	National Coordinating Committee for Repatriation
NEC	National Executive Committee (of the SACC)

NGK	Dutch Reformed Church (Nederduits Gereformeerde Kerk)
NGO	Non-Governmental Organization
NIC	National Intelligence Service
NP	National Party
NPA	National Peace Accord
NRC	Native Representative Council
OAU	Organization of African Unity
PAC	Pan Africanist Congress
PCR	Program to Combat Racism (of the World Council of Churches)
SABC	South African Broadcasting Corporation
SACBC	Southern African Catholic Bishops' Conference, Pretoria
SACC	South African Council of Churches, Johannesburg
SACP	South African Communist Party
SACPO	South African Coloured People's Organization
SADF	South African Defense Force
SAIC	South African Indian Congress
SAIRR	South African Institute of Race Relations, Johannesburg
SANC	South African Native Convention
SANNC	South African Native National Congress (precursor to ANC)
SAP	South African Police
SASO	South African Students Organization
SFT	Standing for the Truth, a joint SACC/SACBC campaign launched in 1988
SPOBA	St. Peter's Old Boys Association
SSC	State Security Council
SWAPO	Southwest African People's Organization, Namibia
TAC	Theological Advisory Commission (of the SACBC)
TRC	Truth and Reconciliation Commission
UCM	University Christian Movement
UDF	United Democratic Front
WARC	World Alliance of Reformed Churches
WCC	World Council of Churches, Geneva, Switzerland
WPCC	Western Province Council of Churches
ZANU	Zimbabwe African National Union

1

Politics, Ideas, and Institutions
Explaining Church Change in South Africa

O N APRIL 27, 1994, millions of South Africans, of all racial and class back-
grounds, voted in that country's first democratic election, thereby ending
forty-five years of apartheid rule and over three hundred years of segregated
rule. The 1994 elections swept to power by an overwhelming majority the African National Congress (ANC), the continent's oldest liberation movement.
The system of apartheid was perhaps the most highly institutionalized and legalized system of segregation known to humankind, and was accompanied by
a level of human rights abuses that is similarly unparalleled. In order to understand the collapse of apartheid, it is vital to take into account not only international events, such as the success of the sanctions movement, but also internal
factors, including the growing strength of the domestic liberation movement.
It is difficult to fully appreciate the events surrounding the demise of apartheid
without understanding the role that church organizations played in this movement. Over 70 percent of South Africans are Christian, many of whom joined
in the struggle against apartheid's racial and economic oppression. And yet,
scholars examining the collapse of apartheid have generally paid insufficient
attention to the impact of religion on political developments. Given the thorough treatment of several other subjects, such as trade unions, political parties,
and the press, this oversight at first seems puzzling. More often than not, this
omission is not an exception but the rule in analyses of South African politics.
Attention to religious factors is warranted, however, because the political involvement of some religious organizations contributed in a significant way to
the growing mass protests that were a major factor in forcing the South African
regime to abandon its policy of apartheid, unban the ANC in 1990, and enter
negotiations. It seems intuitively clear that the churches should be more closely
examined as one source of apartheid's decline. The world became increasingly
familiar in the 1980s with the prominent role that some religious leaders played
in the effort to end apartheid, through pictures of Archbishop Tutu receiving
the Nobel Peace Prize and television stories of church leaders leading protest
marches.

Religious leaders, working under the influence of new religious ideas, served as a force for social change in South Africa, and tens of thousands of Christians, through resistance and defiance, joined in the struggle against oppression. Religion and politics meshed at a particular moment in South African history. One specific issue in particular, the question of declaring the illegitimacy of the South African state, was debated by two church organizations which eventually became two very important actors in the domestic liberation struggle: the South African Council of Churches (SACC) and the Southern African Catholic Bishops' Conference (SACBC). While both organizations challenged the apartheid government with increasing determination during the 1980s, the SACC became more politicized than the SACBC. One example of the more intense politicization of the SACC was its diagnosis of the South African regime as illegitimate.

The Churches and Legitimacy

In the mid-1980s, the SACC and the SACBC wrestled with the questions of whether the state was illegitimate, and if so, whether it was their duty to declare the illegitimacy of the state, thereby taking a confrontational political stance. In the end, the SACC concluded that the South African state was not legitimate and had forfeited the moral right to govern. The most famous and controversial legitimacy statement was made at a conference in Lusaka, Zambia, in May 1987, held under the auspices of the World Council of Churches (WCC). The theme of the conference was "The Churches' Search for Justice and Peace in Southern Africa." Present at this conference were representatives of the African National Congress (ANC) as well as members of other exiled organizations. At this meeting, the following declaration of the illegitimacy of the South African state, which the SACC later formally adopted, was issued:

> It is our belief that civil authority is instituted of God to do good, and that under the biblical imperative all people are obliged to do justice and show special care for the oppressed and the poor. It is this understanding that leaves us with no alternative but to conclude that the South African regime and its colonial domination of Namibia is illegitimate.[1]

In keeping with this pronouncement, the SACC called for mass civil disobedience. For the SACBC, however, the outcome was different. While there were clearly elements within the Bishops' Conference that felt the state was indeed illegitimate, the conference *as a whole* was not convinced that it was the church's right or duty to make a public pronouncement on the matter.

The Lusaka Statement, as the above declaration came to be known, was issued midway through a four-year-long debate, beginning in 1985 and culminating with a major international conference in 1989, over the issue of the legitimacy of the South African state in legal, academic, and theological circles in South Africa. At least two major conferences were held on the subject, along with several smaller ones. The first major conference devoted solely to the subject of legitimacy was held in June 1987, entitled, "Legitimacy of Governments: Is the South African Government a Legitimate Government? Legal, Political and Moral Perspectives and Opinions." It was sponsored jointly by the Centre for Applied Legal Studies (CALS) at the University of Witwatersrand in Johannesburg and the Institute for Contextual Theology (ICT). The bulk of this conference was devoted to a discussion of the legal and political perspectives of legitimacy. The second major conference was much larger in size and scope than the first and was international. It was held in September 1989 in Harare, Zimbabwe, and was sponsored by the SACC, the SACBC, the ICT, the Zimbabwe Council of Churches, the World Council of Churches, and the Ecumenical Documentation and Information Center (EDICESA). Speakers from around the world were invited to address the question of "The Legitimacy of the South African Government." In addition to these two conferences, several others were held specifically on the issue of the legitimacy of the South African state, including the 1988 SACBC Plenary Session, which devoted its study days entirely to this subject, as well as a smaller colloquium held on "The Legitimacy of the State" in June 1988.

These conferences brought together the opinions of a wide range of people, from lawyers with expertise in international law to Catholic and Protestant theologians to political scientists. What emerged after years of debate, dozens of conferences, papers, and lectures held on the topic in the latter half of the 1980s, was a common set of criteria that these South African scholars, lawyers, and theologians applied to their own situation, and with which they diagnosed the illegitimacy of the South African state. Ultimately, the concept of legitimacy was examined from three perspectives: political, legal, and theological. The political perspective was forwarded by academic scholars, who tended to favor a traditional social science, i.e., "consent-based" definition of legitimacy, such as those of Max Weber, Juan Linz, and others.[2] These scholars argued that the criterion of popular sovereignty (as consent of the governed is often referred to) is intimately tied to the issue of obedience.[3] Disobedience and popular sovereignty are negatively correlated—the higher the level of consent, the lower the level of disobedience. Stated positively, the more a majority of the people believe that the system is legitimate, the more they are likely to voluntarily obey that system's laws and policies.[4]

The legal understanding of legitimacy was provided by lawyers, who argued from a "rule of law" position.[5] The greater the level of authority, which is commonly referred to as noncoercive rule of law, the less likely it is that coercion will be required. Indeed, when a government uses excessive coercion it runs the risk of losing all authority derived from law. Therefore, the less rule by law and the more rule by force, the less legitimate the government is.[6] Rule by a military dictatorship, by arbitrary decrees, emergency regulations, intimidation, and brute force, are all signs that the concept of authority has been undermined.

Finally, theologians were most concerned with defining moral legitimacy, which they identified as "governing for the common good."[7] A government does not serve the common good if it engages in the policy and practice of discrimination, therewith serving the interests of some people rather than the interests of all, or serving the private good of some rather than the common good of everyone. Furthermore, a government does not serve the common good if it undertakes a consistent and systematic denial of human rights. Some scholars further argued not only that the guarantee of human rights is indispensable for the common good, but that these rights must be safeguarded by the establishment of economic justice.[8] A second issue of the common good, one related to the concept of human rights, is that of citizenship. According to Mervyn Frost, a South African political scientist, a state is legitimate only to the extent that it provides citizenship. Moreover, that citizenship must be equal—the state cannot allow one class of superior citizens to rule over and above a second class of citizens.[9] A wholesale denial of citizenship to an entire group of people would clearly constitute the loss of legitimacy. In general, a government that in principle does not accord equal human rights to all and does not provide equal citizenship for all, but consistently and systematically denies these rights to a large number of people, has forfeited any claim to legitimacy.

Guided by these various interpretations of the concept of legitimacy, the SACC concluded by the end of the 1980s that the South African state was illegitimate, while the SACBC participated fully in the debates surrounding this conclusion. The process leading to this conclusion forms the core investigation of this book.

Patterns of Change

While church organizations may adopt missions of promoting social change, the degree to which different organizations do so varies tremendously. In assessing the relationship between religion and politics, church leaders face a series of increasingly difficult tasks, from simply denouncing injustice, to challenging the state to share power or even yield authority. In the South African case, one can divide church commitment to the anti-apartheid struggle in the 1980s into three levels, representing increasing political involvement. The first level can be labeled "Sympathetic," which involved condemnation of apartheid in principle and was accompanied by statements issued in support of the victims of apartheid's injustices. The second level can be designated "Human Rights Involvement," in which church organizations became active in the struggle on the level of human rights by engaging in such activities as supporting trade union organizations, objecting to detention without trial, and serving as refuges and sanctuaries. The third level of involvement can be termed "Overt Political Activity," in which church organizations committed themselves in the political arena in cooperation with other organizations to protests and civil disobedience. With the exception of the white Dutch Reformed Churches, almost all religious denominations became involved at the first, sympathetic, level. The Catholic bishops, through the SACBC, went a step further and became very active on the second level, advancing the defense of human rights, especially through the SACBC's national and regional Justice and Peace Commissions; the SACBC went so far as to engage in selected modes of civil disobedience, such as supporting draft resisters. The SACC, however, embraced the highest level of commitment through its declaration of the illegitimacy of the state and its call for mass civil disobedience. It is clear, though, that certain individuals in the SACBC moved precipitously close to the brink of this level of political commitment.

Changes in a church's or an ecumenical organization's relation to politics can be traced to a more general redefinition of self-identity, which is the lens through which the organization evaluates its mission and proper relation to society as a whole. An important question is how these two organizations adopted the specific self-identities that they did. Although both the SACC and SACBC identified themselves as more than just religious organizations which happened to be committed to the anti-apartheid struggle at the level of human rights concerns and occasional condemnations of apartheid, the SACC saw itself as having responsibility for an explicit commitment to the liberation struggle. However, in the end, both the SACC and the SACBC undertook a process of theological and moral questioning (and in the case of the former, condemning) of the state's legitimation structures. This was, above all, a *political* exercise.

Some initial questions come immediately to mind. Why did the South African Council of Churches choose to declare the state illegitimate, while the Catholic Bishops' Conference did not? What factors contributed to these different levels of politicization? Stated differently, why did two church organizations, which were faced with the same political context, have divergent outcomes on this and other political questions? Moreover, why did the legitimacy debate arise at that particular moment, in the mid-1980s? Arguably, there were other times in South African history when this debate could have surfaced, but did not; neither during the Defiance Campaign of the 1950s and the subsequent banning of the ANC and many other anti-apartheid organizations, nor after the second major wave of anti-apartheid protest, led by the black consciousness movement (BCM) in the 1970s. The latter resulted in the banning of BCM organizations, several black newspapers, and the Christian Institute, an ecumenical organization which cooperated closely with the SACC. Thus, rather than seeing the decision to declare the state illegitimate as a natural or automatic reaction to the political events of the time, this might better be viewed as an aberration from past policy and practice.

Determining that the SACC and the SACBC underwent some sort of change is insufficient; the question still remains: change *from* what *to* what? In other words, what was the pattern of change? The transformations in the self-identities of these two South African organizations were not as radical as those seen in some Latin American countries, where the Catholic Church underwent a fairly dramatic about-face between the mid-1960s and the late 1970s. It moved from a conservative position of supporting and reinforcing existing social arrangements to a courageous stance of challenging the status quo and articulating intense criticism of political leaders. Church change in South Africa was more subtle, for it cannot be said that either the SACC or the SACBC ever supported outright the apartheid regime.[10] In contrast to a radical transformation, as in many Latin American cases, what occurred in South Africa was rather a reorientation in the degree and seriousness of social analysis and a concomitant change in behavior, enabling these two organizations to move beyond simple paternalistic statements (however seriously they were intended) condemning the apartheid leadership, to a rigorous analysis born out of the context of actual resistance. These organizations, especially the SACC, broke out of more traditional theological methods of analysis, and by the late 1970s and early 1980s adopted a much more critical, focused, and less naive exploration of social injustice.

Charles Villa-Vicencio, a South African theologian, would label this reorientation a turn from the dominant theological tradition of the church in Western Christian civilization to an alternative tradition. According to Villa-Vicencio, a double theological tradition coexists, somewhat uneasily, in the Western church.[11] Under the dominant tradition, dating back to the Emperor Constantine and the Edict of Milan in 313 of the common era, Christianity became an important part of the ideological framework of the ruling class. From this early era, the institutional church has been a conservative supporter of ruling elites, espousing a social analysis which questions the legitimacy of a government or state only as a last resort. Following such conservative standards, churches resort to radical means of working for liberation only after ensuring that all other methods for bringing about justice have been exhausted. Working in this tradition, Christianity has sometimes indiscriminately legitimated ruthless regimes which claimed to uphold "Western Christian" values. However another, alternative, Christian dimension exists, one which is based on egalitarian, biblical values. This is a minority tradition, a theology of resistance, which Johann Baptist Metz terms a "dangerous memory" of the gospel which will not be ignored.[12] No matter how hard the dominant theological tradition may try, it can never completely suppress this residual revolutionary theology, which works in favor of the poor and the oppressed. The transition away from the dominant theological tradition and towards the adoption of the alternative tradition is the crux of the change experienced by the SACC and, to a lesser degree, the SACBC. Debating issues such as civil disobedience, violence, and the illegitimacy of the government would not have been possible in these organizations, had they not recovered and embraced the memory of the alternative tradition. While both the SACBC and SACC began to consider how doctrinal issues might be translated into explicitly political responsibilities, the SACBC did not see the legitimacy question as its political responsibility, although it did wrestle with the question of this responsibility in other areas, most notably South Africa's occupation of Namibia. This indicates that while the SACBC did not undertake as complete a reorientation in its self-identity as the SACC, it moved closer to embracing the highest level of church involvement, that of overt political activity.

Two examples illustrate the extent to which the SACC underwent this process of change. The first concerns a comparison of two statements condemning the apartheid regime, one issued by and the other supported by the SACC. In June 1968, the Christian Institute, a progressive ecumenical organization, and the SACC jointly issued *A Message to the People of South Africa*. This theological statement was a clear condemnation of the theological justification of separate development. The Message stated that Christians were obliged to adopt lifestyles based on a Christian, nonracial understanding of community, even though this contradicted apartheid laws. This position reflected early discussions within church circles of the moral obligation of civil disobedience; and indeed, the Message represented an important turning point in the theological focus of the SACC. As Peter Walshe states, the Message "pointed in the direction of political and liberation theology, furthered the evolution of theology in South Africa and helped to raise political consciousness among a small minority of whites and many blacks."[13] Nevertheless, it still fell under Villa-Vicencio's dominant theological method of social analysis; it was essentially paternalistic because it was directed to those in a position of privilege and power, urging whites to work for justice for the poor. There was no sense of the need to empower the oppressed, nor was there a call for the poor to liberate themselves.[14]

By 1985, however, when *The Kairos Document: Challenge to the Church* was published, the transition to the alternative theology was clearly evident. This document, issued by the Institute for Contextual Theology, an organization which, like the Christian Institute in the 1970s, worked closely with the SACC, took the critique of separate development in the Message a step further by issuing a clear imperative to action. In the Message, theologians and church leaders still deemed the apartheid regime reformable. In fact, the Message was a basic call to reform society. With the Kairos Document this call was abandoned. The state was no longer deemed reformable, and Christians were called to act decisively to overthrow the apartheid structures of society.

The second example concerns the SACC support for liberation movements. In 1969, under the auspices of the World Council of Churches (WCC), the Program to Combat Racism (PCR) was formed. Part of its mandate was to establish a Special Fund from which grants would be made to groups working to overcome racism. The first of these grants was distributed the following year, when $120,000 was given to various southern African liberation movements, including the ANC. At this point, the SACC was critical of both the PCR and its grant. It condemned the support of movements which espoused the use of force as a means to an end. The Council stated that "We are disturbed by the way in which the Churches . . . are called upon to initiate the use of means usually associated with the civil power in the struggle against racism. These are the weapons of the world rather than the Church."[15] The SACC was quick to point out, however, that by criticizing the grant it was not supporting the status quo, for it had always been committed to change and to bringing an end to the racist regime. The reluctance of the SACC to engage in any serious theological questioning and analysis of whether force might be necessary, in order to work for liberation and to counter injustice, put the organization squarely in what Villa-Vicencio describes as the dominant theological tradition.

This situation had drastically changed by the time of the Lusaka Conference in 1987, again convened by the WCC, when the participants, including the SACC, declared: "While remaining committed to peaceful change we recognize that the nature of the South African regime which wages war on its own inhabitants and neighbors compels the movements to the use of force along with other means to end oppression."[16] Although the SACC remained committed as an organization to peaceful methods of change, it finally recognized the possibility of legitimate counterviolence, aimed at overthrowing the established order and replacing it with a more just social and political system. The SACC had clearly arrived at a new self-identity which embraced the confrontational alternative theological tradition. Interestingly, the SACBC never adopted a conference resolution in support of the Lusaka Statement.

Explaining Church Change

Both the SACC and the SACBC changed, yet still adopted different levels of involvement in the South African political sphere. What combination of external and internal factors was responsible for the different responses of these two organizations? More generally, why are some church organizations more able to promote internal change and develop new links to the political system than others? And why do churches undertake political action in some cases and not in others? The answer that emerges in South Africa is that three specific factors interacted to form two distinct self-identities: a changing sociopolitical context, an evolving religious context, and the institutional contexts in which debates took place. The interaction of these three factors explains both areas of convergence and areas of divergence between the SACC and the SACBC. This book examines the interrelation of all three factors and the implications of this dynamic process for action. The changes experienced by these organizations were closely linked to turns in the political cycle. Churches respond to changes in society and politics, which almost always results in concomitant change in the internal dynamics of the organization.

Much of the theoretical literature on why churches change—and specifically how they come to challenge a regime—has focused on changes in the Catholic Church in Latin America.[17] The model used to explain changing church self-identities in South Africa is necessarily informed by theories developed to explain church change in Latin America, and draws heavily on Latin American comparisons. There are two reasons why so much of the theoretical literature on progressive church change has concentrated on Latin America. In addition to the fact that the Catholic Church in several Latin American countries underwent profound changes in a relatively short period, from a position of generally supporting the status quo to a leadership role in the fight against social injustice, the Latin American Catholic Church is one of the largest churches in the world. At the time of these changes, the Latin American Bishops' Conference (CELAM) and the National Council of Brazilian Bishops (CNBB) constituted the global Church's strongest regional and national ecclesiastical organizations. Despite the fact that research on Latin America has tended to concentrate almost exclusively on the Catholic Church, enough similarities exist for the literature to provide a useful theoretical framework for analyzing the South African case, which includes both a Catholic and a Protestant organization.

Changing Religious Context: The Importance of Ideas

A growing number of scholars look to "ideas" as explanations for policy, suggesting that ideas can be critical in explaining different organizational outcomes.[18] Although these studies focus on different questions in various countries at different times, all conclude that the adoption of new policies cannot be explained solely by changes in objective conditions or material interests. Rather, explanations incorporate a concern with how ideas, institutions, and individuals interact to produce policy outcomes. In general, the emphasis is on the importance of ideas held by individuals, especially top policymakers.[19]

These ideas make up the "universe of political discourse."[20] This universe comprises beliefs about the way politics should be conducted and the kinds of

conflicts resolvable through political processes. Thus, whether an issue is regarded as "political" is dependent upon the existing universe of political discourse. If an issue falls outside this discourse, it will not be included in the
realm of political debate. Only when this universe is challenged and changed
are formerly "nonpolitical" issues taken up for debate. The universe of political discourse acts as a filter in inhibiting or forming organizational identity—
within any given universe of discourse, an organization will see itself as having
a specific self-identity. The same process occurs when the *universe of religious
discourse* is altered, so that issues that were formerly not considered appropriate
for religious debate now become so. This is one explanation for changing self-
identities in the South African case, where a new religious discourse known as
contextual theology formed the basis for new agendas for some church organizations, especially the SACC. Various terms have been used to describe this
theological movement. It is not usually referred to as "liberation theology" in
South Africa, because those involved in the movement wish to distinguish the
religious and political situations in South Africa from those in Latin America,
the region most associated with the term. Often the movement is referred to
as "Prophetic Christianity," in recognition of the fact that this theology draws
heavily from the Old Testament prophets, who consistently stress God's concern
for action and justice. A third term, one espoused here, is contextual theology.
The term is used because the theological analysis taking place in South Africa
was heavily influenced by the social and political contexts in which it occurred.
The ideas coming out of this theology challenged the existing religious discourse and ultimately offered a new one. Under this new discourse, churches
were obliged to adopt a more explicitly political level of commitment and to
act on it. By accepting the values of this new religious discourse, the leadership
of the SACC and, to a lesser extent, the SACBC adopted a new identity, and
this reconstituted self-identity provided the impetus for the declaration of illegitimacy.

Much of the recent literature on the importance of ideas comes from the
field of political economy, but there have been several excellent contributions
in the area of religion and politics generally, and on the importance of ideas
for the emergence of a progressive church, specifically. Again, these studies have
generally focused on Latin America.[21] The core ideas of this new theology,
especially as they evolved in Latin America, illustrate just how important ideas
can be for influencing church action. Prior to the mid-1960s, the Catholic
Church in many Latin American countries, especially in Brazil, Chile, El Sal-
vador, Nicaragua, and Peru, was considered a pillar of the established political order, an ally of the rulers both politically and economically. By working
hand in hand with governing elites, the church perpetuated an oppressive social
structure which favored the accumulation of wealth for a very small percentage
of the population at the expense of an impoverished majority.[22] In reinforcing

existing social arrangements, the church was a conservative power in society. It supplied religious legitimation to governing practices and structures. However, beginning in the mid-1960s, the church as an institution became engaged in public controversy with repressive regimes and began to serve as a shelter for activists involved in social and political dissent. In the span of just a few decades, significant elements in the Latin American Catholic Church moved from a position of support for and identification with the established political order, to one of intense critique of regime leaders. In varying degrees, the Catholic Church in many Latin American countries spoke out against injustice, and some of its members, especially in Central America, resorted to violence in this quest. In the aftermath of the Second Vatican Council, convened from 1962 until 1965, and several follow-up Latin American Episcopal conferences, new religious ideas emerged which help explain this rather drastic about-face. As will become evident, these ideas, originating in Vatican II and further developed in the Latin American context, were to have a profound influence in South African theological circles as well.

Several landmarks, not all originating in Latin America, can be distinguished in the emergence of a new religious discourse. The Second Vatican Council represented the beginning of a period of extensive change for the church as a whole, and exercised a profound influence on the Catholic Church in Latin America. One major outcome of the Council was a revised self-identity. The church minimized its traditional model of an unchanging and hierarchically ordered institution in favor of a new model: the "Pilgrim People of God."[23] Several ideas resulted from the adoption of this model, perhaps the most important of which was the acceptance of temporal, historical change both as a fact and as a source of new and valid ideas. This understanding, that the church should learn from the world, grew from the Council's stress on the need for the church to read and adapt to the "signs of the times." This emphasis, which underpins a position that is open to change, has implications for the long-term interaction of religion and politics.[24]

The modest idea of accepting change as normal had far-reaching and unexpected implications for the Catholic Church. First, it allowed the church to potentially free itself from identification with existing structures and social arrangements, under the notion that if all situations and institutional arrangements are historically determined, no particular arrangement is necessarily the "correct" one.[25] The idea of change was important for a second reason as well— it led to a concern for understanding *how* societies developed as they did. If no particular societal arrangement was predetermined by God, by what was it determined? This question opened a floodgate, for in seeking to answer it, the church turned to secular disciplines for explanation, especially the social sciences. Sociological theories of modernization and development were suddenly "discovered" by some Catholic theologians and church leaders. With the starting point of analysis now being social rather than religious, new ideas about violence, "structural change," and dependency came to the fore. A final consequence of accepting the idea of change is that it led to new ideas about Catholic activism.[26] Under the old model of the church, individuals were expected to simply endure repressive societies in the hope of a better life to come. However, with the recognition that societies can be changed by human will, a new emphasis on praxis became important. Action towards change was necessary and legitimate; in fact, for some theologians action became a necessary consequence of authentic faith, "a kind of validation of the reality of that faith."[27] When the implications of religious faith were expanded in this way to encompass action, spirituality became linked to politics.[28]

Perhaps the most important impact of Vatican II for the Latin American situation was that the bishops were forced to work out the implications of the Council in their own context. Indeed, the motivating force behind the Second General Conference of the Latin American Episcopate at Medellín, Colombia, in 1968, was to apply the insights of Vatican II to Latin America.[29] In the area of ideology, the most important outcomes of the conference were reconceptualizations of the poor and poverty (ideas which were already changing under Vatican II, but developed further at Medellín), and of force and violence. The prevailing understanding of poverty changed from the product of personal failure to the result of structural conditions in society. Notions about alleviating poverty necessarily changed as well. Charity was no longer considered a sufficient or sole means of alleviation. Instead, the structures causing poverty had to change, and this was considered a matter of power and political action.[30] Poverty was no longer deemed inevitable; it was recognized as the result of human-made structures of power that ought to be challenged. Because poverty was defined in structural terms, the church was forced to come to grips with class issues. New understandings of poverty were further refined at CELAM's third general meeting held at Puebla, Mexico, in 1979—a gathering often associated with the phrase "Preferential Option for the Poor." This new understanding had important implications for the evolving understanding of Christian mission. First, a focus on radical restructuring of society to help meet the needs of the poor was accompanied by an emphasis on participation. Consequently, the church came to support a variety of political actions in the name of "participation," believing that mobilization and organization of social tension and even conflict were inevitable concomitants of change.[31] Hence, the Catholic Church was placed in the midst of conflict which severely tested its traditional message of reconciliation and forced it to deal with new understandings of another concept: violence.

The reconceptualization of violence included the recognition of "institutionalized violence," growing out of the day-to-day operations of unequal, unjust, and oppressive social structures. Like poverty, violence was no longer seen solely in terms of individual or collective acts. This redefinition went hand in hand with yet another new idea, this time of sin. No longer did sin simply cover individual morality; now it could be applied to entire social systems whose "injustice, oppression, and institutionalized violence were sinful because they imposed social conditions making a fully moral and decent life impossible."[32] The implications of these new ideas were significant. If entire social, economic, and political structures could be sinful, then religious grace, or freedom from sin, had to be tied to changes in—and sometimes the replacing of—these structures. Political action on the part of churches was legitimated in terms of liberation from sin, which is clearly a central mission of the church.[33]

These ideas that arose from Vatican II, their application at Medellín, and their further refinement at Puebla, together formed a Latin American context-specific universe of religious discourse. When elaborated and systematized, these insights were formed into an innovative Liberation Theology,[34] a theology concerned with the meaning of religion for social and political liberation and vice versa. The resultant protest movements related biblical values to the analysis of a particular society and the search for justice, calling on churches to work with the poor for the empowerment of the oppressed. The importance of context is clear. Juan Luis Segundo argues, "the continuing change in our interpretation of the Bible is dictated by the continuing changes in our present-day reality, both individual and societal."[35] Thus, a major characteristic of liberation theology is a fusion of religious understanding, social analysis, and activism; lines between religious and political responsibility as well as between sacred and profane spheres are eliminated. Gustavo Gutierrez, one of the foremost proponents of this theology, argues that a church with this self-image must necessarily become involved at the level of overt political activity. He states, "the Church cannot occupy neutral ground in the exercise of its influence: it must act either for or against the unjust social order." Moreover, "prophetic denunciation can be made validly and truly only from within the heart of the struggle for liberation."[36]

Without these new ideas, church initiatives, in the form of challenging repressive governments and actively working towards social justice, would never have been possible. The old "universe of discourse" simply would not have allowed it, indeed might never have imagined it. When liberation theology was applied to the South African case, the results were profound. Indeed, the questioning of the legitimacy of the state simply could not have occurred without new thinking about such concepts as poverty, violence, and action. In fact, the theoretical underpinnings of the legitimacy declaration were not even considered "religious" issues in the previous discourse of "church theology." Daniel Levine, a scholar of the Latin American Catholic Church, states that the clearest impact of ideological change "has come through its capacity to shape discourse, creating and promoting issues as legitimate topics of debate in society, politics, and in churches."[37] In other words, debating whether a state is illegitimate, which was formerly considered a purely political issue, might now be legitimately discussed as a theological topic.

Few authors have studied the comparable changes within Protestant churches in Latin America during this period, although several hint that the Protestant contribution to the new discourse was not unimportant.[38] Consequently, very little systematic comparison of the emergence of a new religious discourse and its impact on changing self-identity between the Latin American Catholic and Protestant churches exists. Yet if, as several scholars argue, different organizations have different capacities for implementing new ideas,[39] then this comparison becomes crucial in explaining different outcomes by different church organizations. These authors suggest that institutional structures and procedures either facilitate or inhibit the emergence and maintenance of new ideas. G. John Ikenberry, for example, argues that ideas cannot be disengaged from the institutions in which they emerge and that the institutional setting of policy-making is crucial to the influence that ideas are likely to have.[40] If institutions are indeed important for the implementation of a new discourse, there is no better way to study institutional mediation than to compare them.

Turning to the South African case, part of the explanation offered for the different approaches the SACC and SACBC took to the legitimacy debate is the way in which South Africa's own context-specific religious discourse, i.e., its contextual theology, became embedded in each of these two organizations. How did the leaders of the SACC and the SACBC interpret and understand new ideas about social or structural sin, justice, poverty, violence, as well as tyranny, reformability, and most importantly, legitimacy—concepts which were highlighted in, for example, the Kairos Document of 1985, which clearly identified the ideas, norms, and values of contextual theology? Were different meanings assigned to new religious ideas by church leaders, and did these translate into different reactions to contextual theology as a whole, and to the Kairos Document specifically? The answers to these questions suggest that while both the SACC and the SACBC had to consider the new theological discourse, the SACBC was much more reluctant than the SACC to institutionalize new ideas. It was precisely the acceptance of these new theological ideas that allowed the SACC to adopt the highest political level of commitment and thereby to declare the state illegitimate.

Changes in ideology, however, represent only part of the story of why a church's self-identity evolves. While this change is necessary, it is clearly not sufficient. Another factor was also at work in both the South African and Latin American situations. When trying to understand how a church arrives at a particular self-image one must look beyond religious changes to developments in the political context.[41]

Changing Political Context

The political context contributed to ongoing changes in the church because it led to a "spiral of involvement." As autonomous units of civil society are silenced by a repressive regime, churches often become the vehicles for freedom of expression. Ultimately this leads to harassment and worse for church members. If churches hold their ground and denounce the state, this in turn sets off a spiral of still greater repression directed against the church by the state. The increase in repression reinforces and legitimizes even greater involvement in politics by the church, whose broad responsibility by this point has become the representation of the masses. This situation clearly affects a church organization's conceptualization of its own mission. A spiral of involvement was evident in both the Latin American and the South African cases. In both situations, the basic ideology guiding the state was the doctrine of national security.[42] Although unlike many Latin American countries, South Africa did not experience a military coup, the apartheid regime was dominated by a national security ideology with its twin concepts of total onslaught (against all potential threats facing South Africa) and total strategy (the multifaceted response by the regime to these perceived security threats).

Catholic bishops in Latin America not only denounced overt human rights abuses carried out by these regimes, but in some countries, like Chile, provided a protective umbrella for a whole range of humanitarian programs after other social institutions were repressed in the aftermath of a 1973 coup. Additionally, bishops pointed to what they considered the underlying causes precipitating these violations, including prevailing economic structures with their maldistribution of land and wealth.[43] However, even relatively mild statements by the bishops provoked sharp responses from the state; then, as the bishops held their ground, a theological deepening and radicalization took place within the church. Thus, at the same time that new ideas about the social sin of institutionalized violence were circulating under the growing influence of liberation theology, the amount and degree of violence in society was escalating. The consequent intersection of religious change and the emergence of national security regimes proved to be a "critical conjuncture"; what began as a response to human rights violations evolved into a consistent pattern of criticism of the national security ideology as a whole. Once only embraced by a few individuals, this critical voice became a common response of the institutional church. The national security doctrine was most systematically elaborated in Brazil and Chile, and not coincidentally, the Catholic churches in both of these countries represented the most progressive Latin American churches at that time. Throughout Latin America, more than a thousand bishops, priests, and religious were threatened, arrested, kidnapped, tortured, killed, raped, or exiled. These figures do not include Catholic lay leaders.[44]

In both the Latin American and the South African cases, the state acted swiftly and harshly to repress any political expression by various sectors in society which challenged state policies; and in both cases, progressive elements in the church emerged under these authoritarian regimes. This led to initial conflict with only a minority of "radical" Christians; however, soon a growing number of church activists were imprisoned, tortured, and sometimes killed, to which church leadership reacted with statements denouncing the governments. Thus a spiral of greater repression against the church followed by further church denunciations against the state, was set off.[45] As previously organized political actors were completely excluded from political participation, church leaders were placed in a position of filling the political vacuum. At this point, the church took on the responsibility of becoming the "voice of the voiceless," speaking out not only for the poor but for all of civil society. Its sense of its own social mission was transformed.

Two characteristics of the domestic political situation in South Africa set the 1980s apart from any preceding time. The level of repression by the apartheid government was higher than at any other time, and there existed a national liberation movement of unprecedented scale and organization, known by the late 1980s as the Mass Democratic Movement. When meetings were banned, church buildings became centers for protest, and as all outlets for nonviolent protest other than the churches were silenced by repression, increasing numbers of Christians were eventually "drawn into the front-line of resistance."[46]

As churches took on this increased responsibility, and as several Christian leaders turned to activism, government attacks on church members and leaders took place with increasing frequency. In denouncing such actions, these two organizations opened themselves to government reprisals and repression. While both the SACC and SACBC were government targets (both headquarters were bombed, for example), the government seems to have considered the SACC more "radical" or "dangerous," cracking down more heavily against it than the SACBC.

The changing religious and political contexts are treated as two distinct factors here, but in reality the two cannot be separated. Each set of changes impinges upon the other, with mutually reinforcing results. New religious ideas are worked into the prevailing political context; in the process, these ideas themselves acquire new meanings, generating yet greater commitments to resistance and change. This synergistic interaction also provides an answer to the question of why churches change at the particular time they do. Although repression in South Africa was not new, what was unique in the 1980s was that this repression eventually meshed with new ideas about injustice and the need for a prophetic critique of it. Political repression, far from scaring off church activists, came to reinforce their newfound commitments to the poor and oppressed; it only served to make religious ideas about resistance and justice all the more meaningful in daily life.[47] In their effort to achieve redefined religious goals and to implement activist ideas, the churches suddenly seemed subversive to authoritarian regimes, which acted swiftly in cracking down on the churches. Church leaders did not independently seek out an overtly political level of involvement; rather, it was a result of this process.

Institutional Context

New religious ideas and changing political contexts are not sufficient to explain the adoption of a new self-identity. If they were, we would expect to see similar degrees of change in both the SACC and the SACBC. Both organizations were faced with the same political context and both responded to new religious ideas. However, the outcomes differed—the SACC became more overtly political than the SACBC. Why? The answer to this question appears to lie in the organizational characteristics of the SACC and SACBC, and in the ways in which these organizations mediated new religious ideas.

Despite its transcendent character and mission, a church is still an institution, and institutional characteristics help explain a church's ability to change.[48] In Latin America and in South Africa, the interaction of religious change and political change was mediated by specific church organizations. What must be investigated is how specific organizational characteristics can lead to different patterns of social and political action and how they shape and limit the impact of new ideas. This approach to the study of churches draws from institutional literature which sees institutions as autonomous political actors in their own right and not simply as mirrors of social forces. Processes internal to these institutions can affect policy outcomes. A central claim is that institutional structures mediate the interests and capacities of the groups and individuals within them; in addition, these structures (such as norms, roles, rules of behavior, physical arrangements, and archives) are seen as relatively resilient to the idiosyncratic preferences and expectations of individuals.[49] It is not enough to determine the preferences of individual elites (such as individual Catholic bishops, for instance), because those preferences will be constrained and shaped by the larger institutional setting within which they are situated.[50] In this way, institutions exert a powerful influence over the ways in which people formulate their interests and work to attain them. Additionally, institutional arrangements can constrain individual behavior by rendering some choices unviable, precluding particular courses of action, and restraining certain patterns of resource allocation.[51] What becomes clear in the South African case is that some church institutions act as constraints more than others, while some institutional structures actually empower individuals in their quest to promote change.

Much of the work on the shaping and constraining role of church organizations has tended to concentrate on the specific characteristics of the Catholic Church, and less so on Protestant churches.[52] While this book draws on these insights about the Catholic Church, it also compares the specific characteristics of a Catholic organization with a Protestant one. The importance of organizational characteristics in mediating ideas is set in sharp relief through this comparison.

Conclusion

Why do religious organizations change in their relationship with the political world? Why do religious organizations change in different ways? What are the consequences of these changes? These are the broad theoretical questions addressed in this book. Several issues in the field of religion and politics which have not previously been addressed are examined here. First, relatively little research has been done on how organizational characteristics of churches contribute to a changing self-identity. This is especially true in the South African case. What existing studies inadequately address is the crucial intermediary step of how new religious ideas work through and become embedded in church organizations, which are instrumental in forming policies. Any understanding of new church self-identities must take organizational characteristics into account. This study, therefore, assumes there is a link between two types of explanations of church change, one focused on factors external to church organizations and the other on factors internal to them. Moreover, this study is deliberately comparative. As noted above, most researchers, especially on Latin America, where the bulk of the work on progressive church change has been conducted, tend to concentrate on one specific denomination. This study compares the reaction to the political and religious contexts of the time by leaders of both Catholic and Protestant church organizations, with the expectation that this wider scope can contribute to an understanding of how specific organizational factors influence the adoption of a new self-identity.

It is necessary at this point to examine an important distinction. This study focuses on two church *organizations:* the South African Council of Churches, an ecumenical umbrella organization of Protestant churches (i.e., denominations), and the Southern African Catholic Bishops' Conference, the administrative "secretariat" and decision-making organ of the Roman Catholic Church. It is important to bear in mind that the SACC is *not* a single denomination or administrative body of a denomination, but a separate organization with several member churches. In this sense, it can be considered a supra-denominational organization, existing above the level of any individual church, including the Catholic Church. This study, in other words, does not examine the debates surrounding the legitimacy of the government, the Lusaka Statement, and other political issues which took place within the individual member churches of the SACC. Whether these debates ever progressed beyond the level of the SACC into its various member churches is certainly an interesting problem, but not the focus here. Likewise, for example, this study does not compare the process of change within the Catholic Church with that of the Church of the Province of South Africa, the Anglican Church. While there are potential methodological problems of comparing two dissimilar entities which exist at two different levels—an individual church's administrative body and an organization which operates at a higher level—this is, in fact, a fruitful comparison. In many ways, although the Catholic Church was an observer member of the SACC until the mid-1990s, the SACBC enjoyed a status that was fundamentally different from that of other member churches or even observer churches. The Catholic bishops long insisted on retaining this observer status, repeatedly refusing to become full members. They therefore functioned as a somewhat separate organization, often coexisting alongside the SACC. That the SACC itself acknowledged the near-equal status of the SACBC was evident in the fact that it (the SACC) very rarely issued a statement or initiated a program without first consulting the SACBC.

This work focuses on church elite. Religious elites, although shaped by the institutional setting, also act as conduits for church/state relationships, and the self-images of religious leaders tend to determine the direction, intensity, and style of action that members undertake. Different opinions by church elites regarding their church's religious mission help explain the church's official stance towards political involvement.[53] Therefore, understanding why one organization declared the state illegitimate while the other did not, necessitates examining the views held by elites, since the way leaders understand the church shapes how they see themselves, their institutions, and their proper relationship to social and political issues.

The next two chapters examine the changing political context, as well as its impact on the churches. The first of these (chapter 2) is an examination of historical periods of protest against the government, so that Christian activism in the 1980s can be properly situated in South African political culture. The decision of the churches to take up the legitimacy issue did not occur in a historical vacuum. Rather, there were several periods in South African history, beginning with the formation of the state in 1910, in which both the constitution and government policies were questioned and challenged by various organizations. Chapter 3 examines the political context of "revolution and counter-revolution" of the 1980s, and how the churches were drawn into overt political involvement through a "spiral of involvement." Chapter 4 addresses the rise and institutionalization of new religious ideas, while chapter 5 examines how these new ideas interacted with the political context of the 1980s to allow the issue of state legitimacy to be considered a valid topic for debate within churches. Chapter 6 then analyzes the institutional characteristics of the SACC and the SACBC and how new ideas were mediated by them. Chapter 7 analyzes the ideological and institutional changes inside the SACC and SACBC which took place as a result of the profound political changes in South Africa from the period of Nelson Mandela's release through the 1994 general elections.

2

A Legacy of Protest and Challenge

WHEN THE South African Council of Churches and the Southern African Catholic Bishops' Conference entered into the legitimacy debate in the mid-1980s, resulting in the SACC's declaring the South African state illegitimate, many observers considered this to be a "radical" church statement with little precedent. However, the decision of the churches to take up this debate did not occur in a historical vacuum. There were several periods in South African history, beginning with the very formation of the state in 1910, in which the government was questioned and challenged by black[1] political organizations. This process of questioning gradually eroded the state's legitimacy in the eyes of many black political leaders. While blacks were mainly reacting to increasingly racist and exclusionary policies, there has always been a strong Christian ideological influence on protest movements throughout the twentieth century. Many of the early leaders of the African National Congress (ANC) were also leaders and ministers in their respective churches. The first president of the ANC, John Dube, was a clergyman, as were four of the eleven members of the first executive committee. Indeed, from its inception the ANC based its political demands on Christian morality and values. The legitimacy debate was not new in South Africa, and early on, it involved committed Christians who joined the protest movement. What was new, however, was that by the 1980s this debate was taken up by primarily white-led, mainline, institutional church structures. By the time the institutional church explicitly posed the question of legitimacy in the mid-1980s, it had a rich legacy upon which to draw, one which served as a potential source of support for church leaders in their debate over whether they had a responsibility to speak out on the issue.

The legitimacy issue provides a new framework or lens through which to view and analyze South African historical events. Although several excellent analyses of twentieth-century South African politics exist,[2] none address the issue of the political legitimacy of the government or how this issue affected the actions of the various liberation movements throughout the century. This chapter is an interpretation of political events—both in white and protest politics—from 1910 until 1980 from this perspective.[3] In interpreting South African history from the point of view of legitimacy, I draw on the interpretations of this concept arrived at by South Africans themselves. Many South African

scholars, lawyers, and theologians spent considerable time and energy interpreting the concept from within their specific South African context. Their various
interpretations were not defined until the legitimacy conferences of the 1980s.
However, their understandings of the moral, legal, and political dimensions of
the legitimacy of the South African state serve as guidelines, and South African
political history can be analyzed from the perspective of how scholars within
South Africa might interpret the history of the evolving legitimacy of the state
themselves. The lens used here is one constructed by South African scholars
themselves in assisting church leaders in the 1980s in their decision whether to
declare the state illegitimate. While these scholars and church leaders made the
discussion concerning the legitimacy of the state explicit, the discussion itself
was begun some seventy years earlier. As Villa-Vicencio has said, "History is
ahead of the churches."[4]

The Roots of Challenge

Several periods in South African history in which legitimacy was challenged
suggest that it was an evolving process, dating back to the very formation of
the Union of South Africa in 1910. Initially, large sections of black society did
not challenge the right of the state to exist per se; rather, organizations and
movements were more concerned with questioning specific policies of successive governments. Within a changing political context, however, this opposition
to governmental policies gradually and subtly evolved into a challenge to the
apartheid state itself, and the changing nature of this challenge was accompanied by new tactics employed by protest groups. Consequently, by the time the
churches took up the question in the 1980s, the black liberation movement
already regarded the state as illegitimate, and had long adopted the goal of
creating a nonracial and hence fundamentally new state.

Crises in legitimacy are most obvious during periods of political upheaval.
A crisis can provide the opportunity for prospective leaders to articulate disen-
chantment with the system and offer possible alternatives. In this way, crises
often serve to motivate people in active opposition to the regime or to support
individuals and movements who attack the legitimacy of the regime. Periods
of crisis can also reveal suddenly and dramatically the extent to which the system has failed to justify its claims or to keep its promises.[5] At several moments
in South African history, developments in white politics generated periods of
crisis in black politics. These watershed periods mark the stages in a mounting
challenge to the legitimacy of government policies and then of the South African state itself.

Black protest against white domination occurred long before the formation
of the South African state in 1910. However, since the focus of this book is on

the challenge to the legitimacy of the state, analysis begins with the formation of that state.[6]

The Formation of the Union of South Africa—1910

In October 1908, nine years after the outbreak of the Anglo-Boer war and six years after the end of that war at the signing of the Treaty of Vereeniging, a National Convention assembled to draft the South Africa Act, the blueprint for a new state. The act subsequently passed through the British Parliament, and the Union of South Africa came into being on May 31, 1910. The ink of the draft was not yet dry before Africans began protesting its contents.

In response to the all-white National Convention, African elites joined in protest of their exclusion from the political process. The draft act contained provisions confining the nonwhite vote to the Cape province, and completely prohibited nonwhites from sitting in Parliament. For all four provinces, parliamentary representation was determined on the basis of their white male adult populations.[7] The act offended African elites who were committed to nonracial ideals, both in theory and in the practice of Cape politics, where they enjoyed equality under the constitution as well as a nonracial franchise through a common voters roll. Under the draft act, the common voters roll was entrenched constitutionally, but could be altered or abolished through a two-thirds majority of a joint sitting of the Senate and the House of Assembly. It was the threatened destruction of this Cape nonracial tradition, as well as the creation of a color-bar constitution at Union, against which Africans, who had hoped for the extension of the Cape system to the other three provinces, so vigorously protested.

Budding African political organizations coalesced to oppose the act and protested to South African authorities and to Great Britain, the country granting statehood to South Africa.[8] Protest focused on the color bar clauses of the constitution and the failure to extend a nonwhite franchise to the other three colonies.[9] Africans tried desperately to influence the delegates of the white National Convention through letters and petitions, all to no avail. As one scholar states, "it is clear that [they] had no effect whatsoever on the deliberations of the delegates, who, gathered in secret discourse, and unknown to the country at large, had already reached finality on the matter of the franchise for Africans."[10] With this failure, and with the gathering of the union-wide South African Native Convention (SANC) in Bloemfontein in March 1909, comprised of sixty elected delegates from the four colonies, Africans began to question the legitimacy of the constitution by calling for a new one in which "all persons within the Union shall be entitled to full and equal rights and privileges subject only to the conditions and limitations established by law and applicable alike to all citizens without distinction of class, colour or creed."[11]

Once the act was ratified by all four colonies, with none of the changes demanded by Africans incorporated, the draft constitution was submitted to Britain for approval by Parliament. The locus of African protest likewise shifted to London, where a deputation of Africans, Coloreds, and one sympathetic white opposed its passage by attempting to influence the British government into making amendments to it. The British government, however, chose not to interfere in the domestic affairs of an emerging dominion, and Parliament passed the bill without amendment.[12] Unwilling to intervene, the British Parliament thereby legitimized discrimination. As a result, in three of the four provinces Africans could not vote on a common voters roll, and in all four they were denied the right to sit in Parliament, a right which they had always theoretically enjoyed in the Cape colony but had not yet exercised. Moreover, the clause in which Cape Africans could be disenfranchised was legalized, a provision that was unique in British parliamentary history.[13] Africans had been rebuffed every step of the way. Having lost the battle for a new constitution, however, Africans wasted no time in protesting the policies of the new government.

The formation of the SANC was a seminal event in the emergence of black resistance politics, because it was the first occasion on which African political leaders and their newly formed political associations in the four colonies formally cooperated.[14] The Convention was the first step towards the formation of a permanent national African political organization. In 1912, the South African Native National Congress (SANNC), which in 1925 became the African National Congress (ANC), was formed, setting the stage for resistance on a national scale.[15] Hinting at the issue of legitimacy and the criterion of consent, one ANC founder stated that they were protesting "a union in which we have no voice in the making of laws and no part in their administration."[16] The citizenship issue and its relationship to legitimacy was also immediately recognized by early black politicians. As one leader insisted, "No South African nation could be formed which did not include the non-white races as an integral part, having 'full recognition of all claims to citizenship.'"[17] African complaints about injustice were based on real suffering, for in the two years between the creation of the Union and the founding of the ANC, several other discriminatory statutes were passed which perpetuated white power, including laws regulating labor, restricting immigration, and restricting skilled jobs in mining and engineering to whites only, to name a few.[18]

Faced with these problems, and the fact that they had no direct political outlets to voice their grievances, the ANC was formed for the express purpose:

> to record all grievances and wants of the African people and to seek by constitutional means the redress thereof, to agitate and advocate by just means for the removal of the colour bar in political, education and industrial fields and for equitable representation of Africans in Parliament or in those bodies

that are vested with legislative matters affecting the coloured races; to be the medium of representative opinion and to formulate a standard policy on Native Affairs for the benefit and guidance of the Union Government and Parliament.[19]

Africans were never consulted in the drafting of the constitution, and the resulting constitution severely curtailed their ability to participate in the decision-making process of the government. In effect, the South African Parliament would represent the wishes of whites, and the legislation passed would reflect their interests, no matter how detrimental they were to the well-being of Africans. Clearly, the new government did not enjoy the consent of the majority of the population. In contrast to the African elites' ideal of political rights for all citizens, regardless of race, the reality was a constriction of existing African political rights and the permanent exclusion of Africans from South African political institutions. The new government also immediately showed its intention of governing for the good of whites at the expense of nonwhites when, as noted above, several discriminatory statutes were immediately passed.

Some analysts have labeled early African politics as essentially naive, unduly optimistic, too moderate, and cautious and compromising, mainly because of the tactics chosen by its leaders. They preferred to seek redress for their grievances through constitutional means, and at times even appeared overly gracious to the government.[20] The emphasis was on "prudence, restraint, and a dutiful respect for the rulers God had placed over them."[21] The hope was that whites would have a change of heart as a result of African "perseverance, patience, reasonableness, and the justice of their demands."[22] The ANC worked for change through dialogue and eschewed all violence. Although there were sporadic acts of civil disobedience, on the whole, early tactics were to work within the confines of the law. The ANC registered its protest through petitions (submitted both locally and to the British Crown), deputations, appearances before government bodies, pamphlets, the election to legislative bodies of white sympathizers, and on occasion through "passive action." However, there was a foreshadow of the challenge to come when one newspaper, the *Ilanga lase Natal,* stated that "if racial prejudice persisted and Africans continued to be regarded only as exploitable labour units, the prospect for a future filled with bitter hatred and even violence, loomed ahead. There was 'a great body of natives who never will be ready to submit themselves to the tyranny of the minority.'"[23] As this tyranny increased and all legal efforts to stem it ended in failure, so too, the challenge by Africans and their allies increased.

The Natives Land Act—1913

A second watershed in the evolution of black political activism occurred with the passing of the 1913 Natives Land Act, which created separate "Native and European Homelands," under which blacks could not reside in white territory unless they obtained permission. A mere 7.3 percent of the land was reserved for Africans, whose population total was five million, as opposed to one and a half million whites.[24] The implementation of the act was accompanied by human rights abuses, including wide-scale evictions of Africans from farm land outside their designated reserves. The ANC repeatedly declared its opposition to the act, especially the resultant human rights violations. Delegations were sent in protest both to the Union's prime minister and to Great Britain to present grievances to the king. Again, the British Parliament refused to intervene in South Africa's domestic politics. In spite of frequent disappointments, Africans continued for some time to regard Britain as the defender of their rights of freedom and justice. Finally, in 1922, the ANC passed a vote of no-confidence in the British as well as South African governments.

The Land Act coincided with the First World War. Africans juxtaposed the steady decrease in the legitimacy of their government with evolving international norms, embodied especially in Woodrow Wilson's Fourteen Points. On the issue of the consent of the governed, the U.S. president stated:

> No peace can last, or ought to last, which does not recognize that governments derive all their just powers from the consent of the governed and that no right anywhere exists, to hand peoples from sovereignty to sovereignty as if they were property. Self-determination is not a mere phrase. It is an imperative principle of action, which statesmen will henceforth ignore at their peril.[25]

In the aftermath of the war, Africans drew on these new norms, challenging the government to "extend to them these inalienable rights of citizenship in their entirety," and urging Africans to "launch a big Constitutional fight for this divine right of peoples, for it was God himself who gave man the right of self-determination and self-government."[26] With increasing frequency in the following years, Africans cited international norms to support their opposition to South African government policies and, eventually, to validate their challenge to the very legitimacy of the state itself.

The Hertzog Bills—1932–1936

Throughout the 1920s and 1930s, the privileged position of whites was further entrenched as the color bar was extended into more and more areas. By 1920, the ANC was deprecating the fact that "the poor black man is consequently reduced to a position of utter voicelessness and votelessness, hoplessness, powerlessness, helplessness, defencelessness, homelessness, landlessness. . . . "[27] The ANC continued to protest specific legislation, legitimizing its demands by placing them in the context of inalienable democratic and human rights that were being articulated internationally. The ANC still emphasized constitutional means and, on the whole, avoided large-scale protest campaigns. In other words, the trend continued in which the ANC would pass resolutions, which were then forwarded to white authorities.[28] As in earlier decades, these protests went unanswered.

This pattern of behavior changed at the next watershed of black resistance, when the government promulgated and eventually passed the most comprehensive legislation in its segregation policy. Known as the Hertzog Bills after Prime Minister J. B. M. Hertzog, the legislation was two-pronged, covering both political rights and the land issue. Politically, the Representation of Natives Act abolished the Cape common voters roll, creating instead a separate roll on which Africans could elect three whites to represent them in the House of Assembly and four whites in the Senate. While several very capable and sympathetic Native Representatives were elected until even this token representation was abolished in 1959, they were never successful in reversing or even stemming the tide of increasing segregation. Additionally, the legislation created a Native Representative Council (NRC), on which twelve indirectly elected Africans would sit, with four Africans chosen by the government along with white Native Commissioners, to advise on manners concerning Africans.[29] The second statute was the Native Trust and Land Act, which marginally increased the amount of land allocated for Africans in their "Native Reserves," while prohibiting them from purchasing land outside these areas. It also included a repressive labor section, which resulted in forcing African squatters from white-owned land and driving them into the cities, where they became cheap labor for the white-owned economy.

The two "Native Bills" (as the Hertzog Bills were known), first promulgated in 1932, resulted in a new surge of African political activity. Reaction to the bills was "unequivocal in its opposition and Union-wide in its expression."[30] Before their passage, African opposition coalesced into the All-African Convention (AAC) in 1935. It was attended by over four hundred delegates, who gathered on the same site where the Native Convention had been convened in 1909 to protest the draft constitution.[31] Although the two proposed bills were the main focus of the convention, opposition to the entire post-Union trend of government was obvious. The bills were a blow to the ANC, which had steadfastly remained committed to the goal of eventual direct representation in Parliament for Africans throughout South Africa. This goal was set down in the ANC "Bill of Rights" of 1925, which demanded the "democratic principles of equality of treatment and equality of citizenship irrespective of race, class, creed, or origins."[32] The Hertzog legislation was a final blow to these goals. Delegates at the AAC denounced the further erosion of government based on the consent of the governed, by demanding the "right of partnership in the management of the affairs of the country and in determining and

shaping its course."[33] Human rights abuses were also acknowledged and protested in various convention resolutions, including the increasingly restrictive
pass laws; the appalling living conditions under which Africans were forced to
live in the cities, as well as the increasingly poor land conditions in the "reserves," caused by severe overpopulation; the all-pervasive racial discrimination
in the labor market, especially in the mining industry; and the establishment
of separate African "townships" or "locations" to enforce complete residential
segregation.

The issues of governing for the common good, and particularly of citizenship, were also addressed by the AAC, which lamented the fact that "Union
Africans have been treated like aliens in their own country," especially through
the implementation of the Native Land Act. This law violated human rights,
it was argued, because Africans had, "as human beings, the indisputable right
to a place of abode in this land of their fathers . . . [and] as sons of the soil,
God-given rights to unrestricted ownership of land in this the land of their
birth."[34]

Even after this resounding rejection of African political representation, the
emerging protest movement continued using peaceful tactics, including consultations with white authorities and cooperation with the new system of representation. As Tom Lodge, a preeminent scholar of South African black politics, states, "the AAC and its constituent organizations settled down into a
familiar routine: wordy protests through consultative machinery, delegations,
vague calls for African unity, and national days of prayer. . . . its protestations
were punctuated by affirmations of loyalty to South Africa and the Crown."[35]
There were, however, indications that Africans were becoming frustrated and
disillusioned about the possibility of any meaningful change. This resulted in
a reevaluation of tactics by the ANC, which eventually led to accepting the
futility of relying exclusively on appeals to the morality of whites and traditional pressure group politics, and "a determination . . . to prepare a position
of strength from which non-racial justice could be wrung from the white power
structure."[36] The subtle shift from challenging specific statutes to contesting
the legitimacy of the state had begun.

World War II and Its Effects—the 1940s

Although restricted to non-combatant roles, thousands of blacks served
South Africa in World War II and returned forever transformed by the experience. Having worked to free Europe's citizens from Nazi tyranny,[37] blacks were
soon demanding the same liberation for themselves. They became more adamant in their demands for representation in all governing bodies, recognition
of their trade unions, abolition of passes, better educational opportunities, and
the repeal of discriminatory legislation. During this period, too, there was a

growing intransigence towards ever increasing human rights abuses; hence, on the criterion of the common good, the legitimacy of government policy was being challenged as well. Each tightening of the color bar and its extension into new spheres was met with protest.

The impetus to an irretrievable break with the old patterns of compromising and working within the structures of existing legislation occurred when the ANC interpreted the Atlantic Charter of 1941 in light of the situation in South Africa. The ANC drew specifically on the "self-determination clause" of the Charter's "Third Point," which stated explicitly that "They [the United States and the United Kingdom] respect the right of all peoples to choose the form of government under which they will live; and they wish to see sovereign rights and self-government restored to those who have been forcibly deprived of them."[38] The result was a 1943 document entitled *African Claims in South Africa* and an accompanying Bill of Rights. While long-standing Congress aims were reiterated, when it came to the franchise the ANC took a more radical position than at any time previously by endorsing unqualified universal suffrage for all adults.[39] Point by point, the document dealt with various human rights issues, including the right to choose the form of government; the abandonment of the use of force; the granting of full citizenship rights; a fair redistribution of the land; freedom of residence and of movement; and equal rights in property and education.[40] In *African Claims,* the ANC invoked the language of international human rights standards long before they were identified in various international declarations such as the Universal Declaration of Human Rights (1948) and the two International Covenants on Human Rights (1966). The Bill of Rights that accompanied *African Claims* codified African demands in the form of both civil and political rights as well as cultural and economic rights.

Prime Minister Smuts, upon reading the document, declared it propagandist and refused to even discuss it with any member of the ANC. He declared that it had totally misinterpreted the Atlantic Charter and had stretched its meaning to "make it apply to all sorts of African problems and conditions."[41] After three decades of fruitless working within the system, and in the face of complete rejection by the government, a frustrated and humiliated ANC moved toward a tactical shift that would lead to civil disobedience.

African Claims, while a ground-breaking statement of ANC ideals and goals, did not fundamentally call for a change in tactics to achieve these ends. This did not occur until the creation of the Congress Youth League in 1944, which reflected the more militant ideas of a younger generation of leaders. The Youth League stated its goal as the creation of a "true democracy, in which all the nationalities and minorities would have their fundamental human rights guaranteed in a democratic Constitution." It committed itself to the fight for "the admission of the Africans into the full citizenship of the country" so that they would have "direct representation in parliament on a democratic basis."[42]

To achieve this the League advocated the adoption of new tactics, because it believed the approach of the ANC's leadership was too submissive and incapable of advancing the cause of freedom. Pushing for this more aggressive approach, the Youth League was responsible for the promulgation by the ANC in 1949 of a "Programme of Action" which embraced civil disobedience, including boycotts and strikes, and declared the ANC to be waging a "struggle for National Liberation."[43]

Thus, the period from 1910 to 1948 witnessed the growing recognition among politically active Africans that the South African government was becoming increasingly illegitimate. By 1948 it was obvious, through the steady elimination of any rights Africans had ever possessed in the decision-making process and the governance of the country, through the attack on the Cape common voters role, and through the totally inadequate forms of representation under the Hertzog legislation, that the government cared little for gaining their consent. The emerging resistance movement continued to push the government on the question of the franchise. At the time of Union in 1910, African demands on this point were taken to the British Parliament. In 1936, the AAC petitioned for a qualified franchise for African men. At the same time, the NRC was rejected as an illegitimate substitute for the African franchise. Finally, in 1943 the ANC's Bill of Rights called for a universal franchise. In every case, African demands and petitions fell on deaf, unsympathetic ears, and peaceful protests proved ineffectual in the face of increasing governmental oppression.

And yet, despite the fact that African rights had not been widened, as the ANC had hoped, but significantly curtailed, the ANC held fast to the goal of reform prior to the advent of the apartheid government in 1948. It sought "by rational argument and pressure within the framework of the constitution to persuade the white electorate to reverse the discriminatory tide."[44] Its methodology was cautious and its objectives modest in the light of future tactics and demands. Tactics indicative of challenging the state, those of civil disobedience and even violence, had not yet been adopted. Until 1948 the ANC had been either unable or unwilling to mount mass protest campaigns against the government. It is likely that until this time, African politicians believed that the state was not yet irretrievably identified with segregation. Africans felt that the institutional structures were at least potentially flexible and open to reform. This hope guided protest tactics, not acceptance of what were seen as immoral policies.

1948, however, proved to be a critical juncture in the history of resistance politics. The period between 1948 and 1960 was one of ambiguity and transition for the ANC, when—in the face of increasing repression and severe erosion of the rule of law—it increasingly questioned the reformability of the state. This was the period in which civil disobedience was adopted on a mass scale.

Apartheid—1948

In 1948, playing on white Afrikaner fears of a "black peril" and the loss of white supremacy, the National Party came to power on the slogan of *apartheid*. This at first meant little more than increased coordination and extension of the racist laws of segregation already in existence. However, because the theory behind apartheid (literally, separateness) was the physical, political, cultural, socioeconomic, and religious separation of the races, what started as a slogan soon developed into a "systematic program of social engineering."[45]

The new government quickly revealed that it was giving up any pretense of caring about the consent of the governed. While the Hertzog legislation of 1936 had removed Africans from the common voters roll, the representation of Africans in Parliament by specially elected whites and the establishment of the Native Representative Council implied at least tacit recognition that Africans had the right to some voice in the governing of the country. Yet even this modest gesture towards Africans was unacceptable to the new apartheid government. The Bantu Authorities Act of 1951 abolished the NRC, and Africans were to be henceforth represented by government-chosen and government-friendly Bantu Authorities in the eight (eventually ten) ethnically separate "homelands" (the former reserves), which were meant to represent different "ethnic nations." This ethnic engineering—the basic premise of apartheid—was resoundingly denounced by the ANC, which had always supported nonracial ideas and worked as a nonethnic "supratribal" organization, in which all Africans were seen to be one national group with national spokespersons. The ANC recognized the homelands system for what it was: nothing more than a "divide and rule" strategy of the Afrikaner government, designed to engender prejudice and suspicion among different so-called tribal groups in an effort to prevent a united black majority.

In 1959 every last vestige of black participation in the central political system was abolished. The white representatives of African voters were eliminated and Africans were effectively stripped of their citizenship in South Africa—both ends being achieved by the Promotion of Bantu Self-Government Act, in which the ten homelands were to be given self-government which would ultimately lead to their "independence." If universal citizenship is considered one hallmark of legitimacy, then the creation of homelands marked the death knell of the legitimacy of the South African state. Under the Homelands Citizenship Act of 1970, every African became a citizen of one of these homelands, even if he or she had never lived outside of a "white" area. Those living in cities outside of the rural homelands would henceforth be considered temporary visitors with the status of migrant laborers, without the civil rights enjoyed by whites. One of the most heinous acts of human rights abuse in South African history resulted from this policy, when over three and one half million "surplus" people—that is, people who were unemployed, old, disabled, or otherwise of no use to the white state—were forcibly removed from areas they had lived in for generations and dumped into homelands they had never seen.

The South African government also increased activity in the area of human rights abuses by continuing to pass legislation which was in principle meant to benefit the white population at the expense of blacks. Under the 1953 Bantu Education Act, for example, the government, in per capita terms, spent ten times as much on white as on African students;[46] moreover, the inferior education Africans received was designed to condition them to accept positions of subservience. Furthermore, blacks were forced to leave "white" universities and to attend newly created and separate African, Indian, or Colored universities. The Reservation of Separate Amenities Act (1953) legalized the "separate but not necessarily equal" state of affairs that was already commonplace, when it provided that separate facilities need not be "substantially similar to or of the same character, standard, extent or quality."[47] Other abuses included the allocation of one of four racial categories—White, Indian, Colored, or African—to each individual at birth, and the outlawing of marriages across categories. The Group Areas Act of 1950, which created separate residential and business areas for each of the four racial categories, resulted in "nothing less than a complete unscrambling of the residential patterns in South African towns"[48] as whole communities were forcibly removed to comply with the law. The pass system was intensified and the requirement to carry a pass was extended to African women for the first time in 1952. Finally, under the Industrial Conciliation [Job Reservations] Act (1956), certain occupations were reserved for specified racial groups. As a result of these acts, the South African government fostered one of the most inequitable distributions of income in the world, with almost two-thirds of the African population living in official poverty.

Thus, what in 1948 had only been the theory of a new South African state, had by 1960 become a reality—one which featured an independent white-dominated republic, surrounded by a cluster of economically and politically dependent black client states. This new apartheid state was distinguished from pre-1948 regimes in that it took segregation a step further in "ruthlessness, more elaborate separatism, and determination to achieve its ends without consideration of the means used or the consequences to those affected by the process."[49]

The Liberation Movement Responds

Following the National Party victory and the advent of apartheid, all hope for reform through traditional legal tactics steadily evaporated. Indeed, the ANC responded immediately with the adoption of the Programme of Action at its 1949 Annual Conference, committing it to the use of civil disobedience. Some Congress Youth Leaguers were prepared to go even further, talking of "creating a revolutionary national front."[50] The Programme included a statement of long-term goals, which were national freedom, political independence, and self-determination; the short-term goal was the abolition of all "differential political institutions"; and the means for achieving these ends included boycotting these institutions, strikes, and "a national stoppage of work in protest of the reactionary policy of the government."[51]

The Defiance Campaign of 1952 marked the ANC's first attempt, in alliance with the South African Indian Congress (SAIC), to implement the Programme of Action and to build a mass movement.[52] The ANC maintained its commitment to nonviolence and imposed a code of conduct to ensure that this commitment would be upheld. Actions of civil disobedience included strikes, bus boycotts, the refusal to carry passes, the breaking of curfews, entering segregated facilities, and the defiance of bans on public meetings. The Defiance Campaign was the largest and most sustained organized resistance ever initiated by the ANC. Over 8,500 nonwhites were jailed for defying apartheid laws, and the ANC official membership, it has been estimated, increased from 7,000 to over 100,000 by campaign's end,[53] which did not even begin to reflect the influence the ANC held over many times that number of supporters. As Thomas Karis and Gwendolen Carter state, "Although the number of its adherents could not be measured reliably, there could be no doubt that the ANC was the pre-eminent African political organization in southern Africa and that its annual conferences were a kind of African parliament."[54]

The next major phase in resistance politics was the 1955 formation of the Congress Alliance and the convening of the Congress of the People. The Alliance was a broad-based multiracial mass movement consisting of the ANC, the SAIC, the South African Coloured People's Organization (SACPO), and the Congress of Democrats (an organization of liberal whites). In the representation of nationwide grievances, over three thousand people attended the Congress of the People in June 1955, where a Freedom Charter was read and unanimously adopted. This Charter amounted to a basic restatement of long-standing ANC aims in demanding a nonracial, democratic system of government and equal protection for all before the law. The Charter was a milestone in defining the ANC's interpretation of legitimacy. On the issue of the consent of the governed, the preamble of the Charter declared that "South Africa belongs to who live in it, black and white, and no government can justly claim authority unless it is based on the will of the people."[55]

Through the end of the 1950s, various acts of civil disobedience were carried out, including protesting the forced removal of 58,000 Africans from the city of Johannesburg under the new Group Areas Act, education boycotts in protest of the Bantu Education Act, continued protests against the pass system, and boycotts against bus fare increases, such as the Alexandra bus boycott of 1957. Throughout these campaigns, the ANC leadership never wavered from its commitment to nonviolent tactics; and yet in each and every case the government acted swiftly in its repression against protesters.

The government did not react kindly to the growing challenge to its authority, and the period of the 1950s was marked by increasingly repressive and coercive rule. The more the black protest movement challenged the legitimacy of apartheid laws, the more the government responded with force. This in turn led to an even greater level of civil disobedience. The more the government repressed and the greater the level of human rights abuses, the more the liberation movement intensified its challenge. As a result, what started out as an effort to reform the government turned into a cry for the repeal of legislation, which then culminated in a challenge to the legitimacy of the state itself. The ANC did not start out as a "liberation movement" but, in effect, became one through the actions of the state. This is what one author labels the "Action, Reaction, and Counteraction" process of apartheid,[56] in which increasingly discriminatory laws provoked reaction from those most affected by them. Faced with this opposition, the government responded with punitive measures and more laws to counteract further opposition, and thus a spiral was set in motion. As the government increasingly lost legitimacy in the eyes of the majority of the African population, its ability to maintain control over that population through a residual element of consent diminished. The control it did maintain was due to the use of force. By the end of 1959, the Minister of Defense, F. C. Erasmus, in explaining the role of the South African Defense Force, declared to a gathering of army officers, "you must not think we are arming against an external enemy. We are not. We are arming in order to shoot down the black masses."[57]

Throughout the 1950s, on the justification of "national security," the government passed a series of acts, under the guise of "security legislation," that ignored the principles of civil liberty on which South African public law was theoretically grounded. The first security law was the 1950 Suppression of Communism Act, with its broad definition of communism.[58] In 1976 this law was replaced by the Internal Security Act, which allowed for periods of indefinite detention and for the detention of potential state witnesses for up to six months. By 1977 over 150 children under the age of sixteen were being detained under this act. Through this legislation the government initiated a systematic effort to cripple or immobilize the most active ANC members, by prohibiting meetings and harassing, banishing, banning, or imprisoning its leaders. By 1954 almost the entire National Executive of the ANC had been removed from power in this manner. As the range of repressive legislation was extended, its catalog included the Riotous Assemblies Act (1930), the Unlawful Organizations Act (1950), the Sabotage Act (1962), the General Law Amendment Act

(1955),[59] the Terrorism Act (1967), which legalized indefinite detention without trial, the Public Safety Act (1953), which allowed the government to declare a state of emergency and the police to assume emergency powers if the "public safety" appeared to be threatened, and the Criminal Law Amendment Act (1953), which allowed sentencing of up to three years for the violation of any laws in protest against government policy. Additionally, anyone who committed any offense as a means of protest could be whipped as well as fined or imprisoned. Between 1963 and 1965 over two thousand people were convicted for offenses under one or more of these security laws.[60] Individuals were held indefinitely in solitary confinement without trial, without having their identities revealed, and without having access to anyone except government officials.[61] In a sign of even greater repression to come, in 1958 the ANC was declared an "unlawful organization" in certain areas of the country because it was "detrimental to the peace, order, and good government" of Africans. In addition to these human rights abuses, the enforcement of legislation to prevent any disruptions of the status quo resulted in the violation of other rights as well, including freedom of speech, assembly, press, due process, and movement.[62]

In these difficult circumstances, the 1950s were a test of the efficacy of nonviolent extra-parliamentary tactics, a test the ANC and its allies could not pass. None of the goals of the Defiance Campaign were achieved, in that none of the laws that were the subject of the campaign were repealed. Not only was the government unwilling to accommodate any of the requests of the emerging protest movement, it responded with increasing repression and by tightening and extending apartheid. As a result, by the end of the 1950s the ANC abandoned its sole reliance on nonviolent tactics as a means to bring about change, and for the first time violence was tentatively discussed as a viable option for achieving ANC goals. In the 1960s, disobedience escalated to the use of violence—the transition from moderation to militancy was complete—and the ANC was engaged in a full-scale challenge to the legitimacy of the state itself. The switch to new forms of political struggle was justified by South Africa's having become a virtual police state for all who challenged its policies.

In the shift from relying solely on nonviolence to the use of violent tactics, the 1950s must be seen as a transition period, but also as a period of ambiguity. It was marked by continually shifting attitudes among the leadership about just how revolutionary the ANC really was. A fundamental challenge to the state can be clearly seen in some speeches, while others are more cautious. It appears that the 1950s represented a time of confusion for the ANC. It was becoming obvious that the nature of the state was changing under apartheid, and yet the leadership was unwilling to declare the ANC a revolutionary organization.

In discussing the Freedom Charter, Nelson Mandela wrote in 1956, "The Charter is more than a mere list of demands for democratic reforms. It is a revolutionary document precisely because the changes it envisages cannot be won without breaking up the economic and political set-up of present South Africa,"[63] clearly implying that the state itself was illegitimate and would have to be replaced or at least restructured. At other times the ANC seemed much less adamant on this issue. In 1952, Albert Lutuli stated that the ANC "is not subversive since it does not seek to overthrow the form and machinery of the State but only urges the inclusion of all sections of the community in a partnership in the Government of the country on the basis of equality."[64] The Freedom Charter itself, some believe, had revolutionary implications—it was a blueprint for a fundamentally different society. Certainly, if all reforms were simultaneously applied, it would have had a revolutionary impact on South Africa. Yet the ANC itself denied that violence would be necessary, and at least one academic states that the Charter was "essentially reformist rather than revolutionary," because it aimed at winning political and civil rights within the basic framework of South Africa's existing parliamentary system.[65]

Another area of ambiguity concerned the issue of boycotting. The Programme of Action clearly called for the boycotting of "all differential political institutions." However, throughout the 1950s the ANC continued to participate in the elections of white Native Representatives as well as to run for seats on township advisory boards. While it did so for tactical reasons, the refusal to adopt an outright boycott of these structures was an indication that it was not yet ready to completely abandon its attempt to reform the existing state or to give up what few remaining legal outlets it had at its disposal.

The government recognized that the ANC was beginning to challenge the legitimacy of the state and yet was also caught up in the ambiguity of the period. This was never more evident than in the South African Treason Trial. In 1956, in the aftermath of the Congress of the People and the dissemination of the Freedom Charter, 156 people of all races were arrested and charged with high treason. The main issue of the trial was whether or not the policy of the ANC and its allies was the use of violence, and whether they were motivated by "hostile intent." Not surprisingly, the Freedom Charter was the key evidence of the prosecution, which argued that its aims—the abolition of discrimination and the granting of equal rights to all—could not be accomplished without the use of violence, and that the ANC was therefore advocating the revolutionary overthrow of the state. For the defense, Mandela denied that the ANC advocated violence, but he did admit that the Charter was "a revolutionary document. . . ."[66]

After the trial had dragged on for over four years, the number of those charged had been reduced to thirty individuals, all of whom were acquitted when the presiding judge ruled that there was no evidence of intent to violently overthrow the state. The verdict did recognize, however, that the ANC "intended to bring the Government to its knees and to establish a 'radically and fundamentally different' form of state through mass action."[67] The fact that the government's charge was high treason indicates that it was well aware that the ANC's goals were shifting from working for reform by challenging individual policies, to working for the overthrow of the apartheid state. Many commentators believed at the time that, even without conviction, the trial demonstrated that there were many in the Congress Alliance who were operating close to the edge of treason. Yet the fact that all those tried were acquitted indicates that the government itself was unable to prove that this transition was complete.

The Turn to Armed Resistance—the 1960s

Throughout the 1950s, despite increased rhetoric about the state, the ANC did not fully consider itself a revolutionary organization. Not until the banning of the ANC (and its newly-formed rival, the Pan Africanist Congress [PAC])[68] in 1960, did the liberation movement finally abandon hopes for a peaceful change and turn to violence in an effort to achieve its goals. From this time on, from the point of view of the ANC, the policies of the government and the state had become inextricably linked—South Africa had become an "apartheid state." The ANC abandoned all efforts at reform and turned its full energy to the creation of a new state. The long history of refusing to resort to violence had ended; force was to become one weapon in a complex range of tactics employed to destroy apartheid.

The immediate cause of a reevaluation of goals and tactics was the killing by the police of sixty-seven people during an anti-pass campaign, in what has come to be known as the "Sharpeville Shootings," and its aftermath—the banning of the ANC and PAC, which forced both organizations to operate underground. The March 1960 anti-pass campaign, launched in protest against the exploitive and humiliating system of labor control which these laws facilitated, was to be disciplined and nonviolent. Africans would surrender themselves for arrest.[69] When 20,000 people turned up at the Sharpeville police station to protest and surrender their passes and be arrested, the police opened fire, killing sixty-seven and wounding an additional 186 people, most of whom were shot in the back. Riots broke out throughout the country in the ensuing weeks, and within days the government declared a state of emergency, giving the police broad powers to arrest and detain indefinitely any person suspected of anti-government activity. At this point, the Treason Trial defendants were rearrested and jailed, along with 2,000 other political activists, and the crackdown concluded with the banning of the ANC and PAC in early April under the recently passed Unlawful Organization Act. Using the same line of argument as the prosecutors in the Treason Trial, the government now concluded that these organizations far exceeded the limits of legality because their fundamental aim was the violent overthrow of the state.[70]

The result was the formation of *Umkhonto we Sizwe* (Spear of the Nation, also referred to as MK) and the shift to incorporate force as an integral part of the struggle. In justifying this shift, Mandela later stated at his 1964 trial for sabotage, for which he was sentenced to life imprisonment, that "All channels of peaceful protest had been barred to us. . . . The government has deliberately created the atmosphere for civil war and revolution."[71] The form of violence chosen by *Umkhonto* was sabotage of the economic infrastructure and targets of symbolic political significance, an approach adopted because it would injure or kill as few people as possible, yet it would put a strain on the country's economy through discouraging investments. *Umkhonto* was not publicly linked with the ANC until 1963, when it was described as the "military wing of our struggle." In the first eighteen months after *Umkhonto*'s formation, over two hundred acts of sabotage were executed. In addition to sabotage, however, *Umkhonto* also began preparations for the military training of guerrillas, declaring that "if war [is] inevitable, we [want] the fight to be conducted on terms most favourable to our people."[72] The ANC obviously anticipated a protracted war with the government in its efforts to bring about a new or restructured state.

If an increase in civil disobedience signals an erosion of legitimacy, then the adoption of force—the ultimate form of disobedience—indicates that in the eyes of the ANC leadership the state had, by 1960, lost all vestiges of legitimacy. Past methods had failed to bring about the goals of liberation, with the result that the ANC finally concluded that "fifty years of non-violence had brought the African people nothing but more and more repressive legislation, and fewer and fewer rights." In this context, the Congress was left with only two choices—"submit or fight."[73]

The fact that the ANC now considered the state illegitimate was expressed by Nelson Mandela during both his 1962 and 1964 trials. In 1964, when ultimately sentenced to life in prison, Mandela stated, "My lord, it is not I, but the Government that should be in the dock today. I plead not guilty."[74] Alluding to the state's illegitimacy on the basis of lack of consent among the governed, Mandela declared:

> That the will of the people is the basis of the authority of government is a principle universally acknowledged as sacred throughout the civilised world, and constitutes the basic foundation of freedom and justice. It is understandable why citizens who have the vote as well as the right of direct representation in the country's governing bodies should be morally and legally bound by the laws governing the country. It should be equally understandable why we as Africans should adopt the attitude that we are neither morally nor

legally bound to obey laws which were not made with our consent, nor can we be expected to have confidence in courts that interpret and enforce such laws.[75]

Black Consciousness and Exile—the 1970s

During the 1970s, the challenge to the South African state was twofold: internally from the black consciousness movement (BCM), and externally from the earlier liberation groups that had been forced into exile in 1960. Unlike the ANC, the BCM was not composed of a single organization but was rather the name given to several organizations dedicated to the psychological and cultural conditioning of blacks to effect their own liberation.[76] The two major BCM organizations were the South African Students Organization (SASO), established in 1968, and the Black People's Convention (BPC), established in 1971 as an umbrella organization coordinating the activities of other black consciousness organizations.

The aim and philosophy of the BCM was to recondition the minds of the oppressed people to prepare them to forcefully demand what was rightfully theirs. This reconditioning was known as black consciousness, and its adherents were concerned with overcoming what they perceived as the tendency towards acceptance and resignation among blacks that resulted from prolonged subjugation. Blacks had to be made aware that the conditions under which they lived were deliberately created by the government, and that these conditions could be fought and removed. The short-term goal of the BCM was therefore psychological liberation, a precursor to the long-term goal of mobilization for sociopolitical emancipation.

The BCM discouraged its adherents from cooperating with governmental institutions until its demands for an egalitarian society, with an equitable economic system based on the principle of equal sharing of wealth and a universal franchise, were met. In recognition that the present state was illegitimate, the BCM demanded a completely new constitution. Blacks, the BCM asserted, were no longer interested in reforming the system, as this implied accepting the major premises on which it was based. They were working towards the creation of a new state, decrying the fact that "in a land rightfully ours we find people coming to tell us where to stay and what powers we shall have without even consulting us. The whole idea is made to appear as if for us, while working against our very existence."[77] As with the ANC and the PAC almost a decade earlier, the state responded to the BCM with force in an effort to eliminate it. This was especially true after the "Soweto uprisings" of 1976, although harassment had begun well before that time.[78] On June 16 of that year, when school children from the conglomeration of African townships known as Soweto demonstrated against the imposition of the Afrikaans language as a medium of their instruction, the police fired into the crowd of 15,000, killing two. Within a week, 176 students had been killed in the surrounding areas. This set off a nationwide chain of protests, and again the government had to resort to an ever increasing use of force in an effort to maintain control. Class boycotts by grade school and high school students were joined by workers boycotting in solidarity, and riots spread to several urban areas. By mid-1977, an estimated seven hundred people had been killed by the security forces, thousands injured, and tens of thousands detained or imprisoned. The BCM was blamed for the uprisings, and in October 1977 all movements associated with it were banned, including SASO and the BPC.

In addition to being challenged internally by the BCM, the South African state also faced opposition from the liberation movements in exile.[79] In 1960, the ANC established both a foreign mission and a military training program, and with the trial of Mandela and others in 1964, the political and military leadership of the ANC moved from within South Africa to outside. Although its underground network was broken up and crushed by security forces in the 1960s, the ANC began to reestablish a small underground presence in the country during the 1970s. In the aftermath of the Soweto uprisings, it reemerged as an enormously popular group in the townships. *Umkhonto We Sizwe,* whose ranks had swelled in the aftermath of the uprisings and the resultant exodus of approximately 8,000 youths, then reembarked on a campaign of sabotage and guerrilla warfare. Although the scale and frequency of *Umkhonto* attacks were limited, rising to approximately three hundred incidents a year, this armed struggle ensured increasing support for the ANC, particularly among the younger generations in the townships. While the military threat was never a serious one for the apartheid state's armed forces, it did play an important role in sustaining and developing support in the townships for the liberation struggle that was to reach new heights of intensity in the 1980s.

Conclusion

It is possible to discern certain watershed experiences in the evolution of black protests against the entrenching of white domination in South Africa. This was clearly the case in 1910 with the formation of the Union, in 1913 with the Land Act, and in 1936 with the two Hertzog Bills, the Representation of Natives Act, and the Native Trust and Land Act. This reactive process was also present in the aftermath of the 1948 election with its Afrikaner victory and the rise of the Defiance Campaign, and in the 1960s with the turn to violence in the aftermath of the ANC and PAC banning. By the 1980s, when the government promulgated its reformed apartheid constitution, the entire black protest movement mobilized to undermine this constitution and thereby further challenge the structures of the apartheid state. Thus, the agenda for black politics was constantly being established by the actions of the white government. In this process, the goals and tactics of black protest evolved from challenging specific government policies to challenging the very legitimacy of the state itself. The ANC, at the same time, grew from a political "pressure group" to a full-fledged popular liberation movement. Its tactics changed from cautious and deferential appeals to the government, to a commitment to the violent undermining of the state. Three periods in this mounting challenge to white authority and power can be demarcated, each coinciding with a different form of struggle: constitutional protest politics, extra-constitutional civil disobedience, and finally, armed struggle.

The period from 1912 to 1949 was one of protesting the policies of successive governments using the tactics of constitutional reform. From the beginning of this period, while Africans were seeking an extension of political rights to all qualified individuals, regardless of race and according to traditional British democratic principles, the reality in South Africa was a trend towards restriction of existing rights and the permanent exclusion of Africans from an essentially all-white political system. Throughout the period, the ANC remained steadfast in its commitment to nonviolent tactics to bring about reform, for African leaders still considered the state reformable. Although the policies of the government were moving increasingly away from the ideal of a nonracial common society, blacks still held out hope that a particular government might relent and change direction. In the first four decades of the Union of South Africa, Africans did not believe that the state itself was set in concrete as a "segregationist state," and so from 1912 until 1949—the pre-Afrikaner period—the ANC adhered strictly to a constitutional struggle, putting forward petitions, demands, and resolutions, and sending endless delegations to politely request justice from successive governments.

By the beginning of the second period of 1949 to 1961, however, in the aftermath of Afrikaner victory, blacks were becoming increasingly disillusioned with nonviolent appeals to intransigent white governments. This was a period of ambiguity and transition, when the ANC and its allies began to seriously question the nature of the state, while remaining committed to nonviolence in the ever more forlorn hope of peaceful reform. With the adoption of the Programme of Action, the ANC undertook a tactical change from strictly constitutional methods of protest to peaceful but unlawful protests against apartheid legislation. This Defiance Campaign proved to be the last major effort at a wholly nonviolent challenge to the government's policies. With the forceful crushing of the Campaign by the state, Africans began rejecting the sole reliance on nonviolent tactics, arguing that the South African system was inherently violent and could only be destroyed with the aid of revolutionary violence.[80] This period of ambiguity was best highlighted in the Treason Trial in 1960, in which all the accused were acquitted. The government clearly recognized that the nature of the state was being seriously questioned by the protest movement, but was unable to prove that the state itself was being challenged with revolutionary intent. In general, however, black politics in the 1950s consisted of exerting increasing pressure on the system, rather than the complete destruction of that system.

Within a few short years, this situation changed dramatically, particularly after 1964, when the state in effect convicted Nelson Mandela and other ANC leaders of treason.[81] The third period, 1961 through the 1980s, was therefore marked by an overt challenge to the state. By 1961 the state was irretrievably identified with apartheid policies and was no longer deemed reformable. Exactly when this shift occurred is obviously a matter of interpretation, but the year 1959 must be considered a critical juncture in the liberation movement's perceptions of the South African state, for in that year the government enacted the Promotion of Bantu Self-Government Act. The act had two blatantly negative consequences for legitimacy in the eyes of Africans. First, it abolished the white Native Representatives in Parliament, marking the culmination of a long process of eroding African political rights: starting in 1910 when Africans were excluded from eligibility in Parliament, to 1936 with their removal from the Cape common voters roll, in 1951 with the abolition of the ineffective but symbolic Native Representative Council, and finally in 1959 with the removal of the last vestige of African participation in the central parliamentary structures.

Secondly, the 1959 legislation provided for the creation of the eight (eventually ten) Bantustans and also marked the first move towards eventual independence for these "homelands," with a concomitant loss of all citizenship rights for Africans in the so-called white areas. With this legislation, the Afrikaner Nationalist "Model State" was becoming a reality. Although this outcome was inherent in the government's commitment to apartheid in 1948, it was not achieved until 1959. Earlier apartheid legislation, such as the tightening of segregation in townships and the Population Registration Act, for example, did not fundamentally alter the nature of the state. Rather, these laws merely tightened discriminatory practices that had been prevalent much earlier. The creation of legal "homelands," the most overt manifestation of the theory of apartheid, fundamentally altered the playing field for Africans. It was now undeniably obvious that nonviolent protest had not only failed to influence the government; it had produced ever deepening intransigence.

The creation of the homelands coincided with the banning of the ANC in 1960 and the turn to violence by that organization. At this point, all forms of anti-apartheid protest had become illegal, and the only mechanism for legal participation was through the newly created homeland structures. If the ANC were to remain nonviolent, it would have had to do so by operating within the rigid institutions of a confining context it had spent fifty years fighting against, namely "separate development." Rather than joining the system and giving in on its fundamental principles, thereby legitimating the apartheid state, the ANC chose to confront that state through the use of violence. When the nature of the apartheid state became clearer with the creation of these new homeland structures, and when the patterns of repression that were required to force that system into existence and maintain it intensified, the period of ambiguity ended. The state itself now became the focus of attack, and *Umkhonto We Sizwe* and the guerrilla struggle were born. This changing political context deeply impacted the liberation movement. It affected progressive elements within churches as well. Churches along with secular movements were forced to consider questions of resistance and violence.

Twenty-five years after the banning of the ANC, the South African churches, challenged by the Kairos Document, were forced to take up the legitimacy issue. While this debate was new to these churches, it was not new to other groups. Although theologians now posed the question of legitimacy, this questioning clearly had roots in the liberation movement.[82] The institutional churches interacted with this culture of protest, were conditioned by it, contributed to it, and were able to carry on a dialogue with it. This occurred only after activist elements within the churches became entangled in the changing political context, and after they adopted new ideas which led to shared values and like-minded political judgments that merged with those prevalent in black political culture.

Black political culture in the twentieth century has been open to and conditioned by religious influences from the very beginning. The task of the churches in the 1980s was made easier by the precedent of biblical language and Christian theology being used in resistance. Walshe argues that African political leaders from the early days of the protest movement espoused what might now be termed a "nascent liberation or contextual theology."[83] Dating to the first ANC president, there has been a long precedent of mixing religion and politics—although not in an institutional sense. The institutional involvement of the churches in challenging the state did not occur until the 1980s.

3

Changing Political Context

The Spiral of Involvement

WITH A SHARPLY deteriorating domestic political situation in the 1980s, several activist elements within the institutional churches, influenced by new religious ideas, finally took a cue from the liberation movements and actively entered the legitimacy debate. Although these church leaders did not explicitly set out in the early 1980s to declare the South African state illegitimate, by the end of the decade they had engaged the issue, having been politicized through a process of spiraling involvement in civil society and increasing church/state conflict. This chapter explores how the distinctive political characteristics of the 1980s contributed to changing self-identities of the SACC and the SACBC. In essence, these characteristics resulted from the government's complete disinterest in garnering the consent of the governed. Levels of repression reached an all-time high, and the masses responded with unprecedented levels of civil disobedience. By the late 1980s, activist Christian leaders were in the forefront of the struggle, leading protest marches, boycotting elections, and meeting with banned organizations at home and in exile. The SACC and the SACBC, as organizations, intensified their overt involvement, coming to play an active part in ensuring the collapse of apartheid, and seeing this commitment as an integral part of their Christian mission. While the role of theology is not the main focus here, it should also be recognized that this evolution was not simply the result of a changing political context: both the SACC and SACBC were simultaneously influenced by new religious ideas.

The Political Context: The 1980s

By the late 1970s and early 1980s, the government under P. W. Botha was beginning to realize that the system of apartheid, as it had been pragmatically assembled after 1948, was no longer viable. Apartheid's structures were coming under increasing pressure from several areas, producing a response from the government that was a combination of reform and repression. The popular reaction to this new government activity and the government's counter-response define the political context of the 1980s.

One pressure area for the South African government was demographic. As explained in chapter 2, under the theory of apartheid Africans were supposed to live in "independent homelands," which were to have their own economies and political systems. This was proving to be untenable. The population growth rate for Africans was 2.7 percent and rising, while the growth rate for whites was only 1.5 percent and declining.[1] The increase in the African population was contributing to rapid urbanization and straining the South African economy, which was already feeling the pressure of incipient international economic sanctions. Added to this was the fact that after the Soweto uprisings in 1976, capital flight began to take place in reaction to the belief that South Africa was no longer a safe climate for investment. Other pressures were felt regionally from the disappearance of apartheid's buffer zone after the sudden collapse of Portuguese rule in Angola and Mozambique in 1974, the concomitant rise of the MPLA and FRELIMO, respectively, and the increased activity of SWAPO in Namibia. Finally, the independence of Zimbabwe in 1980 under Robert Mugabe's ZANU—rather than under Bishop Muzorewa, a puppet of the Smith regime—dealt a blow to South Africa's control of the region. Moreover, the South African government feared the potential radicalizing effect of these changes on domestic South African politics. Already, thousands of blacks had fled from South Africa after the Soweto uprisings to join the ANC in exile, which was beginning to infiltrate its cadres back into the country. By the early 1980s, therefore, the apartheid regime was facing a set of crises that could no longer be ignored. Under these new political circumstances, the existing version of apartheid had become a costly and ineffective way of preserving white hegemony.

The South African government responded to this crisis with a strategy that combined both repression and reform. This Reform/Repression approach, also known as "Winning Hearts and Minds" or WHAM, was designed to implement managed change while keeping political expectations within acceptable limits. As this strategy proved unsuccessful, the government increasingly abandoned the pretense of rule by law and relied ever more heavily on force. This was met each step of the way by a decrease in the consent of the governed, evidenced by a strengthening protest movement whose explicit goal was to "make apartheid ungovernable."

As noted in chapter 1, South Africa during the 1980s, like many Latin American countries, was dominated by a national security ideology. In South Africa this ideology was epitomized by the twin concepts of total strategy and total onslaught. This required a huge increase in defense expenditures throughout the decade as well as an increase in the role played by the South African Defense Force (SADF) in internal repression. The underlying ideas and assumptions of the concept of total onslaught were that the survival of the state was threatened by unrest that served the ends of communism, and that all internal criticism was either inspired or fostered by communists. This attitude was described by P. W. Botha in 1978:

> The ultimate aim of the Soviet Union and its allies is to overthrow the present body politic in the Republic of South Africa and to replace it with a Marxist-oriented form of government to further the objectives of the USSR. Therefore all possible methods and means are used to attain this objective. This includes instigating social and labour unrest, civilian resistance, terrorist attacks against the infrastructure of South Africa, and the intimidation of black leaders and members of the security forces. This onslaught is supported by a world-wide propaganda campaign and the involvement of various front organizations, such as the trade unions and even certain church organizations and leaders.[2]

The state and all its people, according to the government, lived in a permanent state of war. Consequently, any means which enhanced national security were justified. To meet the challenge of this total onslaught, a total strategy had to be devised to guide the operation of all areas of life, and within this strategy the military was located at the center of state power. According to Botha, the strategy would be "applicable at all levels and to all functions of the state structure, incorporating political, economic, psychological, technological and military means."[3] As is the case with security states throughout the world, South Africa in the 1980s was characterized by the following phenomena: a well-organized and lavishly financed military, secret police, detentions without trial, torture, bannings of people and organizations, counter-insurgency operations, covert operations, and assassinations.[4]

Although these ideas had been in place since the late 1970s, it was only with the 1986 state of emergency that they became fully institutionalized. The organizational mechanism in which the total strategy was embodied was the revived State Security Council (SSC), which had been created in 1972 but was not utilized until Botha's ascension to power in 1978. In 1979 its role was redefined to "conduct" rather than to "advise upon" the "national planning process."[5] The SSC could not be considered a legitimate governing body: it was not democratically elected, nor was it responsible to Parliament.

The second aspect of the government's strategy was to introduce a series of reforms intended to dismantle certain aspects of apartheid. The intention was to gain a veneer of legitimacy by co-opting a segment of the black population into the existing framework of power. These reforms were also an attempt to convince the world, which was becoming increasingly skeptical, that the National Party enjoyed the consent of the majority of the population. One of the most popular strategies for achieving these objectives was "deracialization"—dismantling those laws mandating segregation in social, personal, and public life. This was accomplished through such reforms as the repeal of the

Prohibition of Mixed Marriages and the Immorality Acts, as well as the abolition of officially mandated race segregation in public amenities. In all this, the government was careful to end only "unnecessary" racial discrimination, and was not so quick to dismantle racist laws when they were deemed necessary to the maintenance of the political, economic, and social position of whites. As F. W. de Klerk stated, "Separation that is necessary to maintain self-determination and to protect the rights of minorities will always remain. But separation that is irritating and unnecessary discrimination will go."[6]

An early reform introduced by the government in 1979 was the legalization of African trade unions—although it was stipulated that they could not act politically. The theory behind this initiative was "labor control through co-optation," the government's hope being that registration would bring organizational benefits to unions, which would be an incentive for moderation.[7] As will be seen, this hoped-for moderation did not occur with legalization.

Reform also led to the creation of Township Councils, set up through the Black Local Authorities Act of 1982. The Councils were responsible for raising their own revenue. They did so by taxing residents, who also had to pay rent to the Councils for their state-owned homes. Pretoria's goal in the creation of these Councils was to shift immediate control over the black population from the central government to elected representatives of this segregated population, and in so doing reduce the political costs to the state of exercising repressive control.[8]

The primary goal of these wide-ranging reforms was always the co-optation of blacks, for the government never intended to forfeit control of the political system. Nowhere was this more obvious than in the new constitution in 1983. This reform was introduced to widen the state's power base and to give the government a semblance of legitimacy; however, it made no fundamental change in the structure of apartheid, and whites alone were allowed to vote in a referendum on the constitution. Under the new dispensation, Indians and Coloreds were permitted to elect candidates to their own, ethnically segregated, houses of Parliament. In this new tri-cameral parliament, whites were to elect 178 members to the House of Assembly, Coloreds 85 members to the House of Representatives, and Indians 45 members to the House of Delegates.[9] With this same 4:2:1 ratio, members of parliament were elected to a presidential electoral college, which thus was comprised of 50 whites, 25 Coloreds, and 13 Indians, thereby guaranteeing whites control over the state presidency. Most importantly, Africans were given no role in this new constitution. Instead, they were to vote for apartheid's homeland political structures and the township councils to exercise their political rights. More than any other reform, this new constitution revealed the true nature of the government's strategy—to adapt in order to avoid a loss of control.[10]

While the Reform/Repression strategy was supposed to produce co-optation, collaboration, and acquiescence, it failed to do so. Instead, it produced insurrection. The introduction of the new constitution served as a stimulus for mass mobilization by government opponents, especially among Africans but also among Indians, Coloreds, and whites. Moreover, the reforms were rejected by the very group, the black middle class, they were designed to placate. In fact, those groups who were the object of the co-optation policy moved to the forefront of black unrest—including trade unionists, students, church people, community workers, teachers, and journalists. Their reaction to the repression and reforms was to create a variety of new organizations, including community, youth, women's, labor, student, and political groups, to oppose the reforms. These associations formed the organizational foundation for a countrywide liberation movement.[11] The impetus for the growth of these civic associations was the hardships imposed by the township councils, especially the escalating rent charges. The state responded to these protests by detaining leaders and deploying police to break up demonstrations, which in turn only generated more organization and protest. The protest movement adopted a strategy of "refusal politics," including consumer, school, and bus boycotts, rent strikes, and political stayaways.

A move to "alliance politics" led to the creation of the United Democratic Front (UDF) in 1983, the first nationally organized mass movement of black opposition since the ANC and PAC had been banned in 1960.[12] The impetus for its formation was twofold: the creation of the township councils, which came into effect in August 1983, and the new constitution, to be voted on in a whites-only referendum in November of the same year. The UDF was launched nationally on August 20, 1983, by representatives from 575 organizations, with the underlying principles of

> an unshakable conviction in the creation of a non-racial unitary state in South Africa undiluted by racial or ethnic considerations, an adherence to the need for unity in struggle through which all democrats—regardless of race, religion or color—shall take part, and a recognition of the necessity to work in consultation with and reflect accurately the demands of democratic people wherever they may be.[13]

The UDF saw itself as a nonviolent mass movement of extra-parliamentary opposition formed to prevent the implementation of the new constitution and to paralyze the township councils. The grass-roots, community-based organizations which had proliferated in the 1980s formed its organizational core, and this offered a certain protection in the face of mounting state repression. Although its national leaders could be detained, and indeed they were, it was difficult to completely cripple the UDF because of its grass-roots character. It was therefore much more difficult to remove than it had been to repress the ANC and the PAC in 1960, as well as the BCM in the 1970s.[14] Through the

UDF, which eventually embraced the ANC's Freedom Charter as its guiding principles, the ANC's presence was vastly enhanced within internal black politics, where it became almost as active as it had been before its banning. The organizers of the UDF were careful to maintain links with the pre-Sharpeville resistance movement, for example, by appointing a veteran ANC activist, Archie Gumede—active in the Defiance Campaign of the 1950s—as UDF president, to indicate to South Africans that they saw their mission as continuing the struggle to delegitimize the South African state that was begun by the ANC.

By 1986 a large majority of the black population was involved in the insurrection, which drew support from virtually the entire social spectrum. One of the main characteristics of the UDF's mobilization was "issue linkage," in which organizations as varied as student organizations, civic associations, and trade unions joined together to protest issues ranging from rent increases to community councils and the elections to the new parliament. Geographically and functionally diverse organizations were linked together under the umbrella of the UDF, which gave the movement a national political direction. Multiple forms of UDF-coordinated nonviolent mass resistance, including school boycotts and political strikes, were combined with escalating armed sabotage by the military wing of the ANC. Between August 1984 and the end of 1986, political work stoppages known as "stayaways" were staged four times more often than in the previous three and a half decades combined.[15] The mounting popularity of the UDF—in its first four years, UDF membership had grown to 700 affiliates, involving from two to four million people—is testament to the fact that by the mid-1980s, the South African government had lost all vestiges of legitimacy in the eyes of the majority of its people, who were neither asked for nor gave their consent to the government.

The South African state's response to the growing protest movement was swift and brutal, abandoning the rule of law and relying, in black townships, solely on force. The government's strategy was characterized by its propagandists as counterrevolution, detailed in the SSC manual, *The Art of Counterrevolutionary War*. According to the SSC, the first step in this new strategy was the "annihilation of the enemy."[16] With the imposition of the second state of emergency on June 12, 1986, the "Reform" dimension of the Reform/Repression strategy was abandoned, giving way to the implementation of straightforward military measures regardless of their political consequences. This new campaign of repression had several elements, the first of which was simply an increase in the manpower deployed to counter the insurgency and to enforce "law and order." This included the deployment of both the SADF and the South African Police virtually as occupation forces in black areas.[17]

By the 1980s, the primary role of the police was to destroy black opposition rather than to fight crime. This was accomplished through the twin strategies of criminalization and suppression. Criminalization occurred through making actions criminal which were previously regarded as legal, and by labeling an ordinary act (such as a funeral) "political" in order to allow it to fall outside the realm of normal behavior, thereby giving the police wider discretion to act. In 1985, 22 percent of the almost 19,000 people detained for "unrest offenses" were under sixteen years of age, and there was widespread mistreatment and torture of minors and others. Besides criminalization, the SAP were also heavily involved in suppression. The police were given powers of arrest and search without warrant anywhere in the country. They were also given the right to use force "resulting in death" if people refused to heed instructions given in "a loud voice," as well as a myriad of other powers to control all facets of resistance and organizational activity. In reality, the state of emergency removed all controls on police conduct by giving members of the police and security forces indemnity from civil and criminal prosecution, so long as they acted "in good faith." In tense circumstances, the police were also issued submachine guns and shotguns.[18]

Another characteristic of the repression strategy was an increase in the apprehension and detention of political activists. By the end of 1986, over 29,000 people were detained, which was almost three times more than in the post-Sharpeville period, twelve times more than the post-Soweto period, and four times more than during the first state of emergency in 1985.[19] Of these, 75 percent were members of UDF affiliates, 25 percent were under the age of twenty-five, and 10 percent were women. By the 1980s South Africa had the highest per capita prison population in the world, and from 1984 through 1990 it had almost 50 percent of recorded government executions worldwide.[20]

The few remaining legal means of opposition were effectively removed in February 1988, when the government conducted perhaps the most draconian security clampdown ever. After months of preparation and the accumulation of evidence, Botha proclaimed sweeping new emergency powers, under which the UDF and seventeen of its affiliates were banned. Additionally, the Congress of South African Trade Unions (COSATU), the country's largest trade union organization, was ordered not to engage in "external political activities." These bannings were supplemented by a campaign of covert harassment, disruption, and assassinations, exemplified by the bombing of COSATU headquarters in May 1987.[21]

In the aftermath of the 1988 bannings, it became illegal to "promote the public image or esteem of an organization which is an unlawful (or restricted) organization (such as the UDF)."[22] Nevertheless, by 1988 the liberation movement had reached such strength that it simply refused to be banned. On August 2, 1989, a Defiance Campaign (so named in recognition of the role of the ANC and its Defiance Campaign of the 1950s) was launched by the Mass Democratic Movement (MDM), a loose alliance of organizations with the UDF and

COSATU at its core. The campaign quickly spread throughout the country, bringing workers, students, and civic organizations together to defy laws. Other symbolic actions included press conferences, services, and rallies to publicly defy the restrictions placed on individuals and organizations, as well as organizations simply declaring themselves unbanned. Banned rallies were attended by tens of thousands of people, and elections were boycotted to the tune of a 70 percent stayaway in September 1989.

Church Involvement in the 1980s

Three characteristics of this political situation set the 1980s apart from any preceding time. The first was the intensity of the opposition to the government, with the diffusion of protest throughout all aspects of everyday life. The uprisings of the 1980s were "more radical, more violent, more widespread, and more sustained than anything witnessed in modern South African history."[23] Along with the intensity of protest, the 1980s were marked by an organizational sophistication that was unprecedented. The explosion of grass-roots organizations and their embrace of "alliance politics" laid the foundation for a nationwide liberation movement of such strength that the government was never able to fully control or extinguish it. The third distinguishing characteristic of the 1980s was the harshness of state repression in its efforts to quell the rising protest. In these attempts, "[t]heir systematic campaign of repression combined a number of elements that in both their intensity and combination were new to the South African scene."[24]

The SACC and SACBC responded to these characteristics. Both organizations became increasingly politicized because they were drawn into a "spiral of involvement," described in chapter 1. Broken down into its component parts, this "spiral of involvement" consisted of three interrelated processes: The first was being "jarred into action." The sheer level of repression shocked the SACC and SACBC into examining the roles they might play in ending this brutality. This examination led them to the conclusion that they had to become more politicized. Second, this resulted in a growing church/state conflict, in the form of state reaction against church leaders and counter-reaction by these organizations. As church leaders and workers became targets of the state's repression, their level of politicization increased dramatically. By continuing to speak out against an increasingly repressive government, church leaders incurred the wrath of the government, which responded by harassing, detaining, deporting, and sometimes torturing church personnel. The final component of the spiral is that church leaders were increasingly becoming the "voice of the voiceless." As the leadership of civil society was slowly but surely removed and silenced through repression, the churches increasingly became the only space left for internal legal opposition, which forced them to accept a more political self-identity.

Thus, in the early 1980s the political activity of the SACC and SACBC, such as it was, primarily took the form of condemning repressive legislation and the human rights abuses of the government; by the late 1980s church leaders had become highly politicized. They continued to respond to the worsening political context, *plus* they were involved in a conflict with the state which took on a life of its own, *plus* they were filling a political void caused by the removal of political leaders from society. The sum of these three processes resulted in the SACC declaring the state illegitimate, and the SACBC coming close to doing so as well.

I. 1980–1983

Even before the government introduced the 1983 constitution, both the SACC and the SACBC had been outspoken opponents of the government, and an incipient church/state conflict was underway. Several incidents are worth mentioning. In the first few years of the 1980s, the primary targets of the state's anger in the SACC were Bishop Desmond Tutu (then General Secretary of the SACC) and Reverend Allan Boesak (an SACC vice-president)—long-standing and vocal opponents of apartheid. Bishop Tutu angered the government by issuing rather cautious statements calling for "economic pressures" (the word "sanctions" was far from being used at this point) to promote political change in South Africa. In October 1979, the government responded by summoning Tutu to the Ministry of Justice and issuing him an ultimatum to stop such calls or to face possible action against both himself and the SACC. Bishop Tutu responded by exhorting churches to move beyond the level of simply denouncing apartheid and to adopt overt political action. At the 1980 SACC National Conference he stated, "We cannot be content only to protest verbally: the Church must do more than just talk. The survival of South Africa is at stake. . . . We must oppose the total strategy with all the fibre of our being."[25]

By 1981 Tutu had become the main target of a bitter and sustained campaign by senior government leaders, politicians, and pro-state media. After confiscating his passport, which generated widespread international protest, the Minister of Police sharply attacked Tutu by accusing him in Parliament of "supporting subversive elements and encouraging the build-up of a revolution in South Africa." Under threat of being silenced, Tutu responded that he would refuse to observe any banning orders, and the government would have to jail him to stop his activities.[26]

Thus, in the early 1980s, some members of the SACC were themselves aware that the SACC was involved primarily at the level of making statements which were not often backed up by action. In fact, in 1980 the SACC voted against a proposal (by one vote) to make a corporate act of witness in Pretoria (which would have been classified as a "riotous assembly" and therefore illegal). Moreover, while the SACC was calling for some acts of civil disobedience, it was still operating under the belief that the government could be reformed and that the best way to ensure this was through negotiations. However, individual church leaders, preeminently but not solely Bishop Tutu and Reverend Allan Boesak, were becoming increasingly aware of the need to become more politically involved, in the sense of actually working through public confrontation for the end of apartheid. Within a month of voting against the proposed act of witness, fifty-three bishops, clergy and a few lay people were jailed overnight for protesting against detention without trial.[27] The SACC was moving towards an ever greater confrontation with the state. In 1981 Tutu announced that he would not attend any further meetings between the SACC and the government until the state president apologized for constant attacks on the SACC and the state's "unrelenting campaign of vilification and denigration." Two months later, the security police detained the SACC's Minister of Refugees, to which the SACC responded by accusing the government of blatant interference in the affairs of the churches.[28]

By 1981, statements by the Catholic Bishops' Conference were also beginning to change in tone, going beyond declarations of denunciation to calling for specific actions to resist the state. During that year the bishops refused to participate in the official celebration marking the twentieth anniversary of the establishment of the Republic, because "the vast majority of the people . . . who are deprived and oppressed, . . . see no cause for celebration."[29]

The SACBC, however, was drawn much deeper into the spiral of church involvement in May 1982, when it published its *Report on Namibia*. This exposé, issued after a six-person delegation visited Namibia in September of 1981 with the goal of securing first-hand experiences of the attitude of black Namibians, stated that atrocities were being carried out by members of the armed forces and that most Namibians viewed the South African military as an army of occupation. The report was immediately denounced by the South African authorities, primarily because it painted a picture of conditions that was in striking contrast with that presented by South Africa's heavily censored media.[30] As a result of the report, what started out as a desire of the SACBC to fulfill its mission of ministering to its constituents in the political context of increasing human rights abuses in Namibia, which is a member of the SACBC, resulted in the SACBC being drawn into further conflict with the state. Calling for a "Day of Prayer" for Namibia in November 1982, the SACBC circulated a four-page abridged version of the original report. Two months later this was declared undesirable literature by the South African Publications Board, "bordering on high treason."[31] This marked the first time that an entire SACBC report had been suppressed. In his response to the banning, Archbishop Hurley, president of the SACBC, called on the Conference to play a more active role in sociopolitical affairs in Southern Africa: "The evolution of the Church towards an ever increasing concern about the social, political, economic and cultural dimensions of human life, is a fact of our time. . . . The evolution is slow. The process of moving from declarations, resolutions, findings and recommendations to implementation and action is painful and precarious and at times scarcely perceptible."[32]

A second event which served to politicize church leaders, in this case the SACC,[33] was its 1982 conference resolution, which declared that apartheid was not simply a sociopolitical order but must also be seen as a theological issue which was in total contradiction of the gospel, and was therefore a heresy. This had immediate political consequences for the SACC, not least because of the state's subsequent actions. The government responded by instigating an investigation into SACC finances, which evolved into a four-year-long major campaign against the Council. Known as the Eloff Commission of Inquiry into the South African Council of Churches, the investigation drew worldwide attention. The year following the SACC resolution, the World Alliance of Reformed Churches (WARC), challenged by the Reverend Allan Boesak—a vice-president of the SACC at the time—not only declared apartheid a heresy, but suspended the powerful and influential pro-apartheid white Nederduits Gereformeerde Kerk (NGK or Dutch Reformed Church) from its membership. At the same Ottawa meeting of the WARC, Boesak was elected president. The SACC's, and subsequently the WARC's, declaration of apartheid as a heresy should be viewed as one of the most significant watersheds in church-state relations in South Africa, because it challenged the churches to leave the realm of abstract speculation and to start seriously contributing towards making a new political dispensation in South Africa a reality.[34] As one scholar argued, the declaration's implicit call to action—"If apartheid is a heresy theologically, its practice must be challenged politically"—became an important rallying cry for Christian resistance.[35]

II. 1983–1985

Just as the promulgation of a new constitution in 1983 prompted a resurgence in the liberation movement in the form of the UDF, so it—along with the increasingly repressive political situation—jarred the SACC and SACBC into adopting a more overtly political level of involvement in the anti-apartheid struggle. Moreover, in the course of the discussion about the Namibian issue, members of the Bishops' Conference remarked that they could hardly become so involved in Namibia without showing equal concern for what was happening in South Africa. Thus, in 1983 both the SACBC and the SACC turned their attention to denouncing the new political developments, specifically the country's new constitution.

One reason church leaders felt they were obliged to engage critically and actively in the debate over the constitution was because the state claimed divine sanction in the preamble, by referring to "Almighty God and His protection of His people in times of stress."[36] Since the SACC had already declared the theological justification of apartheid a heresy, it saw itself as having no choice but to oppose a constitution which further entrenched apartheid.[37] The SACBC, too, vociferously protested the new constitution.[38] However, despite the fact that these organizations exhorted their constituents not to support the new constitution, 66 percent of voters in a whites-only referendum later that year approved it. This approval drew a sharp attack from the SACBC president, Archbishop Hurley:

> We cannot accept the new constitution because, far from recognizing the right to participation of all in the economy, in politics, education and culture, it continues to enshrine the apartheid principle of separation . . . separate, unequal and powerless. Until the principle of genuine participation is recognised it is not possible to accept a constitution, nor is it right to expect those adversely affected to pay to an apartheid constitution the tribute of a vote that would appear to legitimate it.[39]

The seeds of politicization were sown in speeches such as this, with their implicit support for acts of civil disobedience and passive resistance.

The move towards becoming more engaged politically was also evident in the conference resolutions of each organization. In 1983, the SACC was slowly edging beyond making statements, by passing resolutions which actually required a measure of action by its membership. First, it undertook a much more serious consideration of the feasibility and desirability of economic sanctions than it had done previously. Although it had not yet reached the stage of calling outright for economic sanctions, it did pass a conference resolution calling on member churches to refrain from "supporting or investing money in industrial, commercial and other institutions that are directly engaged in defending the present apartheid system in South Africa."[40] The Council also increasingly supported the boycott of institutions, calling on its member churches to "encourage their membership to evaluate their participation in bodies, agencies, organisations and institutions that constantly undergird the unjust political apartheid system, and to refrain from such participation wherever practical."[41]

While statements by church leaders, as well as conference resolutions such as the above, were enough in and of themselves to incur the government's anger, the church/state conflict was further heightened when both the SACC and SACBC joined the UDF. Indeed, the very idea of the UDF originated with

Allan Boesak, who had already angered the state by spearheading the move to declare apartheid a heresy. Of the original thirty organizations attending the launching of the UDF in Johannesburg—pledging to "fight together side by side against the Government's constitutional and reform proposals"[42]—two were the Witwatersrand branch of the SACC and the Johannesburg Justice and Peace Commission of the SACBC. In response, the state chose to threaten Catholic archbishop Denis Hurley as a general warning to churches not to "meddle in politics." Hurley was then charged and prosecuted for statements he made regarding alleged atrocities carried out by South African–trained security forces in Namibia.[43] The government also harassed other church workers, For example, Father Smangaliso Mkhatshwa, SACBC General Secretary, was forcibly detained barely four months after a banning order against him had been lifted.

Thus, by the end of 1983, several interrelated processes were underway which served to draw both the SACC and the SACBC into the social and political struggle in a way they had never before been. First, some church leaders became more aware of their own responsibility in speaking out against human rights abuses. This recognition alone served to politicize these individuals. Second, by acting on these new convictions, these leaders drew the anger of the state, which reacted by banning reports and generally harassing church workers. The ensuing church/state conflict further contributed to the politicization of leaders and their organizations. Third, by 1983, as the state relied increasingly on the rule of force, leaders of the resurgent liberation movement were beginning to be detained, jailed, exiled, or killed. In this context, the churches, without really wanting to, steadily drifted into becoming the vehicles for the expression of black political aspirations.[44] They were being called upon, although not to the extent of the late 1980s, to provide leadership and articulation for black South Africans, the vast majority of whom were Christians. A final source of politicization was that several church leaders themselves were directly involved in the rekindled liberation movement. Both Allan Boesak and Smangaliso Mkhatshwa (while General Secretary of the SACBC) were elected UDF patrons along with Beyers Naudé, who succeeded Tutu as General Secretary of the SACC, while Frank Chikane (then General Secretary of the Institute for Contextual Theology, but later General Secretary of the SACC) was vice-chairman of the Transvaal Branch of the UDF. In short, the changing political scene of the early 1980s led to spiraling involvement of the SACC and SACBC in the political realm.

Several events in 1984 further caused the SACC and SACBC to reevaluate their missions. The first was the February tabling in Parliament of the Eloff Commission report with its recommendations. The commission, which originated with a limited mandate to investigate suspected mismanagement of SACC finances, evolved into an investigation of any aspect of the organization which was deemed "in the public interest." That the government itself viewed the Inquiry as its response to the increasing politicization of the SACC, with the intention of silencing the SACC, was evident in the submission by the South African Police:

> It is the task of the SAP to be on the alert against people or organisations which intend to bring about fundamental change in the South African political and economic system by unconstitutional means. The SACC is alleged to be an organisation of this nature. . . . Furthermore, the SACC covers up its work of 'destabilising' South African society and the South African State by religious arguments and activities and by a particular type of theology.[45]

In his oral evidence, the chief of the Security Police, the state's key witness, alleged that the SACC was cooperating closely with and supporting the ANC, and accused Bishop Tutu in particular of helping to improve the ANC's credibility. After five days of testifying, he concluded that

> there is no doubt that the SACC has as its substantive and only primary goal a striving after fundamental change for the South African society in order to free the so-called oppressed. In order to achieve these secular goals the SACC is active in a number of areas in society, which activities are calculatedly supportive for the achievement of the main goal, namely freedom.[46]

In a 128-page report of evidence against the SACC, he recommended that it be declared an "affected organisation" under the Affected Organisations Act of 1974, which would prevent it from receiving foreign funds. Although the Eloff Commission did not agree, it did recommend that the Council be brought under the discipline of the Fund-Raising Act, which would seriously hamper its ability to raise funds internally.[47]

The SACC was antagonized by statements that it only spent a minimal percentage of its funding for theological purposes, and that the money it did spend was not motivated by Christian compassion but by political considerations. During his testimony before the Eloff Commission, Bishop Tutu challenged the very right of the commission to exist, and stated that the SACC did not recognize its authority to make pronouncements on theology and therefore on any aspect of the Council, since all aspects of its life were determined by its theology. He further accused the state of using a backhanded way of silencing the SACC: "If we have contravened any laws of the country then you don't need a Commission to determine that. There is an array of draconian laws at the disposal of the Government and the Courts of Law are the proper place to determine our guilt or innocence. This Commission, with respect, is totally superfluous."[48] Moreover, Tutu informed the commission that he intended to defy the state, should it come to that: "I want to declare here as forthrightly as I can, that we will continue to do this work come hell or high water."[49]

Through the Eloff Commission, the government attempted, by administrative means rather than through overtly political methods such as a trial, to curtail those activities of the SACC which it considered political. The government could have cracked down much more harshly against the SACC, and many wondered why it did not do so. In addition to the sensitive issue of religious freedom, the state did not want to further tarnish its reputation. During the commission's hearings, worldwide attention was focused on its repressive activities. Nevertheless, world opinion regarding both the South African government and the SACC became clear through the subsequent awarding of the Nobel Peace Prize to Bishop Tutu. This accolade, implying international approval of the SACC's activities, served as a further impetus to politicization, which was indicated in the SACC's response to the award. The SACC saw it as "a call to all churchmen who were in doubt about Bishop Tutu and the SACC to confidently join hands and intensify the fight against apartheid and its evils even if it means becoming so-called 'political priests.'"[50]

The SACC responded angrily to the Eloff Commission's final report. Tutu charged that it was "blasphemous" for the commission to pass judgment on the SACC, and totally rejected its findings. He criticized the commission for having no theologian or black members, even though most of what had been examined related to blacks. He further antagonized the state by saying that he wholeheartedly supported the aims of the ANC, if not its methods, and that nothing would stop him from talking to the ANC.[51] Finally, in a statement on the role of the SACC's Dependents' Conference—which monetarily supported the dependents of political prisoners as well as those banned and detained without trial—he stated:

> I have no doubt that it is this work that has annoyed the government officials more than anything else the SACC does. They obviously don't like our being a thorn in their flesh, constantly opposing this or that iniquitous action or piece of legislation on their part. The appointment of this commission [i.e., Eloff] is purely and simply a political ploy. The government is determined to destroy or seriously handicap the SACC.[52]

In effect, Tutu was acknowledging that by responding to the deteriorating political conditions, the SACC became embroiled in an escalating conflict with the state. In the state's counter-attack, the Minister of Law and Order issued a categorical warning to the SACC that if it continued in its confrontational approach, the state would be forced to act against it.[53]

The second "politicizing" event of 1984 was the joint SACBC/SACC report on forced removals in South Africa, entitled *Relocations*.[54] Published in February (the same month the Eloff Commission report was tabled), this report detailed the number of people forcibly removed by the apartheid regime, the repressive methods used by the government to achieve removal, and the deleterious effects on those forced to be internal refugees. The report specifically challenged the churches to act against this abuse of human rights, encouraging them to accept their "responsibilities of working for radical social change of this socio-economic system."[55] Both the SACC and SACBC were now pledged to resist further forced removals (although it was not specified how). The report drew widespread attention, sold over 20,000 copies within South Africa, and was translated into twelve languages.[56] Additionally, a joint SACC/SACBC delegation traveled to several European countries, briefing government officials and giving conferences on the report, as well as to the United Nations and the Vatican.

Another issue that gained prominence in 1984, drawing church leaders even further into the spiral of involvement, was the End Conscription Campaign (ECC). The Campaign was formed to protest the 1983 Defense Further Amendment Act, which recognized the principle of conscientious objection only for religious pacifists. All other objectors were liable to a six-year prison term—substantially longer than the length of required military service.[57] The state's narrow definition combined with the increasing use of the South African Defense Force to quell unrest within South Africa (especially after the imposition of the 1985 state of emergency) sparked the October 1984 nationwide movement to abolish conscription. As both the SACC and SACBC had a history of supporting conscientious objection, it was a natural choice to support the ECC.[58] That Hurley recognized this stance would draw the anger of the state was obvious in his statement that, "in the South African situation, conscientious objection should be adopted as a principle by the churches. I believe that the churches should adopt this view, even at the risk of open confrontation with the government. Confrontation has to occur some time."[59]

Support for the ECC had a strong politicizing effect on the Catholic Bishops' Conference, because it led them to take up the debate of whether to declare the war in Namibia unjust—especially since many Catholic conscientious objectors used a "just war" argument at their hearing before the Board of Religious Objectors. This came to a head in the 1986 hearing of conscientious objector Philip Wilkinson, at which Archbishop Hurley testified. When asked point-blank whether he considered the activities of the SADF, both inside and outside South Africa, as constituting an unjust war, Hurley replied, "Yes, personally I think that we are in a situation of an unjust war, promoted by the SADF as the armed-force of the South African Government against the oppressed people of South Africa."[60]

By the end of 1984, both organizations were moving towards integrating a political dimension in their self-understanding. However, both organizations were still rather cautious, and not yet willing to publicly state that they had a role to play in the political developments of South Africa. For example, in its response to the Eloff Commission Report, the SACC's Presidium, while denouncing the state's conceptualization of the role and mission of the SACC, nevertheless went to great lengths to deny that it was slowly becoming more politicized: "The Presidium denies that there was ever a campaign of civil disobedience and non-cooperation with the State or support of a disinvestment campaign."[61] During the Eloff Commission hearings, SACC president Peter Storey testified that "the SACC denies in the strongest terms any allegiance to or alliance with the ANC. . . . " Within a few short years, much of this caution—especially on the part of the SACC—was thrown to the wind. Soon, many church leaders and SACC office-holders were publicly calling for economic sanctions, actively supporting and eventually participating in acts of civil disobedience, and meeting with and declaring support for the exiled liberation movements. Thus, the state accused the SACC of activities (including "civil disobedience, evasion of military conscription, and the international disinvestment campaign") that it denied in 1984 but indeed undertook in the late 1980s.

III. 1985–1988

In 1985 the political situation took another turn for the worse with the July imposition of a partial state of emergency, which was renewed and widened in June 1986 and yet again in 1987. Between July 1985 and July 1986, almost 1200 political deaths were recorded, and over 30,000 people had been detained.[62] In November 1985, COSATU was formed and promptly pronounced itself in favor of disinvestment. In the same month the UDF was declared an "affected organization," in an attempt to deny it foreign financial support. In this political context, the SACC and SACBC adopted a much more determined and overt level of political action.

Beyers Naudé, who had by this time taken over as General Secretary of the SACC, urged member churches to undertake resistance to the government, including well-planned acts of civil disobedience. He warned that they would lose their credibility if moral denunciation was not accompanied by nonviolent actions to "break the power of an oppressive and unjust system and thereby bring it to its knees."[63] The Council responded to Naudé's call by issuing a resolution that for the first time officially called for "disinvestment and similar economic pressures." Not only was this a more confrontational stance on disinvestment than the SACC took during the Eloff Commission, but through the resolution the SACC actually broke the law, because by this time it had become illegal even to discuss economic sanctions.[64] Before the end of its 1985 Conference, Naudé received a message from the Minister of Law and Order which threatened action against him and the SACC: "The present campaign which you are conducting to encourage civil disobedience can lead to illegality, licentiousness, confrontation with the authorities and eventually violence. . . . There is no lack of clarity regarding the implications contained in civil disobedience."[65] A week after the conference, President Botha wrote an open letter to Naudé, stating "you have no mandate to assume this arrogant attitude on the national affairs of South Africa. You should decide whether you are a church organisation or a political activist group."[66]

Several other campaigns in 1985 drew the SACC and SACBC into further confrontation with the state. In May, the SACC issued a "Call to Prayer for an End to Unjust Rule" to be observed on June 16, the anniversary of the Soweto school uprising. (The SACBC issued its own, comparably worded call to "pray more earnestly and hopefully than before that all the evils of apartheid may be brought to a speedy end.")[67] The campaign was the result of the SACC's frustration with the ineffectiveness of its appeals for reform in the face of a worsening political situation:

> We have prayed for our rulers, as is demanded of us in the Scriptures. We have entered into consultation with them as is required by our faith. We have taken the reluctant and drastic step of declaring apartheid to be contrary to the declared will of God, and some churches have declared its theological justification to be a heresy. We now pray that God will replace the present structures of oppression with ones that are just, and remove from power those who persist in defying his laws. . . . [68]

The document had serious implications for church/state relations because it requested Christians to cease praying *for* the Government and instead to pray *against* it, that is, for its removal. This had potentially serious political ramifications, for if the call was carried through to its logical conclusion, all delegations to the government or any requests from the regime's representatives had to be questioned. Some argued that the churches could not, with any integrity, have any dealings with the government, once they had asked God to remove it from office.[69]

Two other events in 1985 drew church organizations, especially the SACC, still further into the country's now tumultuous politics. The first was the September publication of the Kairos Document, and the second was the December consultation of church and political leaders held under the auspices of the World Council of Churches. The Kairos Document was the product of a group of some 152 theologians who came together to assess the way in which churches were involved in the political crisis of the time, contrasting this with how they ought to be engaged. While the document's major impact was on the development of new theological ideas (examined in greater detail in chapters 4 and 5), it also contributed to the political activism in the churches for a variety of reasons. To begin with, for the first time church leaders explicitly debated the legitimacy issue. The document labeled the South African state a tyranny, and argued that it was therefore illegitimate from a moral and theological viewpoint and could not be reformed. Rather, the apartheid-structured state could only be replaced by another, whose government had the explicit mandate to rule in the interests of all people. Although the Kairos Document was not an SACC publication (it was signed by Beyers Naudé in his capacity as minister in the N. G. Kerk in Africa and not as General Secretary of the SACC—and no Catholic bishop signed it), its discussion of tyranny and reformability, as well as the political situation, formed the basis of the SACC's renewed self-evaluation and its eventual declaration of illegitimacy.

The document also challenged church organizations to adopt an overtly political level of action, stating that it was insufficient for churches to merely pray for a change of government; rather they "should also mobilise their members in every parish to begin to think and work and plan for a change of government in South Africa." Churches were challenged to actually participate in acts of civil disobedience, in the full realization that if they took their responsibilities seriously in the present circumstances, they would have to confront and disobey the state in order to obey God.[70] The SACC and SACBC were criticized in the document for carrying out "mere ambulance ministry"—not the "ministry of involvement and participation." The only way to rectify this, they were told, was to wholeheartedly join in the struggle for liberation.[71]

Church leaders appear to have taken the Kairos Document's challenge to heart; and in a dramatic show of civil disobedience, church leaders from all over the country participated in protest marches, which by that time had become illegal. In a march in Cape Town led by Beyers Naudé and Allan Boesak, 300 church leaders descended on Parliament to deliver a petition demanding that police be kept out of black townships, and that the government negotiate with leaders chosen by the people. When the police arrived to break up the march, the procession knelt on the pavement and began singing hymns. Subsequently, Naudé, Boesak, and close to 270 others were arrested, although no charges were filed. In Durban, Archbishop Hurley led a 300-strong dawn procession, carrying a six-foot cross on his back, to a prison where UDF members accused of treason were being held.[72]

Shortly thereafter, in December 1985, church leaders from South Africa and other countries, under the aegis of the World Council of Churches and the South African Council of Churches (the SACBC sent an observer), held a consultation in Harare, Zimbabwe, on the South African crisis. During this conference, representatives of political organizations as well as trade unions were given the opportunity to present their analyses of the root causes of the current crisis, and to present the churches with options on how to contribute towards fundamental change. At the final session, the churches stated that they could no longer make a distinction between prayer and political action. While just a few years earlier church leaders were calling on the government to reform its policies, in the Harare Declaration this was now rejected as a viable option:

"Apartheid can in no way be reformed; we therefore reject categorically all pro-posals for modification of apartheid. . . . A radical break has to be made with the present."[73] In order to accomplish this, the Declaration called for the "churches inside and outside South Africa to support movements working for the liberation of their country," for an end to the state of emergency, the release of Nelson Mandela and other political prisoners, and the unbanning of all political movements. It also called on the international community to impose immediate and comprehensive economic sanctions and to refuse to refinance South Africa's foreign debt.

The SACC responded to the challenge by adopting the Harare Declaration at its 1986 National Conference. At this point, the SACC's stance on sanctions had shifted, illustrating its increasing political activism in the face of an intran-sigent apartheid regime.[74] While it had refused to call for sanctions in 1984 on the basis of legal advice concerning legislative prohibitions, with the partial state of emergency in 1985 it called for "disinvestment and economic pressure." By the imposition of the nationwide state of emergency of 1986, it was ready to call for comprehensive sanctions as the only remaining nonviolent method for ending apartheid and forcing the regime to negotiate.

Although the SACBC also became increasingly politicized on the sanctions issue, it remained more cautious than the SACC. In the wake of the Harare Declaration, the bishops held an extraordinary Plenary Session in May 1986 on "The Role of the Church in the Present Day Situation in South Africa," to explicitly debate the sanctions question. During the conference, the bishops were informed by an economist that a statement on sanctions would primarily have the political effect of motivating overseas pressures, which would likely have a tremendous impact in bringing about a "radical change in government policy."[75] The Conference also heard from Beyers Naudé, who, in an impas-sioned pro-sanctions talk, asked:

> If the argument is used that there are other methods of bringing about re-form, my question is: What are the methods that will avoid an escalation of uncontrolled violence? I abhor violence, but it no longer has any real meaning to use that argument and leave it at that. Are these economic pressures not the last resort left before violence?[76]

Despite these arguments in favor of calling for sanctions, the bishops did not comply. In the end, they never called for comprehensive sanctions. In fact they avoided the word "sanctions" altogether and never made a clear "call" of any kind. Instead, in their "Pastoral Letter on Economic Pressure for Justice," they pronounced that in their view, "economic pressure" was a *morally justifiable* means of bringing about an end to injustice which, when applied, should be qualified and selective and should be implemented in such a way as to not destroy the economy.[77] The conference agreed that if the government did not set in motion a meaningful negotiations process in the near future, it would call for an intensification and extension of economic pressure.

Despite this pledge, when the SACBC held a follow-up conference in 1989 to decide whether such a call should be made, the bishops simply reiterated their cautious approach and again avoided recommending specific pressures. This weak response came despite the fact that the SACBC's own appointed Committee on Economic Pressure (created at the 1986 extraordinary Plenary Session) urged the bishops to take a stronger stance, since no meaningful political changes had taken place since the original pastoral letter of 1986 and since the "government has proved to be more than intransigent."[78] The committee was critical of the bishops' insistence that they were not competent to make such a "political judgment" and stated, "it is our view that it is within the bishops' competence not only to condone sanctions but to propose specific forms of action, and itself to engage in appropriate action."[79] The committee concluded its report by recommending that the bishops adopt a less cautious stance and call for comprehensive and mandatory sanctions. This they never did, continuing to insist that "we are not competent to indicate how or when economic pressures should be increased."[80]

In the face of such mounting pressure from the SACC, SACBC, and other church leaders—no longer just in the form of statements and pronouncements but increasingly in direct political engagement—the state hardened its attitude towards church activists. In early marches headed by clergy, every effort was made to process and quickly release those religious arrested; for example, the Cape Town march ended in the release of all 267 arrested without bail. In stark contrast, by the end of 1985 during another mass march, clergy were beaten (one almost losing his eye), nuns were stripped and searched on arrival at prison, bail was opposed, and clergy who arrived at court singing in the back of a police van were teargassed while still locked inside.[81] This hardening of attitude was seen in many instances across the country. It became clear that a deliberate decision had been made at cabinet level to crack down and counter the increase in Christian resistance to apartheid. Church leaders from around the country were monitored, harassed, detained, interrogated, and sometimes—as in the case of Frank Chikane (who succeeded Naudé as SACC General Secretary) and Smangaliso Mkhatshwa (General Secretary of the SACBC)—severely tortured. Lower-level church workers tended to be worse off than eminent church leaders, because less international attention could be focused on them, and the church thus had less leverage with the government. At one point in 1986, the Catholic Church was represented among political detainees by twelve priests, three deacons, four religious sisters, twenty seminarians, and seven lay persons active in church work.[82] Not coincidentally, in May 1986 the Catholic bishops published a pastoral letter in which they declared, "Let there be no mistake—we are not neutral in the current conflict in South Africa. We support fully the demands of the majority of people for justice."[83] Clearly, the fact that church members were now being carefully targeted for state repression had a politicizing effect on the bishops and on many Catholics throughout the country as well. As one church worker stated, "One priest in prison did more to conscientize Catholics than a thousand sermons or statements."[84]

The more hard-line attitude towards the churches was also evident when the state finally brought Archbishop Hurley to trial in February 1985 for accusing South African–trained security forces of perpetrating atrocities in Namibia. This was the first time in thirty years that a Catholic archbishop had been tried anywhere in the world, and the Vatican sent representatives to South Africa to attend the trial. After three years preparing the prosecution, the state withdrew its charges thirty minutes into the trial, because of insufficient evidence. Given that the state must have been aware of its lack of evidence, one can only surmise that the primary reason for charging Hurley in the first place was intimidation. In that case, the state was sorely mistaken, for the trial only served to further entrench within the SACBC a commitment to fighting apartheid. Hurley himself was disappointed at the outcome, because he had hoped the activities of *Koevoet* (a particularly brutal division of the security forces) would be publicly exposed. Indeed, it may be that the state dropped the trial for fear that the international publicity would draw attention to its activities in Namibia. After his acquittal, Hurley responded by suing the state for malicious prosecution and was awarded almost $11,000 in an out-of-court settlement.[85]

There is another reason why religious people were increasingly becoming the targets of state violence. By 1985 many clergy and lay leadership were directly involved in resistance politics, and close ties were being established between church members and civil society groups. Indeed, by 1986 the UDF was asking the churches to play a spiritual leadership role to "ensure that the struggle for peace and justice be observed with discipline and dignity."[86] When the leaders from the UDF and other protest organizations were removed through detention and trials, activist church leaders were thus in a position to move from spiritual leadership to political leadership, through filling the ensuing political vacuum. When the state increased its repression against what was now being called the Mass Democratic Movement, this necessarily affected clergy and lay leaders as well. Because of their community involvement, it was now virtually impossible to delineate whether action by church activists was primarily "church action" or "political action"; either way, the result was the same: it fueled the spiral of SACC and SACBC involvement in confronting the apartheid regime. As more and more ministers, priests, sisters, and lay Christians were arrested for their activities in the liberation movement, it began to be seen as an attack on the church itself. By this time, the actions of the state against the church could no longer be isolated from the broader context of general repression taking place in society as a whole. For example, in May 1985 Frank Chikane, while General Secretary of the Institute for Contextual Theology, was arrested and charged with high treason—not because of his activities as a minister, but on account of his role in the UDF's anti-election campaign.[87] Chikane's home was bombed and he was repeatedly detained. He was a restricted person under house arrest, and was later nearly fatally poisoned. Thus, the church/state conflict was escalating for two reasons, both of which served to further politicize the SACBC and SACC: the state deliberately attempted to crush the growing commitment to action by the SACC and SACBC; and church workers functioning within protesting communities were being caught up in the general repression against civil society.

The state attempted to silence church action in other ways, for example, by placing restrictions on actual religious liturgies. By 1986, many funerals were banned because they were "too political." The Minister of Police sought to prevent services in commemoration of the tenth anniversary of the Soweto uprisings, and was defied by Bishop Tutu and Allan Boesak. Several churches were invaded and desecrated, and teargas canisters were thrown into a mosque. As a result of these invasions by the security forces into sacred space, the SACC recognized that its member churches were being "thrust into overt and explicit confrontation with the state."[88] In recognition that they were quickly becoming "the voice of the voiceless," the SACBC decided in 1986 to allow church building and facilities to be used by resistance organizations, stating:

> black people, whose political expression is so hampered and restricted by their exclusion from all meaningful decision making, are further restricted in a variety of ways from gathering to express legitimate grievances and to organise resistance to injustices. There is, in fact, frequently no other place for people to meet than in a church or church hall. . . . We realise that the use of church buildings may expose the church to various risks, . . . but making church buildings available is an opportunity for the church to identify itself with the people's struggle for liberation.[89]

By 1987, some churches and church leaders felt they could no longer side-step the legitimacy question, and publicly entered the debate. They engaged the issue in detail as the result of a conference held in May in Lusaka, Zambia, again under the auspices of the World Council of Churches. The theme of the conference, which came to be known as the Lusaka Conference, was "The Churches' Search for Justice and Peace in Southern Africa." Its purpose was to dialogue with the liberation movements in an attempt to come to terms with the role of the church in the increasingly violent crisis in Southern Africa.

Almost two hundred representatives of churches, the exiled liberation movements, the United Nations, and other foreign political dignitaries attended. Once again, this overtly political act of meeting with the ANC and PAC was spurred by the deteriorating political scene. Specifically, the eighteen months since the Harare Conference had witnessed continued political confrontation in South Africa, an ongoing state of emergency, and the detention of some 20,000 apartheid opponents. In the face of this worsening context, the SACC felt it had no choice but to become more deeply involved in the political struggle.[90] In the final "Lusaka Statement," the institutional church for the first time declared the South African state illegitimate,[91] stating:

> It is our belief that civil authority is instituted of God to do good, and that under the biblical imperative all people are obliged to do justice and show special care for the oppressed and the poor. It is this understanding that leaves us with no alternative but to conclude that the South African regime and its colonial domination of Namibia is illegitimate.[92]

The Lusaka Statement had perhaps the greatest impact on the politicization of the SACC of any statement issued in the 1980s, for once the legitimacy of the state was questioned, it followed that the police and defense force were also illegitimate. It was only with this recognition that the SACC could deal with the possibility that the use of counterforce by the liberation movements might be legitimate. Hence, the statement that "while remaining committed to peaceful change we recognize that the nature of the South African regime which wages war on its own inhabitants and neighbors compels the movements to the use of force along with other means to end oppression."[93] Up to this point the SACC had been somewhat hesitant to openly support the ANC, as this might imply that it was supporting violence. The Lusaka Statement allowed the SACC to "move beyond the debate." It did not have to agree with the use of violence, nor did it have to advocate violence itself. By recognizing the felt need by the ANC for counterviolence, the SACC had finally opened itself to full support of the goals (if not the means) of the liberation struggle. As both the SACC and the ANC had a long history of working against apartheid, this new understanding of the use of force allowed for a growing cooperation and, indeed, a united front between the two. The SACC could now move from the support of church action in theory (a position increasingly adopted in the wake of the Kairos Document) to actually carrying out that action. After an intense debate at the SACC's 1987 National Conference,[94] the Lusaka Statement was finally adopted, and for the first time the Conference moved from its historically "neutral" position on violence to one intended to challenge the churches and their political options.

Adopting the Lusaka Statement also allowed the SACC to more seriously question the legality of the government. In his speech to the 1987 National Conference, outgoing General Secretary Naudé stated that:

> if from the point of view of the gospel this [illegitimacy] is conceded, another question immediately arises i.e. to what degree this government can any longer be seen to be constitutionally legal? . . . Where a state of emergency has become such an almost permanent feature as a pre-requisite for effective government rule, the legality of such a rule is decidedly at stake.[95]

In the aftermath of adopting the Lusaka Statement, the 1987 SACC Conference recommended to its member churches that they question the assumed moral obligation to obey a number of unjust laws, including the Population Registration Act and the Group Areas Act. Declaring the state illegitimate and calling for disobedience had profound implications for the politicization of the SACC, for it opened the door for an unprecedented level of determined political activity in the wake of the worsening political situation in 1988.

The SACBC, as a conference, never adopted the Lusaka Statement. It was judged too political and not sufficiently theological. In preparing a response for the SACBC, the bishops' Theological Advisory Commission stated that it "was most dissatisfied with the low level of theology displayed in the manifesto. It was tragic that a good cause was undermined by sloppy arguments and poor theology. It was more a party political statement full of clichés than a thought-out theological document; it gave the impression of wanting to curry favour with SWAPO and ANC, rather than being a church statement."[96] However, at a later meeting the TAC softened its stand, stating that "our negative comments about its manner of presentation should not be taken as a disagreement about its main concerns. In many cases the points it raised had already been discussed by the SACBC."[97] It did, though, begin more seriously to debate the legitimacy issue in 1987, while remaining more cautious than the SACC and delaying any pronouncement. At the end of a Special Consultation in March of that year, the bishops stated that they were "not in the position to make a comprehensive statement about the illegitimacy of the present government because of a lack of information and research, more time [is] needed."[98] Despite its wariness, the Consultation did conclude that the majority of the people regarded the government as not only irrelevant but also illegitimate. In direct contradiction to the SACC, however, the consultation concluded that "the present South African government is clearly the *de facto and de iure* government of the country. No other power is at present being treated as the real government—a government in exile. But it is busy losing its moral legitimacy both in the eyes of its own people and in the eyes of the world."[99] Furthermore, unlike the vigorous stance of the SACC, the consultation did not urge the church to become involved in acts of nonviolence.

By March 1988, this view had been slightly modified, and members of the

TAC were willing to grant the illegitimacy of the South African government but not the state: "certainly no one was asking that South Africa be abolished. In declaring the government illegitimate one was requiring that certain of its policies be abolished, but not that the state organs be either abolished or radically changed."[100] Clearly the SACBC's attitude at this point lagged behind the SACC's as well as the UDF's and ANC's. Three months later, after the political situation had significantly deteriorated and the church/state conflict escalated, the TAC altered its understanding of legitimacy and stated that, "in view of the distinction made between the state and the government at the last meeting, it needs to be said that the South African state *as now constituted* is illegitimate, not just the present government."[101] Thus, the Advisory Committee, somewhat belatedly, brought its views of legitimacy in line with that of the SACC's. Despite this advice from its own theologians as well as from its Justice and Peace Commission, the SACBC *as a conference* (unlike the SACC) never declared the South African government or state illegitimate. The bishops undertook a "study day on legitimacy" at its Plenary Session meeting in January 1988 to specifically discuss the issue of legitimacy. Again, they were more cautious on the issue than was the SACC, deciding that "in the end even if the government is illegitimate we can't change or overthrow it and so must live under it and yet try to bring about change."[102] Moreover, their timidity was evident in the conclusion that:

> in reply to the question concerning obedience to laws and regulations of a government that is considered illegitimate but cannot be removed, though that government is not entitled to demand obedience, people may have no choice but to conform and even to accept that in certain ways the government serves the common good—by preventing crime to some extent, providing roads, regulating trade and so on. For the sake of the common good and to avoid a greater evil, the evil of anarchy, in these matters obedience may be unavoidable.[103]

No such language about the unavoidability of obedience was ever present in the SACC discussions surrounding the legitimacy issue. In the end, no definitive statement ever came out of the Plenary Session study day on legitimacy, and the entire issue was deferred to the Conference's administrative board for further review. Eventually, the matter faded into the background and was quietly dropped by the SACBC.

Alarmed by the open discussion of its legitimacy by the SACC and SACBC, and by mounting church-based political action, the government moved to crack down even further on Christian resistance. In April 1987, the Commissioner of Police announced a state of emergency regulation prohibiting campaigns for the release of political detainees, including prayer services. When several prominent church leaders reacted to this direct interference in religion, the government tried to backtrack by stating that it was permitted to pray for detainees in a "bona fide church service," but any action that might "incite" the public to "participate in a campaign" aimed at the release of detainees would remain illegal—thus implying that while individual efforts and prayers might still be legal, concerted actions and campaigns were not. Tutu, now archbishop of Cape Town, reacted by saying he could no longer keep religion and politics separate. "I will continue," he declared, "to call both within and outside services for the release of detainees, despite the regulations."[104] Church leaders increasingly used the only free space left at their disposal for legally opposing the government—the pulpit. Catholic archbishop Wilfred Napier (who had taken over the SACBC presidency from Hurley), in his reaction to the regulation, underscored the fact that not only was the state trying to silence the liberation movement, it was also trying to silence churches: "these latest restrictions are draconian by any standards. But now they affect the work of the Church directly in that they presume to determine what the Church can or cannot do in its care for those in need. . . . This we cannot and will not tolerate. . . . We must obey God rather than men."[105]

The state also continued its harassment of church workers. By May 1987, at least fourteen SACC national and regional office workers were in detention. In October 1987, the SACBC-sponsored newspaper *New Nation* became the first of the "alternative" newspapers to be hit by new censorship regulations. After detaining its editor without trial for more than a year, raiding its offices, and harassing its staff workers, the state increased its pressure by banning the paper for three months because of its "subversive" propaganda, which was "causing a threat to the maintenance of public order."[106]

In short, by the end of 1987 both the SACC and SACBC had adopted a highly politicized self-identity. This occurred for various reasons, including the country's deteriorating political conditions, a closer meshing of these organizations with the liberation movements (particularly by holding various meetings with the ANC in exile, and by accepting the legitimacy of counterviolence), and because personnel were being drawn into conflict with the state as more and more church workers were detained and increasing restrictions were placed on the work of church organizations. As a result, the SACC and SACBC were well-positioned to take major initiatives in the next wave of the liberation struggle—the defiance campaign of 1988–1989.

IV. 1988–1990

On February 24, 1988, the South African political situation took a dramatic turn for the worse when the Minister of Law and Order banned seventeen anti-apartheid organizations (including the UDF) and eighteen individuals (including both the vice-president and president of the UDF). These measures represented the largest clampdown on legal protests and civic rights movements in the history of South Africa. With this final attempt at crushing opposition, almost all mass, nonviolent, legal means of opposing apartheid were closed, leaving the churches and church leaders as the only viable organizations able to generate further resistance. Many of these leaders along with lay Christians took upon themselves the challenge to move to the forefront of the fight against apartheid.

An emergency meeting of church leaders, including the leadership of the SACC and SACBC, was held the day after the bannings. The result was a strong statement which declared that "the ban on the activities of the 17 organisations is a blow directed at the heart of the Church's mission in South Africa, because the banned organisations are organisations of and for our people, the majority of which belong to our churches." Not only did the church leaders urge people to intensify their struggle against apartheid, they also declared that they were prepared to lead it. Since the prohibited activities of banned organizations were in fact "central to the proclamation of the Gospel," church leaders now felt compelled, irrespective of the consequences, to take over their activities. They concluded that "if the State wants to act against the Church of God in this country for proclaiming the Gospel, then so be it."[107] Church leaders were now explicitly involved in the politics of liberation. Issuing a statement was insufficient; they had to back it up with action. Church leaders dismissed the suggestion of meeting with the state president because of his past intransigence towards negotiating for peaceful change (this refusal in itself represented a new approach for these leaders, who had been more than ready in the past to talk to government officials in the face of crisis). They agreed to march to Parliament as a public witness against the bannings. They also planned to present a petition to the state president, urging him to take several immediate actions including lifting the recent bannings, ending the state of emergency, unbanning the ANC and other illegal political organizations, releasing political leaders, and entering into negotiations.[108]

On February 29, a day which has gone down in South African history, twenty-five church leaders, accompanied by more than a hundred clergy and several hundred lay Christians, held a short service in the Anglican Cathedral (which adjoins Parliament). There they read the contents of the above petition, gave instructions on the principles of nonviolent action, and informed the congregation of the possible consequences of the march upon which they were about to embark—which subsequently became known internationally as "the clerics' march." As they left the cathedral, but before they had reached the end of the surrounding wall, the police intervened. Confronted in this way, all three hundred or so marchers knelt on the ground, whereupon the leaders were arrested and forcibly removed to a police station (they were released within several hours). The remaining clerics and other marchers, still kneeling, were bombarded by a water cannon and arrested as well. This police action not only shocked the country but also the international community. It precipitated a spiral of church/state conflict that escalated at an unprecedented rate. In a press conference held within hours after their release, the clerics acknowledged that the church was now truly the "voice of the voiceless." Reverend Peter Storey stated, "it is the task of the church to demonstrate, as has been demonstrated today, through its leadership, that you can't destroy the deep hunger for liberty. And neither, in the end, can you put the whole church in jail. . . . Because there is a commitment on the part of the church leaders here, that while this vacuum exists then the words must be spoken and the actions must be acted out by ourselves." Likewise, Reverend Frank Chikane declared that it was the churches' responsibility to speak out on behalf of banned organizations, and "we will continue doing it, irrespective of the consequences."[109] February 1988, therefore, marked a watershed for these organizations. Not only were they protesting the collapse of the rule of law underscored by the 1988 bannings; they were also recognizing their responsibility towards those who were once again being denied any legal opportunity to voice their opposition. Finally, because of this event, they were also drawn into direct and sustained confrontation with the state.

Archbishop Tutu sent a copy of the petition to the state president, who released his reply to the press. This set off an almost dizzying exchange of communication between the president and church leaders. As a result of the letters, church leaders were forced to clarify their position and thereby gained a deeper insight into their understanding of Christian mission in the crisis. President Botha dismissed the "so-called march on Parliament" and the petition as mere "ANC propaganda," stating in his response to Tutu, "the question must be posed whether you are acting on behalf of the kingdom of God, or the kingdom promised by the ANC and the SACP [South African Communist Party]? If it is the latter, say so, but do not then hide behind the structures and the cloth of the Christian church. . . . "[110] Frank Chikane, as General Secretary of the SACC, responded to the president's open letter to Tutu, charging that church members had never experienced suppression and brutal repression by Marxists, the ANC, or the SACP, but "under your government."[111] In his response, Botha called Chikane irresponsible and a liar and repeated his charge that the SACC was merely a communist front. Moreover, he found it alarming that

> individual members of the clergy who claim to be messengers of God, are in reality messengers of enmity and hatred while parading in the cloth, and hiding behind the structures of the Church; and instead of pursuing reforma-

tion, they are engaged in the deformation of religion, through the proclamation of false so-called 'liberation theology' . . . through its acceptance of the Kairos Document, Harare Declaration, and Lusaka Statement.[112]

The hostile exchange continued with Tutu's response to the president's attack on the SACC's theology: "the Bible and the Church predate Marxism and the ANC by several centuries. . . . We are law abiding. Good laws make human society possible. When laws are unjust then Christian tradition teaches that they do not oblige obedience."[113] Tutu ended his rebuttal with the question: "I work for God's Kingdom. For whose Kingdom with your apartheid policy do you work?"[114] A few weeks later, during a discussion on the budget in the House of Assembly, the president made a lengthy statement regarding the exchange of letters, during which he stated, "the government is not in confrontation with the churches and does not wish to be so. But it so happens that a few church leaders go out of their way to seek confrontation with the government."[115]

This exchange of letters was one of the most dramatic and direct confrontations between the churches and the state in the 1980s. As the SACC and SACBC moved to fill the vacuum created by state repression and the restriction of democratic organizations, the state attempted to denigrate and thwart their initiatives by attacking their actions as communist-inspired, insisting that the regime itself upheld the values of Christianity. To these ends, state-run television programs on "liberation theology" maligned Tutu, Hurley, Boesak, and Chikane, questioning their integrity as Christians.

The state cracked down on the SACC and SACBC in other ways. One week after the February bannings, the Promotion of Orderly Internal Politics Bill was introduced in Parliament, the intent of which was to restrict foreign funding to any anti-apartheid organization, as well as funding for humanitarian aid carried out by churches to victims of apartheid. The bill authorized the Minister of Justice to declare both individuals and organizations "affected" (thus requiring them to obtain permission to raise foreign funds)[116] if he was satisfied that "politics are being engaged in."[117] Although the SACC had narrowly escaped being declared an affected organization in the aftermath of the Eloff Commission report—thus continuing to raise money both inside and outside South Africa—it was again being threatened. This had serious implications for the SACC,[118] because by the late 1980s it had become so politicized that its activities clearly would have been considered "political" under the legislation. Even if the SACC were granted the authority to raise funds, it could still be prosecuted if the money was used for purposes which the state regarded as political. In effect, the bill applied sanctions against the SACC. At its 1988 National Conference, the SACC took the following position on the bill:

> Since the people who are at present in control of the South African state
> use the concept of order to legitimize injustice and the maintenance of the

apartheid system, South African churches and the SACC are obliged to expose and resist what is called the promotion of orderly government as the promotion of disorder and the disruption of justice and peace in human relationships.[119]

As pressure mounted on the state to withdraw the bill, an official letter was sent to inform the SACC that it was no longer exempt from taxes, since it was "neither an ecclesiastical organisation nor engaged in religious functions."[120]

As a result of both the deepening political crisis, the increasing attacks on high-profile individual church members, and the state's attempt to silence the churches, the SACC and SACBC lurched headlong onto a collision course with the state with the May 1988 launching of the Standing for the Truth Campaign (SFT). The Campaign was the product of a Convocation of Churches attended by 230 participants from 26 churches, 21 regional councils, and 14 other church organizations. It was convened to commit a broad coalition of churches and religious organizations to developing effective nonviolent actions, the intention being to force the state to abandon apartheid and to participate in a negotiated settlement to establish a nonracial democracy. It was called *Standing for the Truth* in recognition that crimes against humanity were being committed with impunity as a result of the secrecy surrounding the state of emergency. The church leaders wanted to expose, to "tell the truth" about this reality.[121] In the Convocation's final statement, the leaders acknowledged that they were "called to proclaim and witness to truth in living, and even by dying."[122] Through the Campaign, church leaders asserted that they were not obliged to obey unjust laws which militated against the truth; rather, in their obedience to God they would be forced to disobey the emergency regulations and apartheid laws. In effect, they were saying that unjust laws were not laws at all, and had no claim on their obedience. These church leaders then committed themselves to ignore the emergency regulations by using all means at their disposal, including their church news networks, church courts, and their congregations, to inform South Africans of the truth.[123] A national committee of twelve was set up consisting of three people elected at the Convocation, three representatives of the SACC, three from the SACBC, and three from the newly formed Church Leaders Meeting. Their mandate was to "plan, coordinate and promote the campaign; set up regional structures, mobilize churches and create grassroots networks for mass action; to set up training programs, and to generate the necessary resources for the campaign."[124] Areas of possible nonviolent actions included acts of noncollaboration and noncooperation with apartheid, in social, economic, and political fields such as supporting rent and tax boycotts, defying group area restrictions, and withdrawing chaplains from the SADF; as well as nonviolent interventions, such as putting oneself in the way of the unjust system, for example, having church leaders present at possibly violent situations. The Campaign's "Theological Rationale" recognized that in the political context of the late 1980s, churches no longer had an option but to become the voice of those silenced and to thereby take on a political role: "Many organisations attempting to bring to light and to redress wrongs have been banned or restricted, leaving the Church to guard and struggle to restore essential civil liberties, such as the rights of freedom of assembly and access to information."[125]

In 1988 the SFT Campaign's most defiant and far-reaching nonviolent action was a call for a boycott of the October municipal elections. Anticipating this move, the state had simply declared any such call illegal and punishable.[126] For the first time ever, a broad coalition of church leaders stood together and, in defiance of the law, called for a boycott. In support of this defiance, Chikane drew on the legitimacy debate and stated, "on the basis of the practice and constitution of this government we are compelled to regard it as illegitimate and to declare that we are thus not obliged to obey its unjust laws."[127] The SFT Campaign was opposed to Christians' taking part in the elections, either as candidates or voters, because it felt that elections would be neither free or fair and thus would be illegitimate. The state responded by seizing 30,000 copies of the Western Province Council of Church's (WPCC) newsletter, *Crisis News,* which had published this "Statement of Faith" in defiance of emergency regulations, and the Minister of Law and Order threatened to "clip the wings of certain church and community organizations." The national SFT committee responded by repeating the call to boycott the elections. Faced with this serious challenge, the state retaliated with a police raid on Archbishop Tutu's home and the offices of the SACBC. While no action was taken directly against the twelve leaders of the SFT, the secretary of *Crisis News* was arrested and charged both as a representative of the WPCC and in his personal capacity for publishing a "subversive statement." Four other WPCC members were subsequently detained, and two issues of *Crisis News* were declared banned for possession, to which the SACC responded by asking:

> Why does the government not charge all the church leaders who issued the statement? Why does it pick on an individual pastor? This is only a test-case. The end result may be the unthinkable future of a church without leadership. The State still believes in the strategy of detaining and imposing leadership of opposing organizations. History has shown that the State applies the same security logic to churches that they developed for acting against community organizations. . . . What is on trial here is the utterance of the truth in South Africa.[128]

Thus, as the state could no longer remove the leadership of civil society, it now focused on the church, which by this time had taken over that leadership in many cases.

The SACC and SACBC barely had time to get the SFT Campaign off the ground before their headquarters were hit by bombs and arson. Christians were stunned; their nonviolent acts of civil disobedience—statements, marches, and boycotts—had been countered with state-backed violence. In August, Khotso ("Peace") House, the headquarters of the SACC, was bombed. Some press reports referred to the bombing as "one of the most powerful if not the most powerful blast yet in South Africa."[129] The building sustained serious damage, making it impossible to use. No arrests were ever made in connection with the blast, but the Minister of Law and Order did state that the building had probably been blown up in error by "ANC terrorists," and asserted that Khotso House had long been used by guerrillas for the storing and manufacturing of explosives. Rejecting this charge, the SACC issued a statement which placed the attack squarely in the context of the church/state conflict:

> The bomb blast at Khotso House needs to be put into perspective. It takes place against a background of a consistent and deliberate strategy by the SA government, the SABC [South African Broadcasting Corporation], and other apartheid-supporting institutions to hinder the legitimate activities of the Church. . . . We know that this strategy is being pursued with unceasing ruthlessness because the SACC continues to expose the moral bankruptcy and evil of apartheid. . . . We are therefore shocked, but not surprised by this act of violence against the Church. . . . While we are under no illusions that this has been the last such attack upon us, we reaffirm the commitment to see apartheid destroyed today.[130]

In October, Khanya House in Pretoria, SACBC headquarters, was set alight. Again, no one was arrested for the arson attack, which did extensive damage. Afterwards, Archbishop Napier, SACBC president, acknowledged a pattern, namely, that increasing conflict with the state only served to further politicize the SACBC and SACC. He said, "The attack on Khanya House and the subsequent pathetic attempt to discredit the SACBC, far from succeeding in intimidating into silence those committed to justice, will lead to the resurgence of an even more vigorous engagement in the promotion of peace through justice."[131]

The year 1988 thus marked a turning point in the life of the church. The institutional church became much more committed to effective nonviolent action to end apartheid; or, as Chikane put it, it moved from "passive non-violence to active non-violence." The SFT Campaign both encouraged and was in turn given a strong sense of purpose and direction by the launching of the Mass Democratic Movement's Defiance Campaign on August 2, 1989, a struggle directed against the upcoming September elections for the tricameral parliament. Both the SACC and SACBC were now prepared and willing to step into a leadership position, declaring that the Defiance Campaign's program of action was compatible with their commitment to peaceful nonviolent actions to bring about change.[132] In openly supporting the Defiance Campaign, the Standing for the Truth Campaign declared, "The role of the Church is to create peace. But on the road to negotiations, reconciliation and peace, it will be necessary to confront, pressurise and defy."[133] Two days after an official "Heads of Churches of the SACC" meeting, which stated that during the Defiance Campaign some actions would be initiated by the church while others would be supported by it, church leaders organized a service in Cape Town at which twenty activists who were restricted under the state of emergency defied their restrictions. In the course of the Defiance Campaign, therefore, a new sense of unity was forged between church and secular organizations.

The state responded harshly to the Defiance Campaign, and it increased its repression not only against huge numbers of ordinary people involved in the Campaign, but against its leadership—which included community members and church members. Church leaders were arrested, teargassed, and sprayed with purple dye. In September, Tutu and his wife were each arrested twice in the span of one week, once for trying to enter a police-barricaded church. On one occasion, the Security Police desecrated the archbishop's cathedral by entering it carrying firearms, attempting to remove everyone from the building, and prohibiting entrance. Homes and offices of many other church leaders were raided, as were the offices of the Pretoria Council of Churches. Additionally, in May 1989, Frank Chikane was poisoned. An independent Board of Inquiry into attacks on anti-apartheid groups and activists later provided evidence implicating an SADF hit squad in the poisoning. Furthermore, the Commission of Inquiry into Certain Alleged Murders uncovered an SADF-affiliated hit list of sixteen people, including Boesak, Chikane and Tutu.[134]

Clearly, the church/state conflict was further heightened with the decision of the SFT to join the Defiance Campaign. The days leading up to the election saw the SFT Campaign in Cape Town at the forefront of protest and resistance, active in pickets, marches, meetings, and other acts of defiance, during which Christians and others were beaten and detained. The state responded by banning all rallies. The newly constituted Church Leaders Meeting counter-responded by organizing a worship and protest service in a Methodist church, to which the police reacted by claiming that the ban covered church services as well as rallies. Nailing the banning order to the church door, they surrounded the church, using teargas to keep people from entering. The Central Methodist Mission took the Commissioner of Police to the Supreme Court to have the banning order set aside. While the police argued that church services were consistently being used to promote illegal political goals, a judge ruled, "I am not prepared to ban a church service," which proceeded at 11 p.m.

The churches had won this particular battle, and the most determined attempt to date by the state to eliminate the space opened up in the churches for resistance under the state of emergency was defeated, at least temporarily.[135] However, levels of police brutality increased dramatically in the days following the service. On September 13, church leaders led a "Peace March" in Cape Town, the largest march since the one led by the PAC which precipitated the banning of the ANC and PAC in 1960. Within a few weeks, similar protests were held in all the major cities and several rural areas, with ANC flags being openly displayed and bishops, clergy, women religious, and lay Christians leading and supporting marches. In the three weeks following the Peace March, it is estimated that over 350,000 people participated in marches.[136] Organizations had simply "unbanned" themselves. Less than a month later, eight top ANC leaders were released from prison. This was followed by the release of Nelson Mandela, less than five months after the Cape Town Peace March.

    The SACC and SACBC had come to recognize that with 77 percent of the population claiming to be Christian, and with the severe repression occurring in the country, the church itself was being repressed. Most of the people spearheading defiance actions were members of some Christian denomination, and the SACC and SACBC had finally accepted the responsibility of the institutional church in this context to be a vehicle of resistance. Moreover, this responsibility was now expected of the church leaders. As one marcher said, "They have an obligation to be caretakers until our leaders return."[137] In September 1989, the event took place which symbolized the culmination of politicization: the moral, theological, *and* legal illegitimacy of the state was declared at an SACC- and SACBC-sponsored "Conference on the Legitimacy of the South African State" in Harare.

Conclusion

    The political context of South Africa in the 1980s—characterized by increasing repression, decreasing legitimacy of the state, and a loosely organized yet highly cohesive anti-apartheid movement—contributed to a reevaluation by the SACC and SACBC of their mission. I have argued in this chapter that throughout the 1980s, church action was the result first and foremost of the worsening political crisis. With each wave of human rights abuses, and with the collapse of the rule of law, the SACC and SACBC responded by becoming increasingly politicized. The process is seen most clearly in 1985 and 1988. Not coincidentally, these two years marked major downturns for civil society: in 1985 the first state of emergency was declared, and 1988 witnessed the "final bannings," when eighteen civil society organizations were silenced.

    This first process—being shocked into action—produced a second, unintended consequence, which further contributed to the politicization of the SACC and SACBC: state reaction against church leaders, and the counter-reaction by these organizations. As church leaders and workers became targets of the state's repression, their level of politicization increased dramatically.[138]

Thus, carrying out of their traditional mission of speaking out against human rights abuses resulted in a spiraling church/state conflict, which in some ways had an independent effect on politicizing these two organizations.

Ultimately, the SACC and SACBC became so highly politicized that repressive action by the state against "political" organizations necessarily and directly impacted them. By the late 1980s, it had become increasingly difficult to separate out the two above-mentioned sources of politicization (i.e., an increasingly repressive political context and the church/state conflict). In the early 1980s, state action directed specifically against the church could be separated from that directed against organizations in civil society. By the late 1980s, these lines had blurred. Action against one group necessarily affected action against the other; nor could one distinguish repression against anti-apartheid activists from repression against church workers.

Finally, South Africa in the 1980s was characterized by both the increasing rule of force and the decreasing consent or obedience by the majority of the people. This resulted in a huge increase in arrests and detentions without trial. As the leadership of civil society was removed and silenced, the churches became the only space left for internal legal opposition. As church leaders moved to fill civil society's vacuum, or as one church worker put it, "grabbed the baton from the activists and continued the race to liberation," they increasingly were forced to assume the role of political leadership. Accepting this broad responsibility of political representation fostered a new, more political self-identity. The interaction of these three processes resulted in what I have termed a "spiral of involvement," with the end product a highly politicized SACC and SACBC.

For a brief time in the late 1980s, the institutional church and the prophetic church came close to being one and the same. By the end of the 1980s, this transformed self-identity was obvious in a variety of areas. For example, on the issue of the possible legitimacy of counterviolence employed by the ANC, a difference is apparent in the pre– and post–Lusaka Conference SACC. In his 1983 submission to the Eloff Commission of Inquiry, the SACC president, Reverend Peter Storey, stated with some confidence that the Council "could not walk that way [i.e., support those who used violence]. I could not belong to a body advocating violence as a means of change and I am confident that neither would any of our member churches. I am convinced that the acts of violence perpetrated by the ANC are neither necessary nor helpful in bringing about change."[139] Storey's position was basically one of standing on the sidelines, defending nonviolence and denouncing the violence of both the ANC and the government. This stance was no longer considered legitimate for the SACC after 1988. With the launching of the Standing for the Truth Campaign, neutrality was no longer considered appropriate. Rather, the SACC took sides, and while it never advocated violence, it did openly support the ANC in the understanding that it was pursuing both violent and nonviolent tactics. This was in sharp contrast with Storey's claim in 1983 that "the SACC denies in the strongest terms any allegiance to or alliance with the ANC. . . ."[140]

A second area illustrating this new politicization was that of sanctions. Storey was very clear in his 1983 testimony that "the SACC does not advocate disinvestment."[141] The Harare Declaration had the effect of changing SACC policy on this issue, so that at its 1985 National Conference, delegates resolved "to express our belief that disinvestment and similar economic pressures are called for as a peaceful and effective means of putting pressure on the South African government to bring about those fundamental changes this country needs."[142] Similarly, on the issue of legitimacy, the process of spiraling involvement resulted in a shift from caution to outright rejection on the part of the SACC. In his 1983 testimony, Storey had taken a cautious approach: "while the legality of the South African government is always in question and is often in debate, the SACC has never declared the S.A. Government illegal, although it is certainly clear that it is unrepresentative."[143] However, with the 1985 promulgation of the Kairos Document, which focused so strongly on the question of legitimacy, the SACC and SACBC could no longer avoid coming to terms with the issue. As a result, and in contrast with Storey's stance in 1983, the 1987 SACC National Conference questioned not only the moral legitimacy of the state, but its legal legitimacy too. The SACC could have taken a decisive stance in 1983 and declared the new reformed apartheid constitution illegitimate, but it did not do so. Only as the country's political crisis deepened did it reach this point.

In general, while SACC national conference resolutions of the early 1980s remained primarily on the level of human rights involvement—supporting refugees, denouncing abuses of migrant laborers, and helping detainees and prisoners—resolutions of the late 1980s dealt with political issues that challenged the authority of the government: sanctions, civil disobedience, and the illegitimacy of the state. It is worth recording that very few people, either inside or outside of church circles, predicted that the SACC and SACBC would have become as highly politicized as they eventually did. In fact, in 1983 Charles Villa-Vicencio appeared pessimistic about this very possibility: "there is little likelihood of the mainline English-speaking churches—or, for that matter, the Roman Catholic church—being prepared as institutions to stand readily with uncompromising firmness against the present government."[144]

While the spiral of involvement affected both the SACC and SACBC, the SACBC remained more cautious than the SACC on most issues. In almost all of their pronouncements, the bishops went out of their way to state that they were not competent to make political judgments. On issue after issue, the bishops, as a conference, were less outspoken than the SACC. For example, while the SACC by 1988 was calling for the imposition of comprehensive sanctions, the SACBC at the same time took the hesitant (Archbishop Hurley's term was "middle-of-the-road")[145] position that while "selective pressures" might be justified, comprehensive sanctions would devastate the economy and add substantially to the problem of unemployment. In a rare open display of disagreement between the two organizations, the SACC replied that while sanctions would be painful, the pain was not comparable to that caused by the continued and prolonged violence that would result if the state were not forced to abandon apartheid.[146] The bishops' guarded approach was in line with their unwillingness to adopt either the Harare or Lusaka Statements. While they praised the Lusaka Statement as a reminder of the issues faced by the church, they concluded that the statement itself was not one which they could fully endorse.

Because the bishops, as a conference, did not support the Lusaka Statement, they never made a public declaration on the possible legitimacy of counterviolence. However, Archbishop Hurley in his individual capacity came very close to doing just that, particularly in his pronouncements on whether the ANC was involved in a just war. Because of the injustice of the system of apartheid, Hurley claimed in 1986, the SACBC had no right to make simplistic judgments about just or unjust wars: "To single out the behaviour of the ANC for labeling unjust when the total context in which that behaviour is occurring is a bear-pit of injustice, is an injustice in itself."[147] At another time, he stated, "It is not the job of the church to tell men to turn to violence, but we can say we understand when men reach the point of utter frustration."[148] Thus, speaking as an individual and not as the president of the SACBC, Hurley supported the SACC's stance on the legitimacy of carefully considered counterviolence which was highlighted in the Lusaka Statement.

The bishops also displayed more caution than the SACC on the issue of boycotting elections. In 1987, the SACC National Conference resolved to "whole-heartedly" endorse a boycott of the upcoming October elections. Speaking on the same elections, the SACBC stated, "we have to choose between two evils. In this case the two evils would be, on the one hand, participating in an unjust election, on the other, abstaining from voting or campaigning when we judge in conscience that voting or campaigning may produce some good. Participating may appear the lesser evil."[149] While they believed that Catholics could, as a matter of conscience, boycott the elections, the conference was not going to exhort them to do so.

Similarly, the stance of the SACBC on the issue of civil disobedience was more guarded than that of the SACC. The Bishops' Conference never vowed to engage in acts of civil disobedience. Although the SACBC was represented on the SFT's executive committee, the Conference as a whole did not formally resolve to support the SFT until rather late—in 1990. Even when it did support the SFT Campaign, and thus was forced to address the question of civil disobedience, the bishops gave the issue only qualified support. The SACBC's

Theological Advisory Commission went to great lengths to distinguish between civil disobedience as a right and as a duty,[150] and advised the bishops, when it came to the Standing for the Truth Campaign, to "make quite clear that people are not obliged in conscience to disobey but are indeed free to do so."[151]

Finally, as noted above, the bishops were reluctant to commit themselves on the issue of declaring the state illegitimate. While many of their statements can be construed as an implicit diagnosis of illegitimacy, they never moved beyond *questioning* legitimacy to explicitly making a negative declaration. Eventually, Catholic theologian Albert Nolan questioned how long the bishops would be able to avoid any adverse reactions to their refusal to make a statement, which he interpreted as "sitting on the fence."[152] The bishops defended their position by continually claiming that they needed more time to conduct research into the question before they felt they were competent to make a statement. They continued to delay any pronouncement until it was eventually unnecessary—political events of the 1990s overtook the need for one.

The one issue on which the SACBC was consistently more active than the SACC was the question of South African occupation of Namibia. In fact, the bishops came closer to examining the illegitimacy of the state in this roundabout way, through their focus on Namibia, than through any examination of the domestic situation in South Africa. One possible reason for the higher politicization of the SACBC on this issue is that Namibia falls within the jurisdiction of the Conference, which is composed of the bishops of South Africa, Namibia, Botswana, and Swaziland. The Namibian Council of Churches, however, is a completely separate entity from the SACC.

Despite its more hesitant stance, the SACBC, like the SACC, *did* become more politicized in the course of the 1980s. While the two organizations usually worked separately, they did produce highly political joint statements on several occasions, such as the 1984 report on forced relocations. Although their responses differed in a matter of degree, both organizations rose to the challenge presented to them by the political context of the 1980s, characterized by an increasingly brutal national security state. Caught up in the struggle of the 1980s, both organizations were influenced along the way by a theology of resistance and liberation.

4

Changing Religious Context
The Role of Ideas

THE CHANGING POLITICAL context of the 1980s, although necessary, was not sufficient in itself to ensure that the SACC and SACBC would adopt a more assertive political identity. In the face of an increasingly repressive regime, religious elites were becoming aware that some response on their part, for the sake of interpreting the situation theologically for their constituency, was necessary. However, the form that such reaction would take was by no means predetermined. Indeed, one might argue that the particular response made by these religious leaders was extraordinary. They had long been on the sidelines in political conflict in South Africa. Although they may have condemned apartheid, they had refused for decades to actively take sides in popular confrontations with the state. Given the history of hesitant and tepid organizational response by English-speaking churches, it would not have been surprising to many had the SACC and the SACBC become increasingly otherworldly in their religious conviction and prescriptions. Indeed, some denominations did become increasingly "pie in the sky," maintaining that religion and politics should be kept separate and that the role of the church was to comfort people who could not change their situations in this life, while preparing them for rewards in the next. Alternatively, both organizations could have accepted the regime's adaptations of apartheid, urging their constituencies to be patient in the hope that further reforms would decrease racial domination and bring increased political power in the years to come.

The leadership of the SACC and the SACBC did not, however, respond in either of these two ways. As described in chapter 3, both organizations became progressively more active throughout the decade of the 1980s, to the point of not only supporting nonviolent acts of civil disobedience to force the apartheid regime to the negotiating table, but actually leading such campaigns themselves. The question that remains to be answered is why they adopted the particular self-identities that they did, identities which argued that fulfilling their Christian mission required an explicit commitment to the liberation struggle.

The reaction of the leaders of the SACC and the SACBC was conditioned by their theology, and both organizations responded the way they did because their leadership was working from a set of new theological concepts which encouraged them to do so. This chapter explores the emergence of these ideas, while the next chapter analyzes how these ideas guided the choices made by the leadership of the SACC and the SACBC throughout the 1980s, and combined with the spiral of church involvement to produce overtly political self-identities. Specifically, a discourse known as contextual theology gathered strength in the 1980s and formed the basis for new agendas for both organizations. This theology did not arise overnight out of a religious vacuum. Rather, its fundamental ideas, specifically those concerning the responsibility of churches to work for social justice and the need for Christians to engage their social environment—which in South Africa meant confronting apartheid—were circulating within South African theological circles in the two decades preceding the 1980s. Consequently, by the beginning of the decade a religious subculture had arisen which argued that the theologically correct method of reacting to the repression of the 1980s was overt political activity. While the theological development, or contextual theology, was conditioned by outside influences, in particular, European political theology, Latin American liberation theology, and United States black theology, it was nevertheless an indigenous religious movement, born out of South Africa's gathering internal crisis and the personal experiences of certain religious leaders. Initially, only a core group of religious elites was influenced by the new ideas concerning the Christian responsibility to challenge an unjust status quo. However, in a political context in which injustice became much more blatant, these ideas were refined, clearly articulated, and finally acted upon. In other words, SACC and SACBC leaders were drawn into increased political activism not only as a result of political crisis and the resulting spiral of involvement, but also because they were acting under the influence of a specific set of theological arguments and biblical interpretations that had arisen in the 1960s and 1970s.

Although I treat the impact of a changing political context and a changing religious context as two separate influences in explaining increased political activism, in reality the two factors interacted in a dialectical model to produce new self-identities. Each set of changes impinged on the other, with mutually reinforcing results. The deteriorating South African political context of the 1980s resulted in the further evolution of religious ideas; this in turn generated greater political activity on the part of the SACC and SACBC, which served to further increase the spiral of popular confrontation with the state and its repressive powers. Contextual theology by definition has to evolve; it is conditioned by the particular and changing context in which it arises. Thus, as the political scene changes, the theological response evolves. The emergence of contextual theology in South Africa, therefore, not only contributed to the spiral of involvement; it was itself an ongoing reinterpretation of, and response to, the political situation. What remained constant throughout this evolving discourse, however, were the core theological ideas about social justice and the need for a prophetic critique of existing economic and political structures. Thus, the political context of increased state repression resulted in the reconstituted self-identities of each organization both directly, through the spiral of involvement, and indirectly, through the refinement of religious ideas in reaction to the worsening political situation. As both organizations were drawn by the political context into increasing activism, their theological understanding of this context changed in the process.

Having come through the crucible of the 1980s, the universe of religious discourse by the end of the 1980s was qualitatively different than it had been a mere decade earlier. It was the culmination of this evolutionary process that allowed both organizations to question the state's legitimacy in the 1980s, and to adopt a hard-edged confrontational approach that was in sharp contrast with church/state relations in earlier periods of South African history.

The Origins of Contextual Theology

The leadership of the SACC and SACBC did not suddenly begin discussing the need to actively work for a more just world in the early 1980s. Rather, certain elements within these organizations had been exposed to and influenced by these ideas in the two previous decades. At least four sources of early influences existed on the South African religious scene.

Catholic Social Thought

South African bishops, like many clergy around the world, were profoundly influenced by the teachings emanating from the Second Vatican Council, as well as by other, post-conciliar, Vatican statements.[1] Several important documents emerged from Vatican II. Early on, in 1963, the Vatican published *Pacem in Terris* (*Peace on Earth*), which insisted that there is an obligation of international social justice, as well as of national social justice, and that social justice could not be achieved until the gap between development and underdevelopment was narrowed.[2]

Perhaps the most-well known document from the Council was *Gaudium et Spes*, or the *Pastoral Constitution on the Church in the Modern World*, which held that Catholics had a Christian responsibility to learn from the world, involve themselves in the problems of society, and work to overcome them. Fulfilling one's Christian responsibility meant serving the world in a never-ending effort to bring about God's kingdom on earth. *Gaudium et Spes* was a watershed document for the Catholic Church. The document's preface itself is important for understanding the magnitude of transformation, for it introduced two ideas which contained the seeds which spawned a new class of theologies around the world known as liberation theologies, of which South African contextual theology is one example. These two themes were the "preferential option for the poor" and the ecclesial idea of a "pilgrim people of God."[3] The underpinnings of later ideas adopted by several national bishops' conferences concerning the need to fight social and economic injustices were clearly evident in this statement; according to *Gaudium et Spes,* wherever fundamental rights of humanity were at stake, the church had the right and the duty of "passing moral judgment even in matters relating to politics."[4] The idea that the church should be involved in social problems amounted to a quantum leap in Catholic social thought, as it represented a new understanding of what it meant to be involved in social processes, and resulted in a new religious paradigm, one which stressed the need to read and respond to "the signs of the times" in light of the gospel. Although the translation of these ideas into overt political action was still years away, the idea that action was indeed necessary and legitimate was clearly expressed in *Gaudium et Spes.* In the next few decades, political action was facilitated by the formation of Justice and Peace Commissions, the creation of which was a significant result of *Gaudium et Spes.*

This new religious discourse, with its concern for justice and church activism, was further developed in several Vatican documents from 1967 to the beginning of the 1980s. These statements contained ideas which would later come to the fore when the SACBC attempted to respond to the repressive context of the 1980s. Of particular importance for the later development of contextual theology in South Africa was Pope Paul VI's 1967 encyclical *Populorum Progressio (On the Progress of Peoples)*, which added several new insights to the growing teaching on Catholic social justice.[5] As a result of this document, the issue of the moral validity of the established economic and political system became a legitimate topic for religious debate. Also, for the first time the issue of revolutionary violence was addressed in a papal document, an idea which later played an important role in the development of contextual theology in South Africa. Four years later, the pope added to the growing body of teachings on the Church in the world in his encyclical *Octogesima Adveniens (Eightieth Anniversary [of Rerum Novarum])*, which again supported involvement in "political" issues.[6] In that same year, the Vatican's Synod of Bishops issued an important document entitled "Justice in the World." In it, the bishops declared that "action on behalf of justice and participation in the transformation of the world fully appear to us as a constitutive dimension of the preaching of the Gospel, or, in other words, of the church's mission for the redemption of the human race and its liberation from every oppressive situation."[7] The next advance in the development of Catholic social teaching was the 1975 encyclical *Evangelii Nuntiandi (Evangelization in the Modern World)*, in which the word "liberation" appeared for the first time.[8] By this point, the scope of issues which were considered to be legitimate topics for theological discussion had been considerably enlarged to include the problem of poverty, the gap between rich and poor, human rights, and the active participation by all people in decision-making structures. In addition to discussing the need for changes under the rubric "social justice," by the early 1980s the Vatican had also addressed the question of how these changes were to be brought about, and by whom. In his 1981 encyclical *Laborem Exercens* (*On Human Work*), Pope John Paul II discussed the issue of solidarity, by which he meant the legitimacy of opposition—especially of trade unions—in overcoming tyranny. He also called on the church to support movements of solidarity.

The Southern African Catholic Bishops' Conference, like its sister conferences in Latin America, was profoundly influenced by these new theological ideas. In their response to these ideas, the South African bishops contributed, not necessarily intentionally, to the emerging prophetic movement in South Africa. Even before the convening of Vatican II, the SACBC had made a bold pronouncement concerning the need to work for social justice in South Africa. In 1957, in response to the tightening of segregation,[9] the bishops took a leading role in denouncing the government's interference in the right to build human community across racial lines. In its plenary session of that year, the SACBC condemned the policy of apartheid on the grounds that it was artificial, divisive, and thus unchristian. The Conference also issued its landmark "Statement on Apartheid," which was the bishops' first outright condemnation of that policy. The statement, which proclaimed apartheid a "fundamental evil and blasphemous,"[10] contained the seeds of later theological and ecumenical debates which would come to the fore in the 1980s, such as that which led to declaring apartheid a heresy.[11]

In 1962, in a pastoral letter announcing the forthcoming Vatican Council, the bishops indicated that they viewed it as part of their mission to become involved in social issues, stating that:

> We dare not remain silent and passive in face of the injustices inflicted on members of the unprivileged racial groups. . . . We must use every lawful means suggested by our Christian conscience in order to counteract and overcome the injustices pressing down on the underprivileged groups . . . particularly when the people who belong to these groups are denied the elementary right to organize in defense of their legitimate interests.[12]

Thus, challenged by the ideological racism of the apartheid regime, and in some ways anticipating the recommendations of Vatican II, the SACBC had begun to reevaluate its mission—at least tentatively acknowledging that its Christian mission required it to become involved in worldly issues such as political and economic injustices (albeit using only "lawful means"). This awareness was deepened as the SACBC responded to the challenges of the Second Vatican Council. In 1966, the bishops issued a pastoral letter whose purpose

was to apply the insights of *Gaudium et Spes* to the specific South African context. Attention was paid to a variety of injustices, including the denial of
human rights, racial discrimination, and the migratory labor system, with the
bishops reiterating that all legal means should be used to change unjust laws.[13]
A significant development resulted from this letter, one which would have an
important influence on the bishops' evaluation of appropriate action in the
1980s: the SACBC Justice and Peace Commission was formed, which played a
crucial role in linking the bishops with local groups and individuals struggling
against apartheid.

In 1972, the SACBC issued another statement, "A Call to Conscience," in
which not only did the bishops attack unequal educational and economic opportunities as well as the migratory labor system, they also proclaimed that they
had a duty to champion the right of the masses to a living wage. In addition,
for the first time the bishops addressed the issue of injustice within their own
hierarchical structures, concluding that social justice did not prevail there.[14] A
final statement which illustrates the evolution of thought towards increasing
activism within the bishops' conference was their 1977 statement, "Commitment on Social Justice and Race Relations within the Church." This was their
most outspoken statement to date, and through it the bishops tentatively moved
towards recognizing the need to confront the state. The statement defended
the right to conscientious objection, an implied challenge to the legitimacy of
the South African Defense Force which did not become overt until the bishops'
statement on Namibia in 1982.

Through this emerging theology of social justice, some bishops entered
the 1980s with a predisposition to be open to overt political action. This small
group of progressive bishops was headed by Archbishop Denis Hurley, the most
consistently outspoken bishop against apartheid. Even before Vatican II's conclusion, Hurley was applying the Church's increased emphasis on social justice
to the South African scene.[15] Time and again, he made prophetic statements,
touching upon ideas and issues which would not be taken up by the institutional
church for another two decades.

Prior to the 1980s, this burgeoning commitment to social justice, at least
on an institutional level, rarely moved beyond the level of statement into that
of practice. For example, the bishops' groundbreaking 1957 statement was issued during the height of the ANC's Defiance Campaign, yet the SACBC, as
an organization, never directly supported the campaign, stressing instead the
need for the maintenance of order. Additionally, very little discussion of structural changes could be found in the early statements, where the bishops focused
primarily on individual conversion. Since changes on an individual level were
called for, the bishops did not feel the need to call for active political opposition
to the government. These early statements were relatively mild, and highlighted

the extreme caution insisted upon by the bishops.[16] Moreover, the pastoral letters never became material for regular church instruction and teaching, and no attempt was made to influence the Catholic electorate. Finally, although the Catholic Church had condemned segregation as far back as 1957, it did not, in fact, practice what it preached. The bishops did not address the issue of the integration of seminaries until 1972, and this integration did not become an established fact until 1979. Catholic schools throughout the country had only been integrated (some would say in a token fashion) a few years prior to this, and segregation was still practiced in other Catholic institutions such as hospitals until 1979. While these acts of integration did challenge apartheid laws, it had taken the bishops twenty years to implement in practice what they had declared in principle in the "Statement on Apartheid."

Most bishops lacked the prophetic vision of Hurley, and the new ideas were rarely translated into action. By the beginning of the 1980s, however, there *was* an identifiable South African theological strand of "Catholic Social Justice."[17] The Conference as a whole was moving towards an identification with the oppressed and their social and political liberation. This emerging, more political, self-identity was nowhere more obvious than in the following statement from the 1977 "Commitment on Social Justice and Race Relations," a statement issued as the bishops came under pressure from the black consciousness movement:

> We commit ourselves to give practical expression to the conviction that the Church's mission includes work for complete human liberation and to the teaching of *Evangelii Nuntiandi* that evangelisation includes transforming the concrete structures that oppress people: and in the light of this, to strive that the Church be seen in solidarity with all those who work for the promotion of human dignity and the legitimate aspirations of oppressed people.[18]

Later, when faced with increasing injustice, the bishops' choice of actions were guided by this new understanding of their mission. In the 1980s, the combination of new theological ideas with an increasingly deteriorating situation translated into the implementation of commitments they made in 1977.

The Christian Institute

A second landmark in the development of an indigenous liberation theology in South Africa was the creation of the Christian Institute[19] in 1963 by the Reverend Beyers Naudé, a minister of the Nederduits Gereformeerde Kerk (NGK), the largest white Dutch Reformed Church (DRC). Naudé was later to be barred from membership in that church because of his religious and political convictions. The Institute was founded in the aftermath of the Cottesloe

Consultation, convened by the World Council of Churches and its South African members in Johannesburg in 1960. One result of the Consultation, formed to examine the responsibility of the churches in the post-Sharpeville context of mounting unrest and repression,[20] was a division within the DRC and between the DRC and other churches, prompting the withdrawal of the DRC from the SACC and the WCC. The conflict was sparked by the final statement of the Consultation, which, although not strongly worded, was basically critical of apartheid.[21] Specifically, on the issue of apartheid the Consultation's final document stated, "the spiritual unity among all men who are in Christ must find visible expression in acts of common worship and witness. . . . "[22] Despite the fact that the NGK had a policy of segregated churches, its delegates signed the document. The Afrikaner establishment, including the prime minister, reacted harshly and decisively against both the document itself and the signing of it by the NGK delegates, ordering them to recant. While most did so, a handful of delegates, led by Naudé, refused.

Because of the failure of the DRC to stand by the Cottesloe resolutions, Naudé took a prophetic stance, establishing the Christian Institute as a nonracial ecumenical organization dedicated at first to converting the Afrikaner establishment. Proving unsuccessful at this goal, the Institute moved in a new direction in the 1970s, towards a deeper interaction with both black political leaders and black theologians. Founded with a membership of 180 individuals, the Institute had grown to over 2,000 by the time of its banning in 1977.

The Christian Institute's contribution to the development of a new theology in South Africa occurred when it reoriented itself away from a reliance on the liberal illusion that fundamental change could take place through education and moral persuasion of whites; instead, it embraced ideas emanating from the emerging black consciousness movement and the movement's accompanying black theology (of which more will be said shortly). The new ideas endorsed by the Christian Institute included the belief that Christians should identify with the poor, seeking a redistribution of power in society through supporting widespread participation in decision-making structures. This, it was argued, would then result in the necessary radical redistribution of resources. Thus, the Institute's primary focus shifted in the course of its development from an attempt at influencing whites to an identification with the poor and oppressed, the overwhelming majority of whom were black. Moreover, the Institute had by now also grasped the crucial difference between working *for* these oppressed to working *with* them, and came to firmly believe that liberation would have to be a black initiative, with only assistance from whites. This change in emphasis was noticeable in the pages of its journal *Pro Veritate,* whose editorials increasingly reflected on issues raised by Latin American liberation theology, black theologies of South Africa and the United States, and the WCC's Program to Combat Racism. In the journal, radical South African theologians began articulating the connection between race and economic exploitation and the need for a complete restructuring of society to end this oppression. Moreover, several prominent black theologians, such as Manas Buthelezi and Allan Boesak, were employed by the Christian Institute, which thereby played a facilitating role in the dissemination of their ideas to the black community. The Institute thus facilitated a new language of protest—one which was biblically grounded—in which the challenge of the Scriptures was articulated as service to the poor. The SACC and SACBC drew upon this language in the changing context of the 1980s.

These developments clearly represented a challenge to the state. The more the Christian Institute responded to the insights of black theology, the more the state reacted by harassing Institute members and by eventually attempting to silence the Institute through an official Commission of Inquiry, similar to that used against the SACC in 1983.[23] If the Christian Institute was born in the aftermath of the 1960 Sharpeville crisis, its death was marked by the aftermath of the 1976 Soweto crisis. Having identified itself on the side of the student protesters, in October 1977 the Christian Institute, together with sixteen other organizations of the black consciousness movement, was banned. The Institute's leader, Beyers Naudé, was served a banning order which was to last for seven years. Because of its incisive social analysis, its willingness to serve as an outlet for the ideas of silenced black leadership, and the ecumenical contacts it made, the contribution of the Christian Institute to the articulation of an indigenous prophetic Christianity cannot be overstated.

The Christian Institute was profoundly influenced by the emerging black theology movement. In turn, the Institute provided a forum for the development of this new theological movement, which was thus itself influenced by the white Christian left. The black theology movement represents the third source of pre-1980 ideological influences upon the SACC and the SACBC.

Black Theology

"Black Theology," according to one its most prominent theoreticians, "is the theological reflection of black Christians on the situation in which they live and on their struggle for liberation."[24] The ideas propagated by black theologians matured throughout the 1970s and continued to evolve within the larger movement called contextual theology in the 1980s. The movement underwent several distinct phases, paralleling the changes in the surrounding political context.[25] Prior to the early 1980s, at least two phases can be distinguished: the first dating from the late 1960s to 1976, which can be characterized as a theology of consciousness; and the second dating from approximately 1976—the year of the Soweto uprisings—to 1981 (the year I argue marked the beginning of contextual theology proper), which can be characterized as a theology of power.

The first phase can be traced to the early days of the South African black consciousness movement. The theology accompanying this political movement was primarily concerned with bringing a consciousness of the black situation to black people. The theological ideas which emerged from black theology at this time, and their subsequent impact on the development of contextual theology in the 1980s, cannot be understood without reference to the black consciousness movement (BCM), which was the experiential base from which black theology arose.[26] In fact, both the BCM and black theology originated with the same organization: the University Christian Movement (UCM). Moreover, many leaders in the BCM core organization, the South African Students Organization (SASO), were seminarians.[27] During this early phase, the primary ideological emphasis in the BCM, and hence in black theology, was internal liberation—the fostering of a healthy self-respect, and liberation from a slave mentality. As such, the category of "black" was redefined to include all people of color in South Africa, those suffering from white racist oppression. Although theologians writing at this time would consider themselves liberationists, the type of liberation they stressed was racially and psychologically based.[28]

These ideas had to evolve substantially before they could comfortably be taken up by more than a small minority of people in the predominantly English-speaking churches of the SACC as well as the Catholic Church. Black theology at the time embraced a strategy of exclusivism, and the multiracial approach of English-speaking churches was condemned as superficial, if not hypocritical, for it had produced a situation in which black Christians rarely acquired leadership positions of any power. Thus, in their concern to promote a positive self-image and their skepticism that multiracial structures could aid in this effort, black theology reflected the basic tenets of the BCM of the 1970s. Moreover, black consciousness leaders such as Steve Biko lambasted the Christianity practiced by most whites as being irrelevant to the lives of blacks.[29]

Several ideas which would later become prominent in contextual theology had their roots in this period. Although there was no discussion of overtly challenging the state, the seeds of this challenge were indeed present. Part of the purpose of black theology at this stage was to make blacks psychologically aware that they were not poor, powerless, dominated, and oppressed by accident. Rather, this condition was the result of the white power structure, which was dependent on their powerlessness.[30] Once this psychological liberation was achieved, it was but a small leap to political action, a core concept of religious ideas a mere decade later.

Although the government tried its hardest to quell black protest, it could not silence ideas, and black theology continued to evolve in the aftermath of Soweto. However, in the face of violence and death, black theologians began to recognize that the avoidance of political confrontation in the name of psy-

chological renewal was no longer sufficient. The preparatory stage to action—
the theology of consciousness—was over, and it was replaced by a more radical
theology of power. Whereas the first phase was mute on theological reflections
on such topics as action, violence, and revolution, this second phase confronted
these issues head-on by focusing on the issues of black power and political liberation.

This second phase is perhaps best represented by theologian Allan Boesak
in his seminal work *Farewell to Innocence,* which was one of South Africa's first
academic contributions to black theology. Influenced by U.S. black and Latin
American liberation theologies, as well as European political theology, Boesak
set out to apply ideas from these sources to the South African context. His
major contribution to the evolution of theological ideas in South Africa was
his refinement of the concept of "black power," and his capacity to link it to
the broader theme of liberation. Although Boesak was still in favor of an enlightened black consciousness, this was no longer his ultimate goal, which for
him had now become human liberation.[31] If liberation was sanctioned by Scripture, the use of power to attain it was also a theological imperative because,
argued Boesak, "Power in its purest form is indeed obedience to God who calls
for justice and liberation."[32]

As this theology moved beyond an emphasis on black consciousness, the
door was opened for an increased cooperation and acceptance of the potential
contribution of whites. In addition to this more nonracial approach, Boesak
was also concerned about the issue of reconciliation, an issue that would resur-
face again in a powerful way in the 1980s.

Thus, in the second phase of black theology the concept of "blackness"
began to fade away and was subordinated to the concept of "liberation." While
the emphasis was still on "black," the word took on a different meaning by this
time. Black theologian Simon Maimela expressed this evolved understanding
of the concept, stating:

> "black" has a wider and universal meaning, because it connotes every situation
> of human deprivation, suffering, exploitation and oppression. Here people
> who suffer and are thus referred to as "black" may happen to have black skins,
> as it has been the case historically in South Africa and North America. But it
> may very well happen that people who have white skins may actually also
> suffer injustices at the hands of the exploiters and the oppressors. Such suf-
> fering people are understood in black theology to be "black", because their
> fate is similar to the historic experience of all the people of colour who lived
> under the situation of enslavement and domination.[33]

This new, nonracial approach was necessary before black, and later contextual, theology could be an impetus to action on the part of the SACC and the

SACBC. In the 1980s, class oppression became a more reliable basis for ecumenism than race. For Boesak, oppression was primary, and color (although the cause of oppression) was incidental.[34] Boesak continued his move beyond black consciousness towards non-racism with his support of the UDF. During his 1983 speech at the UDF's launching, Boesak stated, "The nature and quality of our struggle for liberation cannot be determined by one's skin color, but rather by one's commitment to justice, peace and human liberation. . . . Let us, even now, seek to lay the foundations for reconciliation between whites and blacks in this country by working together, praying together, struggling together for justice."[35]

The South African Council of Churches

Although much theological innovation in South Africa in the 1960s and 1970s, such as black theology, did not originate within official church structures,[36] on occasion the institutional church did contribute to the development of a more prophetic theology. As noted above, this was occasionally true in the Catholic Church. It was also at times true of the SACC. Moreover, the SACC itself was increasingly dominated by members influenced by black theology. As the organization's agenda came to be more and more set by those reflecting from a black experience, the theology of the SACC eventually moved from an emphasis on reformist liberalism to one based on the need for fundamental change.

The best example of an early prophetic statement that originated inside the SACC (in close cooperation with the Christian Institute) was the June 1968 publication of *A Message to the People of South Africa*.[37] The Message was a basic condemnation of those who were prepared to justify separate development on theological grounds, by showing how this was "a denial of the central statements of the Gospel."[38] The statement's central argument was that Christians had to work for God's kingdom in history, a statement which would pave the way for later activism by the institutional church. Although the Message was clearly important for the evolution of contextual theology, it was not without its shortcomings. It was essentially paternalistic in that it was directed to those in positions of privilege and power, urging whites to work for justice for the poor. There was no sense of empowerment of the oppressed, nor was there a call for the poor to liberate themselves.[39]

Despite these shortcomings, the Message was in many ways a precursor of developments to come, and themes covered in this early document were returned to time and again in the 1980s. For instance, while neither the SACC nor the SACBC were willing to actively call for civil disobedience in the late 1960s, the seeds of such a call—which would be a cornerstone of their activism some twenty years later—could be found in the document:

we believe that it is the Church's duty to enable our people to discriminate more carefully between what may be demanded of them as subjects or citizens of the State of South Africa and what is demanded of them as disciples of Jesus Christ. . . . Where the Church thus abandons its obedience to Christ, it ceases to be the Church. We confess, therefore, that we are under an obligation to live in accordance with the Christian understanding of man and of community, even if this be contrary to some of the customs and laws of this country.[40]

In addition to civil disobedience, several other themes to be addressed by contextual theology in the 1980s had roots in this document, including the heretical nature of apartheid, the obligation for Christians to struggle against an oppressive regime, changing attitudes towards the liberation movements, the legitimacy of the state, the use of violence, and a new understanding of reconciliation. However, while the document spoke of the need to work for the poor and oppressed, those who wrote the document were neither, and these themes remained subdued. They were not to be pursued or acted upon until the political situation had significantly deteriorated and both the SACC and SACBC had become dominated by leaders heavily influenced by the emerging South African liberation theology in the 1960s and 1970s.

In addition to the SACC's adopting a more prophetic theology as a result of the influence of black theology, it also did so in reaction to theological events occurring on a global scale. Specifically, the SACC began to reorient its theology in the aftermath of the World Council of Church's establishment of the Program to Combat Racism. Although the SACC did not initially support the granting of money to Southern African liberation movements[41] (even if they were for ostensibly humanitarian purposes), because of the implied support of violence, this event nevertheless had an impact on the radicalization of the SACC. The grants and the controversy surrounding them forced the SACC to analyze its own attitude towards the liberation movements and consequently towards the state. The structural result was the establishment in 1972 of the SACC's Division of Justice and Reconciliation. Under the leadership of Wolfram Kistner through the 1980s, the Division of Justice and Reconciliation played a central role in theologically guiding the SACC's adoption of an overt political self-identity. It was through this division that all ideas and decisions concerning the question of legitimacy were studied and referred back to the ecumenical body for action.

Almost immediately, the Division of Justice and Reconciliation's transformative effect on the SACC's challenge to the state was evident. At the 1974 SACC National Conference, the issue of participation in military action to defend South Africa was raised. At the conference's end, after serious debate, the SACC adopted a resolution supporting the right to conscientious objection.

While the resolution was not accompanied by acts of overt political activity on the part of church leaders,[42] its theological rationale did include an early discussion of a central issue in Latin American liberation theology which was to come to the fore a decade later in South Africa—the issue of structural violence. The preamble stated that "South Africa is a fundamentally unjust and discriminatory society and this injustice and discrimination constitute the primary, institutionalised violence which has provoked the counter violence of the terrorists or freedom fighters." The seeds of later civil disobedience were also to be found in the resolution's second clause, which read, "the Conference . . . calls on its member Churches to challenge all their members to consider . . . whether Christ's call to take up the Cross and follow Him in identifying with the oppressed does not, in our situation, involve becoming conscientious objectors."[43]

Thus, throughout the 1970s, especially under the influence of black theology, the SACC increasingly acted as a prophetic catalyst. It set the agenda for its member churches' response to theological debates which were becoming ever more political.

Overlapping Sources

Although I have treated Catholic social thought, the Christian Institute, black theology, and the SACC's early prophetic stance as distinct sources of theological innovation, it should by now be obvious that there was a tremendous amount of overlap and diffusion of ideas between all four, and between domestic South African innovation and theological trends occurring globally. For example, there was a growing cooperation between the Christian Institute and the SACC, and both were increasingly influenced by people working from a black theology perspective. Although the Institute had more freedom to operate than the SACC—which was accountable not to individuals but to member churches—the relationship between both remained close and cooperative. From 1967 onward, the Christian Institute was an associate member of the SACC, and some believe that with the Christian Institute's banning, the SACC served as the main institutional locus for the development of South African liberation theology (at least until the development of a specific organization for that purpose, namely, the Institute for Contextual Theology). There was also cooperation, although not as close as with the SACC, between the Christian Institute and the Catholic Bishops' Conference, most notably through Archbishop Denis Hurley, who sat on the Institute's board. Additionally, the Christian Institute helped to conduct workshops for the newly formed SACBC Justice and Peace Commission.[44]

The Catholic bishops were also being challenged to listen to the message of black theology by the newly formed Black Priests' Solidarity Group (BPSG), an organization of black Roman Catholic clergy created in 1976 from the early black priests' group known as SPOBA (the St. Peter's Old Boys Association).[45] The BPSG was at the forefront in the push for contextualizing seminary training, and was a leading force in the eventual integration of seminaries. A key figure in the BPSG was Father Smangaliso Mkhatshwa, who was the SACBC's General Secretary throughout most of the 1980s.

The SACC was influenced by black theology in a variety of ways. Black theologians were invited to deliver keynote addresses at annual National Conferences, thereby exerting an influence on decisions taken by the Council. Others were appointed as staff members, and so were able to influence the Christian response to political events. One of the most important appointments in this regard was Bishop Desmond Tutu, an outspoken protagonist of black theology, who became the SACC's first black General Secretary in 1978. Finally, the SACC's link with black theology was evident in specific conferences it held, such as the 1980 "Consultation on Racism in South Africa," a review of the first ten years of the WCC's Program to Combat Racism. The Consultation was addressed by two prominent black theologians, Allan Boesak and Bonganjalo Goba.[46] Thus, at a time when the organizations of the black consciousness movement were banned, the SACC was able to serve as a vehicle and platform for the theological ideas coming from this movement.

Clearly, by the end of the 1970s, several theological ideas had emerged in South Africa which together constituted a new universe of religious discourse. In this discourse, the Christian mission was seen as working with the poor and oppressed, and an emphasis on working for social justice was now the focal point of the emerging theology. This theology was uniquely South African. It was an amalgamation of ideas coming from the Christian Institute, Vatican II, black consciousness, black theology, Latin American liberation theology, United States black theology, European political theology, as well as ideas which originated within both the SACC—including the *Message to the People of South Africa*—and the SACBC—including the 1977 Declaration of Commitment. These various influences came together in the 1980s to create an indigenous South African liberation theology, which later came to be called contextual theology. The ideas of the preceding two decades continued to evolve throughout the 1980s and were further refined, as well as institutionalized, in the Institute for Contextual Theology.

Despite the beginning of a theological reorientation, however, both the SACC and SACBC had not moved much beyond the level of statements in the early 1980s. They remained vague and reticent in terms of action. Still, a core group of church leaders entered the decade of the 1980s profoundly influenced by this new theology. These included, among others, Desmond Tutu, Beyers

Naudé, Denis Hurley, Allan Boesak, Smangaliso Mkhatshwa, and Frank Chikane. They were the leaders of both the SACC and SACBC in the 1980s, who
became caught up in the spiral of involvement.

Theological Evolution: From Race to Class

A clear evolution in the emphasis of contextual theology can be traced from
the 1960s through the 1980s, with each adaptation reflecting the changing political context. In the period prior to the Soweto uprisings of 1976, the primary
emphasis in black theology was on race. The period from 1976 through 1983,
when the government introduced its new constitution and further entrenched
racism, can be seen as a transition period. Theologians still spoke and wrote of
"black" theology, but the concept was given an essentially nonracial meaning.
At this time, theologians tended to espouse a theology of liberation for black
people. During the 1980s, two distinct changes in contextual theology occurred. First, in the post-1983 period there was much less use of the term
"black" in theological statements; rather, the primary reference was to class
and to the economic structures underpinning apartheid. In this period, one no
longer spoke of "black theology," but increasingly of "contextual theology."[47]
Many theologians in the 1980s who cut their theological teeth on the black
consciousness strategy of racialism moved towards embracing the nonracial
contextual theology of the 1980s, including Desmond Tutu, Frank Chikane,
Allan Boesak, and Smangaliso Mkhatshwa. They made this theological transition along with a political transition from black consciousness to the UDF and
the charterist position—a shift that allowed for both continuity and evolution
in prophetic theology in South Africa. These theologians took up leadership
positions in the SACC and the SACBC in the 1980s, thus ensuring that the
theological influences in those organizations would be of the contextual (and
not black) theological variety.

The evolution towards a primary emphasis on class in the 1980s permeates
most theological writings from that period. Theologians became aware, partly
through dialogue with Latin American liberation theologians, that theology
could not be separated from social analysis. Issues became defined less in terms
of race and more in terms of class; hence the struggle was seen less in terms of
whites versus blacks, and more in terms of rich versus poor. Some theologians
pointed out that racism could not be separated from economic exploitation and
incorporated both in their analysis.[48]

A second change in contextual theology involved its goals. In the first period (that is, the late 1960s and early 1970s), black theology viewed the fostering
of a healthy consciousness as its theological goal. Little attention was given at
this point to political action by blacks to change the status quo, for this was
considered premature before consciousness was raised. In the second period

(from the early 1970s through the early 1980s), theologians recognized that the implications of an increased consciousness was liberation (best summed up in Boesak's conceptualization of "black power"), but still no specific action on the part of the church was spelled out. In the third, post-1983 period, which coincided with the spiral of involvement, theologians reflected further on the implications of the second stage, and argued that liberation required revolution.[49] Thus, in this period Christianity moved beyond inspiring to demanding a foundational restructuring of unjust political, social, and economic structures. Consciousness had moved to protest, and protest to challenge in the period from the early 1960s to the late 1980s. If earlier black theology was conscious of the need to transform political structures, contextual theology in the 1980s was more militant—it wanted these structures abolished. Likewise, where earlier theologians challenged the church to be an "instrument of social criticism,"[50] later theologians challenged the church to go beyond criticism to action. It is not coincidental that increasing activity on the part of the SACC and SACBC both mirrored changes in theological thought and resulted from an increasingly deteriorating political situation—for these more radical religious ideas were themselves a response to the political context in which theologians found themselves. As black politics of the 1980s increasingly turned to confrontation with the state and civil disobedience, this change came to be reflected in the theological writings of the time. Only with these new theological ideas could both organizations become overtly political.

One of the clearest examples of the theological evolution from race to class and from consciousness to revolution was the Kairos Document, about which more will be said below. Not once does the document make reference to "blacks"; rather, it speaks of the "oppressed," with all Christians being exhorted to participate in the struggle to bring about new political and economic structures.

Contextual Theology

Just as the Christian Institute served as a platform for and think tank of black theology in the late 1960s and through the 1970s, so contextual theology became institutionalized in the Institute for Contextual Theology during the 1980s. The Institute was formed in 1981, and its first steering committee was indicative of the heavy debt it owed to earlier theological influences, being composed primarily of two groups: veterans of the Christian Institute and black theologians.[51] The Institute was founded with the specific goal of "contributing towards a theological base for the realisation of a new society in Southern Africa,"[52] as well as the political goal of "preparing people for a participatory democracy in a liberated South Africa."[53] Clear strains of Latin American liberation theology can be heard in the ICT's description of its work, which is carried out in a variety of ways, all of which reflect the political emphasis embedded in this theology. The ICT sponsored many projects in the 1980s, including the Black Theology project; Ministry in a Situation of Conflict; Theology of Labor; Education for Democracy; The Women's Kairos; and Land and Restitution. The ICT also sponsored conferences which produced the following publications: "Churches and Violence," "The Illegitimacy of the South African Government," and "Negotiations, Defiance, and the Church."[54]

What were the theological ideas underpinning contextual theology? How did these ideas contribute to an increasing level of politicization within the SACC and SACBC? Finally, how did these ideas interact in a dialectical fashion with the changing political context to spur these religious organizations to political action, the result of which was a further refinement of these ideas, which only emboldened the organizations to become yet more actively involved? As with the examples of theological innovation in the previous two decades, sometimes these ideas originated within the structures of the SACC and SACBC, while at other times they originated outside.

Contextual theology, according to the ICT's own definition, is "the conscious attempt to do theology from within the context of real life in the world."[55] Although this is a rather broad definition and does not give many clues to the major ideas underlining this theology, it does point to the one major idea that all contextual theologians adhere to: all reflection must begin from within a particular context, or life situation. As de Gruchy states, "the fundamental task . . . is to reflect on how God's self-disclosure has been discerned in those situations to which Scripture bears witness in relation to the issues facing us in our present context and our response to them."[56] In addition to this overarching theme, there are at least four other themes, all interrelated, that comprise the religious discourse known as contextual theology.

The first idea is that contextual theology relies on biblical exegesis[57] and on two specific themes in the Bible—liberation and the teachings of the prophets. Hence, contextual theology is often referred to as prophetic theology.[58] The task of contextual theology is to read and interpret the signs of the time in light of the gospel teachings. The signs themselves are human events, and the process of reading these signs is that of discovering the religious significance of public events, by "discerning, differentiating, and interpreting them in relation to God." In other words, the gospel becomes contextualized in an attempt to understand its meaning in the situation of conflict and crisis in South Africa.

Contextualizing the gospel to South Africa means taking up the theme of liberation, and several liberation themes in the Bible are stressed. Social and political oppression is interpreted in light of the Bible, the most quoted biblical story being that of the Exodus, which is described as one of political liberation. Jesus's liberating mission is seen as directed towards the oppressed, and an oft-quoted passage which describes what Jesus will do for the oppressed is Luke 4:18: "The Spirit of the Lord has been given to me, for he has anointed me. He has sent me to bring good news to the poor, to proclaim liberty to captives, to proclaim new sight to the blind, to set free the downtrodden, to proclaim the Lord's year of favor."[59] The descriptions of "setting free," "proclaiming liberty," and "bringing good news," are read as clear signs that the gospel's mission is one of social and political liberation. When read from the perspective of the poor, the Bible is read as a book *of* the oppressed and *for* the oppressed.

This theme of drawing on biblical stories of liberation and the teachings of the prophets is related to the second characteristic of contextual theology: the need to interpret the gospel from the perspective of the poor and oppressed, which in South Africa means opting for the victims of the apartheid system. Opting for the poor means working not only for racial but also for economic justice, the two being inextricably intertwined. It does not refer to the choice of recipients of the gospel message (i.e., to whom the gospel should be preached); rather it is a matter of the content of that message itself. Opting for the poor means examining the sin of oppression and what Christians, both rich and poor, should be doing to eradicate this oppression.[60] This is a theology which is critical of any Christian tradition that simply accepts the economic and political institutions of the day. As Tlhagale states, "Christian symbols of brotherhood and love resound with emptiness. Images of God as a just, loving and merciful Father do not correspond with the harsh reality of racism, landlessness, economic exploitation and political powerlessness."[61] Opting *for* the poor means opting *against* any form of oppression or exploitation. It is an uncompromising commitment to the cause of the oppressed as the cause of God. This means not only denouncing injustice, but also working for a future liberated society.

Closely related to this second theme is the third: the need for social analysis. As Nolan and Broderick assert, contextual theology requires a new language to "mediate the word of God to people."[62] The language chosen is that of the social sciences, and the "signs of the times" are thus read from a social scientific perspective. Specifically, in the 1980s contextual theologians began to see South Africa in terms of structural problems which required structural solutions. Armed with this type of analysis, they recategorized sin to include not only personal but also social sin. Hence, apartheid structures themselves were sinful. Social analysis would then serve to make Christians aware of their role in allowing this structural injustice to continue, as well as their role in ending it.

The final theme that binds all contextual theologians together is an emphasis on a particular type of methodology, which can best be summed up as "doing theology." Chikane terms this "hermeneutical praxis," while Nolan prefers the terminology of "hermeneutical circle."[63] Both mean that theology must begin with the experiences of those actually involved in the struggle. This

implies involvement in efforts to bring justice; and as will be seen below, this
is one reason that the SACC and SACBC, working under the influence of contextual theology, became actively involved in the struggle in South Africa. This
is also the reason for the dialectical model discussed above, for if one begins
with experience and moves to theory, theological thinking becomes influenced
by the everyday realities of life, which in turn influences the way that Christians
become involved in that reality. That involvement in turn influences all further
theological reflection. Nolan states this model thus:

> Theory and practice go hand in hand. Right thinking and right acting in-
> fluence one another. There is no one way movement from one to the other
> but a two way movement or mutual influence that continues through life as
> we grow in truth of living and believing. . . . It is an on-going process that
> moves through practice and theory, action and reflection towards a deeper
> understanding of our faith and a more committed practice of it.[64]

For Chikane, there is no such thing as a "universal" theological interpretation. Rather, each interpretation is dependent upon the situation in which
theologians find themselves, and each interpretation supports, rejects, or legitimizes certain forms of praxis. He rejects any theological interpretation of the
South African situation which comes from the perspective of the rich and privileged, because they advocate a status quo praxis. Rather, he states that "theology not grounded in liberating praxis is not liberating theology."[65] Nolan
agrees, and is critical of Western Catholic theologians who have abandoned the
theological principle of *sensus fidei,* or the instinct of faith, which is so important to contextual theology. Traditional theology, Nolan believes, is fundamentally distrustful of experience, and hence views any attempts to do theology
from the context of lived experience as unreliable and "not real." For both
Chikane and Nolan, all other interpretations of the gospel in South Africa,
because they are not made from the perspective of the poor and the oppressed,
are misleading. Such false or distorted interpretations have included everything
from the theological justification of apartheid, to the belief that religion and
politics should be kept separate, to religious acceptance of liberal attempts at
modifying the system.

Given these tenets of contextual theology, it is not difficult to see how this
new religious discourse contributed to the politicization of the SACC and the
SACBC. For if one were to live out the implications of these teachings, one
would have no choice but to act. Contextual theology is not a part-time hobby,
nor can it be confined to academic writings. It is not just a way of thinking;
rather, it is also a way of acting. This is expressed as *taking sides.* In South Africa
in the 1980s this involved taking sides with the oppressed, exploited, and victims of apartheid; and contextual theologians were unequivocally clear that re-

maining neutral in a conflict situation was tantamount to taking sides with those who supported apartheid. As Nolan states, "those who stand on the sidelines and observe the struggle between good and evil from a distance or take a mere academic interest in how it is going to work itself out, are giving their support, by omission, to the aggressor."[66] Not only was remaining neutral a rejection of the message of contextual theology, but working for compromise and moderation in the context of apartheid was also a contradiction of the Bible. Nolan acknowledges this is an extreme position, but he argues that caution and "false prudence" on the part of those working for reform lead to compromise and hypocrisy. All those committed to the message of contextual theology are by faith committed to social change, and this makes this message, according to Chikane, "subversive by nature."[67] Nolan concurs, and states that by opting for the poor, Christians have automatically taken sides in a situation of structural conflict. He also firmly believes that it is imperative not only to support the cause of the poor, but also to support organizations that genuinely work to bring about that cause, including trade unions. (This was later also extended, albeit controversially, by the SACC and the SACBC to support of the liberation movements.) For Nolan, Chikane, and others, it is impossible for Christians to experience personal conversion (i.e., a change of heart) without simultaneously working for a change in structures.

Herein lies the crux of how these new ideas contributed, both directly and indirectly (through stoking the spiral of involvement), to a more political self-identity not only for Christians but also for Christian organizations. If the entire underlying social and economic structures of the apartheid system were unjust, then they could not be changed from within. They had to be abolished, and Christians soon came to realize that working for this would not come without confrontation and a heavy cost. Chikane best expresses how living this theology amidst a worsening political context directly contributed to the spiral of involvement. He states:

> The new methodology means becoming involved in the struggle for a full humanity. . . . It involves being in detention with the victims of the system where one will be forced to ask realistic and concrete theological questions about God. It is demanding because it means theologians must relinquish their position of privilege and choose rather to suffer with the people of God. . . . It is costly because one might become a victim of detention in solitary confinement without trial. It could mean being banned, restricted or banished It could mean death in detention or even assassination. . . . To do theology in a situation of conflict demands carrying the cross.[68]

In the course of the 1980s, then, a new "universe of religious discourse" evolved. Issues not formerly considered appropriate for debate, including theological discussion of the legitimacy of the state, became so by the end of the decade. As a result of this discourse, the SACC and the SACBC leadership felt obliged to enter the field of political activism. The ideas of contextual theology inspired the policies and commitments of the SACC and the SACBC.

5

Contextual Theology and
the Spiral of Involvement

THROUGHOUT THE 1980s, contextual theologians challenged the status quo from their religious perspective. An analysis of each successive issue they embraced indicates that as the political situation deteriorated, they increasingly stressed that their theology required them to confront the system of apartheid and to work for the implementation of an entirely new system. As their ideas motivated Christians to action, these ideas themselves evolved, and this evolution empowered yet further action by those committed to the struggle. The result was a yet more refined set of religious ideas by the beginning of the 1990s.

Issues in Contextual Theology in the 1980s

Apartheid Is a Heresy

One of the first issues taken on by contextual theologians during the 1980s actually originated inside institutional structures, in this case the SACC. In June 1982, during its National Conference, and while the Eloff Commission of Inquiry was still in session, the SACC declared explicitly that apartheid was sinful and its moral and theological justification a heresy.[1] Almost fifteen years after it published the *Message to the People of South Africa,* the SACC finally took that message—that apartheid was a pseudo gospel—a step further, by calling for ecclesiastical action. The first dramatic sign of such action occurred two months later. Under the newly elected presidency of Allan Boesak, the World Alliance of Reformed Churches at its international meeting in Ottawa agreed with the declaration of heresy and suspended the powerful and influential NGK for theologically supporting apartheid. The Ottawa events gave an international legitimation to the SACC's embrace of contextual theology, precisely at a time when the SACC was embroiled in a growing church/state conflict. At the time of his election to the presidency of the WARC, Boesak was a member of the SACC executive, who were being maligned at that very moment by the Eloff Commission.[2]

In his address to the WARC, Boesak explained why that world body, like the SACC, felt it imperative to declare apartheid a heresy. Both organizations wanted to make clear that the political policy of apartheid was dependent for its very existence on its theological legitimation. Both organizations were recognizing, therefore, that to confront the political policy, it was also necessary to wage war on its theological justification. In this way, reflection on the role of religious organizations in the political arena became more pressing. Once apartheid was definitively declared a sin, Christians were exhorted to confess their participation in it and commit themselves, in obedience to God, to eradicating the sin. The political implications of the heresy declaration were made explicit by Boesak, who posed the following questions:

> Can you be a Christian, and can you say with your church, "Yes, apartheid is a heresy," and still continue to vote for that government? Or can you say "apartheid is a heresy, it is a denial of the gospel, it calls upon me as a Christian to become involved in the struggle for human dignity and freedom and liberation and justice and genuine reconciliation"—and still remain silent and simply benefit from that system as so many English-speaking Christians think they can do? Can we say that apartheid is a heresy and speak language as clear as all that, and then turn around and remain silent because we are afraid, or because we may in some way have economic gains from the system? . . . The only thing that is left is the deeds to follow the words.[3]

For Boesak, the message was clear: having declared apartheid a heresy, Christians had no other choice but to become involved in the struggle. The heresy declaration was a challenge to the institutional churches to reexamine their understanding of Christian mission.

A Call to Prayer for an End to Unjust Rule

The next major development in contextual theology occurred in 1985 with "A Theological Rationale and a Call to Prayer for an End to Unjust Rule" (hereafter referred to as the Call) in the weeks leading up to the June 16 commemoration of the ninth anniversary of the Soweto uprisings. The Call was extremely controversial both inside and outside of church circles; indeed, very few South African theological documents have produced such public outcry. This time theological innovation did not originate inside the SACC; rather, it came from an ecumenical study group independent of the SACC. The seed of the Call, however, originated with Allan Boesak at the SACC's 1984 National Conference. During an address to the delegates, Boesak stated:

> What the poor need in this country is not meaningless reforms but a new government that will love justice, hate evil, and do what is right for all the people of South Africa. This present government does not seem able to do this, and therefore . . . I call on all Christians and churches to set aside a day

on which to pray for the downfall of this government. If the rulers will not hear the cries of the people, if they will not change, if they continue to prevent justice, let us pray them out of existence.[4]

During the following year, an ecumenical working group, which had been established to prepare a theological statement in defense of this prayer, slowly came to realize that it would be naive to pray seriously and honestly for the end to unjust rule without simultaneously praying for the removal from power of those who were responsible for this rule. The result of this realization was the birth of the Theological Rationale, which was published in May 1985 by the WPCC—a regional council of the SACC, although with independent authority.[5] As Boesak's earlier call for the "downfall" of the government was thought to be too radical, even for many progressive Christians (it was apparently interpreted as support for revolutionary violence), the study group agreed to change the wording to "remove from power."

The Call itself was clear and specific. Its most important, and therefore most controversial, passage read:

> We have prayed for our rulers, as is demanded of us in the scriptures. We have entered into consultation with them, as is required by our faith. We have taken the reluctant and drastic step of declaring apartheid to be contrary to the declared will of God, and some churches have declared its theological justification to be a heresy. We now pray that God will replace the present structures of oppression with ones that are just, and remove from power those who persist in defying his laws, installing in their place leaders who will govern with justice and mercy.[6]

Drawing on contextual theology's emphasis on structural injustice, the Call continued:

> We have continually prayed for the authorities, that they may govern wisely and justly. Now, in solidarity with those who suffer most, in this hour of crisis we pray that God in his grace may remove from his people the tyrannical structures of oppression and the present rulers in our country who persistently refuse to heed the cry for justice, as reflected in the Word of God. . . .[7]

On June 16, 1985, thousands of people attended hundreds of church services across South Africa, in which petitions were made to God to end unjust rule. In Cape Town over one thousand people attended a service, despite police blockades of buses arriving from the surrounding townships. Ceasing to pray *for* the Government and praying instead for its removal had serious political implications for those who took the Call to heart, for it required them to become engaged in a new level of opposition.[8] Christians were now required to ground their prayers in a corresponding commitment to work for bringing about just government. Consequently, serious questions arose regarding Christian duties to disobey the government. As such, the document contributed to the church/state conflict in a way few previous documents had done, serving as a precursor of further conflict engendered by future documents.

The prayer also signaled a new phase in the legitimacy debate, although that debate had not yet been explicitly acknowledged by the SACC or SACBC. At this point, theologians were saying that the particular government of the time had to be removed. It was not long before they were claiming that in order for God's will to be done in South Africa, the very structures of the apartheid state itself had to be dismantled. An explicit discussion of these questions would not occur, however, until the political situation had further deteriorated and contextual theology had further evolved. Both occurred the following year with the imposition of the state of emergency and the publication of the Kairos Document.

The Kairos Document

Nowhere was the call to Christian action issued as strongly and as clearly as in this document, published in September 1985 by the ICT, independently of the institutional structures of either the SACC and the SACBC.[9] The Kairos Document is recognized as *the* definitive statement of contextual theology in South Africa.[10] It makes use of the methodology of the "hermeneutic circle," starting its analysis from the sociohistorical context of the repression of 1985. It also draws heavily on the Bible for support, especially on the message in Romans 13 regarding the legitimacy of governments. It makes use of social analysis, diagnosing apartheid society in structural terms. It serves as evidence that not only do religious ideas influence the role of churches in political situations, but that these situations themselves also impact the production of new religious ideas, for the document was a theological response to the specific political context of South Africa in the mid-1980s.[11] As one theologian stated, it was essential in the political context of both increasing repression and mounting defiance to provide a critical theological analysis that was conversant with both the perceptions and demands of the masses as well as with the political agenda of the government, not least in terms of explaining its total strategy.[12] The document not only drew on the theological ideas of previous documents and statements, it also moved these ideas onto a higher plane: never before had such an explicit call for political action to end apartheid been justified on theological grounds. Coming at a time of political turmoil and crisis, the Kairos Document's starting point was an analysis of this crisis by those who had lived and suffered in the situation.[13] One of the major contributions of the document is its identification of three distinct types of theology present in South Africa—State Theology, Church Theology, and Prophetic Theology. It thoroughly critiqued the first two while espousing the third.

State theology, a theological justification of the racist, capitalist, and to-talitarian status quo, was rejected for its deliberate misuse of theological con-cepts and biblical texts for political ends. It gave an absolute and divine author-ity to the state, while at the same time branding anyone who rejected this authority as "communist."[14] Moreover, by depicting the discriminatory laws of apartheid, the institutionalized repression, and the indiscriminate use of violence to maintain it, as "normal," the state designated all those who re-jected this type of law and order as sinful. The Kairos Document's critique of state theology exposed the regime's attempt to assert its theological justifica-tion of apartheid in order to maintain power in the context of increased resis-tance.[15] No longer did the state try to justify apartheid on the basis of racial segregation (which had been declared a heresy); rather, as the Kairos Docu-ment pointed out, this justification was now based on the ideology of a na-tional security state. Phrases such as "law and order," "national security," and "anti-communism" peppered the state's theological interpretation of South Africa.

The document's critique of church theology was considerably more con-troversial than its critique of state theology. It declared for the first time that liberal churches were part of the problem in South Africa. It did so by call-ing into question the central features of traditional Christian resistance: ideas about reconciliation, nonviolence, and justice. Mainstream interpretations of these were critically analyzed and found wanting. While the Kairos theologi-ans wanted true reconciliation, peace, and justice, they did not want these in the form of the same old liberal opposition to the state that had characterized many of the English-speaking churches, with the praxis that accompanied these churches' interpretation of the concepts of mediation and reform. The Kairos Document rejected any such attempt to forge a compromise. Since apartheid had already been designated as evil, unjust, sinful, and heretical, no compromise with this system was deemed possible. For the Kairos theologians, reconcili-ation through compromise could never be made into an absolute principle that must be applied in all cases of conflict. Rather, they argued that there are some conflicts that can only be described as a struggle between justice and injustice, or good and evil. In such cases, attempts to reconcile both parties through negotiated compromises would be a betrayal of the gospel. For South Africa, this meant that reconciliation, and thus peace, were impossible without the total dismantling of apartheid.[16] In contrast to reconciliation, the Kairos Docu-ment challenged churches to respond with a theology of confrontation and resistance.

Thus, the justice of reform, one that is "determined by the oppressor and is offered to the people as a kind of concession," was rejected. The Kairos theolo-gians opted for a more radical justice that "comes from below and is determined by the people of South Africa."[17] These theologians pointed to the structural injustice of South Africa and maintained that it would never be alleviated by reforms instituted from the top down; true justice could only come from below. Having acknowledged this, the document then rejected church theology's blanket condemnation of violence. It drew a distinction between the structural, institutional violence of the South African police and army and the violence used by the people, especially in the townships, to defend themselves. (However, it did *not* state that this latter type of violence was permissible in all instances.) Thus, one of the major flaws of church theology was its superficial and counterproductive critique of apartheid, resulting from a lack of in-depth social analysis. It was seen as a theology that does not take account of the particular political context.

Having rejected state and church theologies, the document turned towards a prophetic theology, one that is rooted in social analysis and includes *reading the signs of the times*. The time (*Kairos*) that the writers of the document "read" was one of "structural inequality (political, social and economic) expressed in discriminatory laws, institutions and practices [which] has led the people of South Africa into a virtual civil war and rebellion against tyranny."[18] For the first time, the legitimacy of the South African state was theologically called into question: "if it is a tyrannical regime, it is, from a moral and a theological point of view, *illegitimate*."[19]

The document ended with a clear acknowledgment of the necessity of a political level of commitment by the church. "Changing the structures of a society is fundamentally a matter of politics. There will be a Christian way of approaching the political solutions, a Christian spirit and motivation and attitude, but there is no way of bypassing politics and political strategies."[20] Prophetic theology itself adopts this explicitly political commitment, and exhorts Christians to take an unequivocal stand with the concerns of the oppressed in their quest for liberation. The question that undergirded the document, and that was brought to light in its last section, was, "whose side is the church on?" The document was unequivocal that one could not remain neutral and be prophetic. It was clear, however, that taking sides should not be accomplished through revolutionary violence but by other means, including civil disobedience. Campaigns for liberation, including consumer boycotts and stayaways, should be supported by the church. The Kairos Document was a charter for radical Christian praxis as opposed to the moderation and pietistic non-involvement of even "progressive" churches.

Post-Kairos Theological Development: Harare and Lusaka

The Kairos Document not only made waves inside South Africa, it also received widespread attention in international church circles. A mere three months after its publication, the World Council of Churches, with the assistance of the SACC, organized an emergency consultation in Harare, Zimbabwe, to reflect on the challenges presented to them by the Kairos Document.[21] The theological pronouncements which resulted from this meeting have subsequently come to be known as the Harare Declaration. The delegates affirmed that "the moment of truth (KAIROS) is now. . . . We have heard the cries of anguish of the people of South Africa trapped in the oppressive structures of apartheid. . . . We agree that the apartheid structure is against God's will, and is morally indefensible." In keeping with the Kairos Document's challenge to action, the Harare Declaration called "on the Churches inside and outside South Africa to support South African movements working for liberation of their country."[22] In addition to supporting the Kairos Document, the Harare Declaration also made reference to earlier declarations, stating: "We understand and fully support those in South Africa who are calling for the resignation of the government. . . . We call on the Churches inside and outside South Africa to . . . observe June 16th—the 10th anniversary of Soweto—as a World Day of Prayer to end unjust rule in South Africa."[23] Furthermore, in acknowledgment of the need to produce a prophetic statement that reflected the basic tenets of contextual theology, the delegates stated, "we recognise that there is a crisis of relevance in applying traditional theological concepts and formulations to the situation in South Africa. We are challenged to give fresh understanding to concepts like love and reconciliation."[24] Finally, the conference reconfirmed contextual theology's insistence that apartheid could not be reformed but had to be completely abolished. The statement read, "We reject categorically all proposals for modification of apartheid. Apartheid is to be dismantled fully and completely. A radical break has to be made with the present."[25]

A year and a half later, in May 1987, the WCC held another conference, this time in Lusaka, Zambia, on the theme, "The Churches' Search for Justice and Peace in Southern Africa." The conference's purpose was to review progress on the implementation of the Harare Declaration and to discuss the responsibility of the churches for effecting justice and peace in Southern Africa. In addition to church representatives from both Africa and the international community, participants were also present from the ANC, PAC, and SWAPO. Whereas at Harare the liberation movements had been present as observers, now their representatives were delegates, with both the ANC president and the PAC chairman addressing the conference.

The conference's final document, the Lusaka Statement, reaffirmed the message of the Harare Declaration, while pushing the theological debate on political issues onto a higher plane. Strains of the heresy declaration, the prayer for an end to unjust rule, and the irreformability of apartheid structures could be found in the statement. Additionally, at least two new issues emerged from the conference as subjects for theological debate. These included a firm declaration of the illegitimacy of the South African state and a discussion of the legitimacy of the violence employed by the liberation movements in their fight against apartheid. While the Harare Declaration declared that the South African government had "no credibility" and therefore supported "those calling for the resignation of the government," the Lusaka Statement was much more unequivocal. As noted earlier the delegates stated: "It is our belief that civil authority is instituted of God to do good, and that under the biblical imperative all people are obliged to do justice and show special care for the oppressed and the poor. It is this understanding that leaves us with no alternative but to conclude that the South African regime and its colonial domination of Namibia is illegitimate."[26] Declaring the state illegitimate had definite consequences for Christians, for having made this statement, they were now under an obligation to disobey the laws of government. By implication, Christians were required to engage themselves in an organized manner to remove the government from power. Thus, widening the scope of theological debate had the potential of contributing to increased civil disobedience. This increase, in turn, would contribute to the spiral of church/state conflict.

The public declaration of illegitimacy made news, but more controversial by far was the familiar second statement: "While remaining committed to peaceful change, we recognize that the nature of the South African regime, which wages war against its own inhabitants and neighbors, compels the movements to the use of force along with other means to end oppression."[27] Thus, a new theme was taken up and later refined by South African contextual theologians, that of the theological legitimation of certain types of violence. As a result of this understanding of the concept of violence, a much closer cooperation between these theologians (and their respective organizations) and the liberation movements (including the UDF) was forged. Contextual theology's understanding of this issue had clearly evolved throughout the 1980s, for the Kairos Document's discussion of violence impacted the debate at the Lusaka Conference. This statement in turn led to a conference inside South Africa, sponsored by the ICT, on the theme of theology and violence.

Theology and Violence

1987 was not, of course, the first time that the issue of violence was taken up as a topic for theological debate. However, this time the debate surrounding the use of violence, both by the state and by the liberation movements, was influenced by the accumulated ideas of contextual theology, especially those in the Kairos Document and the Lusaka Statement. Consequently, a more complex understanding of the issues surrounding the use of violence emerged.

South African theologians had long wrestled with the question of when violence could be legitimately used, as well as the appropriate response by churches to the violence of the liberation struggle.[28] In their discussions, they were influenced by similar debates about violence which had taken place in Latin America. By the 1980s, contextual theologians had recognized that violence might be inevitable in the struggle. Still, they were hesitant when it came to the issue of the legitimacy of that violence. Boesak's opinion in 1977 represented the early view in theological circles on this issue. He stated, "Whereas we do not deny that a situation may arise where retaliatory violence is forced upon the oppressed and no other avenue is left open to them, we do so with a clear hesitancy, knowing full well that it will probably prove a poor 'solution' and that *violence can never be 'justified.'* "[29] Soon after, however, the pendulum began to swing in the opposite direction. In 1980, during the SACC's Consultation on Racism, this shift was evident, as indicated by the statement, "it appears as if much more thought needs to be given to the reasons for rejecting revolutionary violence."[30] In the decade to come, contextual theologians were to further revise their position on this issue. The watershed was the Kairos Document, which condemned the absolute principle of nonviolence, pointing out that in South Africa's situation, violence was not a neutral term. Kairos theologians specifically objected to the equation of police aggression with insurgent response, and made a very clear distinction between the structural, institutional violence of the state, and the violence of resistance in the townships that was occurring on a vastly different scale. The Kairos Document pointed out that the churches tended to unwittingly justify, or at least overlook, the former type of violence, while condemning the latter. The refusal of contextual theology to compromise, and its insistence on the need for a radical restructuring of society, necessarily lead to a different view of the legitimacy of insurgent violence. The document rejected nonviolence as an absolute Christian ideal. It argued that a blanket condemnation of all violence was tantamount to refusing to make a judgment about who was right and who was wrong. Pacifism, which ignored the state's use of violence (an approach which was embodied in "church theology," Kairos theologians argued), enabled the status quo of violence to continue.

In an effort to bring together the various theological statements on violence and to reflect upon the implications of these for action, the ICT sponsored a workshop on theology and violence in November 1987, which was attended by 125 church workers and lay persons from various denominations and religious organizations.[31] The explicit goal was "to work towards a positional direction on Christian theology and violence in the South African context."[32]

The tradition of condoning the state's use of violence while condemning the use of violence against it was severely criticized. One participant argued that the prophetic tradition of responding to the demands of the socially marginalized and politically oppressed members of society allowed for a theological understanding and, at times, a theological legitimation of revolutionary violence, so that anyone claiming to take a preferential option for the poor would have to side with this tradition. Violence could be used, therefore, only if it brought justice to the poor.[33] Participants pointed out the hypocrisy of many churches: they indirectly participated in the militarization of the state by allowing their chaplains or ministers to give spiritual support to Christian soldiers, while at the same time preaching restraint to the masses in the townships—often the victims of those same soldiers.[34] This latter policy was seen as particularly offensive, since the South African state, and thus its Defense Force, had already been declared illegitimate in the Lusaka Statement. Participants offered several hypotheses regarding the nature of violence in South Africa, including the idea that a state's legal right to use violence degenerates into a license to enforce tyranny once that state is no longer legitimate. In such cases, it might be legitimate to use force to destroy the tyrannical regime. It was also argued that as long as oppression exists, violence is inevitable, so that the only way to honestly face the issue of political violence in South Africa was to address the fundamental cause of it: the structures of apartheid which lead to political oppression and economic exploitation.[35]

By workshop's end, the participants had reached consensus on several broad issues and recommendations, which together amounted to a theological justification of political action, although *not* of violent action, by those religious institutions which chose to adopt them. The workshop challenged the institutional church to declare the South African government illegitimate; to adopt the Lusaka Statement; to support the liberation movements, while affirming primary obedience to the gospel of Jesus Christ; to provide ministry to the liberation movements while withdrawing chaplains from the South African Defence Force; and to support the call for economic sanctions as a means of isolating the South African regime.[36]

Perhaps the most important ideas of the workshop, however, ideas that contributed to a higher level of cooperation between the SACC and SACBC and the liberation movements, were those embedded in Frank Chikane's speech entitled "Where the Debate Ends." Chikane chided religious institutions, including his own SACC, for spending so much time debating the issue of non-violence versus violence, and so little time engaging in effective nonviolent actions to end the apartheid regime. Nonviolence could mean two things, Chikane said. It could either mean the absence of conflict, or it could mean a nonviolent struggle for justice. He criticized the former while calling for the latter. Chikane's message was profound in its simplicity: the debate about violence and nonviolence had reached a point at which it simply had to end. There was a point beyond which such debate was no longer possible. Those who wanted to continue debating the issue while putting off action were not taking the side of the poor, for they could carry on the debate only from their positions of peace and comfort far away from the violence of the townships. What good did it do, Chikane asked, to spend endless hours debating the morality of the ANC and PAC taking up arms, without at the same time doing something to end the necessity of their taking up these arms? Chikane implored the churches to stop debating and to begin acting, or to move from "non-involvement to critical involvement."[37] Chikane later reissued this challenge to the SACC and its member churches, imploring them to "stop the debate on violence and non-violence, stop debating whether people should have taken to an armed struggle or not and concentrate on developing and implementing non-violent strategies of change to end apartheid. This will make the violence and non-violence debate unnecessary."[38] For Chikane, nonviolence at all costs was miles apart from a position of strategic nonviolence.

Chikane's vision of the responsibility of churches contributed in a major way to the evolving religious discourse in South Africa during the late 1980s. Time and again he offered a direct challenge to Christian individuals and institutions to become overtly political actors on the side of the liberation movements, both inside South Africa and out. By the end of the 1980s, both organizations were committed to a contextual theological position.

Evidence of Influence

It is insufficient to simply demonstrate that a new religious discourse gathered strength in South Africa in the 1980s. The existence of these new ideas do not, in themselves, explain why the SACC and the SACBC chose to confront the state. It is necessary to demonstrate that both organizations were acting under the influence of these evolving religious ideas. The evidence is discernible in three ways: through an examination of the SACC's and SACBC's understanding of theology, as expressed in their own separate statements; through the reaction of both organizations to the various theological statements detailed above; and through an analysis of joint SACC/SACBC statements and activities to determine whether these reflected the message of contextual theology.

The Theology of the SACC and SACBC

To make a definitive statement of the theologies of these organizations is difficult for the simple reason that both continued to evolve their understanding of mission during the 1980s; by the end of the decade, this understanding was vastly different than it had been at the beginning. However, both institutions had structures set up for the explicit purpose of theological reflection on the role of the church in society (in the SACC, the Justice and Reconciliation division, and in the SACBC, the Theological Advisory Commission). There are several examples which, while not "absolute proof" that both organizations were adhering to contextual theology at all times, nevertheless do serve as evidence of this influence.

The SACC was forced to clarify its theology, both for itself and for the world, as a result of the Eloff Commission of Inquiry.[39] While this commission was ostensibly formed to investigate alleged mismanagement of SACC funds, it quickly evolved into an evaluation and critique of SACC theology by the South African state.[40] In the process of responding to the state's onslaught against it, the SACC came to a much clearer understanding of its own theological position. The testimony by its officials (especially by Wolfram Kistner, head of the Division of Justice and Reconciliation, and Desmond Tutu) during commission hearings amounted to a theological justification of the SACC position on every "political" issue raised by the state. Ironically, even state witness South African theologian David Bosch confirmed through his testimony that the SACC adhered to many of the ideas of contextual theology. After evaluating the SACC's actions and statements, Bosch concluded that it was impossible to understand these without simultaneously understanding that body's theology. This theology, he explained, was based heavily on the Old and New Testament prophets, with the result that the SACC believed it had a divine calling to challenge and censure the authorities.[41]

Wolfram Kistner is considered by many as the SACC's "primary theologian" during the 1980s. His fifty-page response to the South African Police's findings was a careful analysis of the SACC's theology, and gives insight that the SACC was indeed being influenced by the theological ideas coming from contextual theology at the time. Kistner states:

> The activities and the thrust of the Division of Justice and Reconciliation in rejecting the policy of the South African government which has already led to the deprivation of approximately eight million South Africans of their citizenship have to be understood in the context of the effort to interpret the Gospel in relation to the experience of the people of South Africa and to the insistence that Christians are under an obligation to resist this policy.[42]

Bishop Tutu, in his presentation before the Eloff Commission, reaffirmed that it was impossible to understand the activities of the SACC without first understanding its theological presuppositions. In particular, Tutu was adamant that those "political" issues which the Eloff Commission insisted should not be the domain of the SACC were in fact deeply theological matters. In an impassioned speech, Tutu declared:

> Our God cares that children starve in resettlement camps, the somewhat respectable name for apartheid's dumping grounds for the pathetic casualties of this vicious and evil system. The God we worship does care that people die mysteriously in detention. He is concerned that people are condemned to

a twilight existence as non-persons by an arbitrary bureaucratic act of banning them without giving them the opportunity to reply to charges brought
against them.[43]

Moreover, Tutu said, the SACC was obliged to take sides with the poor, because
"God can't help it. He always takes sides. He is not a neutral God. He takes
the side of the weak and the oppressed."[44] What was perhaps most important
in Tutu's presentation was his demonstration of the linkage between the political activities of the SACC and its theology. The SACC's work on behalf of
political prisoners, detainees, and banned persons, as well as for their families
and dependents (through the Detainees' Parents Support Committee [DPSC]
and the Dependents' Conference, two of the Eloff Commission's major targets), was a direct result, Tutu argued, of the SACC's obedience to Christ's
commands.[45]

The theology of the SACC, which required it to take sides with the poor
against the structures of apartheid, was made evident as a result of the Eloff
Commission. However, the commission was held in the early 1980s, before the
states of emergency and before more outspoken contextual theology statements
had been written. Consequently, the SACC was somewhat ambiguous. It also
showed signs of more traditional theology, some might say "church theology,"
at the time of the Eloff hearings. This was true, for example, on the issue of
violence. In failing to distinguish between the violence of the state and of the
liberation movements, Tutu's stance reflected a much less radical understanding
of the issue of theology and violence than that of the SACC at decade's end.

The SACBC was never "forced" to explicitly state its theological underpinnings in the same manner as the SACC, under pressure from the Eloff Commission. Nevertheless, there were clear indicators throughout the 1980s that
several bishops, although not the Conference as a whole, had adopted the ideas
of contextual theology. The SACBC is a member of the Inter-territorial Meeting of Bishops of Southern Africa (IMBISA), an organization composed of
Catholic bishops from several Southern African countries, that meets regularly
to coordinate policy on a broader, transnational scale. Its 1983 Plenary Assembly
was devoted to a discussion of "The Prophetic Mission of the Church." At that
meeting the bishops declared, "The People of God in Southern Africa, as elsewhere, has this calling and duty of speaking out prophetically. In the present
circumstances of our history in Southern Africa, more than ever before, we feel
compelled to answer this call to prophetic witness."[46] This prophetic mission,
the bishops declared, began with reading the political, economic, social, cultural, and religious signs of the times, which were interpreted as a series of
contrasts—between wealth and poverty, war and peace, freedom and oppression, and fear and hope. In clear reference to the ideas of contextual theology,
the bishops stated:

> To be a prophet today is to take up the cause of the poor, to proclaim their God-given dignity and to denounce the social structures that trample on them. We are the Church of the poor that will not be silent and neutral in the struggle between man and the unjust structures, between the poor and the powerful. . . . Poverty is a structural problem. It is a direct result of an economic and political system that favors some and deprives others. . . . Because the Church's prophetic message has the dignity of man as its starting point, in practice it will be from the position of the poor in Southern Africa that the Church judges itself and the social structures and social practices of the various countries in this sub-continent.[47]

The bishops also recognized that simply speaking prophetically was insufficient, for "deeds speak louder than words."[48] Hence they strongly reaffirmed the need for action. Since the SACBC participated in this plenary session and contributed to its final statement, one can infer that at least some bishops had taken these theological ideas to heart.

Further evidence of the influence of contextual theology was provided a few years later. Each year, a Theological Winter School, which is sponsored by the SACBC, is held as an intensive workshop devoted to studying one particular theological issue facing Southern Africa. In 1986, shortly after the state of emergency was reimposed, the seventeenth annual Winter School was held with the theme "To Nourish our Faith: Theology of Liberation for Southern Africa." Each day's program consisted of morning lectures by Albert Nolan and afternoon small-group workshops facilitated by Richard Broderick, a member of the SACBC's Justice and Peace Commission. Although this Winter School cannot be taken as direct evidence that the SACBC supported liberation or contextual theology, it does indicate that the Conference was at least willing to explore the ideas coming out of this religious movement. It is not coincidental that this openness to discussing new ideas occurred in the wake of a serious downturn in the political situation in South Africa.[49]

One final example should suffice to indicate that the SACBC was increasingly committed to the ideas coming from contextual theology. In 1987, in recognition of the need to take sides in the struggle, the SACBC's TAC officially adopted the Freedom Charter, which had been written in 1955 by the ANC and its allies in the Defiance Campaign and later accepted as the policy platform of the UDF.[50] In a policy paper on the issue, the TAC stated that the Charter "should be considered as an outstanding sign of the times for South Africa. Its protest against dispossession, the imposition of apartheid, and the arbitrary use of force by the state still remains valid today."[51]

Response to Contextual Theology

A second method of discovering whether both organizations were acting under the influence of contextual theology is to examine their reactions to the various statements which reflected the development of this new discourse. As in earlier periods, some of this theological innovation took place within institutional structures, especially those of the SACC. In such cases, one can safely infer that the SACC did indeed embrace these ideas. More often than not, however, theological innovation occurred outside the SACC or SACBC. The task thus becomes one of determining whether these ideas filtered through the organizations' decision-making structures, and whether they actually impacted the decisions of both organizations to become more overtly political.

The SACC took the lead in declaring apartheid a heresy, although this declaration did not receive the same publicity as the same statement made later that year by the WARC, which was covered by the international media. Accompanying this theological statement was an increased commitment by the SACC to more overt political action. For example, during the conference in which the heresy declaration was made, the SACC also passed a resolution calling on churches to make their buildings available for trade union meetings.

The SACBC, in contrast, was equivocal in its stand on the heresy issue. At the time of the declaration in 1982, the bishops were silent, issuing no official response and taking no stance on the issue. In fact, it appears that the SACBC did not officially address the topic until at least five years after the initial declaration,[52] as a result of a debate brewing within its own Theological Advisory Commission. In a personal response to the heresy debate, Catholic theologian Brian Gaybba wrote an article in 1987 in which he concluded that based on several criteria, the apartheid regime was indeed guilty of heresy.[53] Although this statement did not represent official SACBC—or even TAC—policy, Gaybba was a member of the TAC, and the article subsequently set off a debate within that body. The TAC cautiously stated that it was difficult to say whether apartheid was necessarily a heresy, because it was not always—strictly speaking—a doctrine or clearly enunciated set of beliefs. The TAC opted to avoid any sort of "condemnatory statement" in favor of a "positive" one.[54] No official statement was ever produced, and eight months later the TAC reported that the SACBC administrative board had decided that "it is not worthwhile to pursue this topic further. It has already been stated by other churches. Also, there is the difficulty of defining exactly what apartheid is, explaining just how it is heretical, providing criteria for judging whether someone upholds it, and applying sanctions such as excommunication."[55] Thus, as in the case of the legitimacy debate discussed in chapter 3, the SACBC appears to have delayed addressing the topic for such an extended period that it simply became irrelevant, thereby relieving the bishops from having to take an unequivocal stance. In other papers, however, the TAC appears to have agreed that any defense of apartheid was indeed heretical.[56] The SACBC's Theological Advisory Commission vacillated in its stance on heresy. The Conference as a whole, however, never officially declared the apartheid system heretical; at least on this issue, it was less prophetic than the leadership of the SACC.

The 1985 "Theological Rationale and a Call to Prayer for an End to Unjust Rule" was controversial, even for the SACC. The controversy stemmed from the uncertain status of the Theological Rationale. This theological explanation was drafted by an ecumenical working group and was published under the auspices of the WPCC, not the SACC, despite the fact that two of the members of this working group were Allan Boesak, a vice-president of the SACC, and Beyers Naudé, its General Secretary. As noted above, the Call contained the following statement: "We now pray that God will replace the present structures of oppression with ones that are just, and remove from power those who persist in defying his laws, installing in their place leaders who will govern with justice and mercy." Several heads of SACC member churches (the Anglican archbishop of Cape Town and the president of the Methodist Church being the most notable) felt distinctly uncomfortable with calling for the removal of the present government. A debate followed over whether the SACC executive committee would support the rationale, in opposition to several of its member churches. The SACC executive committee met in April, two months prior to the June 16th day of prayer, to discuss the issue, and this was followed by a meeting of an expanded presidium on June 3. At this latter meeting it was decided to support the Call to Prayer for an End to Unjust Rule and, in keeping with a 1984 SACC conference resolution, the abolition of all apartheid structures. The call for the removal of the government was not adopted as official SACC policy but was merely "submitted related to the call for prayer," and referred to member churches for their consideration. Finally, just three days before the actual day of prayer on June 16, a meeting of the leaders of SACC member churches endorsed this decision.[57]

At a service in Cape Town on June 16, a message was read from Beyers Naudé, who was in Europe at the time. It stated, "I reaffirm my total support for the document entitled, 'A Theological Rationale and A Call for the End to Unjust Rule [*sic*].' We need to be guided by the theological tradition in which we stand, . . . to remove from power those who persist in defying His laws."[58] The controversy surrounding this issue highlights the complexity in determining whether the SACC was embracing this theology. While several members of the SACC executive committee clearly felt comfortable adopting the most radical elements of the emerging theology in South Africa, these ideas were not wholeheartedly supported by all of the SACC's member churches.[59]

The debate over the Call did not stir any similar controversy for the Catholic bishops. The SACBC issued its own, albeit more mildly worded, statement. Rather than demanding an end to unjust rule, the bishops said, "we call upon all Catholics in South Africa to observe Sunday June 16 as a special day of mourning and prayer. . . . However, as we pray for the dead and for the bereaved, we also join together to pray more earnestly and hopefully than before that all the evils of apartheid may be brought to a speedy end."[60]

The Kairos Document originated completely outside both the SACC and SACBC, although the list of signatories includes a mixed group associated with both organizations. The General Secretaries of both organizations—Beyers Naudé of the SACC and Smangaliso Mkhatshwa of the SACBC—signed it, although not in their official capacities but as individual clergy. In contrast, neither Tutu nor Boesak signed it. Tutu, a high-level church leader in the Anglican Church, was distinctly uncomfortable with the document's attack on the underlying theology of institutional churches, which he characterized as unfair.[61] Both Albert Nolan and Frank Chikane of the ICT were intimately linked with the writing of the document, and both subsequently signed it. Wolfram Kistner also played a significant role in the document's drafting, and he too signed it—although not as the director of the SACC's Justice and Reconciliation Division, but as a member of the Lutheran Church. Twenty-three of the 156 signatories were Catholic, many in the employ of the SACBC. However, no Catholic bishop endorsed the document.[62]

The SACC, as an organization, never officially adopted the Kairos Document. However, two years after the document was published, the person most associated with it, Frank Chikane, was elected General Secretary of the SACC. The SACBC (especially through the TAC) did devote a fair amount of discussion to it. The result was an official SACBC response which was fairly supportive of the document, with a mixed response "behind the scenes." In the official response issued two months after the document's publication, the bishops took the criticism of church theology to heart and confessed their own guilt, saying: "We recognize the essential message of the Kairos Document as urging us to address ourselves more forcefully and clearly to the black population of South Africa, to spell out the justice of the cause in the struggle for liberation and to indicate how we see that struggle in the light of the Gospel, to indicate too, that we are in solidarity with the oppressed. . . . " In addition, they stated, "we have to admit that we have relied too much on appeals to the white community, obviously not seeing clearly what role the black community should play in its own liberation. . . . "[63] Despite several criticisms of the document, especially of its "sweeping generalisations," the SACBC's official response was that they "welcomed the challenge" presented to them by the Kairos theologians.[64]

The Lusaka Statement did not originate in either the SACC or SACBC; it was the result of a World Council of Churches' sponsored conference. The SACC, however, was a cosponsor of the conference and its final statement found a more welcome home in that organization than with the bishops.[65] At its 1987 National Conference, the SACC voted by a large majority to adopt the Lusaka Statement. The SACBC, by contrast, never officially endorsed the statement. While the Theological Advisory Commission agreed that the conference and its statement raised many important issues, it did not feel that the bishops could wholly endorse it. The TAC criticized the document for its low level of theology, regarding it more as a party political statement than a well-thought-out theological document. Although the conference's theme was "The Churches' Search for Justice and Peace in Southern Africa," the TAC felt that there was little or no independent thought on what truth, justice, or peace required.[66]

Joint Statements and Actions

1988 marked a turning point for both the SACC and SACBC. As described earlier, the political context took a further turn for the worse with the banning of seventeen anti-apartheid organizations (including the UDF) and eighteen individuals (including the president and vice-president of the UDF). The more intense level of political activity on the part of these religious organizations occurred, it was argued in chapter 3, as a result of this changing context. It also occurred, probably not coincidentally, a few months after the Lusaka Statement's acceptance of the legitimacy of violence employed by the liberation movements, and after the workshop on theology and violence. The door was opened for the SACC (and even the SACBC) to move from merely supporting campaigns of civil disobedience to actually leading these campaigns. As a result of this interaction of context and ideas, a new sense of unity was forged between these religious organizations and secular ones. Moreover, as the SACC and SACBC cooperated as never before to fight apartheid, they did so with a clear understanding of the theological justification of their actions, a justification which had contextual theology written all over it. In a meeting held a few weeks after the bannings, the leadership of the SACC, SACBC, and several SACC member churches declared that the activities of the banned organizations were central to the proclamation of the gospel, and that they thus felt compelled to take over these activities. They concluded the meeting with these sharp words: "Our mandate to carry out these activities comes from God and no man and no government will stop us. If the State wants to act against the Church of God in this country for proclaiming the Gospel, then so be it."[67] In spite of earlier hesitations, both the SACC and SACBC were now committed to the theological position that not only was apartheid against the will of God, it must also be removed through nonviolent acts. This position was evident in all the major joint ecclesiastical actions of 1988: the Clerics' March, the Convocation of Churches, and the Standing For the Truth Campaign.

As described in chapter 3, on February 29 a group of twenty-five church leaders and hundreds of Christians attempted to deliver a petition to Parliament protesting the latest security crackdown. They were stopped, attacked with water cannons, and arrested. In a press conference held shortly after their release, the church leaders insisted that their action was theologically demanded of them. Archbishop Tutu summed up this belief, saying that he and other church leaders would continue nonviolent protests because "We are saying this is what our Lord demands of us when he says: 'Pick up your cross and follow me.' And if the witness that Christians are going to make in a situation of injustice means there may come more suffering, then we have to say we are ready and we hope that God will give us the grace to be able to survive."[68]

This march was followed three months later by the Convocation of Churches, at which the SACC and SACBC committed themselves, along with a broad coalition of other churches and church organizations, to carrying out effective nonviolent actions to force the state to abandon apartheid and to participate in a negotiated settlement to establish a nonracial democracy. Again, this decision was taken not only as a result of the growing spiral of involvement, but also because their theological understanding of their mission now required it of them. In his opening address to the Convocation, Frank Chikane, recently appointed General Secretary of the SACC, confirmed the theological underpinnings of their proposed actions: "The question is not whether we should be neutral or not, the church cannot be neutral as far as questions of justice are concerned. When it comes to justice . . . we cannot do otherwise than to take sides. . . . The question is therefore now not whether we should act or not, but what type of action we should engage in."[69]

The actions proposed by the Convocation of Churches took the form of the Standing for the Truth Campaign. An explanation booklet containing a chapter entitled "A Theology for Standing for the Truth" was produced for dissemination through the churches. The Campaign was seen as nothing less than an integral part of the SACC and SACBC's duty to fulfill the gospel imperative: "In the spirit of Jesus' mission and practice, we must participate with the majority of our people in our common struggle to be liberated from the sins of racism, exploitation, sexism and tyranny. It is a liberation for democracy, non-racialism and the construction of a new humanity."[70]

In 1989 the liberation movement within South Africa gathered further strength with the Mass Democratic Movement (MDM). In August it launched a nationwide Defiance Campaign of civil disobedience. Both the SACC and SACBC were now prepared and willing to step into leadership positions, declaring that the Defiance Campaign's program of action was compatible with their commitment to peaceful nonviolent actions to bring about change. The leadership of the Standing for the Truth Campaign said of the Defiance Campaign, "The churches have declared apartheid, the policy, ideology and its practice a sin and irreconcilable with the Gospel. . . . Resistance to this evil system is both a calling and a duty of the church. We believe that the church must be in support of, and may even have to give leadership to, nonviolent forms of protest."[71] Both the SACC and SACBC officially endorsed the Defiance Campaign.

Thus by the last two years of the decade, the SACC and SACBC viewed overt political activity as integral to the fulfillment of their mission. Through their involvement in the MDM's Defiance Campaign, the leaders of both organizations were finally living out the theological pronouncements they had for so long been making. The decision of the SACC and SACBC to take a lead in the Defiance Campaign of 1989 represented the culmination of years of evolving theological understanding about the role of the church in the apartheid system. This was a far cry from the Defiance Campaign of the 1950s, where high-profile church leaders were conspicuous by their absence.

Overlapping Roles

The fact that the SACC and SACBC came to view contextual theology as synonymous with their theological mission should perhaps not be too surprising. Many of the theologians who were involved in the development of these new ideas, dating as far back as the black theology movement, came to be active not only in the development of contextual theology two decades later, but in the SACC and SACBC as well. Most important was the fact that many of those involved in black theology, the Christian Institute, and contextual theology came to leadership positions in both these organizations during the 1980s. In particular, the black theology movement provided the institutional church two decades later with the radical black leadership of Desmond Tutu, Allan Boesak, Frank Chikane, and Smangaliso Mkhatshwa.

A brief overview indicates the extent of overlap between those individuals most active in the production of radical theological ideas and the leadership of the SACC and SACBC. Archbishop Hurley, arguably the most radical of the Catholic bishops, was an active member of Vatican II, where he was only one of six Africans (his role there was not inconsequential, since he was assigned to the Central Preparatory Commission). He was profoundly influenced by the teachings which emerged from the Council. When the Christian Institute was formed, he was a member of its board. Not surprisingly, Hurley was the bishop who most firmly embraced contextual theology during the 1980s. He ultimately had a profound influence on the SACBC, because in 1981 he was elected president of the Bishops' Conference and held that position until 1988. Within the SACC there was also a tremendous amount of leadership overlap between earlier periods and the 1980s. Beyers Naudé, founder of the Christian Institute in 1963 and heavily influenced by black theology during the 1970s, was SACC General Secretary from 1984 through 1987. During this period the nationwide state of emergency was declared. Naudé guided the SACC through the Call to Prayer for an End to Unjust Rule, the Kairos Document, and the Harare and Lusaka Statements—all of which he played an important role in drafting. Naudé was also a part of early discussions about the need to create an institute promoting a theology that would be relevant to the South African context—discussions which led to the formation of the ICT.

His predecessor was Bishop Tutu, who held the position of General Secretary from 1978 through 1984. Tutu, a product of early black theology, was a participant in the first national seminar on black theology, held in 1971 and organized by the University Christian Movement (UCM). The Eloff Commission of Inquiry was held during Tutu's leadership, and it was Tutu who authorized a huge increase in SACC funding for Justice and Reconciliation programs.

Frank Chikane, who succeeded Naudé as SACC General Secretary, had a long career in the contextual theology movement. As a young university student, he was a member of the black theological students' organization, the South African Students Organization (SASO). The ideas to which he was exposed in SASO continued to influence him years later as General Secretary of the SACC.[72] Between his days as a SASO student and leader of the SACC, Chikane was the ICT's first General Secretary, as well as the vice-president of the UDF from 1983 to 1985, serving on its National Executive in 1984.[73] More than anyone else, Chikane is the person most associated with the writing of the Kairos Document. His appointment as SACC General Secretary heralded a more intense fusion between that organization and the ideas of contextual theology. During his tenure at the SACC, he maintained a position on the ICT's Steering Committee.

Openness to the ideas of contextual theology by the leadership of the SACC and SACBC is perhaps not surprising, given the movement of senior personnel, all of whom were active in earlier periods of theological development, between these organizations and the Christian Institute, black theology, and the ICT. This movement was not always unidirectional (i.e., from the black theology and the institutes towards the institutional church). Father Smangaliso Mkhatshwa, a product of the black theology movement, became the ICT's second General Secretary (replacing Frank Chikane) *after* his tenure as General Secretary of the SACBC.

Conclusion

Did evolving religious ideas constitute a key motivation for the political activities of the SACC and SACBC? I have argued that a changing political context, while necessary, was not sufficient to ensure the adoption of political self-identities. Religious legitimation was equally necessary. Political self-identities reflected the influence of certain religious ideas which evolved, becoming increasingly radical as the decade progressed. The process can be seen in the evolution from the SACBC's 1957 statement that apartheid was intrinsically evil to the 1982 SACC declaration that its theological justification was a heresy. It was a logical step to suggest that a government which continues to exist based on this heresy must be removed from office. This was the message of the Call to Prayer for an End to Unjust Rule in 1984. The 1985 Kairos Document drew on this debate but took it one step further, combining it with social analysis and a clear call for action and challenging the churches to take sides in the escalating struggle. The 1987 Lusaka Statement took the next step by declaring the state illegitimate and allowing for the possibility that violence might be used ethically by some of those struggling to end apartheid. By this point, contextual theology was informing the churches that it was their duty to become involved in acts of civil disobedience. This led to the Theology and Violence workshop in which Frank Chikane challenged the SACC and SACBC (and others) to "go beyond the violence debate" by actually engaging in nonviolent acts of civil disobedience.

The seeds of the declaration of the illegitimacy of the state were planted several decades before the decision was actually taken, and what seemed radical at one point in South African history no longer appeared so at later points. For example, in 1984, praying for the end of unjust rule created an uproar in South African church circles. By 1988 this seemed a rather mild statement which was no longer sufficient. The SACC could not have declared the state illegitimate at any earlier time; the issue was not yet theologically ripe. In other words, theological evolution *had* to occur (above all, the Kairos Document had to be written) before the legitimacy debate could be taken up by the churches.

This chapter also endeavors to furnish a model for understanding how both the SACC and SACBC came to be politically active in the course of the 1980s. Politicization was the result of two sources: a changing political context and new religious ideas, which interacted in a dialectical fashion. Theological ideas which were brewing below the surface in earlier periods became explosive in response to the worsening political context. Theological innovation in the 1980s was both a reaction to *and* a cause of the spiraling church/state conflict. What happened in the struggle affected the process of theologizing about that struggle, which in turn affected church action in the struggle itself. For example, the Kairos Document was published as a theological response to the recently declared state of emergency. As a result of this document, church leaders and other Christians became more involved in acts of civil disobedience. State repression and the spiral of violence resulted in additional theological refinement, in this case the Lusaka Statement and its declaration that the South African state was illegitimate. Although the immediate impetus for the Standing for the Truth Campaign was the February 1988 security crackdown, the churches might not have contemplated such a campaign had they not embraced contextual theology's challenge to actively engage with the liberation movements in nonviolent mass action to bring about a radical restructuring of society. The acceptance of new religious ideas allowed the SACC and SACBC to move into the front line of the struggle. Such action would not have been possible otherwise. That each new political crisis brought further theological refinement was recognized by the ICT itself: "the highest moments of theologising are the peaks of crisis in the particular community. It is in a crisis situation when people begin to ask crucial and seemingly heretical questions that Christians are forced to develop better insights into their situations."[74]

Thus, the interplay of faith and situation led the SACC and SACBC to adopt a new and common interpretation of their identities: that of overt political actors. Although both organizations became more political in the course of the 1980s, this overtly political identity found a more welcome home in the SACC than the SACBC.

6

The Institutional Context of Political Debates

THE SACC and the SACBC exited the 1980s with a more highly politicized understanding of their mission than they possessed at the start of the decade. This reoriented understanding of their role in society, however, was never as fully consolidated in the SACBC as it was in the SACC. Time and again, the Catholic bishops, as a Conference, were more hesitant and less outspoken in their statements and actions than the leadership of the SACC. The bishops insisted throughout each debate that they possessed no competency with which to make political judgments. The language they used and the positions they took were consistently more nuanced, at times ambiguous, and usually less radical than the corresponding resolutions and actions of the SACC. From the tentative assertion that "selective economic pressures might be morally justified" (versus the SACC's call for comprehensive economic sanctions), to the mildly worded prayer that the "evils of apartheid be brought to a speedy end" (as opposed to the SACC's prayer "to remove from power those who persist in defying His laws"), the SACBC remained more restrained than the SACC. Similarly, from its unwillingness to adopt the Lusaka statement, to its refusal to explicitly declare the apartheid state illegitimate, the SACBC repeatedly displayed a more guarded stance.

What explains this differentiated level of politicization? While the impact of changing political and religious contexts explains areas of convergence between both organizations (both became more politicized), what explains areas of divergence? Why did this political self-identity become more firmly embedded in the SACC? Specific organizational characteristics of the SACC and SACBC either encouraged or impeded their politicization; what becomes clear is that certain institutional factors acted as a constraint upon the SACBC, but facilitated more radical statements and action by the SACC. Not only were factors internal to the SACC and SACBC important for determining policy outcomes; their international institutional linkages played a determining role as well. Finally, because the organizational context of the SACC encouraged such overtly political acts as declaring the state illegitimate, the SACC incurred the wrath of the apartheid state on a greater scale than did the SACBC. For a variety of reasons, only one of which was the fact that it was more radical, the South African state treated the SACC more harshly than the Catholic bishops.

The SACC and SACBC: A Difference in Type

The SACC and SACBC are two fundamentally different types of organizations, and this difference has conditioned the actions each undertakes as well as the ease with which they can be undertaken. The South African Council of Churches is not a denomination but an ecumenical umbrella organization of Protestant churches. In contrast, the Southern African Catholic Bishops' Conference is the administrative secretariat and decision-making organ of one particular denomination: the Roman Catholic Church. Thus what is being compared here is an ecumenical body existing at a level above individual churches, with an individual church itself. This difference has consequences in a variety of spheres, including the relationship to their constituencies, the way decisions are made, and the ability of each to implement decisions once they have been taken.

In 1934 the Christian Council of South Africa (CCSA) was formed as the organizational basis of various missionary societies working in the region. In the aftermath of the Second World War, most missionary churches were transformed into independent South African churches, and in 1968 the CCSA consequently became the South African Council of Churches. The membership of the SACC is divided into full member churches (i.e., denominations), associate organizations, and observer churches. Until the mid-1990s, the Council had twenty-one member churches, twelve associate organizations (including, for example, the Institute for Contextual Theology, the Student Christian Movement, and the Young Women's Christian Association International), and three observer churches, of which the SACBC was one.[1] SACC member churches are often referred to as the "English-speaking churches," but this is actually a misnomer. By far the majority of the members of these churches, who are 80 percent black, do not conduct their ordinary church life through the medium of English. Moreover, the label "mainline churches" is also confusing, as it refers to the distinction between European-originated Protestant churches and traditional independent African churches. However, many of these independent churches are represented in the SACC through the Council of African Independent Churches (CAIC), a "member church."

The goal of the Council, as stated in its constitution, is to foster unity between its various member churches by organizing consultations, conferences, ecumenical studies, and joint actions; to enable the church to more effectively carry out its mission; to undertake joint action and service; and to engage in activities on behalf of its member churches that are integral to their worship, witness, and service.[2] This partial list of objectives makes clear that the SACC operates in part as a "supra-organization," existing at a level wholly different than that of an individual church. It is this characteristic that allows the SACC to take a more radical stance on most issues than any of its member churches.

The central policy-making structure of the Council is the annual National Conference of its members. As the supreme governing body of the SACC, the National Conference is responsible for the administration of the Council's affairs, formulation of its policy, and implementation of its programs. The Conference elects a National Executive Committee (NEC) which meets four times a year[3] and is responsible for ensuring that decisions taken at the National Conference are carried out throughout the year, and under which the Council Secretariat as well as the various departments operate. The NEC consists of approximately twenty-five people, who fall into two categories. The first consists of individuals elected by SACC member churches and associate organizations for terms ranging from one to three years. The second consists of the Council's officers, including its President, Senior Vice-President, Vice-President, General Secretary, and Deputy General Secretary, all of whom are elected at the National Conferences for various terms of office. The NEC is composed primarily of male clergy, but lay people, including several women, and a few other church leaders, including bishops, also sit on the Committee. Additionally, twenty-six regional Councils of Churches throughout South Africa carry out the ministry of the SACC at a local level.[4]

In order to understand why the SACC was consistently more radical than the SACBC, it is vital to keep the following distinction in mind: the SACC does not only function as an ecumenical body, whose member and observer churches come together in a Conference once a year. It can also be viewed as an independent organization, with its own staff and its own bureaucracy. As such, the SACC performs functions similar to other nongovernmental organizations. Church leaders, workers, and theologians in South Africa are quick to emphasize the distinction between the SACC *as a council of churches* and the SACC *as an independent organization*.[5] Approximately eighty people are employed in the SACC's headquarters, Khotso House, which is operated along divisional lines. The most important division is the General Secretariat, which is responsible for the day-to-day activities of the Council and answers directly to the NEC. In addition, the General Secretary is ultimately responsible for the hiring of staff. Throughout most of the 1980s, the SACC was divided into twelve additional divisions, one of which was Justice and Reconciliation.[6]

In its capacity as an independent organization, the SACC was one of South Africa's most outspoken anti-apartheid critics and activists. This was due in large part to its leadership (i.e., those working in the General Secretariat as well as the divisional directors), and to the type of staff it employed. Frank Chikane, General Secretary of the SACC from 1987–1994, firmly believes that throughout the 1970s and 1980s the Council attracted to its staff a particular type of person—individuals who were socially progressive and politically active. The reason for this, Chikane says, is the particular role played by the SACC during this period. Because the SACC was involved in such anti-apartheid activities as providing assistance to detainees and their families, those who carried out these programs had to be prepared to risk detention themselves. Those most willing to take on this risk were, not surprisingly, formerly detained people, or those who had suffered other apartheid atrocities, who had in some way been assisted by the SACC. The organization came to be a home for those victimized by apartheid repression, and was consequently staffed by people who were actively engaged in the liberation struggle.[7] David Thomas argues that not only were the staff members of the SACC more radical than the average South African Christian, but the tendency to attract outspoken activists is common to ecumenical organizations in general. They develop a "critical distance" between themselves and their member churches (although one could argue that this "critical distance" is simply another term for misrepresenting the views of members). In describing why ecumenical organizations draw a particular type of person, Thomas notes: "Offering very little in the way of remuneration and 'perks,' they attract not the kind of bureaucrat seeking a comfortable sinecure, but a more committed kind of Christian willing to adopt a pioneering role."[8] Charles Villa-Vicencio argues that the critical distance of which Thomas writes was heightened in the South African context, because the SACC staff during the 1980s was increasingly exasperated by the unwillingness of many of the Council's member churches to reject their cautious "church theology," as exposed by the Kairos Document. Moving outside of these churches, politically radical but frustrated Christians found a more welcome home in the SACC, where they were surrounded by like-minded people. Embodying the aspirations of grass-roots Christians, as opposed to the mind-set of the institutional church, the SACC staff at Khotso House during the 1980s represented, for Villa-Vicencio, the alternative church.[9]

In contrast to the two-tiered reality of the SACC (i.e., as a Council of member churches and as a separate organizational entity), the SACBC is the association of Catholic bishops of Botswana, Namibia, Swaziland, and South Africa. Because it is the regional organization of a single church, it functions along entirely different lines than the SACC. Prior to 1947, Catholic bishops (then vicars apostolic) in the Southern African region had no permanent structure for corporate pronouncements. The Catholic hierarchy was only established in South Africa in 1951 with residential archbishops and bishops, who held their first plenary session the following year. The purpose of the Conference is to provide bishops with a platform for joint consultation, planning, and policy making; to promote united action among bishops; to coordinate the work of the thirty dioceses (or ecclesiastical territories) into which the Conference is divided (these dioceses are grouped into five regional pastoral

Conferences); and to act as a link between the Catholic Church, the Apostolic Delegate, and the Vatican.[10] The policy-forming body of the SACBC is the plenary session, which consists of a full sitting of all bishops, and which is held once a year (although occasionally extraordinary plenary sessions are held to discuss specific issues). An administrative board, consisting of the Conference president, vice-president, and chairmen of commissions, is elected by the plenary session. The board is responsible for implementing the resolutions of the Bishops' Conference and coordinates the work of the various commissions. The day-to-day administration of the Conference is carried out by the General Secretary, who is responsible for the secretariat staff, headquartered in Khanya House in Pretoria. The SACBC conducts its work through several commissions, which are not only responsible for carrying out the decisions taken by the bishops, but also for submitting recommendations to the plenary session. Each commission is headed by a bishop, and usually has a non-episcopal secretary.[11] Most "political" issues are considered in the Justice and Peace Commission, which was headed throughout most of the 1980s by Archbishop Denis Hurley, who also served as the Conference president for much of the decade. The SACBC's Justice and Peace Commission was established in 1981, almost ten years after the 1972 formation of the SACC's Division of Justice and Reconciliation.[12]

Several characteristics of the Roman Catholic Church limit the extent of change that is acceptable in its norms, structures, and behavior. To begin with, the Catholic Church is committed to a church-type rather than a sectarian pattern of incorporation,[13] and as such is an inclusive organization which offers universal salvation, in contrast to sectarian movements which offer salvation to a select few. Because of this universal religious claim, the Roman Catholic Church has constructed a large organizational network to provide continuity and universality for its mission, with the result that it has become the most institutionalized and least flexible Christian church.[14] The effort to appeal to all social classes and to people of widely different political beliefs has tended to make the Catholic Church a conservative and cautious force in secular society. As an organization, the church tends to avoid extremes, and "radical" religious movements have been consistently undermined by the church hierarchy.[15] Eric Hanson notes that "the natural political impact of such universality has been a tendency to stress reconciliation among all people, not prophetic confrontation. *Such style contrasts with traditional Protestantism.*"[16]

One of the defining characteristics of the Catholic Church worldwide is the strictly hierarchical nature of its authority system. This emphasis on hierarchy extends to the SACBC and helps explain why the Conference was consistently less radical than the SACC. The archdioceses and dioceses which make up the SACBC still fall under the control of the Sacred Congregation for the Evangelization of Peoples in Rome. Because of strict episcopal control, which ultimately rests with the pope, the SACBC functions solely as a consultative body. Its resolutions have no binding force on its member bishops, who are responsible only to Rome. It is therefore vital that statements have some degree of support from all bishops, since resolutions are implemented in dioceses only insofar as the bishops consent to them. For this reason, the SACBC works on the basis of consensus, which has implications for its resulting statements and resolutions. These tend not to be radical because of the compromises necessary to get all bishops to agree to them. This leads, as Brian Smith points out, to "Episcopal pronouncements that are hardly prophetic."[17]

The hierarchical nature of the Catholic Church requires its bishops to follow strict doctrinal guidelines handed down from Rome; consequently, they are cautious about issuing statements which are at odds with established doctrine. In the words of Archbishop Napier, former president of the SACBC, "Certain theological positions have official sanction; others are peripheral in so far as they may be the ideas of theologians, but they are not the teachings of the Magisterium—the teaching authority of the Church. This is not the position of Protestant churches. They have no hierarchical structure with an official position."[18]

It is this characteristic, says Villa-Vicencio, which allowed the SACC to embrace contextual theology more easily than the SACBC, for it was difficult for the Catholic bishops to respond quickly to the changing theological issues, without previous doctrinal guidelines from the Vatican. In contrast, the SACC was able to respond prophetically and quickly to the prevailing issues of the day without needing theological approval from any higher body.[19] This issue was instrumental in the debate over declaring the state illegitimate, according to Bernard Connor, former secretary of the SACBC's TAC. Connor believes that if they had had a Vatican document backing them up, this might have become an official SACBC position.[20] The respect for, and the importance of, hierarchical authority on doctrinal issues in the Catholic Church is best summed up by Villa-Vicencio, who states:

> Protestants don't mind attacking the church. I don't bat an eyelid when I take on the bishops in my own [Methodist] church—and they don't take me very seriously, and that's the way it goes. For Catholics, that's a serious business. I've often said that if Leonardo Boff were a Protestant, he'd still be a minister, but he'd simply be ignored.[21]

Thus, the SACC and SACBC are two fundamentally different institutional entities, and this has implications for the type of action engaged in by each. Whereas the SACBC is part of a larger hierarchy, the SACC is not responsible to any overarching authoritative body. And while the SACC serves as an umbrella body for several member churches, it also functions in many ways as a separate organization, adjacent to, and often in conflict with these member churches. One result of these institutional differences was a more radical and outspoken SACC. However, while the SACC compensated for the failure of denominational structures to respond to the pressing needs of the day, and therefore came to embody the "prophetic spirit" or "alternative church" on the cutting-edge of witness in the South Africa of 1980s, there was also a downside to the way it functioned. Some South African theologians have argued that the SACC was in danger of losing touch with the institutional churches, becoming increasingly alienated from them, and sometimes regarding them as "the enemy."[22] Moreover, because of the role played by the SACC, its member churches often shirked their responsibility of speaking with a prophetic voice.

The institutional structure of the SACBC, while resulting in a more wary approach to political issues, also has some positive implications. Because it represents a single church, there is a clearly defined relationship between the SACBC and its constituency, a definition which is sometimes missing for the SACC. Each bishop is responsible for a particular diocese and is therefore directly accountable for decisions on which he has voted to all Catholics in his diocese. In contrast, since many of the delegates to the SACC National Conference are not church leaders, they do not have any constituency to whom they are directly and personally responsible. This difference created considerable tension between the SACC and SACBC. The knowledge that bishops might have to justify and defend their decisions to the more conservative members of their dioceses leads them to push for less radical statements; however, the fact that they are personally accountable for those decisions also has the effect that bishops accept greater responsibility for their implementation. This is another reason for the more conservative tendency of the bishops. Because bishops are responsible for implementing decisions in their dioceses, they become preoccupied with the implications that resolutions will have. Speaking in reference to the debate over declaring the state illegitimate, Bernard Connor of the TAC admits that he was personally hesitant about advising the bishops to take this step. While he would have supported labeling various laws illegitimate, he questioned whether declaring the regime as a whole illegitimate was practically feasible. Connor asks, "If you declare the whole government illegitimate, can you negotiate with it? Can you talk to it about other, non-political things such as health services and communications?"[23] Jude Pieterse, who succeeded Smangaliso Mkhatshwa as SACBC General Secretary, concurs: "the difference is when you've got to take responsibility for decisions you take. The less responsibility you have for the consequences of decisions, the more radical a decision you can take."[24]

One of the primary explanatory factors for the differentiated levels of politicization between the SACC and SACBC is the manner in which decisions are made. A closer analysis of the decision-making procedures of each organization is necessary.

Decision-Making Structures and Their Consequences

The primary decision-making organ of the SACC is its National Conference, composed of representatives of member churches, who send delegates on the basis of proportional representation.[25] Additionally, regional councils and associate members (for example the ICT) also send voting delegates, and observer members, such as the SACBC in the 1980s, can each send two delegates, who have the right to speak but not to vote. Finally, the Council's officers are also voting members of the Conference. The composition of the decision-making bodies of both the SACC and SACBC is one reason for the different types of statements each makes. In contrast to the SACBC, where only bishops are allowed to vote on a resolution, a broad spectrum of people constitutes the voting membership of the SACC. Some Protestant bishops are indeed selected as church representatives, but the vast majority of the delegates are lower clergy and lay people. Representatives are chosen for a variety of reasons. In general, they are selected not because they are in formal leadership positions but because they have been involved in social justice activities, and are consequently interested in serving as delegates. Thus, the most politically active people within the churches end up at the National Conference, voting on resolutions. Delegates tend to be a self-selecting group, a situation which cannot arise in the SACBC. Whereas all Catholic bishops, no matter what their ideological bent, form the SACBC decision-making body, the more conservative members of the SACC member churches are likely to steer clear of the National Conference. This clearly facilitated the passage of politically oriented resolutions by that body in the 1980s.

Resolutions proposed at the National Conference are debated in an open forum and voted on by the delegates, and those decisions receiving a majority vote become Conference policy. Because the self-selecting nature of the Conference tends to produce a core of delegates with a similar ideological outlook, what occurred repeatedly throughout the 1980s was that delegates proposed resolutions with which they agreed personally, but which had not come through the structures of their own churches. Although they were expected to represent their church, delegates often did not distinguish between their personal position and that of the institution they were representing. In fact, it was not uncommon for delegates to the National Conference to vote *for* a particular issue at the Conference, but to vote *against* that same issue once they returned to their own churches. Bernard Spong, one-time director of the SACC's Communications Division, explains why this happened, especially in the 1970s:

> You could understand someone who comes, and in the free atmosphere of ecumenicity, where he is not beholden to anybody and his job is not at stake,

feels able to express and to vote on the deepest of his feelings. When he gets back into his church structure, which at that time was still a majority white, and was run on a white basis, and that freedom wasn't there, he went along with them.[26]

The issue of whether resolutions passed at an ecumenical level were broadly representative of the SACC member churches produced tremendous tension, not only for the member churches themselves, but also between the SACC and the SACBC. While this tension will be discussed below, what is important to note here is that the SACC, through its National Conference, had the power to say and do things that individual member churches could not have undertaken, nor would have wanted to in many cases.

SACBC policy is formulated at the annual plenary session. In contrast to the SACC, where decisions pass by a majority vote, the Catholic bishops place a premium on consensus, for reasons already discussed. Recommendations are submitted to the bishops by the various commissions, who present annual reports to the plenary session. While clergy, women religious, and lay people (especially "outside experts") might attend the plenary session study days, the bishops, after listening to presentations and recommendations, retire behind closed doors to formulate policy. Acrimonious debate may take place there, but what is presented in public is a statement which has been unanimously approved by the bishops. Once a decision has been taken, the bishops present a united front. Not only do they rarely contradict each other in public, it is also an uncommon occurrence for an individual bishop to speak out in his diocese in a different manner than the Conference as a whole. Some individual bishops may be of the opinion that an SACBC statement is too radical, while others feel that it does not go far enough; nevertheless, once it has been agreed on, all bishops stand behind it. Albert Nolan notes that this ecclesiology of unity is wholly absent from the SACC, and this has important consequences: "One of the primary concerns for the bishops is the unity of the church, and that very often outweighs speaking out for justice. The SACC can have terrific fights in Conferences, and nobody sees this as a problem; it is seen as a way of solving problems. For the bishops, speaking together is very important."[27]

One strength of this emphasis on unity is that it was difficult for the regime to isolate any particular bishop from the rest of the Conference, as it tried to do with Archbishop Hurley during his 1985 trial for statements he made about alleged atrocities of South African trained forces in Namibia. The trial was partially a "divide and rule" strategy designed to isolate Hurley by demonstrating to his fellow bishops that he was spreading rumors and lies. Because of the bishops' commitment to unity, this strategy failed; the bishops rallied behind Hurley, assuring the state that he spoke for the Conference as a whole. In 1983 several bishops and priests sent messages of support to Hurley, one of which read in part:

> We are aware of insinuations that it is "Hurley the individual" who is making pronouncements. . . . We wish to emphasise that documents which emanate from the Southern African Catholic Bishops' Conference and which are signed by our president reflect the views of the entire conference. . . . Not only do we regard SACBC statements as statements of the hierarchy as a whole, but also that when you speak in your capacity as president of the bishops' conference, you are speaking for all of us.[28]

Thus, conservative bishops act as a moderating force for the radicalism of progressive bishops, while at the same time the presence of conservatives in the conference may protect the national church (and individual progressive bishops) from severe state repression.[29]

Another characteristic of the SACBC decision-making process is that the bishops engage in lengthy and thorough consultation with various commissions involved in a particular issue (usually, the Justice and Peace Commission and the Theological Advisory Commission on "political issues"), before issuing a policy statement.[30] This consultation occurs for a variety of reasons, including the need to ensure that the bishops are doctrinally correct. In contrast, SACC delegates are usually unaware of the issues to be presented to them before arriving at the Conference. Most see the resolutions for the first time there, and proceed to vote on them, often without consulting the leadership of their church.

Thus, two hallmarks of the SACBC decision-making process are consensus and consultation. In consequence, decision-making is a very slow process. Expressing a sense of frustration at the length of time it takes for bishops to issue a statement, Margaret Kelly, a former Secretary of the Justice and Peace Commission, stated, "what you usually find is that the bishops will commission a study on it, and then investigate it, and then talk about it, and then maybe a few months later they will issue a statement. They might issue an initial press statement, but their policy statement will usually be more nuanced."[31] This frustration was likewise felt by those who hoped the bishops would declare the state illegitimate. After two consultations had already taken place on the issue, the bishops decided that more time, further study, and additional research were still needed. This drew the following response from a Catholic working on the issue:

> I point out that the church continuously finds itself in this dilemma. A crisis develops, and the Church is expected to give an immediate response but it cannot do so without time to consult, analyse and reflect on the situation in the light of the gospel. In other words we always seem to be caught unawares

and unprepared. The only way out of this dilemma is to foresee possible crises and prepare ourselves for them by doing our homework *before* a response is demanded of us.[32]

There are many examples throughout the 1980s in which the bishops delayed taking a decision for so long that the issue simply became irrelevant. On other occasions, when they did finally take a prophetic position after long debate, the resulting statements were less radical than some had hoped they would be. A case in point was the bishops' statement on Namibia. It is undeniable that the SACBC was consistently outspoken on the issue of the South African war in Namibia. In fact, it may be the one area in which the bishops were more prophetic than the SACC. And yet, despite the fact that the SACBC sent a delegation to Namibia long before any other church or religious organization, both the SACC and the British Council of Churches managed to publish their reports months before the Catholic bishops. Moreover, when the bishops' Namibian Report was finally published, it was disappointing to the members of both the Justice and Peace and the Theological Advisory Commissions, who had asked them to declare the war unjust. The Justice and Peace Commission first proposed such a resolution in 1982, the year the bishops' report was published. At the time, the bishops decided that such a step required "due consideration of all the implications of such a statement and the effect on those who would be directly or indirectly affected by it."[33] In 1984, the Justice and Peace Commission was mandated by the Conference to undertake a year-long study on the issue, to be presented for debate and discussion at the following plenary session. Following established criteria for just and unjust wars, the commission concluded that the war was indeed unjust. However, no decision was taken by the Conference at that time. In 1988 the Justice and Peace Commission again asked the bishops to declare the war unjust. By the time the bishops finally decided they would address the issue, the war had ended, and it was no longer necessary to make any declaration. Margaret Kelly believes that this failure constituted "one of the big misses of the SACBC in the 1980s."[34]

The legitimacy issue similarly fell victim to the lengthy decision-making process of the SACBC. Few issues took as long to move through SACBC structures, with so little to show for it. In addition to the various consultations and study days held on the issue, the bishops commissioned the TAC to produce several documents for consideration. These took the form of two papers, entitled "The Legitimacy of the Government" and the "Gospel and Apartheid." They were written in 1987, but quickly became caught in the cycle of postponement. In 1988, the Conference, not being able to agree upon a course of action, passed both documents on to the administrative board, which also took no immediate action. At a press conference in 1988, the archbishop of Cape Town, Stephen Naidoo, explained the delay:

This decision has got to be worked out over a period of time. People have got to be consulted. Its implementation has got to be carefully considered and strategies worked out. That process is going on now. So at a later stage we will certainly be able to say much more than we are saying at the present time.[35]

Frustrated with this lack of action, Bernard Connor, Secretary of the TAC, approached Archbishop Hurley in December 1989 about the statements. Hurley replied that with the situation changing rapidly, it had become "inopportune" to publish them.[36] In the end, the SACBC never published anything for public consumption regarding the legitimacy of the South African state. Connor believes that conservative bishops employed delay tactics, so that it never came up for a vote by the bishops. He suspects that the debate would have been even more divisive than that of economic sanctions, and doubts whether a declaration of illegitimacy would have passed, because it would have been extremely difficult to achieve consensus.[37] In contrast to the SACBC, in the same year that the Lusaka Conference first declared the illegitimacy of the state, a resolution declaring the state illegitimate was proposed, voted upon, and passed by the SACC at its 1987 National Conference—the same year the TAC originally took up the debate.

A third difference in the decision-making structures of the SACC and the SACBC (the first two being majority versus consensus rule, and the high degree of consultation undertaken by the bishops) is that the General Secretaries are given vastly different roles by each organization. The General Secretary of the SACC has been mandated a powerful leadership position, whose responsibilities, as spelled out in the constitution, include specifically "the responsibility of prophetic witness of the Council including, but not limited to, public addresses and press statements and visits to community areas."[38] In contrast, the SACBC's General Secretary, who need not be a bishop, functions primarily as an administrator and does not wield a comparable degree of power. He or she has no similar authority to speak or act on behalf of the bishops, nor is he or she expected to play a prophetic role. The stated responsibility is to "coordinate the work of the Administrative Board and the Episcopal Commission, and to supervise and direct the work of the staff attached to the secretariat."[39] While the SACC's General Secretary acts as the primary spokesperson for that organization, in the SACBC this role falls not on the General Secretary but on the Conference president. However, the SACC's General Secretary has considerably more freedom in making statements than the SACBC's president. The president of the Bishops' Conference will not issue a statement without first having consulted with at least the administrative board, and preferably with the Conference as a whole.[40] It is up to the discretion of the SACC's General Secretary to decide how much consultation should be engaged in before reacting to a situation. No major policy statement is made without the approval of the whole membership of the SACC, but the General Secretary is authorized to issue interim statements on his or her own in reaction to day-to-day events occurring in South Africa. This freedom was made explicit during Peter Storey's testimony to the Eloff Commission of Inquiry. Storey, a former SACC president, confirmed:

> As a Christian leader, the General Secretary is expected also to have a prophetic ministry speaking frequently on behalf of the Council on a wide variety of issues. In exercising his prophetic ministry, there is always the possibility that he will articulate a position or stance which lies beyond that taken officially by the National Conference or the Executive. . . . We do not see such actions as inconsistent with the leadership role to which he is called.[41]

As a result, not only does the SACC react more quickly than the SACBC, it also responds more often.[42] This ability to react immediately, without the need for lengthy consultation, adds to the perception of "radicalness" within the SACC.

Because the position of General Secretary in the SACC is a powerful one, the person who holds it has a tremendous amount of influence in determining the policy direction the organization will take. People like Tutu, Naudé, and Chikane have all left "the stamp of their personality" on the SACC (more so than even Hurley did as president of the SACBC), thereby contributing to the particular reputation it developed. When Chikane was appointed General Secretary in 1987, for example, this was widely interpreted as meaning "that the SACC and its member churches will become even more involved in supporting black South Africans at the grassroots in their conflict against apartheid and the government. . . . It is a major triumph for the United Democratic Front."[43] In contrast, although Smangaliso Mkhatshwa, former General Secretary of the SACBC, was equally outspoken, he was not a bishop, and therefore was unable to leave his prophetic mark on the Conference.[44]

One consequence of the decision-making process of the SACBC is that the sentiments of more radical Catholics are thwarted and official statements become tempered by the conservative voices in the Conference. This occurs in two ways: either the most outspoken Catholics working for the SACBC are those who do not have a vote, or the most progressive bishops are forced to compromise in order to achieve consensus. This results in statements that are more cautious than those emanating from the SACC National Conference, which consists of the more radical elements of member churches in the first place, and where people of differing status, not just bishops, are given the vote. Within the Catholic Church, those people most concerned with social justice issues naturally gravitate towards the Justice and Peace Commission. While the commission is headed by a bishop, the type of person who would accept that portfolio (like Hurley, who held it through much of the 1980s) would most likely be progressive in the first place. The commission thus functions similarly to the SACC's National Conference, as a self-selecting group of like-minded people. It is therefore not surprising that the Justice and Peace Commission (along with the TAC in many instances) was consistently "ahead" of the bishops on most political issues, pushing them to take positions that were bold and assertive. Margaret Kelly describes the relationship between the commission and the bishops as follows:

> The image of bishops should be that of shepherds, because their main function is to keep the flock together. The Justice and Peace people are like the sheepdog. The shepherd may keep the flock together, but they don't go anywhere. The sheepdog moves them along. We have to accept that our roles are different. We have to fulfill ours, but appreciate theirs.[45]

And indeed there were many instances in which the Justice and Peace Commission tried to move the bishops as a whole forward. In addition to their failure to declare the Namibian war unjust, the bishops proved disappointing on other occasions to those working for the commission. One concerned the issue of economic sanctions. The commission had asked the bishops to call for total mandatory sanctions, as the SACC had. What they got instead was an ambiguous statement that, in some cases, economic pressures *might* be morally justified. Because they were not experts in the fields of economics and politics, the bishops insisted, they had no authority to make a political statement. This "watering down" of commission recommendations occurred time and again during the 1980s.[46]

Had Margaret Kelly and like-minded people in the Catholic Church been a part of the SACC National Conference, they would have had a greater voice in determining whether their recommendations passed because they would have been able to vote for them. However, only bishops determine SACBC policy, and because of the hierarchical nature of the Catholic Church, the Justice and Peace Commission complies with their decisions, no matter how disappointed its members are.[47] Progressive bishops are often forced to "tone down" their positions in order to get them accepted by the Conference as a whole. Thus, people like Hurley, in the words of Nolan, "often get their wings clipped."[48] It is likely that if Hurley could have acted as an individual and without the need for consensus, he would have endorsed several actions which the SACBC as a whole did not—including declaring the Namibian war unjust and the South African state illegitimate.[49] In contrast, people like Tutu, Naudé, and Chikane were free of the ecclesial control by which Hurley was bound, and could express their opinions more freely.

Some Catholics (both lay and religious), frustrated with their inability to influence SACBC policy, choose to work outside official Church structures.

Whereas radical Protestants tend to end up working for the SACC, equally radical Catholics often do not feel at home inside the structures of the SACBC. Buti Tlhagale points out that these very structures serve to unintentionally "weed out" the most radical Catholics: "Anyone with any good sense would have to ask him or herself what achievements they could accomplish in that context."[50] A logical place for them to turn in the 1980s was the Institute for Contextual Theology, which quickly gained the reputation of being "the radical wing of disenchanted Catholics" because of the large number of Catholics on its staff.[51]

Ties between the SACC and Its Member Churches

The distinction was made above between the SACC as an ecumenical body, whose membership consists of various churches and religious organizations who have delegated certain functions to the larger ecumenical whole, and the SACC as a separate institutional entity—with its own subculture—headquartered in Khotso House in Johannesburg. The SACC therefore functions at two levels. On the one hand it exists at the service of the churches that created it, and on the other hand it has an ongoing life of its own. This distinction is important because it is the source of considerable tension between the SACC and its member churches; it has also determined the type of relationship that exists between the SACC and the SACBC. Moreover, it sheds light on the degree to which the SACC can be considered more radical than the SACBC during the 1980s. It was certainly more radical than many of its own member churches. When delegates to the National Conference pass a resolution, it is not automatically accepted by the member churches whom they represent. Resolutions are referred back to the governing councils, assemblies, or synods of these churches, which are then faced with several options—to "note" them, accept them, reject them, or to refer them to a committee for further study with the mandate to report back in a year—by which time the crisis has often passed, so that nothing is done with the resolution. An example of the vagueness with which member churches handle resolutions passed down from the National Conference is the Lusaka Statement. At its 1987 National Conference, the SACC voted by a large majority to adopt the Lusaka Statement. The Methodist, Congregational, and Presbyterian Churches all "received" the statement, which does not necessarily mean that they "adopted" or "endorsed" it. They all referred it on to committees for further study and comment. The Church of the Province of South Africa (the Anglican Church) officially "accepted" the statement. This state of affairs has produced charges by the South African state as well as by member churches that resolutions passed in the National Conference are not representative. Many, including Villa-Vicencio and Chikane, are critical of criticisms emanating from the member churches, claiming that they are partly responsible for this dichotomy.

Chikane argues that if member churches are unhappy that Conference delegates tend to be more progressive than church membership as a whole, it behooves these churches to elect representatives that more accurately reflect their views. Villa-Vicencio maintains that member churches may, in fact, benefit from this arrangement, playing a "double game" with the SACC. On one level they are pleased with the degree of radicalness coming from the National Conference. Their attitude is, "You say what we cannot afford to say as an individual church without the resources and power that an ecumenical organization has." However, the minute the institutional churches disagree with Conference resolutions, they respond, "it was not us, it was the SACC that said that."[52] The member churches, according to Villa-Vicencio, use the critical distance between the SACC and its constituency to their benefit, as a way of giving expression to the more progressive tendencies within their ranks, while at the same time getting off the hook with their own conservative membership. Chikane concedes that the member churches also used this argument to their advantage internationally:

> It is known that most SACC member churches were happy to let the SACC undertake risky ministry on their behalf. They did not always disassociate themselves from it; but they also did not involve themselves directly in it. Under pressure from congregations, they would always say, "No it's the SACC." But if asked by international and bilateral partners, they would always claim to be supporting the SACC, saying "we are working *through* the SACC." This was convenient for them.[53]

In this context, according to Villa-Vicencio, the SACC was given the freedom to "respond more sympathetically, more creatively, more imaginatively, more bravely, and—some would say—more recklessly to proposals than would the institutional churches."[54] However, when push came to shove, and the relationship between the member churches and the Council was questioned, as was done during the Eloff Commission of Inquiry—which argued that member churches were alienated from the Council, "a largely bureaucratic organization, kept alive by its overseas donors"[55]—many churches were quick to rally behind the Council and to show their allegiance to it. (Several member–church leaders testified during the Eloff Commission hearings in support of the Council.) Villa-Vicencio believes that one of the reasons the South African state did not crack down even harder on the SACC in the aftermath of the Eloff Commission hearings is precisely because its member churches "rose up and said, 'that's our organization; hands off!' "[56] This, then, is the dialectic of the member churches: on the one hand they support the SACC, while at the same time they hold the Council at arm's length, trying to distance themselves from its radicalness. Because of this dichotomy, the responsibility for following through on decisions taken by the National Conference often falls on the staff at Khotso House who, as discussed above, tend to be far more progressive than the average constituency of any member church. Again, the distinction between the church-oriented ecumenical Council and the program-oriented bureaucratic organization is critical.

The question must then be asked: Whom did the SACC represent in the 1980s? Did it represent its constituency in the form of its member churches, or did it represent some other constituency? When asked whether SACC actions and resolutions during the 1980s reflected the views of its member churches, Villa-Vicencio's answer was unequivocal:

> No. Undoubtedly not. I would want to be dogmatic on that. Time and again over the years things came out of the SACC and were met with either silence, or indifference, or cautious acceptance, or outright rejection by the member churches. One of the problems for the SACC is that the institutional churches don't take what the SACC says very seriously.[57]

Regarding institutional churches, therefore, the SACC can be said to represent only the views of the majority of Conference delegates. The small number of churches who go on to adopt controversial resolutions can be a measure of the distance between the collective sentiment and the individual positions of the churches. The SACC *did* represent the voiceless, in the form of the masses of grass-roots Christians who were not in leadership or administrative positions within the institutional churches, but who were most victimized by apartheid's brutality and who benefited most from SACC activities such as the Dependents' Conference and the Fund for the Victims of Apartheid. And while the SACC was often not in step with the views of some in its member churches, it was, in fact, educating these churches on justice issues.

The relationship between the SACC and its member churches is the primary reason that the SACBC was for years unwilling to move from observer status to full membership in the Council, although it came under increasing pressure to do so. The SACC's constitution states that observer membership is to last no longer than three years, during which time both the particular church and the SACC are to determine whether full membership would be desirable. The SACBC, however, held that position from 1969 until 1995 (although it was decided at its 1967 plenary session that dioceses so inclined could become full members of regional councils, which several did). Discussions between the two organizations took place on several occasions between 1969 and 1995, and on each occasion the SACBC requested more time to consider the invitation. The SACBC's hesitation was striking when compared with activities of bishops' conferences in other areas in the world generally and in the rest of the Southern

African region specifically. Around the world approximately forty-one bishops' conferences are full members of national councils of churches. Additionally, the Catholic Church in South Africa's neighboring countries of Namibia, Lesotho, and Swaziland participated fully in their respective councils of churches at that time.

Why, then, did the SACBC avoid full membership for well over two decades? The reasons given underscore the issues discussed above. The greatest obstacle to a closer affiliation for the SACBC was the manner in which decisions are made at the SACC National Conference, primarily because resolutions are voted on by representatives who are overwhelmingly not ensconced in denominational hierarchies. This, according to the SACBC, means that they do not have to face the consequences of their decisions—the argument being that non-ecclesial leaders have no direct constituency, and are therefore less careful about how resolutions are worded, and less committed to implementing decisions they have taken. Moreover, because delegates put forward motions that have not necessarily come through their own denominations, these resolutions run the risk of being unrepresentative of member churches' views. Because the bishops work by consensus and consultation, they feared that joining the SACC as a full member would force them to be associated with decisions that were representative solely of the majority thinking of those who happened to be present at a National Conference. In 1993 Archbishop Napier expressed the bishops' concern in this regard, saying, "the manner in which resolutions are drawn up and voted on at the National Conference means that any group can come along and propose a resolution. It is then voted on there and then without any reference back or mandate from the member churches."[58] Because some bishops are concerned about their right to distance themselves as a conference from certain positions of the SACC, the bishops felt that provisions first needed to be established allowing for dissent from SACC decisions. In addition, the bishops are not inclined to surrender authority to the General Secretary of the SACC, with his or her ability to make statements on behalf of the Council without first consulting member churches. The question would then arise as to how much they are bound by such statements. This is not an issue within the SACBC, since the way that it makes decisions eliminates the need for any bishop to disagree with a position of the Conference. The bishops' uneasiness was highlighted in a 1991 TAC study on the issue: "What has probably been our main objection to joining the SACC is a nervousness about belonging to what appears to be a 'super-church.' A general perception is that the SACC speaks for its members more forcibly than the members speak for themselves."[59] A final concern for the bishops in the 1980s was the recognition that, with the worsening political situation, the SACC increasingly voiced the "political position" of the banned liberation movements—a reality that made them distinctly uncomfortable.

Despite its unwillingness to become a full member in the 1980s, the SACBC enjoyed a status which was fundamentally different than that of other member churches, both observers and full. By refusing to become a full member, the SACBC existed as a somewhat separate organization, often working alongside rather than beneath the SACC. That the SACC itself viewed the SACBC as existing on an equal level is evident by the fact that it (the SACC) rarely issued a statement or initiated a program without first consulting the bishops. Many more statements were issued jointly by the SACC and the SACBC than by the SACC and any other South African church.[60] However, it was sometimes awkward for the two organizations when international anti-apartheid organizations were looking to the South African churches for guidance, only to receive different, often contradictory, statements from the SACC and SACBC, thereby giving the impression that the two organizations were at odds with each other on their interpretations of the South African situation.[61]

The Race Factor

The issue of race permeates all aspects of South African society, and it would therefore be impossible to analyze the SACC and SACBC in the 1980s without acknowledging how race-related issues played out in each organization, impacting their ability to adopt overtly political self-identities. In 1972 the SACC was officially declared a black organization by the state (like people, each organization in South Africa was given a racial classification); this was symbolic of the changes that were occurring in that organization and would continue to occur throughout the 1970s. These changes partially explain why the SACC was more radical than the SACBC in the 1980s. In 1972 a black majority emerged for the first time in the National Conference as well as the National Executive Committee,[62] and from that time on, the SACC rapidly evolved from being a white-dominated institution—in terms of National Conference delegates, Council officers, NEC members, as well as staff—to being more broadly representative of the black Christian community. Not only were new leaders black, they were also highly politicized and deeply influenced by the ideas emanating from the black consciousness movement and its concomitant black theology. This evolution culminated in the appointment in 1978 of Desmond Tutu as the Council's first black General Secretary, who hurried the SACC along the path of confrontation with the apartheid state.[63] Buti Tlhagale sums up the importance of Tutu's appointment for the SACC thus:

> Things in the SACC took an entirely different turn with Desmond Tutu. He politicized the SACC. His concern was not with liturgy, and church-related issues. That was peripheral. His concern was taking care of the victims of apartheid, and in the process, to oppose the state.[64]

The impact of the transformation from a white-dominated to a black-dominated organization in the early 1970s was quickly apparent, especially at the annual National Conferences. By 1975 these had become a platform and sounding board for the prophetic church in South Africa.[65] That the SACC was becoming increasingly radical under the influence of its black majority was evident at the 1980 "Consultation of Church Leaders on Racism in South Africa." During this gathering, held to assess the first decade of the WCC's Program to Combat Racism, black delegates made clear that they were approaching the breaking point with the white-dominated hierarchies. They drew up a statement which read in part that "if, after a period of twelve months, there is no evidence of repentance [of racism in the institutional churches] shown in concrete action, black Christians will have no alternative but to witness to the Gospel of Jesus Christ by becoming a confessing Church as an alternative to the existing Denominational Churches."[66] Although this threat of a breakaway church was never carried through, it was an indication that blacks were becoming impatient and were increasingly willing to challenge white fellow Christians on their commitment to eliminate racism within their own churches, let alone within society at large. Thus, with a change in the racial composition of the SACC leadership and National Conference, the organization evolved away from a hesitant position on racial issues to one which more accurately reflected the sentiments of grass-roots Christians, the vast majority of whom were black.

This "blackening" of the SACC was reflective of changes occurring in its membership. The changes began in the late 1960s, when several new churches came into existence as missionary bodies handed over their work to local Christians, and several established black independent churches moved into SACC membership.[67] Today, the overwhelming majority (approximately 80 percent) of SACC-affiliated church membership is black. In addition, the majority of clergy and ministers in SACC-affiliated churches are also black. With the exception of the Anglican and Methodist Churches (along with a few others), the highest level of leadership—bishops and archbishops—of these churches is likewise black.

The same situation does not hold true for the Catholic Church. Despite their numerical strength, black Catholics have little control over the policy-making structures of the Church. Approximately 80 percent of Catholics in South Africa are black, but the majority of priests—estimates range from 70 to 90 percent—as well as bishops—over 60 percent—are white, and many are expatriates (over two-thirds of Catholic bishops are foreign-born).[68] Moreover, many of the white Catholics, who make up 20 percent of the Church, are very conservative. The presence of approximately 600,000 Portuguese Catholics who emigrated to South Africa with the independence of Angola and Mozambique partly explains this. Thus, in the Catholic Church, unlike the member churches of the SACC, the number of white priests and bishops is highly disproportionate to the number of white Catholics.

This situation has resulted in underlying tension between black Catholics (especially black priests) and the Church's hierarchy. The tension burst onto the public scene on at least two occasions in the 1980s.[69] The first occurred in 1984 when Prime Minister P. W. Botha, who had been in Europe seeking support for his recent apartheid reforms, was given an audience with the pope. As soon as he left, the Vatican issued a statement denouncing apartheid and calling for the independence of Namibia. Nevertheless, the visit was condemned by several black priests, who sent an open letter written by Buti Tlhagale to Archbishop Hurley, president of the SACBC. They criticized the pope's political insensitivity not only for receiving Botha but for presenting him with a gift as well. Issues of race were prominent in the angry letter, which read in part:

> Perhaps you need to be reminded that he [Botha] heads a government and belongs to a political party that despises black people. They discriminate against black people on the basis of skin-color. . . . This is the racist regime whose head the Holy Father has deemed fit to honor with a gift. There is this empty phrase which Church leaders hurl around saying that the church ought to be on the side of the oppressed. The gesture of the Roman Pontiff contradicts this. Apparently the black man's oppression means nothing to the Pontiff. Blacks are not Polish, so why bother? To come closer to home, one suspects that the white church leadership might also be in the same position, sympathising with blacks but owing loyalty to their own white people.[70]

In his response, Hurley argued that Tlhagale's was not the only interpretation which could be given the meeting between Botha and the pope. Simply because they met did not mean that the pope condoned apartheid. Interestingly, however, Hurley acknowledged that he was not as much in touch with Tlhagale's feelings as were other black leaders: "My good friend Bishop Desmond Tutu has conveyed to me that your interpretation is a common one among the people that he and you can be said to represent." In addition to defending the SACBC's anti-apartheid work, Hurley gently rebuked Tlhagale for his critique of the pope, saying, "I hope that when you have got over the worst of your resentment you will regret the unkind and disparaging language you used about the Holy Father."[71]

The second occasion in which tension arose between the Catholic hierarchy and its predominantly black laity concerned a proposed visit to South Africa by the pope. Originally, the pope's 1988 visit to Southern Africa included a stop in South Africa. The SACBC at first endorsed this proposal, but later withdrew its support for two reasons. First, after discussing the proposed trip with representatives from the UDF and COSATU (the organization of trade unions allied with the UDF), it became clear to the bishops that the Mass Democratic

Movement opposed the visit, which they said would be interpreted as a rejection of the tradition of boycotts and as a legitimation by the pope of the South African government and its apartheid reforms. Knowing that Botha's 1984 visit to the pope was interpreted by the black community as giving implicit recognition to the government and its reform program, the bishops realized how much more a visit to South Africa would be seen as giving credibility to the regime. Secondly, both Archbishop Tutu and Allan Boesak stated that they would call a boycott should the pope visit South Africa, to which the SACBC responded, "whatever the merits of such a call, numerous people regard the two as leadership in our struggle for justice and as such will support the call. . . . The tensions that will flow out of this will make Catholic participation in ecumenical initiatives very difficult."[72] In the end, Archbishop Napier informed the Vatican that the "time was not opportune" for a papal visit, saying: "Eighty percent of South Africa's Catholics are black and they are suffering terrible repression at the hands of the security forces who would be asked to guard the Pope. We felt it would be incongruous and unacceptable in the present situation in South Africa."[73] The bishops thus brought themselves in line with the views of grass-roots Catholics.

What role, then, did race play in determining the politicization of the SACC and the SACBC? The issue of race is a complex one for the Catholic bishops. Bishops are appointed by Rome, not elected by South African Catholics (election determines the leadership of SACC member churches). Bishops are generally chosen for their fidelity to Rome's line and their willingness to comply with Rome's orders, in addition to their potential for administrative work. As such, it is possible for black bishops to be appointed who are in fact more conservative than many white bishops. In general, the more progressive black priests (such as Mkhatshwa) were not chosen to become bishops in South Africa. Because they are not democratically elected, it is therefore not always the race of the bishops that matters, but the *kind* of bishops.

The race factor was influential in several ways. First, as the leadership and staff of the SACC became increasingly black, that organization came to be more representative of the black Christian community and hence came to reflect the views of the majority of Christians in South Africa in a way that never happened in the SACBC. This is especially true because many of those moving into leadership positions in the SACC had been deeply influenced by black theology, with its challenge to work for the liberation of South Africa's oppressed. Through this influence, the resolutions coming from the National Conference and the programs being implemented by SACC staff increasingly reflected black Christian opinion. In contrast, many black Catholics felt that white expatriate bishops did not provide the kind of political leadership they desired, a leadership seen to be present in the SACC. For example, Albert Nolan believes that the racial makeup of the Catholic Church partially explains why liberation theology (i.e., Latin American style with Christian Base Communities) never became a strong force in South Africa. Whereas in Latin America those who most supported liberation theology were priests, in South Africa priests hindered its development. The reason, according to Nolan, is that the large number of European priests brought a missionary mentality with them from Europe, which they then imposed on South Africa. As such, liberation theology never became an ethos, or way of life, in South Africa.[74]

With a majority of the SACC National Executive Committee, National Conference, and staff being black, the SACC was now being run by people who were direct recipients of apartheid's brutality. Frank Chikane and others among the SACC were detained and tortured on several occasions—a profoundly radicalizing experience. No Catholic bishop experienced anything comparable; none was ever detained, much less tortured. At most, their homes were searched.[75] The majority of the bishops never personally experienced the effects of apartheid to the same degree as did the leadership of the SACC, and were thus left to speak *on behalf of* their constituency, rather than *with* them. This difference was recognized by Archbishop Napier:

> The SACC General Secretary lives in Soweto [South Africa's largest black township]. He has tremendous contact there at that local community level. Many of the other SACC leaders are living and ministering in townships. They've got far more direct contact with what is happening, and that has to affect they way they perceive, react, and respond to that reality, and the way that they therefore make statements about that reality. In the SACBC we do not necessarily have that very close tie with the local black community.[76]

Second, because so many Catholic bishops are foreign, they do not necessarily feel the same sense of "having a stake" in the political developments of South Africa. They prefer to concentrate more on ecclesial issues. The fear of being deported leads them to be cautious about meddling in the "affairs of state," which, believes Tlhagale, was one of the primary reasons the SACBC never declared the state illegitimate.[77]

The fact that the different racial composition of the SACC had such important consequences was partly due to its democratic structure. In the 1980s, the SACC represented the distribution of a normal, non-apartheid, South African society. In other words, the SACC was able to break out of apartheid-enforced segregation and more accurately reflect South Africa's population distribution.[78] In some sense, the SACC of the 1980s can be seen as a foretaste of what the churches might become in a South Africa no longer dominated and distorted by white minority power. Moreover, as has already been noted, the SACC decisions at National Conferences are made by people who are not only overwhelmingly black but also overwhelmingly lay men and women, who also make up the NEC. None of this is true for the SACBC, which is completely male-dominated, and where priests and sisters do not hold decision-making positions—let alone lay people. The SACC, therefore, is proportionately more representative of poor black women and men living in the townships and suffering from apartheid. Consequently, the SACC was able to "keep its finger on the pulse of the people," so that when the liberation struggle heated up in the 1980s, the SACC reflected this change with more radical statements and actions.

The authoritarian structure of the Roman Catholic Church has left some black priests with bitter feelings. These were eloquently expressed by the radical priests Smangaliso Mkhatshwa and Buti Tlhagale, who have much to say about the undemocratic nature of the SACBC. Tlhagale argues that even Archbishop Hurley, a long-standing opponent of apartheid who was in the Catholic forefront of the struggle, did little to promote consultation, let alone democracy, within his own organization. The Catholic Church, Tlhagale says, has never been allowed to become a local church, and this is primarily because of a lack of black leadership of high caliber. For him, the SACBC was not a genuinely progressive institution in the 1980s. At best it was liberal. Even radicals like Hurley, who pushed so hard for justice in society, failed to see the lack of democracy within their own organization. Radical statements by bishops, such as declaring apartheid an intrinsic evil, never filtered down effectively into their own clerical structures or into Catholic parishes.[79] For Mkhatshwa, the issue is that of power. All Catholic institutions are now fully racially integrated, but blacks still have very little control in terms of leadership or, more fundamentally, in terms of values. Throughout the 1980s, Mkhatshwa maintains, the values that were instilled in the minds of seminarians and the theology they were taught were not those of liberation, not those of a preferential option for the poor. He states, "After so many years they still can't find enough black lecturers at the seminaries. There is something seriously wrong there. I don't believe there aren't any around. It's that their ideas and ideological preferences are not acceptable to the Church."[80] Until blacks are empowered in the Church, Mkhatshwa claims, the local church will not truly exist independently of European ideological influences—which, according to Rome, is exactly as it *should* be. The idea of an independent local church is anathema.

International Linkages

The Vatican maintains a high degree of control over national churches through its episcopal appointments. It is therefore difficult for bishops' conferences to move the Catholic Church in a direction not supported by Rome. In contrast, although the SACC is affiliated with the World Council of Churches, it is not subject to similar control. Even if the SACC *were* under the direct control of the WCC, however, it probably would have still adopted a more political level of involvement than the SACBC; for, if anything, the WCC was even more outspoken on the apartheid issue than the SACC. In short, the ties between these South African actors and their international partners impacted their willingness and ability to act—yet another explanatory factor for the greater degree of radicalness in the SACC than in the SACBC.

The WCC was established in 1948—the same year the National Party came to power in South Africa—and there has been a long history of contact between it and South Africa ever since. Its most authoritative policy-making body is the Assembly, which meets every seven years. Between Assemblies, decisions are made by the 135-member Central Committee, which meets once a year and is chaired by a General Secretary. The WCC's membership consists of over three hundred member churches in more than a hundred countries, its most conspicuous nonmember being the Roman Catholic Church. The SACC is, in fact, not a member of the WCC and cannot be, as membership is only open to churches. Rather, the SACC is one of thirty-five "associate councils," which means that it is entitled to send one nonvoting representative to the seven-yearly Assemblies. Moreover, whenever South Africa is on the agenda of the Central Committee, the SACC is invited to send a nonvoting representative to the meeting. Nine of the SACC's member churches, however, are also full members of the WCC.[81] Throughout the 1970s and 1980s, the WCC was consistently ahead of the SACC and its member churches on two specific issues: support for the liberation movements and economic sanctions. While the SACC was more outspoken than the SACBC on both of these issues, it lagged behind the WCC by almost two decades.

The WCC's close involvement in South Africa dates back to the 1960 Cottesloe Consultation, which it sponsored in the aftermath of the Sharpeville massacre and the subsequent bannings of the ANC and PAC. This meeting was heavily conditioned by the WCC's 1954 Evanston Assembly, at which the issue of race was a major topic of debate.[82] Cottesloe was convened for the purpose of analyzing the dramatically changing South African situation in light of Christian attitudes towards race relations. From that point on, the WCC heightened its focus on South Africa, issuing increasingly assertive statements.[83]

The radicalization of the WCC on the South African issue came to a head at its 1968 Assembly, held in Uppsala, Sweden, where plans for the WCC's future involvement in fighting racism were adopted. Delegates decided that mere statements condemning racism were no longer sufficient, nor was giving charitable aid to racism's victims. Rather, what was needed was the strengthening of racially oppressed people, with a concentration on institutional racism rather than on interpersonal race relations.[84] These decisions were to have far-reaching consequences not only for the relationship between the WCC and South African churches, but for church/state relations within South Africa itself. These recommendations were translated into concrete action the following year at a meeting in Notting Hill, England, which adopted the radical and controversial statement that "all else failing, the church and churches should support resistance movements, including revolutions, which are aimed at the elimination of political or economic tyranny which makes racism possible."[85] What resulted from this decision was the Program to Combat Racism (PCR). This had two parts: the Program itself, which consists of ongoing research into the causes of racism, and the far more controversial Special Fund, which was established the following year to make grants to organizations supporting the victims of racial injustice.[86] As noted earlier, pre-eminent among these were the liberation movements of Southern Africa.[87] South Africa was chosen as the focus of WCC concern, in part because its apartheid regime justified its ideology in Christian terms. For years, the PCR was primarily associated with Southern Africa in the eyes of the world, and so gained its reputation as an internationally-sponsored church anti-apartheid movement.

The response of the South African churches to the PCR and its Special Fund was hardly prophetic. It created an uproar, not only in South Africa but throughout the world. Although the WCC insisted that there was a distinction between expressing solidarity with the oppressed and supporting violence, its member churches in South Africa, along with the SACC, held that the grants symbolized an "implied support of violence." At an emergency meeting of senior SACC staff and the NEC on the day the grants were announced, the SACC disassociated itself from the WCC action, stating that, "We are disturbed by the way in which the Churches . . . are called upon to initiate the use of means usually associated with the civil power in the struggle against racism. These are the weapons of the world rather than the Church."[88] Despite the fact that all the WCC member churches in the SACC criticized the grants, they decided to retain their membership in the WCC—although each ceased making payments to the WCC. In 1973, the SACC sent a delegation to the WCC Central Committee meeting to express concern about the grants, saying that it rejected violence and terror in all forms as a means to bring about political change.[89]

It appears, however, that the fundamental concern of the SACC and its member churches was not, in fact, the issue of violence. Most continued to provide chaplains to the South African Defence Force fighting the liberation movements while at the same time condemning the PCR grants. It is also worth noting that these churches had not embraced pacifism and had quite readily accepted "just war" arguments in the context of World War II. Rather, the major concern was that grants were being given to groups that had been labeled, not only by the government but by the churches themselves, as terrorists. The PCR challenged this judgment. The WCC was years ahead of the SACC and its member churches in its views on structural violence, and on whether it was theologically justifiable to support organizations which were turning in the last resort to violence as a means for ending apartheid. Although the WCC made it clear that the Special Fund was to be used for humanitarian and nonviolent programs, the grants inevitably raised the question of the legitimacy of counterviolence. The WCC's opinion on this issue was clear. In 1973 the Central Committee issued a statement on "Violence, Non-Violence, and Civil Conflict," in which it stated that the WCC was experiencing "a growing reluctance to condemn categorically those groups which feel obliged to use force in attacking entrenched social, racial and economic injustice." Furthermore, the statement read, the WCC "passed no judgment on those who resorted to violence as a means of securing their liberation. It is recognized that in some situations choice about the use of force and violence cannot be avoided."[90] For the WCC, overcoming racism meant supporting the victims of racism and taking sides with those struggling for justice and liberation, even if they embraced the use of violence. The SACC did not fully come to this same conclusion until its adoption of the Lusaka Statement in 1987 (itself a WCC-sponsored initiative), fifteen years after the WCC statement.

Why was the SACC so reticent in supporting the WCC in the late 1960s and early 1970s? One reason is that the SACC was not yet a fully black-controlled organization. Black opinion was by no means as unfavorable to the grants as white opinion. The increasing influence of a black perspective was evident in 1975, when the SACC conceded that it supported the PCR in principle, although it disagreed with its methods.[91] By 1978, the year of Tutu's appointment, the SACC had moved into a much closer working relationship with the WCC and was beginning to seriously examine the concept of structural violence, as defined by the WCC. This was partly a result of the formation of the SACC's Division of Justice and Reconciliation, itself a direct outcome of the self-examination forced on the Council in the aftermath of the PCR grants.

The second issue on which the WCC acted prophetically, well in advance of the SACC, was that of sanctions. In 1971 the WCC's Finance Committee, in conjunction with the PCR, conducted an investigation of the WCC's portfolio of investments to determine if there were any direct or indirect investment in companies and banks operating in Southern Africa. It also asked WCC member churches to do likewise. In the following year the Central Committee instructed the Finance Committee to sell any holdings and to make no further investments in corporations involved in or trading with South Africa, Namibia, Rhodesia, Angola, Mozambique, or Guinea Bissau; in addition, it was not to deposit funds in any banks with operations in these countries. The WCC also called for a complete withdrawal of multinationals from Southern Africa.[92]

Again, the SACC proved to be less radical at this point in its history than the WCC. It sent three representatives to the 1972 Central Committee meeting, where SACC General Secretary John Rees argued against the disinvestment resolution. He called for selective engagement, arguing that investment was a spur to peaceful change and that it resulted in increased employment and greater financial and educational opportunities for blacks. However, as the

SACC increasingly came under the influence of more radical black thinking, its attitude towards divestment began to change. At its 1976 National Conference, the Division of Justice and Reconciliation was mandated to undertake a study of foreign investment in South Africa. The study made several recommendations which were still mild in comparison to the WCC. In its report, the Division recommended that investments be withdrawn unless industries accepted an obligatory code of conduct. The SACC code drew heavily on the Sullivan Principles, which were published in the same year.[93] With the election of Tutu as General Secretary in 1978, the SACC edged further towards the support of economic sanctions.[94] The Council did not officially support economic sanctions, however, until its 1985 National Conference, in the aftermath of the Harare Conference (which was again a WCC initiative) and the imposition of state of emergency regulations by the government. It thus took the SACC a full thirteen years after the WCC's statement on sanctions to come to the same conclusion.

The WCC continued to make Southern Africa a PCR priority throughout the 1980s. In 1980, it held a "World Consultation on Racism in the 1980s," the goal of which was to review the achievements of the first ten years of the PCR, as well as to list priorities for the next ten. It was agreed that combating racism in Southern Africa should remain the top priority of the PCR. The Consultation offered several recommendations, all of which were subsequently adopted by the Central Committee. These included rejection of attempts at compromise and collaboration, in the form of the Sullivan Principles and homeland leaders, including Gatsha Buthelezi and others who "have fallen prey to capitalist manipulation." The Consultation also called for the imposition of comprehensive economic sanctions and for the total isolation of South Africa politically, economically, culturally, and diplomatically. Finally, the right of the people of Southern Africa to work for justice and peace through liberation movements—even those that resorted to the use of violence—was again affirmed: "In view of the violent situation created in Namibia and South Africa by the present South African government, recourse to retaliatory violence by the oppressed themselves should be seen as the last political option open to a people when stripped of basic human rights and subjected to intolerable injustice."[95]

The World Council of Churches was therefore ahead, at least chronologically, of the SACC in its understanding of the issues of racism, violence, and economic pressure. As a result, the SACC was challenged by the WCC to examine its own attitudes on these issues. This proved to be a radicalizing process. When the SACC's Division of Justice and Reconciliation needed to advise the Council on such issues as the legitimacy of counterviolence, it was able to look to the WCC for guidance and support. As the SACC came to embrace the ideas of contextual theology, it followed in the footsteps of the WCC: taking sides with oppressed blacks, using social analysis in relating racism to structural in-justice, and insisting on action over words.[96] The two gradually moved closer as the SACC and its member churches became increasingly involved in chal-lenging the apartheid regime. This occurred at a rapid rate once the SACC became a black-dominated organization. Prior to this, the theological agenda of the Council and its member churches had been set primarily by those least affected by apartheid, which explains their negative reaction to the PCR and its Special Fund.

The international linkage, then, served first as a challenge and then as a source of support for the SACC, facilitating the adoption of an overtly political self-identity. The same was not true for the SACBC; if anything, the Vatican inhibited the politicization of the bishops in their struggle against apartheid. The SACBC is much more directly tied to the Vatican than is the SACC to the WCC. The Vatican is represented in South Africa by an Apostolic Delegate, who acts as a link on matters of major importance both ecclesiastically and politically, by attending and addressing the bishops' plenary sessions. In general, there is a fair amount of communication between the bishops and the Vatican; for instance, before the SACBC issues a pastoral letter, the bishops communicate its contents to Rome. Making decisions independently of Vatican control be-came an issue for the SACBC several times during the 1980s, and impacted the legitimacy debate. The Vatican is not only a church, it is itself a state. Therefore, actions undertaken by bishops' conferences towards their own states have po-litical implications for the Vatican. Because, in the understanding of the Curia, bishops officially represent the view of Rome, a statement by them declaring the South African state illegitimate would appear to have the Vatican's implicit support. Such a declaration would have been tantamount to one state declaring another illegitimate. For this reason, Albert Nolan suggests, "It is very likely that the Vatican would be thoroughly unsupportive of declaring any govern-ment anywhere in the world illegitimate."[97] Indeed, the Vatican did interfere with the SACBC's debate over declaring the South African state illegitimate. Every five years the bishops of each country report to the pope in their *ad limina* visits, which the SACBC undertook in 1987. This took place six months after the Lusaka Statement had been released, and the question of the legiti-macy of the South African state was being hotly debated in theological circles. This debate had not escaped the SACBC, and the issue was raised during various meetings in Rome. The bishops were told in no uncertain terms by Cardinal Silvistrini, Secretary of the Council for the Public Affairs of the Church, that the Catholic Church was not in the business of declaring other states illegiti-mate. This event was confirmed time and again during interviews in South Africa, both off and on the record. However, many interviewees were quick to point out that such direct orders as that which came from Silvistrini are, in fact, not the norm, and the bishops usually have more independence to make statements than was the case with the legitimacy issue. As interviewees pointed out, the issue "just so happened" to be topical during the *ad limina* visit. Had the timing been slightly different, the Vatican may not have interfered quite so directly. The fact that it did, however, had a determining impact on the outcome of the debate. The SACBC was already hesitant and cautious about making such a declaration, for the numerous reasons already noted. The fact that the bishops would receive no support from Rome turned out to be the deciding factor in the debate's outcome. Although they continued to discuss the issue for the next two years, the lack of Vatican support made it virtually impossible for the outcome to be anything other than it was: the bishops never formally declared the South African state morally or legally illegitimate.

The Vatican directly interfered in the Catholic Church in South Africa on at least one other occasion, although this time not with the Bishops' Conference itself. In November 1990, the Vatican blocked the granting of an honorary doctorate of theology by the University of Fribourg in Switzerland to Reverend Albert Nolan, O.P., of the ICT. As a Pontifical Institute, Fribourg is dependent upon Rome and cannot give honorary degrees without the approval of the Vatican's Department of Education. No reason was given for the Vatican's denial of a degree to Nolan. Angered by this decision, the University of Fribourg refused to give any honorary degrees that year, even to those receiving Vatican approval.[98]

Tension between the Vatican and the SACBC over the increased politicization of the bishops came to a head during the 1987 plenary session (the same year as the bishops' *ad limina* visit). At this session, the apostolic delegate, Archbishop Joseph Mees, "reminded" the bishops that "the church very wisely forbids its clergy from participation in politics." Moreover, Mees reported that it was the pope's wish that the SACBC continue to dialogue with the South African government, "working with patience and tenacity for a peaceful solution to strife caused by apartheid, while conforming to the law."[99] Both the outgoing and incoming presidents of the SACBC (Hurley and Napier) reacted angrily to this statement at a press conference, challenging Mees to explain what he meant by "involvement in politics." Archbishop Hurley asked the pope to issue a document in which he clearly distinguished between promoting gospel values in social, economic, and political life, and seeking political power, saying that he [Hurley] could not support an outright rejection of political involvement. Archbishop Napier concurred, stating, "We certainly have no intention of getting involved in party politics. But I do not see how we as Christian leaders can avoid getting involved in the issues that affect our society. Life in South Africa is governed by politics, and we can't withdraw from life."[100] Newspapers, especially conservative ones, quickly picked up on "the special message" from the pope telling the bishops to stay out of politics. The bishops, in turn, made it clear that no direct message on the issue of political action had ever been received from the pope, and shortly thereafter Mees was recalled to Rome and replaced with another apostolic delegate.

If the Vatican was making noises about the bishops' involvement in politics and pressuring them not to declare the South African state illegitimate, what then were *its* views on apartheid? Although it condemned apartheid in words, it never backed up these condemnations with any actions that even approximated those of the WCC, with its financial support of the liberation movements and its divestment from South Africa. The Vatican stated its views on apartheid most explicitly on two occasions: in a speech by Pope Paul VI to the UN Special Committee on apartheid in 1974, and ten years later in a speech by Pope John Paul II to that same body. At neither time did the pope address the issue of structural injustice, nor was there any discussion of taking sides with the liberation movements. Rather, analyses of apartheid were framed in terms of traditional Catholic social teachings, such as the Christian commitment to promoting human dignity.[101] For example, in his 1984 speech Pope John Paul II said:

> The Holy See does not wish to put forward proposals of a political nature. The Holy See is not unaware of the numerous political implications surrounding these issues, but its interest is on another level: the level of the human person. . . . The good news which she received from her divine founder obliges the church to proclaim the message of salvation and human dignity and to condemn injustices and attacks on human dignity.[102]

In addition to these two speeches, the Vatican spoke out against apartheid on several other occasions. Soon after having met with Prime Minister Botha in Rome, the pope declared apartheid "an offense to human dignity and a possible threat to regional and world peace." In 1985 he said that "no system of apartheid or separate development will ever be acceptable as a model for the relations between peoples and races."[103] Despite these statements, the Vatican never followed through with any concrete actions aimed at forcing the apartheid regime to abandon its policies. Although Pope John Paul II declared in his 1984 speech that "I earnestly hope that a different policy will be established," he did not institute or encourage any actions to bring such policy about. For example, the pope never supported the imposition of economic sanctions against the apartheid regime. During his 1988 trip to Southern Africa, as the black majority of South Africa was facing ever more brutal repression, he said, "Sanctions are a political means. From a global point of view, they are politically acceptable in some situations. But they should be attempted only as a last resort. A search should be made for a solution that is less drastic and more worthy of man."[104] The following year he reiterated his belief that there was nothing the Vatican could do to force an end to the apartheid regime, saying, "The international community does not have any means of coercion at its disposal with regard to countries which, through their legal system, still practice racial discrimination towards their own peoples."[105] In general, he never moved beyond expressions of solidarity, such as a statement in 1985 in which he said, "to those who suffer the violence of such an inhuman situation, I express sentiments of profound support."[106] Given this cautious approach by the Vatican, and given its high degree of control over national episcopal conferences, it is little surprise that the SACBC was itself so cautious on the issue of economic sanctions.

It is possible that the lack of political initiatives against apartheid was symptomatic of a more general move towards conservatism by the Vatican during the 1980s, a move that was evident in various ways. Several South African theologians have expressed the view that the anticommunist attitude exhibited by the Vatican under Pope John Paul II influenced its stance on apartheid, especially because the ANC was perceived in some Western quarters to be communist-inspired. Smangaliso Mkhatshwa's interpretation of how this assumption impacted the Vatican is as follows:

> When the Pope went to Poland he was a regular revolutionary, and very anti-regime. The issues for him were very clear—the Catholic Church stands for democracy, freedom, and human rights, as opposed to communism. In South Africa, there was always the unarticulated fear that if blacks took over the government, what were they going to do with it? Especially before the demise of the Soviet Union, the fear of communism was the fear of blacks.[107]

The conservative tendency of the Vatican in the 1980s was also evident in its growing wariness of liberation theology. In a 1983 pastoral letter to the Nicaraguan bishops, Pope John Paul II declared that it was "absurd and dangerous to imagine that outside—if not to say against—the church built around the bishop there should be another church . . . alternative and as it has been called recently, a people's church."[108] In the following year, the Vatican made its views on liberation theology explicit when Cardinal Ratzinger, Secretary of the Congregation of the Doctrine of the Faith, published an "Instruction on Certain Aspects of Theology of Liberation." The Instruction was aimed at delegitimizing liberation theology from an ecclesial point of view, by accusing liberation theologians of politicizing the gospel and advocating violence. Criticism of this theology has been seen by some, including Peter Hebblethwaite, as an attempt by the current Vatican leadership to return to some of the pre–Vatican II hierarchical discipline and control.[109] Daniel Levine concurs and argues that the changing Vatican attitudes towards these new religious ideas grew from a concern over their implications for democratization within the church. This has led to attempts to withdraw from politics, with the result that the church's capacity to assume a critical, public stance as an institution on issues of political importance has been undercut.[110] Ian Linden of the Catholic Institute for International Relations in London has said that the document was very anti-Marxist and "showed no sympathy or even close acquaintance with the reality of the Church of the Poor and its theology, and seemed to view it as an abstract doctrine replete with errors."[111] If the Vatican was critiquing the theological ideas underpinning liberation or contextual theology, this might well have served to inhibit the capacity of the SACBC to adopt these values, which were becoming increasingly important in the South African political context of the 1980s.

Finally, the increased conservatism of the Vatican in the 1980s affected the Catholic Church in South Africa through the selection of bishops. Throughout the world, Rome was filling vacant dioceses with bishops who were deliberately chosen for their conservatism and their willingness to move the church back to a less progressive era. On the whole, South African radical priests, black or white, were not appointed as bishops. A case in point was Smangaliso Mkhatshwa. As Buti Tlhagale, himself a radical black priest, points out, "Mkhatshwa has demonstrated leadership skills over the years, and he normally would have qualified. But he would have never been appointed a bishop, because he would have been too radical."[112] It would have been difficult to find anyone more committed to the liberation struggle than Mkhatshwa in either the SACBC or SACC; however, he was not a bishop, and therefore never became a part of the decision-making processes of the SACBC. Consequently, his influence on the direction of that body, despite the fact that he was its General Secretary, always remained somewhat limited.

It is plausible that the deepening conservatism of the Vatican in the 1980s acted as a deterrent to the adoption of an overtly political self-identity by the SACBC. The bishops witnessed the disciplining of priests and the warning of bishops around the world, and the prospect of a crackdown against themselves—rather than an actual crackdown itself—in all likelihood served as a moderating force on the Conference.

State Repression: SACC versus SACBC

The SACC incurred the anger of the South African state in the 1980s on a far greater scale than the SACBC. As discussed earlier, the government's Eloff Commission of Inquiry into the South African Council of Churches evolved into a four-year-long, major campaign against the Council. No similar investigation ever took place of the SACBC. In addition, leaders were detained and tortured. Frank Chikane's home was bombed, and he was poisoned—by an SADF hit squad, it was later determined. Even Archbishop Tutu was arrested on numerous occasions, although he was always released almost immediately. No Catholic bishop suffered any similar fate. Why was state repression directed primarily against the SACC and not the SACBC? Was it simply because the

SACC was perceived to be more radical than the SACBC, or were there other reasons as well?

The state cracked down on the SACC, of course, because it *was* more radical than the SACBC—in its statements, actions and programs—for the various organizational reasons discussed in this chapter. The Council spoke out more often on a wider range of subjects. However, the distinction must always be kept in mind between the SACC as a separate organization, with its own staff carrying out its own programs through teams of crisis field-workers in the townships in direct contact with the grass roots, and the SACC as an ecumenical umbrella organization, bringing together several member churches. For example, the Dependents' Conference, with its aid for defense lawyers, bail money, and support for families of detainees, was administered by the SACC headquarters staff. In the minds of the security police, then, Khotso House was one of the most active anti-apartheid organizations of the 1980s, and should pay dearly for this.

The SACBC was slow to make statements, and they were invariably more cautiously worded than statements of the SACC. However, they were more likely to be carried through and acted upon than those of the SACC. Because of the SACBC's hierarchical nature, its statements and programs were more likely to reach the level of parishes, even if they were not always adopted there. While the staff at Khotso House was excellent at action, its member churches were less so; and when decisions were made at the National Conference, it was often left to Khotso House staff to implement them, rather than the member churches. The same was not true for the SACBC; once a decision was taken, the hierarchical structure was in place to make implementation easier. The perception on the part of the state that the SACBC was not particularly radical was therefore not entirely true. Although it appeared less dangerous to the state, it may in the end have had a greater impact on its parish constituency—a fact possibly overlooked by the police.

Despite these differences, however, it would be difficult to deny that the SACC, on a whole, was more overtly political than the SACBC, and this made the Council more dangerous to the state. However, this danger existed for other reasons as well, one being the SACC's size. The SACC is a larger organization, represents more people, and in the 1980s, controlled a vastly greater amount of money than the SACBC. Because the SACC represents a far larger group of Christians (over ten million for the SACC versus three million for the SACBC), it had a greater pool of radical Christians to draw on for its staff positions. The smaller constituency in the Catholic Church also fed the perception that the bishops were less influential and therefore less dangerous than the SACC. By far the most important reason, however, that the SACC was dangerous to the state was the substantial sum of money it had at its disposal for fighting apartheid. During the 1980s, and especially after the bannings of

1988, the SACC was perhaps the primary channel through which international nongovernmental resistance money entered South Africa. Although the SACBC was also a conduit of international funds, it handled a much smaller volume. The SACC was able to carry out a particular type of ministry of which no individual church was capable. When Frank Chikane took over the General Secretariat of the SACC, for example, he had R12 million in discretionary funds at his disposal, which, as Chikane says, "tells you the extent of work the SACC could do."[113] During that same year, the total income of the SACC was slightly over R23 million, of which 96.5 percent was received as grants and donations (the rest coming from affiliation fees and earned interest).[114] Of these funds, approximately 98 percent came from outside South Africa, primarily from European and North American church organizations.[115] Close to 80 percent of this money was spent on programs aimed at helping the victims of apartheid, including providing legal defense, supporting families of detainees and political prisoners, and helping to rebuild homes destroyed by police and defense forces.

Such heavy reliance on overseas support made the SACC vulnerable to repeated government charges that it was unduly influenced by "foreign agents" trying to undermine the South African state, and that this constituted proof that its member churches did not approve of its activities. This was a particularly salient issue for the Eloff Commission, whose final report concluded that the theological arguments given by the SACC were merely an excuse to carry out the work of foreign-funded destabilization. This charge represented another attempt by the state to employ a "divide and rule" strategy, but the SACC's member churches were quick to come to its defense, insisting that although they did not always adopt SACC decisions as their own, the lack of domestic funding in no way represented a division between themselves and their parent organization. The truth is that over 80 percent of the membership of SACC churches are black. In apartheid society, that meant that their economic circumstances made it extremely difficult for them to support their own churches, let alone special Council programs. In contrast, the predominantly white minority of members with wealth were not likely to be pleased with the activities and statements of the SACC, and so were not forthcoming with any financial support. Reliance on overseas funding, therefore, did not symbolize a lack of domestic support; rather, it was the result of poverty suffered by those most willing to support the SACC.

This high degree of foreign support does help explain, however, why the SACC was able to maintain an independent existence from its member churches throughout the 1980s, allowing the organization to carry out radical activities even when they were not fully supported by its constituency. Not only did over 90 percent of funding come from overseas, the bulk of this money was raised by Council officers rather than member churches. As one former SACC official reported to the 1982 National Conference, "Any organization which raises its own funds, with only a token contribution from its members, may claim a measure of freedom in expending those funds."[116] The size of the more radical SACC, in terms of staff, constituency, and financial power, represented a greater threat to the South African state than did the SACBC. As Ian Linden points out, "the SACC was more dangerous to the state by any calculation because it packed a bigger punch across a wider area in all senses."[117]

The state treated the SACC harshly because it was radical and powerful. A third reason was related to its racial composition. Because the Council's leadership was primarily black, it automatically came under suspicion in the eyes of the government, which unfairly assumed that it must be communist-influenced. Smangaliso Mkhatshwa notes, "because the SACBC has always been white-led, it could therefore be trusted."[118]

Given the government's obsessive fear of communism in the cold-war international context of the 1980s, the SACC's relationship with the WCC was a fourth reason the state treated it with so much hostility, as the WCC had long been labeled communist.[119] With the WCC's formation of the PCR and its special fund, accusations flew fast and furious that it was a communist front, providing money to "terrorist organizations" to buy arms. Articles on the vulnerability of the Cape Route and the key position South Africa played in NATO's southern flank began appearing in Western European newspapers shortly after the grants were announced. And even though the SACC and the WCC's South African members in fact disassociated themselves at first from the PCR, in the eyes of the government the SACC was simply an extension of the WCC; because the WCC was communist-inspired, the SACC must be so as well.[120] The government responded by financing right-wing Christian groups such as the Christian League of South Africa (CLSA), whose goal was to discredit, through propaganda and smear campaigns, the SACC and WCC, which it saw as "major sources of ungodly doctrine and action infiltrating the churches."[121] Charges of communism were also made against the WCC because it equated racism with capitalism. At its 1980 World Consultation on Racism in the 1980s, for example, the Council denounced "naive assumptions such as the one that racism is a phenomenon which can be isolated from capitalism and imperialism." The Consultation concluded that the "international capitalist economic system provides the foundation of much of the racism experienced by people in the world today."[122]

Whereas the WCC was vigorously portrayed as communist-inspired, the Vatican was seen as anti-communist by the South African government, in part because of Pope John Paul II's anti-communist background,[123] and in part because of such Vatican documents as its 1984 "Instruction on Certain Aspects of the Theology of Liberation," which was highly critical of Marxism. This impacted how both the SACC and SACBC were treated by the state. The Eloff

Commission's recommendation that the SACC be declared an "affected organization," thereby preventing it from receiving foreign funds, was an attempt to counteract what it saw as overseas influence, both financial and ideological, not least by the WCC.

A fifth reason the state treated the SACC more harshly than the SACBC was simply because it *could*. The SACBC represented a worldwide church, while the SACC was a domestic ecumenical organization (albeit with ties to international churches). It was therefore easier for the South African government to crack down on the SACC than the SACBC. During the 1980s, the government was desperate to maintain as much international support as possible. Had it cracked down on the local Catholic Church, it would have risked alienating those European countries with large Catholic populations, including Germany, Italy, and France, whose citizens might have put greater pressure on their governments to punish the South African regime. Members of Protestant churches in these countries did not feel the same sense of "ownership" of the SACC. Both Archbishop Napier and Smangaliso Mkhatshwa are aware that their church received a measure of protection for this reason. Napier believes that "had the government cracked down on the Church, per se, they would have lost all of Europe—even those countries who underground were trying to be friendly to the National Party."[124] Mkhatshwa concurs: "No matter how conservative the German or Belgian or American bishops may be, they would have felt immediately challenged. Any good politician would be very wary of taking on a worldwide Church."[125]

A final reason for the more assertive crackdown on the SACC was theological, related to the need of the white Dutch Reformed Churches, especially the NGK, to prove that apartheid was theologically legitimate. The NGK had once been a member of the CCSA (the forerunner of the SACC), and it was particularly important to disprove what the Council was saying. Theologian Cedric Mayson sums up this antagonism: "The SACC is Protestant, and considered [by the NGK] 'our people,' and some of 'our people' had actually gone off and joined 'them'—i.e., the black churches of the DRC. Therefore, the SACC had to be proved wrong, and had to be destroyed."[126] Part of the reasoning behind the Eloff Commission, then, was the necessity felt by the NGK-controlled government to denigrate the Council's work. If the state could prove that the SACC was not Christian but communist, then its theologically based anti-apartheid stance could likewise be delegitimated.

Conclusion

By the 1980s, organizational characteristics of the SACC allowed it to carry out a particular type of ministry—that of responding rapidly and directly to the needs of the victims of apartheid. The Council also provided a measure of protection to activist community leaders, who then joined the organization to carry out their work. With a degree of freedom from its denominational constituency that the SACBC did not enjoy, with a vast sum of financial resources at its disposal, and with resolute support from activists whose own organizations were banned, the SACC was able to provide a home and a matrix of broader contacts for radical people to carry out their anti-apartheid struggle. In the process, the SACC became the voice of the alternative church. The SACBC was more constrained: by the necessity to achieve consensus; because it was a denomination with direct ties to its church constituency; and because of constant awareness within its hierarchy of the need to cooperate with the Vatican and to follow established doctrine. Because of these institutional factors, radical voices in the Catholic Church were not as easily heard. The Catholic Church in South Africa produced people as equally radical as Tutu, Chikane, and Naudé. However, these individuals were not given the same freedom to speak inside the institutional confines of the SACBC, and consequently, many of them chose to work outside it. Those individuals, like Hurley, who chose to remain inside official structures, did not have the same degree of freedom to speak on behalf of colleagues as did their counterparts in the SACC. As a result of these organizational differences, it was easier for the SACC to play the role of political actor than it was for the SACBC, which always went to great lengths to insist that its competency did not extend beyond ecclesial issues to political expertise.

Where the SACC was strong the SACBC was weak, and vice versa. The Council was able to speak boldly and prophetically; the bishops were cautious and nuanced. However, while the SACC was often unable to involve its member churches in its decisions, the strength of the SACBC lay in its ability to ensure that decisions and pastoral letters penetrated to the parish level. The hierarchical nature of the Catholic Church tempered its ability to be outspoken, but it also facilitated the diffusion of centralized messages; in contrast, while there is no doubt that the actions of the Council were often prophetic, that vision did not regularly filter down to the life and practice of its member churches. The point is that there was a need for *both* types of actions: quick, radical statements which would grab international attention and support the high emotions circulating at the grass roots, and slower, nuanced responses that were more likely to be implemented. In part, this reflected a difference in goals. The SACC was most concerned with playing a political role of resistance in the 1980s, regardless of whether in the process it transformed attitudes within its member churches. For the SACBC, this goal of transformation was paramount.

Despite the fact that the SACBC was less outspoken than the SACC, it often risked far more than many of the Council's own member churches. These were at times less than courageous in their willingness to challenge the apartheid state. Charles Villa-Vicencio is unequivocal on this point:

In many ways the Protestant leaders of the 1980s were some of the most re-actionary people that I have ever dealt with in my life. Certainly, they were no more enlightened than the Catholic bishops, and in many, many instances, the Catholic bishops as individuals were more enlightened and prepared to go a step further as individuals than were these church leaders. . . . With the ex-ception of Archbishop Tutu, there was very, very little leadership coming from the institutional churches during that time. The leadership was coming from the SACC.[127]

When the full history of South African politics in the 1980s is written, however, both the SACC *and* the SACBC will be shown as having put them-selves on the line. It was a trying but satisfying period in the lives of these organizations. Although fault can obviously be found with both, they actually did something—they helped to mobilize people around political issues, they confronted the state, and they helped contribute to its loss of legitimacy. Both were prophetic organizations in the sense that they spoke out on behalf of justice, the poor and the oppressed. And what they were saying had support among the vast majority of South Africans. Try as it might, the state never succeeded in silencing the voices of either organization.

Briefly, in the late 1980s, the alternative theological tradition described by Villa-Vicencio became the "dominant" one. The institutional church *was* the church of resistance. To be sure, radical Christians remained a minority in most churches, representing the cutting edge of this resistance church. Neverthe-less, it is not an overstatement to say that these organizations changed, in an exceptionally short period, from a position of somewhat self-righteous indig-nation against apartheid which rarely moved beyond the level of statements, to one of self-criticism and committed support for, and identification with, those fighting to abolish the apartheid regime. This support eventually led the lead-ership in these organizations to view politics as a legitimate arena for religious action. That these ideas were taken up by individuals who eventually com-prised the leadership of institutional churches—people such as Beyers Naudé, Desmond Tutu, Denis Hurley, Smangaliso Mkhatshwa, Frank Chikane, and Allan Boesak—was extraordinary, and indicates just how profoundly far these organizations strayed from traditional institutional church actions.

7

South Africa in the 1990s

New Contexts, New Identities

IN 1990 the apartheid regime unbanned the ANC and PAC, released political prisoners, and eventually consented to a negotiated political settlement. These changes culminated in the April 1994 democratic elections, which swept the ANC and its leader, Nelson Mandela, to power by an overwhelming majority. If the hypotheses forwarded here are correct, with the changing political context, one would expect to see a similarly changing religious context. Moreover, because of these new political and religious contexts, one would expect to see the SACC and SACBC adopt different styles of action. South Africa in the 1990s has indeed proven to be fertile testing ground for the framework proposed in this book. All the elements are present: a new political context arose; a new religious context also emerged, one which stressed the importance of mediation as opposed to confrontation; finally, even the institutional context evolved, with the SACC becoming a much smaller organization in terms of resources and personnel. In the face of these profound changes, what model of church do both organizations now follow? In other words, have they reconstituted their self-identities once again, so that their sense of mission and understanding of their proper relationship to society is no longer overtly political or supportive of the post-election regime's initiatives?

Research on Latin America has indicated that when contexts change, a church may go through an "identity crisis" in which it is forced to again reevaluate its mission and its proper role in society. Its level of political involvement is likely to be affected.[1] When a draconian state loses control of society, as occurred in South Africa, churches may be unsure about their purpose. With democratic openings, civil society—the formerly "voiceless"—can now turn to several organizations for representation. Both the needs and opportunities for church political action are constricted. Simultaneously, the church is faced with complex issues, including whether it should attempt to represent civil society under the new conditions. The question also arises, who legitimately represents the "voice of the voiceless"? In the early 1990s, South African church organizations faced a similar dilemma to that faced by Latin American churches in the 1980s. The dilemma is summed up by Mainwaring and Wilde: "if earlier the Church needed to choose between voice and silence, now it had to address a second set of questions: What kind of voice, for whom, how expressed?"[2] These questions have profound implications for South Africa, and the SACC, the SACBC, and other religious institutions throughout the first half of the 1990s have been forced to reevaluate their work. Conscious of the fact that for the previous three decades a prime motivating factor was the struggle against apartheid, the SACC (and to a lesser extent the SACBC) entered the decade of the 1990s with what amounted to a profound existential crisis.

Changing Political Context

In a February 2, 1990, policy speech, South African president F. W. de Klerk—who had come to power five months earlier on September 6— astonished South Africans and the rest of the world by revoking bans on the ANC, its ally the SACP, its rival the PAC, and thirty-three other banned organizations, including the UDF and COSATU. Restrictions on 374 anti-apartheid activists were removed, and de Klerk committed himself to the release of the most famous of these activists, Nelson Mandela. In addition, he called for negotiations with "the representative leaders of the entire population" in order to seek a solution to the country's problems which would "ensure lasting peace."[3] On February 11, Nelson Mandela was released from his twenty-seven-year imprisonment.

Church organizations in South Africa greeted the announcement with cautious optimism. Frank Chikane summed up this tempered excitement by stating, "I welcome with enthusiasm the announcements made by Mr. F. W. de Klerk. . . . He is to be congratulated for meeting at least some of the initial conditions towards creating a climate conducive to negotiations."[4] At the same time, the SACC, along with the ANC, PAC, UDF, and COSATU (and the international community in general), called for the continuation of economic sanctions as a means of forcing the total dismantling of apartheid. In general, church leaders took a "wait-and-see" attitude. Wary of de Klerk's sincerity, they maintained the stance that the events of early 1990 still fell short of creating the kind of climate in which genuine negotiations could take place.

Negotiations

The period from February 1990 until the April 1994 elections was overwhelmingly dominated by two political phenomena: negotiations and violence. The ANC adhered to the Organization of African Unity's (OAU) Harare Declaration, with its specific proposal of ending the conflict in South Africa through a negotiated settlement. From the earliest stages of negotiations, including the "talks about talks,"[5] the ANC insisted that the purpose of negotiations should be the creation of a constituent assembly and the formulation of a new constitution which embodied certain principles.[6] The period from February 1990 through December 1991 consisted mainly of hammering out the preconditions to negotiations[7] and laying out the guidelines for the process. The ANC was also busy during this time organizing itself as a normal political institution of civil society after decades of operating as an exiled liberation organization.

December 1991 marked the launch of the Convention for a Democratic South Africa (CODESA), consisting of nineteen political parties and organizations and headed by de Klerk's National Party (NP) and the ANC. The ANC's main negotiating position was the creation of an interim government with sovereign powers to replace the existing administration, and a popularly elected constituent assembly whose primary responsibility would be the drafting of a new constitution.[8] The NP negotiators hoped to maintain a share of political power through what amounted to veto power over majority decisions concerning such issues as the loss of economic or personal rights by whites. To achieve this, their goal was to place limits on any sort of blanket majority rule, in favor of group rights.[9] Clearly these two antagonists were arguing from positions which had little in common, in a situation which was fraught with distrust among most of the political parties. In order to come to some sort of negotiated settlement with a minimum of conflict, both sides would have to travel far, with each having to forfeit dearly held principles. In this context the churches found themselves asking what role they could play to reduce tension and foster goodwill among the many political players.

This role was to stretch the churches close to the limits of their reconciliation skills. The negotiations soon turned rancorous. In May 1992, negotiations deadlocked over percentages that would be required by an elected constituent assembly for constitutional ratification, the veto powers of a proposed Senate, and the time limit for the transition.[10] Shortly thereafter, on June 17, forty-three people in the town of Boipatong—an ANC stronghold—were massacred, resulting in the ANC's withdrawal from multiparty talks. This marked the end of the CODESA forum, since all negotiations were suspended.[11] The ANC returned to the tactics of the 1980s and called for a campaign of country-wide mass protests in order to force concessions from the NP. The largest of these protests was a general strike called by the ANC and its allies on August 3–4, which was adhered to by over four million workers, and which included a march of over 100,000 ANC supporters to the Union Building in Pretoria.[12] The ANC was quick to interpret this response as a positive endorsement of its policies and as a barometer of its support among the majority of South Africans. The threat of violence always loomed large over these protests, and violence did indeed break out in September in Bisho, the capital of the nominally independent homeland of Ciskei, when troops loyal to the Ciskei leader, Brigadier

Oupa Gqozo, opened fire on unarmed ANC demonstrators, leaving twenty-eight people dead and hundreds more wounded.

1992, therefore, marked a low-point for those desperately working for a peaceful negotiated settlement. The year was marked by the breakdown of multiparty talks, the mass action campaign, and escalating violence, all of which culminated in "the restoration of the pre-February 1990 stalemate."[13] However, despite the breakdown of formal multiparty talks, the ANC and National Party continued to talk privately through several unpublicized meetings. The nature of these talks—i.e., bilateral private consultations—was to have long-term consequences, in that they put Chief Gatsha Buthelezi of the Inkatha Freedom Party (IFP) on notice that he would not be a major player in the negotiated settlement. This decision raised the specter of violence to an even higher degree in the ensuing years. In November 1992, despite public acrimony, the ANC and NP achieved a momentous goal privately, when they agreed in principle to a negotiated settlement. This would eventually take the form of a three-phase transition, consisting of an administrative transitional executive council,[14] an elected constituent assembly, and the formation of a transitional coalition "Government of National Unity," thereby enforcing power-sharing among the two major parties for a set time period of five years.[15] The details of this transition began to be formalized when multiparty talks resumed publicly in March 1993. Tensions remained high in this forum. Debates often turned bitter, and in July the IFP and the right-wing Conservative Party (CP) withdrew from negotiations.

South Africans then began the process of what one scholar has called "slouching towards 'free and fair' elections."[16] After nine months of intensive negotiations, the twenty-one members of the negotiating council adopted an interim constitution which contained a Bill of Rights. This constitution would serve as South Africa's supreme law until a constituent assembly could draft a permanent constitution. The negotiators also formally approved a transitional Government of National Unity (GNU), which would come into existence at the time of the April 27, 1994, elections, and last for a period of five years.[17] Although negotiations were never again derailed, they did face some potentially serious challenges, one of which was a coalition of right-wing opponents who vowed to disrupt the enactment of negotiated agreements if their demands were not met. This group of both Afrikaner nationalists, including the Afrikaner Volksfront (AVF or Afrikaner People's Front) and the CP, and Zulu nationalists represented by the IFP, demanded separate federal states, including an Afrikaner volkstaat and a state of Kwa-Zulu. Both groups of nationalists, joined together as the Freedom Alliance, threatened civil war; and indeed the number of bomb attacks directed against ANC and other offices increased dramatically in the several months preceding the elections. The IFP, under the leadership of Buthelezi, steadfastly maintained its boycott of the elections until

almost the very end: scarcely one week before the April 27 elections, Buthelezi
called off his boycott, thereby averting the almost certain blood bath which
would have occurred in KwaZulu/Natal.

Violence

Early in the 1990s, the ANC and its allies began accusing the de Klerk
regime of embracing a double strategy: supporting negotiations in public,
while privately working towards—or at least turning a blind eye to—the destabilization of the organizing capacity of its main negotiating rival, the ANC.
As evidence, the ANC and others pointed to levels of violence which would
skyrocket in the aftermath of each new negotiated settlement marking a step
towards the end of apartheid rule, and the fact that the violence had a character
which indicated that its primary source was outside the black community.[18]
Moreover, the ANC had the weight of statistics on its side. The average number
of fatalities per day almost tripled in 1990 (10.1 per day), when negotiations
started, compared to 1989 (3.8 per day), the year prior to negotiations.[19] This
double-edged reality of daily life in South Africa has been described by one
scholar as follows:

> While career diplomats and political notables were engaged in a war of words
> over highly nuanced negotiating platforms, township residents were locked
> in a war of bullets with civilian-clothed gunmen who killed and maimed with
> impunity. The chameleon-like character of the negotiations process with an
> ever-changing pace and rhythm all its own, stood in stark contrast to the
> grim, seemingly endless monotony of routinized township violence.[20]

Their accusations proved sadly correct with the revelation in June 1991 that the
government had been secretly funding the IFP, thus indicating partisan support on the part of the de Klerk government for the IFP in what was portrayed
as a struggle solely between the IFP and the ANC. Later revelations indicated
that the government had provided specialized training at secret military bases
for over two hundred IFP members.[21]

The number of deaths during the first years of the decade was staggering:
between February 1990 and October 1992, almost 8,000 people died, and in
the period between September 1992 and the 1994 elections, South Africa suffered an average of 300 deaths a month.[22] In chilling evidence that the violence
was spreading beyond its original site of Natal—the IFP stronghold, between
August 1990 and May 1991 more people were killed in the township of Soweto
alone than had died in the nationwide uprisings in 1976.[23] In the single year of
1992, over 3,600 people died, and an additional 6,000 were seriously injured.[24]
More than 15,000 people were killed in South Africa between the period that
negotiations began and the 1994 elections.[25]

Despite the often tenuous nature of negotiations and the intimidating use of force, South Africans voted on April 26–29, 1994, for candidates from nineteen political parties. The ANC's victory was overwhelming. The ANC captured 252 of the 400 parliamentary seats, a total of 62.6 percent. The National Party won 20.4 percent of the vote and 82 seats; the IFP won 10.5 percent and 43 seats; the Freedom Front (an amalgamation of right-wing Afrikaner parties which decided at the last moment to withdraw from the Freedom Alliance and contest the elections) won 2.2 percent and 9 seats; the Democratic Party won 1.7 percent and 7 seats; the PAC won 1.2 percent and 5 seats; and the African Christian Democratic Party won .5 percent of the vote, for a total of 2 seats. As a result of the power-sharing arrangements decided during negotiations, Nelson Mandela was elected president, and the vice-presidency was shared between Thabo Mbeki of the ANC and F. W. de Klerk of the NP. Eighteen of the twenty-seven cabinet seats also went to the ANC. In the words of Nelson Mandela, South Africans were indeed "free at last."[26]

Church Response to a New Political Context

Two phenomena thus characterized the political context of the first four years of the 1990s: negotiations for a new political dispensation and escalating political violence. This context, marked by the opening up of political space, stands in stark contrast to the political context of the 1980s. In particular, what was absent in the 1990s was the harshness of state repression against those protesting the apartheid government. Draconian legislation was abolished; troops were removed from townships; and the number of arrests, detentions, and tortures diminished. Although violence still plagued the political landscape, it was no longer the overt institutionalized violence of the state. The SACC and SACBC had become politicized in the 1980s in a spiraling reactive process against this very state repression.

The linchpin to this spiraling involvement, then, was increasing levels of state repression. Once it vanished, the spiral of involvement collapsed. As a result, the self-identities which the SACC and SACBC found themselves embracing by the end of the 1980s—overt political involvement in the form of acts of civil disobedience and support of the liberation movements—was no longer appropriate for the changed political context of the 1990s. In an atmosphere of negotiations and at least public goodwill, these two organizations had to reassess their relationship to both the state and the liberation organizations, which were once again becoming viable actors in civil society.

Thus, South Africa in the early 1990s was characterized by dwindling state repression, which resulted in a contracting spiral of involvement. As a consequence of these two changes, religious organizations which had been actively critical of the government were forced to question what their role should now appropriately be. No longer would it be sufficient to simply be an oppositional force in society. A more nuanced role would now be required: one which called on them to continue criticizing political groups when necessary, while at the same time encouraging the same groups to achieve some sort of political reconciliation. In general, just as they had done in the 1980s, the SACC and SACBC again underwent a redefinition of their self-identities.

Just as the political context of the 1980s influenced the overtly political identities adopted by the SACC and SACBC in that decade, so the roles played by both organizations in the 1990s were heavily influenced by the prevailing political exigencies of the time: negotiations and violence. The overwhelming activity undertaken by the leaders of the SACC and SACBC in the first years of the 1990s was mediation. The leaders expended their full energy on trying to keep political opponents talking with each other, while at the same time desperately trying to stem the rising tide of violence.

Negotiations

Even before de Klerk's February 1990 speech, Chikane, Boesak, and Tutu declared their willingness to adopt the role of facilitating potential negotiations. In October 1989 they met with de Klerk, in office for barely one month, and declared that they had come to Pretoria as church leaders, attempting to create the climate for negotiations. At this point, church leaders had apparently decided to become politically involved through embracing a two-prong strategy. The meeting with de Klerk took place a mere month after the huge Cape Town "peace march," led by many of the same leaders now meeting with the government. Thus, the last months of 1989 and the first months of 1990 marked a period of identity transition for church leaders. The Defiance Campaign was in full swing, supported and often led by church leaders, who at the same time were willing to play a facilitating role in preliminary talks about negotiations, a role which would clearly require them to work with the government. While church leaders such as Chikane, Boesak, and Tutu were willing to talk with the government to help it move towards negotiations, they were not prepared to give up their prophetic critique of it. As they declared to de Klerk, "it does not appear to us that your Government appreciates the far-reaching nature of the steps it needs to take to get negotiations off the ground."[27] Moreover, church leaders let it be known that although they were eager to play a role in the negotiated end of apartheid rule, they were not prepared to uncritically support all negotiations. A month after Mandela's release, they stated, "negotiations that will not achieve and entrench justice must be rejected as much as we rejected false reconciliation. Negotiations must be accepted and endorsed only if there is a reasonable chance that they will achieve justice for all."[28]

In reflecting on their potential roles in the "new South Africa," both the

SACC and SACBC produced various statements regarding the task of the church in the period of negotiations.[29] In the new political context, in which the church was but one of many groups in civil society—a society now characterized by freedom of political activity—the churches were adamant that they viewed their role as a supportive one, aimed mainly at educating their constituencies while leaving political activity to political organizations.

Once negotiations did start, they were immediately fraught with disagreements and rising tensions. For example, in April 1991—during the period of "talks about talks" which eventually led to the launching of the official CODESA negotiations—a serious disagreement on the release of political prisoners developed between the ANC and the government. It resulted in the ANC National Executive Committee issuing a statement declaring that "should the Government not meet our demand for the release of political prisoners and the return of exiles, we would have to decide whether to continue talking about further negotiations."[30] In response to threats such as these traded between political opponents, church leaders—working primarily through a newly constituted Church Leaders Meeting[31]—became engaged in classic "shuttle diplomacy," moving hectically between the ANC leadership and de Klerk's office, offering compromises that might be acceptable to both, and hoping to avert a derailment of talks. Church leaders attempted to mediate in other ways as well. For example, when the PAC withdrew from CODESA early in the negotiations, an SACC delegation comprising the SACC General Secretary, his Deputy General Secretary, and two Senior Vice-Presidents, met with a PAC delegation in an attempt to resolve their concerns. Following this meeting, the SACC General Secretary, Frank Chikane, arranged appointments between the ANC, the PAC, and AZAPO (Azanian People's Organization), allowing them to discuss the negotiation process by themselves, away from the public eye.[32]

Frank Chikane referred to this type of activity as "the ministry of mediation."[33] In 1991 alone, the Church Leaders Meeting met with de Klerk three times to propose measures that would curb violence and restore the public's faith in negotiations.[34] Church leaders were especially called on to engage in this ministry after the Boipatong massacre and the disintegration of CODESA. In the aftermath of these two events, the Church Leaders Meeting held an emergency meeting on July 24, 1992, followed by a flurry of meetings between labor, business, the government, and the ANC, in an effort to find deadlock-breaking mechanisms and prevent almost inevitable mass action, which they feared would be accompanied by violence. The church leaders presented various options to de Klerk, who did not respond.[35] Church leaders realized that mass action was unavoidable, and indeed it was soon scheduled for the week of August 3. Shortly thereafter the SACC declared, "we believe that mass action has been necessitated by the deadlock occasioned by the Government's unwillingness to accept genuine democratic processes to take their course."[36] The Church

Leaders then wrote a "Code of Conduct for Mass Protest" for those engaged in protest, the security forces, and the government, in the hope of minimizing violence.

In addition to keeping lines of communication open between the ANC and the government, different church leaders facilitated the period of negotiations in other ways. For example, Archbishop Desmond Tutu held a meeting of black South African leaders at his home in Cape Town in November 1990. This meeting was notable in that it brought together for the first time representatives from liberation movements which had traditionally been rivals, including the ANC, PAC, and AZAPO, with some leaders of the government-created "homelands," who had often been characterized by the liberation movements as collaborators with the apartheid regime. By gathering at Tutu's home, black leaders thereby had a chance to meet for the first time before the CODESA meetings. While Mandela of the ANC attended the meeting, Buthelezi, along with the entire IFP leadership, boycotted it. Nevertheless, the wide-ranging group which did attend exchanged views about preliminary negotiations, in an attempt to present a common position and united front against the government. By meeting's end, delegates had agreed on two important principles: that the dismantling of the homelands should be a goal of a post-apartheid society, and an acknowledgment of the probability of "third force" violence, which included elements of the security forces whose aim in stoking violence was to sabotage the negotiations process.[37] These two agreements went far towards sending a message to the government that black leaders, including homeland leaders, would indeed be united in opposition, and that the government would no longer succeed in a "divide and rule" strategy.

Violence

While church leaders worked furiously to keep lines of communication open during the period of both public and private negotiations, they were also grappling with ways to decrease the rising violence which was proving to be an obstacle to these negotiations. They engaged in a series of activities designed to determine the causes of the violence, to provide their mediating services if possible, and to provide material assistance to the victims of violence. The priority given by church leaders to the issue of violence was voiced by the president of the Methodist Church, Bishop Stanley Mogoba, who stated that "the peace issue is the major issue facing the Churches and . . . everything else is as nothing beside it."[38]

As evidence increasingly indicated the involvement of the government's security forces in the violence, the church leaders initially made repeated appeals to de Klerk to control these forces. They met with de Klerk on the issue of violence four times in the first two years of the 1990s.[39] When it was revealed

in July 1991 that the government was secretly funding the IFP, thereby con-
firming the rumors of the role of the state's security machinery in orchestrating
violence, church leaders immediately issued a statement questioning de Klerk's
integrity and calling for action by the government to restore public faith. This
statement was then followed by individual visits to de Klerk by both Tutu and
Chikane. Finally, a delegation of church leaders, led by the president of the
SACC, Khoza Mgojo, and the president of the SACBC, Wilfred Napier, held
a two-hour meeting with de Klerk, during which they informed him of the
public erosion of confidence in him and his government.[40] By the end of 1992,
church leaders reluctantly realized that appeals to the president were ineffectual,
a realization which led Chikane to declare in December 1992, "I believe now
more than ever before that Mr. de Klerk is a prisoner of the historical evil of
apartheid. That since he is a prisoner of the Generals who know so much about
what he knows, he cannot act against them without bringing about his downfall."[41]

Partly in response to their lack of faith in de Klerk's willingness, or ability,
to stem the violence, and in the aftermath of the public disclosure of state-
funded "third force" violence, church leaders in cooperation with business leaders initiated an independent national peace effort which culminated in the formation of a National Peace Accord (NPA), launched on September 14, 1991.
Its purpose was to counter the "climate of violence" which was quickly en-
gulfing the country.[42] The accord was signed by de Klerk, Mandela, and Buthelezi, along with over twenty trade unions and religious and other civil society
organizations. In the Accord, political, church, and business leaders declared
their intent to seek peace, to use only peaceful means of operations, and to
follow an agreed code of conduct for peace (there were in fact two separate
codes of conduct: one for political parties and one for security forces). The NPA
was intended to provide the basis for the control of violence, and it called for
the creation of Local and Regional Dispute Resolution Committees, which
would be comprised of members from political organizations, churches, trade
unions, business, the police, and the military, and would be coordinated by a
National Peace Secretariat.[43] The National Peace Committee, with representatives from all the major political parties, was co-chaired by Bishop Stanley Mogoba, presiding bishop of the Methodist Church in Southern Africa, and John
Hall, a prominent business leader. The NPA had several shortcomings: it only
had an effect on those who signed it; the committees established by it could
only act on information received; and, most seriously, covert operations therefore fell outside of the NPA's scope. Despite this national effort supported by
groups across the political spectrum, the period following the signing of the
Accord continued to be marred by serious incidents of violence. Over 3,600
people were killed in the year after its launching.[44]

Desperate to arrest the violence, church leaders tried other methods as well.

In April 1992, the Church Leaders Meeting convened an "Emergency Summit on Violence," attended by eighteen predominantly black political organizations and chaired by Archbishop Tutu (at this time Anglican archbishop of Cape Town), Bishop Stanley Mogoba (co-chairperson of the NPA), and Reverend Khoza Mgojo (president of the SACC).[45] While the conference delegates agreed that the government bore primary responsibility for the violence, they admitted that their own political organizations shared responsibility, and committed themselves to holding joint peace rallies and to setting up local reconciliation committees. Another church-sponsored initiative for addressing the violence was monitoring. In October 1991, a consultation was held in Cape Town between the World Council of Churches, its member churches in South Africa, and the SACC. This consultation concluded with a list of proposals for church action, one of which stated that since a strong conviction existed among church members that violence monitoring could not be adequately undertaken by security forces, it was necessary to select and train monitoring teams which would be representative of all major political and community groups, including the churches. Consultation members further felt that the monitoring process should be directed and supervised by an international group with adequate powers to investigate, report, and ensure appropriate action.[46] As a result of this recommendation, in September 1992 the SACC and the SACBC launched an independent church-based monitoring program, called the Ecumenical Monitoring Programme in South Africa (EMPSA). The SACC and SACBC worked with their international partners, the World Council of Churches and the Pontifical Council for Justice and Peace, to bring in international violence monitors through EMPSA's international coordinating office at the WCC in Geneva.[47]

In addition to working as mediators in negotiations and violence, the SACC and SACBC undertook activities which fell under their more traditional roles of church ministry. In early 1990, for example, the SACC and SACBC set up various task forces to deal with issues pertaining to the repatriation of 20,000 political exiles in the wake of the unbanning of political movements.[48] This led to the rise of a new ecumenical experience, with the creation of the National Coordinating Committee for Repatriation (NCCR). Ecumenism was no longer restricted to Christians, since the participation of the World Conference on Religion and Peace (WCRP) brought Hindus, Jews, and Muslims onto the Committee. In addition, the NCCR marked the first time that these church organizations worked directly with liberation movements; the Committee membership was also comprised of representatives of the ANC, the PAC, and AZAPO.[49] Close to 6,000 exiles were assisted in their return by the NCCR before the UN High Commission for Refugees (UNHCR) took over the bulk of the operation in December 1991.[50] Before its dissolution under a cloud of controversy in April 1993, the NCCR had repatriated over 12,000 refugees.[51]

While church leaders were adapting to their new self-identities as concili-
ators, they were not willing to completely forfeit the role they had so painstak-
ingly adopted by the end of the 1980s, that of overt political actors critiquing
the apartheid government. Indeed, in the early years of the 1990s church leaders often found themselves playing both roles at once. In particular, church
leaders were often unequivocal in their critique of the government on the issue
of violence. For example, at its 1992 National Conference held a month after
the Boipatong Massacre and the breakdown of CODESA, the SACC adopted
a resolution whose tone was remarkably similar to the many anti-government
resolutions it passed half a decade earlier. In it the SACC instructed its National
Executive Committee to draw up a plan of action to facilitate (among other
things): disobeying all unjust laws and practices in obedience to God; fasting
and hunger strikes to force the regime to resign; urging church leaders to place
advertisements in their newspapers calling for the resignation of the government; and imposing a moratorium on further talks with the regime and urging
their overseas partners to do likewise.[52] Church leaders also responded harshly
to the revelation in July 1991 of government funding of the IFP. In an address
given in August 1991, Frank Chikane delivered a sharp critique directed against
de Klerk:

> While these revelations gave Mr. de Klerk the opportunity to confess the pain
> and suffering apartheid caused to millions of South Africans, he failed to do
> so. When he was given an opportunity to disclose past covert operations and
> close future operations to start on a new slate, he also failed. When he was
> given an opportunity of dissociating himself from the funding of one party
> to destabilize another, he expressed confidence in those Ministers who author-
> ized these activities. This brings into question the very bona fides of Mr. de
> Klerk himself. . . . Those of us who called him a man of integrity had to swal-
> low our words. . . . [53]

The ecumenical Church Leaders Meeting also took sides with the liberation
movement by unequivocally accusing the government of deliberately stoking
violence. In May 1992 the Church Leaders placed responsibility for the violence
squarely in the lap of the government, declaring:

> We conclude that the minority and illegitimate government had a premedi-
> tated strategy of undermining the influence and effectiveness of the liberation
> movement and their leadership by orchestrating violence in the townships so
> that residents can blame it on the movements. Through this the regime seeks
> to extend its stay in power and to continue imposing schemes which will en-
> trench political power and economic privileges of the minority. It therefore
> manipulates the political playing field by creating an adverse climate for the
> holding of free and fair elections which are to lead to the establishment of a
> democratic South Africa.[54]

In summary, the self-identities of the SACC and the SACBC (along with the Church Leaders Meeting) changed in the first several years of the 1990s. While by the end of the 1980s, both organizations were identifying themselves as overtly political actors dedicated to the removal of the apartheid government, in the early years of the 1990s they identified themselves primarily as conciliating actors, trying to mediate between the various political factions in their negotiations. This identity shift should not be surprising, given that the specific identities church leaders adopt are largely determined by the particular political context in which they find themselves acting. Thus, in the political context of severe repression in the 1980s, the SACC and SACBC identified themselves as taking sides with the goals of the liberation movement in action (albeit not violent) against the government. The mediating identity of the 1990s was similarly a reflection of the political context of the time. The 1990s was marked by decreased levels of overt state repression, with the consequence that the spiraling church/state conflict disappeared.[55] As a result of these two changes, both organizations no longer identified themselves primarily as the church of resistance, but increasingly as the church of conciliation and facilitation. This did not mean, the SACC was quick to point out, that it had stepped out of the political movement; rather, it had "stepped back from the firing line."[56]

Nevertheless, both the SACC and the SACBC continued to demonstrate a willingness to confront the government on various issues. In fact, these organizations often found themselves being asked to play two roles at the same time, a situation which they admitted to finding difficult. This difficulty of adapting to a new self-identity, while still embracing parts of the old, was acknowledged in an editorial in December 1991 in *Ecunews,* the newsmagazine of the SACC: "In the days before February 1990 the lines were clearly drawn. We all knew who we were with and who we were against. The enemy was apartheid and anyone who stood with it and/or sought to benefit from it. That was as clear as the Black and White definition of apartheid itself. That clarity has become smudged and the border line not so easily recognised."[57]

Changing Religious Context

The identities of both the SACC and SACBC were conditioned not only by the changing political context of the 1990s but also by the changing religious context. As described in chapter 4, the overtly political identities both organizations adopted in the 1980s were influenced in part by a new religious discourse which had arisen in South Africa, known as contextual theology. Contextual theology by its very definition must evolve: as the political context changes, so too does the theological response to it. Moreover, religious ideas not only influence the type of actions church organizations undertake, these ideas are themselves continually reinterpreted as a result of these actions. Thus, contextual theologians in the early 1990s were not only interpreting the political changes taking place in South Africa, they were also responding to the new activities of facilitation and mediation in which church organizations were now engaging; and they were soon asking the question, "is it possible for the church to position itself as an acceptable interlocutor by both the liberation movement and those forces that still seek to maintain the status quo, and at the same time maintain its commitment to a prophetic ministry?"[58]

The Evolution of a New Identity

South African church leaders and theologians knew that the self-identities that some activist Christians and organizations had adopted—which required them to not only support nonviolent acts of civil disobedience to force the apartheid regime to the negotiating table, but to actually lead these campaigns—were no longer appropriate. Now that this regime was indeed approaching the table, a new theological interpretation of the role of the churches was necessary. But what should this role be? It would not be an exaggeration to state that in the first years of the 1990s, churches and ecumenical organizations in South Africa were faced with a profound theological identity crisis. Church leader after church leader asked the question, and conference after conference was held with variations on one theme: What should the role of churches be in the new political context? The religious context of the early 1990s was characterized by soul-searching debates around this question. Thus, active engagement in the process of helping to create a conducive climate for negotiations took place hand in hand with an active process of theological reflection.

The question was asked repeatedly and phrased in a variety of ways. Some organizations began to reflect on these issues immediately. For example, four months after de Klerk's speech and Mandela's release, the SACC devoted its 1990 National Conference to an examination of how to redefine its role after the high political profile it had assumed in the past several years. The outgoing president of the SACC, Bishop Manas Buthelezi, presented his view of the future role of the organization to Conference delegates. While churches must reassess their role as being the voice of the voiceless, Buthelezi argued, they must not give up their role as society's conscience: "The prophetic ministry within the church is not purely an incident of apartheid. We believe that the church is the watchdog of whoever is a victim of oppression. As long as human beings are human beings there will be no perfection."[59]

Many of the theological ideas concerning the role of the churches during the 1980s had originated in the Institute for Contextual Theology, and this organization too was forced to reflect on its role. How should contextual theologians now interpret the new "signs of the times?" Smangaliso Mkhatshwa, the ICT's General Secretary during the early 1990s, summed up the identity crisis in which his organization found itself: "one detects some bewilderment and an obvious confusion about how to participate in the present race for the future."[60] While the new situation may pose "problems," Mkhatshwa admitted, he also felt that it provided churches with new opportunities: "We have said over and over again that theology has a role in social reconstruction programmes. We cannot support the struggle for justice and liberation and then dump all social reconstruction into the laps of political organisations! It is tantamount to starting to build a house and then abandoning it before completion."[61] The ICT interpreted the changes of February 1990 in a pamphlet published the following month entitled, "The Release of Nelson Mandela: Reading the Signs of Our Times." The ICT made it clear that while one phase of the liberation struggle may have ended, the struggle was far from over; rather, it had simply entered a new phase: "While the release of Mandela is filled with promise, it also spells out the need for a long and arduous struggle to bring about the structures necessary for a non-racial and democratic society."[62] The ICT continued to focus on the issue of a continued struggle, albeit in a different form, stating, "There is a need for the church to ensure that every step towards the process of negotiations is a moment of struggle. Come the day of negotiations, come the day of intensified struggle. The church must contribute in making negotiations another instrument of struggle in the hands of the oppressed."[63] A few months later, like the SACC, the ICT devoted its 1990 Annual General Meeting to the theme, "The Role of Christians in the Present Political Crisis in South Africa." Again, Mkhatshwa spoke on the need to reflect on its changing identity: "I believe that most of us have come here in order to do a critical theological reflection on the present socio-political crisis in South Africa as well as to identify the responsibility of ICT in this crisis."[64] And again, Mkhatshwa cautioned participants not to think that their work was finished now that apartheid was coming to a close: "our experience is that ICT has more work today than at any other time before. If we take contextual theology seriously, we must realise that our responsibility is immense."[65]

In addition to organizational reflection, individual church leaders demonstrated that they, too, were wrestling with the question of what their new roles should be. For example, church leaders acknowledged at a November 1991 Church Leaders Meeting that there were going to be "many gray areas about where to go, which debates to join, what partners to choose in projects, and about accepting or not accepting invitations."[66] At a later meeting, one church leader expressed the fear that churches might simply not know how to act in the absence of political crises: "If all the residents of Alexandra township were about to be relocated, we would know exactly what to do. But we haven't a clue how to make our people Christian."[67] Archbishop Tutu also joined the debate. Recognizing that a changed political context often translates into new self-identities, he made it clear that in the new political situation his role as religious leader would change: "I am going to keep a lower profile. We had to fulfill a role and I kept saying that I was an interim leader, because our real leaders were either in jail or in exile. Now that we are normalising the political process in this country, and our leaders are out, I will not have to be as prominent, doing things which in a normal country you would not be doing."[68] He was adamant, however, that he would continue to "be the voice of those who will be marginalised and voiceless in new dispensations, when [I] may have to speak critically against those whom we championed earlier." Churches could not, he warned, afford to "be co-opted or to become this or that party at prayer."[69] Yet another prominent theologian of the 1980s, Charles Villa-Vicencio, added his voice to the identity debate: "While hitherto our primary responsibility has been to say 'No' to apartheid and all related forms of oppression, our task is to begin to say 'Yes' to opportunities of renewal, without losing the right to say 'No' when necessary."[70]

Even non-religious leaders offered their opinions on the appropriate role of churches. In a December 1992 address, Nelson Mandela made reference to the identity crisis in the church, stating: "Some have argued that after February 2, 1990 the church took a little lonely walk in search of an identity and a role." Mandela continued by attempting to answer the question of the role of the church: "the church in South Africa cannot afford a retreat to the coziness of the sanctuary, tempting as it may be in these confusing and challenging times. The church in our country has no option but to join other agents of change and transformation in the difficult task of acting as a midwife to the birth of our democracy. . . ."[71]

The debate about the role of the churches in the 1990s was soon sharpened and concentrated on one question: Could the churches successfully be both mediators and prophets at the same time? This, according to John Lamola, head of the SACC's Department of Justice and Social Ministries (formerly Division of Justice and Reconciliation)—which traditionally provided a theological rationale for the activities undertaken by the SACC—was at the heart of the identity crisis facing theologians and churches. According to Lamola:

> The practice of the church is torn apart by a serious tension of theological practice. This tension which threatens to paralyse the ministry of the Church is the tension between a compulsion to dispense a prophetic ministry of condemning nefarious political attitudes which obstruct and frustrate the creation of democratic dispensation, while at the same time the Church realizes the urgent need to bring the end of the current problem of violence by providing itself as a mechanism for political dialogue and conflict resolution. This occasions a tension between two apparently irreconcilable mythological

frameworks of a prophetic theology on the one hand, and a theology of mediation on the other.[72]

Sr. Margaret Kelly, Secretary of the SACBC's Justice and Peace Commission (the SACBC's equivalent of Lamola's position at the SACC), acknowledged that the Catholic bishops too felt the tension of being pulled in two directions: "The Catholic Church [has] felt itself pulled between the roles of the prophet who denounces evil and the servant who becomes involved in attempts to build a good society as a way of building the kingdom of God."[73]

Despite this tension, Lamola did not believe the crisis was insurmountable or that both roles were necessarily mutually exclusive. The SACC, he argued, could indeed play both roles at once, as long as it executed its ministry in such a way that "where mediation is called upon, it shall mediate as a prophet, and where a prophetic ministry is called into place, it shall prophesy as a mediator."[74] This, according to Lamola, could be defined as playing the role of facilitator, a role which would be fraught with more problems and challenges than undertaking either mediation or prophetic critique alone, for it took tremendous skill to "know when to mediate and when to condemn and call for repentance."[75] Frank Chikane also expressed his belief that the SACC and churches could successfully simultaneously mediate and take sides, as long as they mediated from the proper perspective. Chikane identified three forms of mediation: from a position of power, from a position of neutrality, and from a position of commitment to justice. As long as churches mediated from this last position, they could still fulfill the gospel imperative of working for the poor and oppressed while at the same time facilitating reconciliation between all groups.[76] Albert Nolan of the ICT tended to agree with Lamola and Chikane, but he was somewhat more cautious about the mediating role of the church, arguing, "the role of the church is to look very carefully and analyze the nature of the conflict in relation to what is right and what is wrong before we jump in as the professional mediators just because there is a conflict around. We are not professional mediators."[77]

The "mediation versus prophesy" debate made explicit an issue which was increasingly troubling to many theologians and church leaders in South Africa: the fear that churches might forfeit the critical stance of taking sides with the poor and oppressed that they had come to adopt as part of their self-identities by the late 1980s. In other words, some religious leaders feared that the newly constituted self-identities of churches and ecumenical organizations would no longer be informed by the ideas coming from contextual theology, and that the churches would revert back to the more traditional identity associated with what the Kairos Document had labeled "church theology." Such a possibility existed, according to theologian James Cochrane, because "the prophetic role of the Church is always more fragile, more difficult to hold together and more

difficult to promote than its pastoral and priestly role."[78] Cochrane noted that
contextual theology was in a state of crisis, not only because of the promise of
a gradual demise of racial injustice, but because of changes in the global political context which coincided with changes in South African domestic politics.
Specifically, many of the ideas which emanated from this theological perspective
were linked with socialism, a worldview which seemed to lose legitimacy in the
1990s. Cochrane warned, "If it is unable to deepen and adapt its own message
and task, prophetic theology will become marginalised—and for a time it might
even die out."[79] Moreover, Cochrane noted that in the wake of the unbanning
of organizations and the opening up of the political process, activist Christian
groups such as those in the Standing for the Truth Campaign lost some direction which had been gained in the time of the silencing of opposition. Finally,
the newly sanctioned public activity of the liberation movements meant the loss
of church activists who had shifted to straightforward political work, with the
result that "the prophetic elements of the church have had an already weak
organizational infrastructure further weakened, in respect of resources, structured programmes and available, skilled people."[80]

Another theologian greatly concerned with the potential marginalization
of the influence of contextual theology was Charles Villa-Vicencio, who argued
that "history suggests that resistance theology more often than not surren-
ders its prophetic task, becoming yet another legitimating theology."[81] Villa-
Vicencio warned against the retraction of churches from the political sphere:
"to leave politics to the politicians is as inherently dangerous as it is to reduce
theology to a specific political ideology that ultimately results in a marriage
between church and state. The role of the church not only in nations facing
reconstruction, but also in nations engaged in the process of continuing renewal and reform, is of significant theological and political importance."[82]
Villa-Vicencio, in fact, drew parallels with the fate of resistance theology,
known as the Confessing Church Movement, in post–World War II Germany
and issued a clear warning that such an outcome not be allowed to occur in
South Africa. Villa-Vicencio concluded that the Confessing Church Movement
had been "bound together primarily by a need to counter a common enemy.
When Hitler no longer rendered the church this service, it collapsed and was
absorbed into the all-encompassing structures of a new brand of liberal Christianity not easily distinguishable from the dominant culture of post-war Germany."[83] The problem, as Villa-Vicencio saw it, is that a theology useful in
resistance is not always an equally useful instrument in reconstruction. Albert
Nolan was a third theologian who feared the future marginalization of the
theology to which he had devoted his life work. Churches were in danger of
losing the prophetic dimension of their ministry, Nolan claimed, because they
had been prophetic in a superficial way, protesting racism only. Because racism
had been deemed the true evil in apartheid, it was easy for churches to be pro-

phetic. However, Nolan predicted, it would be far more difficult for churches to take courageous stances about other evils such as economic injustices.[84] Beyers Naudé, one of the seminal influences in contextual theology in the 1970s and 1980s, was similarly alarmed about its future: churches and their leaders, Naudé ventured, seemed to be overwhelmed by the complexity of the transition and paralyzed by feelings of helplessness and incompetence. In this situation, many had simply withdrawn to occupy themselves mainly with church affairs, a behavior which he found intolerable. Why, Naudé wanted to know, "were Christians afraid to speak out against the perpetrators of violence and against the government 'for its obvious hypocrisy?' Why were clergy failing to 'preach from every pulpit in the country against the exploitation of the poor?'"[85]

Church leaders, especially in the SACC, also worried that the influence of contextual theology might be waning. Frank Chikane warned member churches to be careful in interpreting the political events in the early 1990s and to be vigilant against losing the contextual edge:

> At times it seems as if the church has interpreted the signs of the times to mean that peace is permanently here and justice prevails. The Church seems to believe de Klerk when he says apartheid has gone. Related to this is the development of a creeping trend of neutrality within the Church and a common misunderstanding that now the organisations of the oppressed have been unbanned, the struggle can be left to them and the Church can retreat to the Sanctuary. . . . The Church exists in a social context and must always seek to remain relevant to that social context no matter how it changes.[86]

John Lamola, arguably the SACC's "theologian in residence" (a role Wolfram Kistner had played as head of the Department of Justice and Reconciliation throughout the 1980s), was even more forceful in his expression of the crisis of contextual theology: "The greatest challenge facing this county is the dearth of theology. We owe SA [South Africa] a good theology. We owe SA a Liberation Theology. We owe SA a theological praxis which will demonstrate where we stand as Christians. The churches all along called for Christian action, criticising armed struggle. Now it is the era of mass action, peaceful action. The church is not there!"[87] Not surprisingly, the ICT, whose very existence revolved around the dissemination of contextual theology, had much to say about what it discerned as a fading influence of these ideas: "An increasing source of concern to ICT members is that of 'neutrality.' While neutrality may be assumed for the laudable role of reconciliation, alternative motives for this strategy [are that] churches want to play it safe and not be seen flirting with socialism. While emphasis is often enough given to charity and relief work, the preaching of justice is beginning to get short shrift."[88]

The issue of the sidelining of contextual theology came to the fore early in the 1990s, when several contextual theologians reacted critically to a major religious event: the National Conference of Church Leaders, held in the town of Rustenburg in November 1990.[89] The purpose of the conference was to attempt to set aside doctrinal issues in a search for a united Christian witness in a changing South Africa, in an effort to create a climate conducive to negotiations and reconciliation. The Rustenburg Conference (as it was called) was a momentous event in the religious history of South Africa. It brought together the broadest range of black and white church leaders ever to convene in South Africa. South Africans were represented by some 230 people from eighty denominations and forty organizations, representing a cross-section of South Africa's religious life.[90] The Rustenburg Conference will be remembered primarily for various confessions of guilt, expressed in the historic *Rustenburg Declaration* adopted by majority vote.[91] Confessions were made from many perspectives, including from those who actively supported apartheid, those who had taken a neutral stance, and those who had condemned it but had not adequately resisted it. Even the victims of apartheid confessed that they had failed in many ways.[92] The Declaration concluded with a call to the government to join in a public confession of guilt and to issue a statement of repentance for wrongs perpetrated over the years.

The Rustenburg Declaration was lauded as an extraordinary document, and many were thus surprised when several contextual theologians reacted somewhat critically to it. James Cochrane, for example, criticized the conference for its "centrist" tendencies, in which participants attempted to accept the "morality of the center" and therefore arrive at a "lowest common denominator" position vis-à vis each other and the state. This, according to Cochrane, would sideline all forms of contextual theology, making them marginal to the "moral majority" within the Christian church. Therefore, "the danger of a new Magisterium of churches who hold sway over the minds and hearts of their members along the lines of minimal prophecy and maximal harmony is great. . . . "[93] Cochrane was particularly skeptical of the rapidity with which the various church groups represented at Rustenburg embraced the call to repentance. He argued that the desire to honor repentance (no matter how worthy a goal) was likely to cover over still existing political and economic agendas previously known to be incompatible. The alliance of formerly anti-apartheid religious organizations with those which had previously exhibited moderation and conservatism, in the desire to establish some common ground for debate and to create some space for goodwill, would mean, Cochrane feared, that these formerly activist organizations would opt for the "lowest common denominator" ethic, which would translate into a desire to return to their "real jobs" of servicing the religious life of members in a secularized state. Cochrane strongly rejected this approach, arguing that "the necessity of confrontation must be reasserted over and against cheap reconciliation."[94] In the end, Cochrane argued, the Rustenburg

Declaration was simply an updated, more liberal, and more comfortable version of the old "church theology" which the Kairos Document had so vigorously warned against. The statement did not represent genuine prophetic theology in the Kairos tradition.[95] The type of reconciliation called for at Rustenburg was cheap, Cochrane argued, because there was little evidence that conservative and right-wing churches or church groups had shifted much in terms of their historic interests.[96] Cochrane worried about the impact of statements such as Rustenburg's on previously radical organizations, such as the SACC: "the effect of [the Rustenburg Conference] on a body such as the South African Council of Churches in terms of public legitimacy is to shift its prophetic position to the margins. . . . " Cochrane was pessimistic, concluding that "the probability [is high] that the prophetic tradition within South African churches will be marginalized as a consensus of the middle ground takes over to legitimate the transformation of South African society."[97] Beyers Naudé also recognized the potential danger for contextual theology implicit in the Rustenburg Declaration. Naudé echoed Cochrane's concern about "cheap reconciliation": "There is a real danger that in our urgent longing to achieve united witness, we may tend simply to deny or ignore these differences or try to paper them over for the sake of reaching an acceptable compromise. Such action would be a grave mistake: it will not lead us to the truth, it will not help us to remove deep-rooted injustices, and it will not pave the way for lasting reconciliation and peace."[98]

Various moments of reflection reveal how the "universe of religious discourse" evolved in the early years of the decade, and how the predominant theological activity during this period was a search for a new theological paradigm and new self-identities. Theological reflection began even before the first major religious conference, the Rustenburg Conference. In October 1990, the ICT held its own conference in preparation for Rustenburg, entitled "A New Kairos: What Is at Stake for the People of South Africa?" At this conference, theologians such as Albert Nolan and James Cochrane began to voice concern over the potential waning of contextual theology's influence. In response to this concern, the ICT issued a public message to the delegates to the upcoming Rustenburg conference, warning them that there could be no reconciliation without justice: "Identity with and supporting the call of the oppressed is the meaning of reconciliation. There is no cheap grace here, there is no easy repentance and hollow forgiveness. There is a cost to discipleship in the face of serious sin and evil, and this cost is the only basis of any really meaningful practice of reconciliation. Until there is justice, no reconciliation is possible."[99] The ICT recognized, therefore, that it would be relatively easy to offer words of repentance while the causes of the need to repent remained in place, and it was this possibility to which James Cochrane and others reacted critically. Thus, one of the first issues that theologians confronted was that of reconciliation and repentance. The debates surrounding this issue, brought to the fore at Rustenburg and the ICT's preparatory conference, were to take on a nationwide character in a few short years with the promulgation by the new government of the Truth and Reconciliation Commission (TRC). Many of the debates which took place throughout South Africa about the TRC were simply secular versions of theological discussions about the need for confession and penance before genuine reconciliation could be achieved.

If debates surrounding the acts of confession at Rustenburg in November 1990 marked the first moment of theological reflection in South Africa, the second was marked by a World Council of Churches visit to South Africa in October 1991, dubbed "Cottesloe II," in reference to the fact that it was the first time a WCC delegation had met with church leaders on South African soil since the Cottesloe Consultation of 1960.[100] An international ecumenical conference was organized in Cape Town to coincide with the pastoral visit of Dr. Emilio Castro, General Secretary of the WCC. The conference was entitled "Towards an Ecumenical Agenda for a Changing South Africa," and provided the occasion for a rigorous ecumenical review of the unfolding situation and for a program of action to guide the churches in South Africa and the ecumenical movement internationally in responding to the situation. The delegates at the Cape Town Consultation released an impressive program of action,[101] but the major theological issue was the marginalization of contextual theology. Specifically, the questions had to be asked of how deep the roots of contextual theology had ever been, and whether they were indeed deep enough to challenge Christians to action against injustice, now that the focal point of racism was apparently disappearing. Charles Villa-Vicencio recognized the sad reality: "to be sure, the Cape Town Statement addressed all the right issues—violence, reconciliation, women, youth, amnesty for political prisoners, sanctions, the political economy, the need for cultural pluralism, and the importance of spiritual renewal. But . . . the 'fire in the belly' was gone."[102] A core issue facing contextual theology in the 1990s was thus identified: how to ensure that impressive ecumenical statements filtered down to the grass roots so that they might inspire churchgoers to move beyond their weekly church services to actively working towards checking political violence and joining in secular debates about appropriate public policies.[103]

In an effort to address the concerns about the waning influence of contextual theology, the SACC General Secretary convened a meeting in January 1992 in an attempt to recover this voice. The conference, entitled "A Theological Colloquium on the Implication of Current Political Developments on the Mission of the Church," represented a third moment of theological reflection. The colloquium's final statement, which came to be known as the "Koinonia Minute," warned that the "Church has to strenuously guard against being caught into a paralysis of being afraid to offend some side of the divergence, thus compromising its obligation to prophetic witness."[104] Theologically, perhaps the most important contribution of the Minute was its economic emphasis. The critical question the colloquium sought to address was: "What does it mean to be on the side of the economically poor and socio-politically marginalized within the CODESA context?"[105] South African theologians were beginning to move beyond an emphasis on the injustices of the apartheid system to address the injustices of a capitalist-based society, whether apartheid or post-apartheid. Colloquium participants reiterated the Cape Town Statement's assertion that the failure of Eastern European socialism was not a vindication of Western free-market capitalism, since neither system had adequately met the needs of the poor. Contextual theology was thus evolving, and it became clear that economic justice was going to become a focal point in the post-negotiations period.

Theological evolution was again evident at an August 1992 "Emergency Conference on the Current Situation," convened by the ICT. At this conference, Albert Nolan made reference to an issue which would soon evolve into a major initiative in post-apartheid contextual theology: the role of churches in reconstruction and nation building. Nolan stated, "We have all been talking about the fact that for a long time we have protested, we have criticised, we have condemned. But now we have to begin the positive side of the process, of structuring something, or building a nation and building a society."[106] In the area of reconstruction, Nolan felt that churches should play a supportive role, rather than actively engaging in building houses or opening new schools, or "getting into things which are the business of other agencies, the business of the state." A more appropriate role for the church in reconstruction would be to critically assess new development projects, and to withhold support for those which were not beneficial to the poor.[107]

Theological evolution did not take place only in the pre-1994 period. Theologians insisted that contextual theology had a role to play in post-apartheid South Africa. This became evident at an ICT conference entitled "Kairos '95: At the Threshold of Jubilee," held to celebrate the tenth anniversary of the publication of the Kairos Document. The stated purpose of the conference was to "advance the quality of the methodology of doing contextual theology and its prophetic tradition."[108] Again, the political context had changed. Negotiations had ended, and free and fair elections had resulted in an ANC-dominated Government of National Unity. The issues focused on at the Kairos Conference reflected the political times. No longer was contextual theology focused on the issue of the legitimacy of the state—conference participants readily acknowledged that the present government was legitimate. However, this did not mean that contextual theology was no longer relevant. Specifically, the conference concentrated on three issues: inadequacies in the new government, the evils of the market economy, and a discussion of traditional authority. On the issue of problems with the new government, the conference concluded that "there is a

perception that the government's priorities are upside down. This is exacer-
bated by what seems to be people in government who are concentrating on
their own enrichment first. Their quality of life has changed drastically for the
better. The quality of life for the majority of people is the same. The church
needs to help government to prioritise."[109] On the issue of traditional authority,
the conference noted that "traditional authority has not shown any capacity to
shed its undemocratic tenets that contradict the spirit of the new order. . . . IF
adequately empowered and properly harnessed, traditional structures could be
used to ensure that we advance into the future with all land disputes laid to
rest forever. But all caution should be taken not to reverse the gains of our
struggle for democracy."[110] The conference, however, devoted most of its energy to a discussion of economic justice, stating, "the Kairos Conference pleads
with the Government of National Unity to protect its people from the effects
of developed and liberalised trade. The influence of Bretton Woods institutions
on the future social policies of the new government must be kept to the minimum."[111] Conference participants argued that the growth-based market model
had failed as a panacea for social and economic injustice. In fact, it had only
aggravated the crisis of the poor, by leading to greater concentration of economic, political, and technological power, and it was, therefore, an unsuitable
model for organizing the South African economy.

The Content of New Contextual Theologies

Much of the theological activity of the early 1990s thus consisted of a
reactive process, with theologians issuing dire warnings against the potential
loss of contextual theology's influence. At the same time, however, these theologians were actively engaged in producing new theological ideas. Theologizing
was, therefore, both a reactive and a proactive activity. What, then, were new
theological ideas? Two contributions of the 1990s were a theology of reconstruction and a theology of economic justice. Both these ideological innova-
tions involved a search for new symbols.

The primary symbol of contextual theology in the 1980s was the biblical story of the Exodus, which was used to guide the churches in the political context of struggling for liberation. Contextualizing the gospel to the new
South Africa meant taking up new themes, with accompanying new symbols.
Several biblical metaphors emerged, including the wilderness experience before
entering the promised land, the exile period prior to rebuilding Jerusalem, and
the return of the Babylonian exiles in the post-exilic period.[112] The period from
1990 through 1994 was often compared with that of wandering through the
wilderness after the crossing of the Red Sea. As Beyers Naudé explained, the
journey through the desert was rife with analogies for the South African transitional period.[113] Post-liberation theology also looked to the post-exilic expe-

rience, when the Israelites returned from Babylon to begin the task of reconstructing Jerusalem. This is a particularly potent symbol in South Africa, theologian Charles Villa-Vicencio argued, because the society that emerged in Jerusalem was almost as repressive as the one it replaced. This should serve as a warning to South Africans not to make similar "post-exilic" mistakes.[114] Moreover, the post-exilic metaphor seemed appropriate in the face of tens of thousands of exiles returning to South Africa, some after close to forty years in exile.

Coinciding with the search for new biblical metaphors was the reorientation of the church from "the negative to the positive," or to some mixture thereof. Villa-Vicencio stated the issue succinctly: "Theology has never got the relationship between saying 'No' and saying 'Yes' correct. It tends either to be part of the resistance process (saying 'No') or to provide religious legitimation of the status quo (saying 'Yes')."[115] The question for Villa-Vicencio and others was whether, in the new political context of reconstruction in the post-apartheid era, contextual theology could make the shift from resistance to reconstruction. The need to transform itself from the negative to the positive church required, according to Villa-Vicencio, a new guiding theology, one which he termed a "theology of reconstruction," which would focus on nation-building in South Africa and the promotion of human rights.

In this new liberatory theology, resistance is no longer the major type of activity required of the churches. Rather, the central task is "theopolitical responsibility," which includes both confronting the new state when necessary and encouraging programs of hope and renewal.[116] In recognition of the new political context, in which South Africa has suddenly found itself again a player in the world arena, reading the "signs of the time" in this new theology means taking into account not only national conditions but international ones as well. Nation-building theology, Villa-Vicencio argued, has to pose tough and sometimes uncomfortable questions about the global economy and international alliances, in addition to reading the national political context, which consists of a country torn apart by generations of race, gender, and class divisions.[117] Villa-Vicencio's "theology of reconstruction" clearly falls within the genre of contextual theologies, in which reflection begins from within a particular context. It emphasizes biblical exegesis, the imperative of interpreting the gospel from the perspective of the poor (which in the new South African context means increasingly not only racial but also economic justice), and a methodology which includes a heavy reliance on social analysis. In the political context of nation-building under the GNU, a theology of reconstruction must necessarily be remedial and compensatory, with a special responsibility of righting past wrongs and healing old abuses. In South Africa, this means lending theological support to efforts at affirmative action, constitutionalism, human rights, freedom of conscience, and a just political economy—with the constant goal of prioritizing those who had been marginalized as a result of past discriminatory laws and practices.[118] In this situation, churches must constantly evaluate their position vis-à-vis support and criticism of the state. This is, in many ways, a more challenging place for the church to be located than when its task had simply been to criticize the apartheid state. As Villa-Vicencio states, "in some situations the 'No' will need to be bold and unequivocal. In others the 'Yes' will need to be decisive and without compromise. In most cases, however, concrete proposals, social programmes and actions involve neither an unqualified 'No' nor an uncompromising 'Yes.'"[119] Thus, even in the 1990s, when even the most radical churches are apt to be located "on the side of the rulers," ministering to a government committed to promoting social justice, they must always do so in solidarity with the poorest members of society. In contextualizing the gospel to South Africa of the 1990s, the theology of reconstruction argues that the essential requirements for a decent human living, such as housing, a living wage, education, and human rights, are integral to fulfilling the vision of God's rule on earth.[120] In the particular social context of post-1994 South Africa, the ideas receiving most attention in this new contextual theology include an emphasis on human rights (including first-, second-, and third-generation rights);[121] the insistence on political and economic democracy; preference for the provision of the basic necessities as opposed to the absolute protection of all property rights; and a concern for ecological destruction.[122]

As the issue of racial discrimination began to fade in the post-election period, it was superseded by a concern over economic discrimination. Emerging alongside, and in fact overlapping with, the theology of reconstruction was another theological innovation in the 1990s: a theology of economic justice. One theme in particular has dominated the search for economic justice: a rejection of Western industrialized nations' vision of economic development, dominated by free-market capitalism. The prevailing international economic order has been critiqued time and again by theologians in South Africa. Frank Chikane, for example, argued in 1995 that in contrast to the theory of comparative advantage, which suggests that all people benefit when economies are open to use their comparative advantage to increase wealth in the world, the reality is that there is a "comparably unequal advantage," which perpetuates the relations of inequality. As long as there is a monopoly of knowledge, skill, technology, and communications by the Western world, the gap will continue to grow between the poor and the rich in the world. The true Kairos facing churches in South Africa, according to Chikane, is to fight the temptation to give in to the seemingly natural order of comparative advantage. Chikane states: "Giving in to the logic of the system—which will be our greatest temptation—will mean that our struggle for the liberation of our country will have been in vain."[123] Chikane subsequently issued a challenge to the churches not to be a captive of the worldwide economic status quo and to force South Africa's leaders to deliver a different system. Chikane set out the mission of the church in this regard: "We do not wait for the leaders to deliver but we cause them to deliver. In this mission we do not look upon the leadership to save us from the forces of injustice and darkness, but we engage in a struggle to 'save' the leadership from being consumed by the system."[124]

The theological emphasis on economic justice was accompanied by both global and South African debates on investments in a post-apartheid South Africa. The ICT felt helpless, it said, because it realized that the GNU was in fact powerless to control economic outcomes in South Africa in the face of multinational corporations and international financial institutions, which were accountable to none but themselves.[125] To counter this feeling of helplessness and to prevent investment which failed to appreciate South Africa's social history, the SACC, SACBC, and ICT convened a conference in February 1992 to address ethical principles and priorities which they felt should inform investment in post-sanctions South Africa. The result of the conference was a Code for Ethical Investment and Corporate Conduct, which these religious organizations hoped would be used by investing countries and companies as guidelines for ethical investment. The Code of Conduct included several components, including a commitment to affirmative action to advance the position of disadvantaged communities, especially black people and women; the obligation of companies to respect the rights of workers, especially the right to union representation; and the responsibility to invest in ways which responded to the country's most urgent needs and social priorities, such as the creation of maximum employment and housing.[126] The Code of Conduct was made available to business leaders both inside and outside South Africa, who were asked to commit themselves to the standards of behavior proscribed therein.

The Impact of New Ideas

Theological innovation in the 1990s sometimes occurred inside the structures of the SACC and SACBC, just as in the 1980s. Often, however, new ideas originated outside of these structures, and it should not simply be assumed that they filtered through these organizations. Evidence does exist, however, that both the SACC and SACBC were being influenced by new religious insights, and that their self-identities were being affected by the evolving religious context as well as by the changing political context. As a result, theological evolution was reflected in the actions of both.

In the early 1990s, the SACC's Department of Justice and Social Ministries (formerly Division of Justice and Reconciliation) produced a set of affirmations concerning the mission and thrust of work that the Council as a whole would undertake in the period of transition. In the new political context, the SACC acknowledged that it had to redefine its identity as "the voice of the voiceless," and would instead adopt the new self-identity of standing in critical solidarity with the former liberation movements now turned negotiators, and with any post-apartheid government. While it would maintain a critical distance from the activities of political parties, the SACC would emphatically *not* remain impartial; rather, it would actively take sides with those negotiating on the side of justice. Flowing from these affirmations, and under the initiative of its General Secretary, the SACC devised for itself a new "Programme of Action," in which it committed itself to work for the end of violence; to maintain a vigilant monitoring of the negotiation process; to work for a climate of freedom and respect for human rights; and to work for the "empowerment of the public." To carry out this new program of action, the SACC established broad-based task groups on economic matters, political monitoring of the negotiations process, violence, and education for democracy.[127] The SACC's insistence on maintaining a position of solidarity with the poor is an indication that the self-identity it chose for itself in the 1990s was one which continued to be influenced by the ideas of contextual theology. Strains of Villa-Vicencio's "theology of reconstruction" could be discerned in Frank Chikane's address to the SACC's 1993 National Conference, in which he offered his vision of the SACC's new role: "Now that the liberation movements have been unbanned and the leaders back, there is no need to speak on their behalf. . . . [However], we will remain as the conscience of the new society critically supporting the envisaged new order when it does justice, and prophetically condemning it should it fail to pursue the justice of God."[128]

An examination of SACBC activity during the same period reveals that it too continued to be influenced by the ideas stemming from contextual theology. A series of pastoral letters issued by the Catholic bishops in the early 1990s indicates that they were not immune to changes occurring in the larger religious context. For example, in a January 1992 pastoral letter entitled "A Call to Build a New South Africa," the bishops stated, "we urgently need a new economic order as well as a new political one. . . . The vision must aim at meeting our two urgent needs: greater economic growth and fairer distribution of wealth." The prevailing economic situation in South Africa was condemned as sinful, as was the evil of consumerism, which led the bishops to remind Catholics of Jesus's words: "You cannot serve both God and money."[129]

Both organizations also reacted to religious developments in South Africa which were occurring outside of their structures. Although, as noted above, the Rustenburg Declaration was criticized by many in the contextual theology movement, it did represent theological evolution in South Africa, and its sections on Affirmations, Restitution, and Commitment to Action did in fact contain prophetic elements; thus, the SACC and SACBC response to it can be seen as an indicator that these two organizations were attempting to respond to the changing religious times. The SACC leadership played a dominant role in organizing the Rustenburg Conference (Frank Chikane was in fact one of its co-conveners). One can perhaps safely infer, then, that the theological ideas contained in the conference's final Declaration—specifically the ideas contained in the Commitment to Action—were embraced by the SACC.[130] Interestingly, the SACC's official response to the Rustenburg Declaration indicates that the organization was indeed well aware of the theological debates of the day. At its 1991 National Conference, an SACC resolution warned that "the confession of guilt may neutralise the prophetic witness of the Church, [and] the confession of guilt may displace the commitment to a non-racial, democratic and just South Africa as the basis for Christian witness and co-operation." In view of these possibilities, the National Conference did not adopt the Declaration as official policy, and rather resolved to "receive the *Rustenburg Declaration* and refer it to its member churches for action."[131] The SACBC firmly supported the Rustenburg Declaration at its plenary session meeting of January 1991, at which they issued a pastoral letter entitled "*Rerum Novarum* and Its Implications for Negotiations in South Africa."[132] In it, the bishops confessed the Catholic Church's guilt.[133]

Despite the fact that both the SACC and SACBC showed signs of being influenced by the continually evolving ideas coming from contextual theology, the SACBC continued a trend which had been evident throughout the 1980s: the bishops remained more cautious in their statements and actions than the leadership of the SACC. They were again quick to assert that they did not possess competency to make political judgments, and they were content to let the newly unbanned political organizations step back into the forefront of speaking for the people. Consequently, the SACBC relinquished its overtly political self-identity earlier than did the SACC. For example, in the drafting stage of the Pastoral Letter on the Centenary of *Rerum Novarum,* the term "constituent assembly" was debated for a considerable length of time. Some bishops argued that it was a political term which could be interpreted as taking sides and favoring particular groups, particularly the ANC. Its use might therefore alienate conservative and even moderate Catholic lay members, and the term should consequently not be used. Others argued that it was crucial that the term be maintained, and the final letter contained the following rather innocuous sentence: "the normal way to achieve [change] is through a gathering of representatives of all the people of a country to work out a constitution. There would have to be negotiations about how to organize the election of such a constituent assembly. . . . "[134] In contrast, the SACC officially adopted a resolution in support of a constituent assembly at its 1990 National Conference.[135] This voluntary relinquishment by the SACBC of its role as voice of the voiceless at an earlier stage than the SACC should not be surprising, given that the self-identity of overt political actor had never been as fully consolidated in the SACBC as it had been in the SACC. This speedy withdrawal from addressing political issues was evident in several instances, with the issue of sanctions being arguably the most pronounced.

As noted in chapter 3, the SACBC had maintained a more cautious stance on the issues of sanctions throughout the 1980s than the SACC.[136] Not surprisingly, when the debate turned towards lifting these sanctions, the SACBC weighed in on the side of ending them at an earlier date than did the SACC. The SACC followed the position of the OAU's Harare Declaration, subsequently adopted by the Commonwealth and the United Nations, which related progress made in dismantling apartheid to the easing of sanctions. To this end, as early as 1990 the SACC espoused the concept of "the irreversibility of change," which stated that pressure on South Africa could only be lifted when the dismantling of apartheid had reached an irreversible stage. The SACC's 1990 National Conference adopted a definition of irreversibility which stated that the dismantling of apartheid would become irreversible only when a constituent assembly had been created and the existing apartheid legislative structures had had their sovereign power removed, for as long as power was vested in those structures, it would require a simple majority of the minority in Parliament to reverse the progress that had thus far been made. In his address to the Conference, Frank Chikane contended that "irreversibility can only be arrived at when the white minority cannot legally reverse the process of the current status quo through the present unrepresentative legislative structures."[137] In June 1991, the government repealed several of the traditional "pillars of apartheid," including the Land Act, the Groups Areas Act, and the Population Registration Act. The government may have expected these changes to result in the lifting of sanctions, and in fact many countries did begin to seriously review their sanctions position. The United States lifted sanctions immediately. The SACC, however, argued that the changes were insufficient. While the SACC welcomed the changes, Chikane told its 23rd National Conference held the same month, it was concerned that a more careful analysis of the government's actions revealed that they did not greatly change the daily situations of apartheid's victims, many of whom were living in the shadows of escalating violence. Chikane concluded that "A strict interpretation of our past resolutions leads to a conclusion that the changes thus far are not irreversible."[138] The following month, July 1991, brought revelations of government funding of the IFP, the so-called "Inkathagate scandal." In his response, Chikane argued that the revelations indicated that the government had not entered into negotiations in good faith, and that the scandal was proof that state power was still vested solely in the hands of a government which was constituted for the express purpose of protecting the interests of one small section of the population. Therefore the whole process of change remained, according to Chikane, "totally vulnerable."[139] Two years later, and a mere two months after the assassination of the popular anti-apartheid leader Chris Hani, a resolution was tabled at the

SACC's 1993 National Conference on the issue of SACC support for the lifting of economic sanctions. Again Frank Chikane spoke against their lifting, saying that the Church Leaders Meeting had hoped that a transitional executive council would have been in place by that point. Since this was not the case, he could not advocate the lifting of sanctions: "morally, it will be wrong to advocate an action which will only empower the present racialistic and minority government, and entrench the existing unjust economic order and structures."[140] In light of the impoverished circumstances under which most of the SACC's constituency lived, Chikane made a point of stating that "we do not consider it a light matter to propose that the economy should continue to be denied foreign capital for what may be a number of weeks or months. We are, however, convinced that the economic crisis of this country cannot be divorced and be solved independent of the political crisis which undergirds it."[141] The Conference heeded Chikane's words and did not call for the lifting of sanctions at that time. Rather, the second resolution of the 1993 SACC National Conference read, "Conference endorses the decision of the NEC that the SACC should call for the lifting of economic and financial sanctions when the date for a general election has been set and a transitional executive council, with provision of joint control of the security forces, has been established."[142] The election date was set within weeks of this July pronouncement, and the transitional executive council began co-governing the country on November 29.

As noted earlier, the debate over the lifting of sanctions provoked a rare open display of disagreement between the SACC and the SACBC. In January 1990, the Catholic bishops issued a "Statement on Economic Pressure and Negotiations," in which they declared that their position on economic pressures remained as it was in 1986, and that "we believe a continuation of economic pressures to be justified."[143] A month later, however, de Klerk unbanned political organizations and released Nelson Mandela. The SACBC was quick to respond. In August 1991, in direct contrast to what the SACC was arguing at that time, the bishops declared that "we believe that the process that has been set in motion is irreversible." The bishops, cognizant that many others in South Africa disagreed with their position, explained, "while respecting the views of those who hold economic pressures to be still necessary to motivate faster change, we consider that these pressures have contributed to bringing about a situation in which they are no longer necessary. . . . We don't say that pressure has to stop, but tactics must change."[144] Frank Chikane reacted to the SACBC statement by declaring again that the SACC did not think the time was ripe for the lifting of sanctions, to which the SACBC president, Bishop Wilfred Napier, responded by saying he was not convinced that the SACC's views reflected the sentiments of its member churches.

Thus, the profound political changes that were taking place in the 1990s in South Africa were reflected in a changing religious environment. Two issues dominated this new religious context: concern over the waning influence of contextual theological ideas in favor of a return to what the Kairos Document had identified as a liberal and moderate "church theology," and the generation of new ideas within contextual theology in an effort to adapt to the changing "signs of the times." Theologians like Charles Villa-Vicencio and James Cochrane were outspoken in their fear for the first issue, while contributing in a major way to the second. Religious organizations in South Africa were caught in this period of religious transition, and at times they responded in ways which seemed to confirm the worst fears of contextual theologians (by, for example, making statements about returning to the sanctuary), while at other times they took up the challenge issued by them (by, for example, committing themselves to working for economic justice). By responding to new theological ideas as well as a new political context, church organizations such as the SACC and SACBC slowly began the process of adopting and consolidating new self-identities. It has proven to be a long and often painful process, one which is far from complete. South Africa itself is in many ways just beginning the difficult work of consolidating its transition.

A New Institutional Context

The SACC and SACBC adopted new styles of action in the 1990s as a result of new political and religious contexts. They also adopted these new styles for another reason: a new institutional context. The SACC was especially impacted by the changes of the 1990s, since it had been consistently the more political of the two organizations. First, the role that the organization played as an organ of civil society was severely curtailed, partly as a result of a loss of funding. Second, as a result of funding shrinkage, the SACC was forced to decrease its staffing, which further impacted the activities it could undertake. Finally, the changes of the 1990s also resulted in an altered relationship with its international partners.

The fact that the SACC may become a less relevant institution in South Africa was acknowledged early on by its General Secretary, Frank Chikane. In 1993 the SACC celebrated its twenty-fifth anniversary, and at the opening address of the National Conference, Chikane observed, "some say that the whole mission of the SACC was a negative one against apartheid, and that once apartheid is gone the SACC will have no reason to exist. Some say, even amongst ourselves, that because the challenge of apartheid is going there will be nothing to worry about."[145] Chikane then acknowledged that the SACC had to assess the nature of its ministry, its structures, and its programs, and would have to answer the question, "how can we build a more effective and historically relevant SACC?"[146] Part of searching for a new relevancy concerned addressing the SACC's ties to its member churches, which had long been an issue for many of these members (and for other churches, including the Catholic Church, which had precisely chosen not to become a full member of the SACC because of the issue over whether the SACC actually represented the views of its member churches). As chapter 6 indicated, the particular type of ministry engaged in by the SACC in the 1980s—as an activist organization in the anti-apartheid movement—opened it up to the criticism of failing to represent its denominational constituency. While the actions of the Council could often be termed radical, frequently the vision expressed by these actions did not filter down to the practice of its member churches. The SACC played a political role of resistance in the 1980s, but it could not foster an attitudinal transformation of its grass-roots membership. The leadership of the SACC was often courageous; the leaders of its member churches rarely displayed an equal measure of courage. In fact, one could argue that the SACC made a bigger impact on the liberation movements in the 1980s than it did on its own church structures. This disjunction between the SACC and its member churches became a cause for concern and greater attention in the 1990s. Christians began to reflect on whether the need still existed for a "para-church" organization (as many critics had called the SACC), with the activist church community residing primarily outside the main constituency of the institutionalized church. The self-identity of the SACC would have to evolve in order to overcome this disjunction. Chikane attempted to articulate a new self-identity at the 1993 National Conference, arguing that "first and foremost, we have not only been united by the struggle against apartheid. As an ecclesiological organisation of the Church, our unity is central to what the Church is all about: one body of Christ." If the church in South Africa did not recognize the primacy of the ecclesial identity, Chikane argued, the SACC would face "the particular danger that as apartheid repression becomes the thing of the past, there is a certain danger that there may be a measure of disintegration."[147] Beyers Naudé devoted a large portion of his speech at the Cape Town Consultation to the negative consequences of weak ties between the SACC and its member churches. Naudé was unequivocal in his opinion that the SACC would become increasingly irrelevant and ineffective if these ties were not strengthened:

> I have been struck in the last few years and constantly agonized within my own heart with this question. What are the root causes that the SACC through its National Conference passes resolutions, makes beautiful and impressive statements, operates on behalf of the member churches, but in so many respects there is not the spontaneous, willing, eager response on the part of the member church? Does the fault lie with the SACC? Does it lie with the member churches? Does it lie with our lack of love and understanding with one another? . . . If it does not succeed at that level, if it does not penetrate the grassroots of the life of our congregations and parishes,

sisters and brothers we may pass all the most beautiful resolutions which there are in the world, but the church will remain weak and ineffective and unconvincing.[148]

The relationship with its member churches was so crucial, Naudé argued, that it represented a Kairos for the SACC: "The moment has come that if we wish to play a really meaningful role as an ecumenical body, we have got to look at every form of weakness and failure which we have made—and I include myself. If we are really serious, we need to address ourselves to that."[149]

Why was the SACC suddenly so concerned with its relationship to its member churches, when the charges of nonrepresentation had existed for a long time? One answer is that the SACC was forced to address the issue in the 1990s as a matter of survival. Specifically, as a key organ of the anti-apartheid movement in the 1980s, the SACC received vast amounts of money from overseas donors. With financial security in hand, the SACC could afford to act without the support of its member churches. However, one of the major changes experienced by the SACC as a result of the changing political context of the 1990s was a sharp drop in funding. Although it was never stated explicitly and publicly, one consequence of financial loss was that the SACC had to take notice—to a degree that it had never had to previously—of where it stood vis-à-vis its member churches.

Much of the foreign assistance entering South Africa throughout the 1980s took the form of resistance money directed at supporting anti-apartheid causes. The SACC, especially after the 1988 bannings, was the recipient of vast sums of this money. Two changes occurred in the aftermath of 1990, which resulted in financial loss for the SACC. First, in the period from 1990–1994, foreign anti-apartheid assistance began to be directly channeled into newly legalized political organizations, such as the ANC. Second, in the post-1994 period, money was no longer sent to assist in bringing about the downfall of an illegitimate government. Rather, the newly elected, now legitimate Government of National Unity became the focus of foreign money, which took the form of private investment and multilateral and bilateral development loan funding. Many nongovernmental organizations (NGOs) suffered when this transformation of international assistance occurred, and overseas funds for NGOs dwindled as the momentum of political transformation accelerated. The SACC, as perhaps the largest single NGO recipient of this assistance, suffered tremendously. In addition to the fact that the SACC no longer received money from foreign governments, who were now dealing directly with the GNU, its funding from overseas NGOs dwindled as well.[150] In 1992, for example, only 38 percent of the Justice and Social Ministries' budget was pledged by foreign partners. John Lamola, the department's head, asked bitterly, "Need I remind you that, in the past when repression hurt most, it was this programme that carried the SACC?"[151]

Due to the evaporation of its primary sources of funding, and given that the economic circumstances of the majority of its constituents were extremely poor, the SACC had little choice but to engage in staff retrenchment and organizational restructuring. The lack of funding resulted in a severe budget crisis in the SACC. It was forced to reduce its operations by 23 percent in 1990 and by a further 30 percent in 1991. Such severe reductions could not but adversely affect the organization.[152] In addition to staff reductions which followed such cuts, the remaining staff were highly demoralized. The double burden of the financial threat to the Council, along with the relatively noncompetitive salaries of the SACC, resulted in a brain drain within the organization. Some of its most talented staff left to take up positions in the newly legalized political organizations. The SACC was thrown into a state of near crisis, with many of its operations reduced, redefined, reorganized, or simply closed. In a damage-control effort, the SACC revised its constitution and restructured itself. One consequence was that regional councils of churches lost their constitutional autonomy and became branches of the SACC. While this change occurred in order to reduce operations, it was only made possible by the political changes in South Africa. The regional council structure was originally created as a means of counteracting threats by the state to declare the SACC an affected organization, which meant that it would have had to report and declare its funding sources. To circumvent the danger posed by these threats, the twenty-three regional councils were given constitutional autonomy from the SACC. With the threat by the state gone, it was no longer necessary to have such a decentralized structure, and it was felt that a more centralized structure would be more efficient. The SACC's budget cuts, staff retrenchments, and organizational restructuring prompted Charles Villa-Vicencio to comment that "The SACC has shrunk overnight, and that's because of 1990 and the changing context. Its heyday is over."[153]

In addition to these internal changes, the SACC also experienced new relations with its major religious partners, both nationally and internationally. As noted in chapter 6, throughout the 1970s and 1980s, and into the 1990s, the SACBC had refused full membership in the SACC, choosing to remain an observer. The reason given for this refusal centered on the way decisions were made at the SACC National Conference, that is, by delegates who were overwhelmingly not members of denominational hierarchies. This resulted, the SACBC argued, in the passage of resolutions which were not necessarily representative of the sentiments of church members, and which more often than not expressed the wishes of the majority of those who happened to be present at the National Conference. The resulting resolutions therefore tended to be more radical than those passed by the SACBC. Unwilling to be bound by such resolutions, as well as by statements made by the General Secretary without full consultation with member churches, the SACBC opted to maintain its observer status. With the political changes of the 1990s, accompanied by new religious ideas about prophetic mediation instead of prophetic confrontation, the SACBC was no longer so concerned to distance itself from positions taken by the SACC. Consequently, in 1995 the SACBC became a full member of the SACC—a position it had rejected since 1969.

The changed political situation in South Africa also allowed new relationships to develop between both the SACC and SACBC and their international partners, the World Council of Churches and the Vatican. The WCC was forced to reassess its role in South Africa the most—more so than the Vatican, the SACBC, and even the SACC—since it had been the most radical in its opposition, as described in chapter 6. The policy of the WCC towards the apartheid regime had stood on three pillars: sanctions, isolation, and acts of solidarity with liberation movements. While the SACC had been more outspoken than the SACBC on all three of these issues, it lagged behind the WCC for many years (the Vatican lagged behind all three organizations). The gap between the WCC and the other organizations grew particularly wide in the aftermath of the creation of the WCC's Program to Combat Racism in 1969, with its controversial Special Fund, which soon established a supportive relationship with the liberation movements of Southern Africa. For years, the SACC held the PCR at a distance because of its implied support of violence, and did not bring its views in line with the PCR on sanctions until it adopted the Harare Statement in 1985, and on violence until it adopted the Lusaka Statement in 1987. As South Africa edged closer to its nonracial elections, the WCC recognized that its relationship to South Africa had to change. Likewise, the SACC and its member churches acknowledged the need to reassess their relationship to the WCC and especially to its PCR. In March 1992, the WCC's Executive Committee met in Santiago, Chile, and decided that it would no longer support the cultural isolation of the people of South Africa, who now needed the active support and presence of international partners. At the same time, the WCC felt that the time was not yet ripe for the lifting of economic sanctions against South Africa (which was in line with SACC opinion at the same time). Finally, the WCC resolved to coordinate its programs with churches in South Africa during the time of transition and beyond.

The PCR's Special Fund came under the spotlight during the Santiago meeting, since the Fund's future was in question. The WCC decided to maintain the Special Fund, albeit with a new emphasis. Henceforth, the criteria for allocating funds would be projects which promoted the unity of the anti-apartheid forces, and projects which promoted peace, unity, and reconciliation, and which effectively addressed the legacy of apartheid.[154] A few months later, SACC General Secretary Frank Chikane requested of his National Executive Committee that the SACC reconsider its hands-off policy regarding the PCR's Special Fund, and that it now become involved in assisting the implementation of the new policy of the WCC.

Relations between Catholics, especially radical Catholics, and the Vatican also improved during the 1990s. As explained in chapter 6, the Vatican often inhibited the adoption of an overtly political self-identity by the SACBC. It was more conservative than many South African bishops on such issues as declaring the state illegitimate and supporting economic sanctions. As the political situation in South Africa improved, however, and it was no longer necessary to criticize the government of another state, tensions between the Vatican and the SACBC over its level of politicization eased. And while the SACBC felt that it could not morally support a visit to South Africa by the Pope in 1988, largely because of opposition to the visit by grass-roots Christians, by the mid-1990s the bishops reversed this opinion. In March 1994 the Vatican and South Africa established full diplomatic relations, and in September 1995 Pope John Paul II visited South Africa, where he was given an overwhelmingly positive reception.

Thus, in the 1990s the institutional context, especially of the SACC, changed as a direct result of the changing political situation. The SACC was no longer required to play the role of the primary anti-apartheid NGO, for other explicitly political organs of civil society could now take up this role. The SACC and SACBC were no longer primary sites of the struggle. As a result of the opening of political space, the SACC lost a great deal of its funding and was forced to drastically cut its budget, with a concomitant laying off of staff and reduction of its operations. At the same time, the SACC began to focus more inwardly on its relationship with its member churches, rather than maintaining the outward-looking focus on the state and civil society—and even the international arena. If the SACC were to remain relevant, it could no longer afford to maintain its autonomous stance, regardless of whether it represented the views of its constituency. As the SACC began to shrink, the National Conference itself took on less importance. Charles Villa-Vicencio summed up this process in 1993, stating, "Many of us who used to make a point to go to Conference every year no long go to Conference. The sense of urgency is no longer focused there, where it was once focused. If you really wanted to turn South Africa around today, who would you talk to? Would you really talk to the Archbishop or to Chikane, or to Nelson Mandela if you had a choice?"[155] In the aftermath of the changes which began in February 1990, the SACC began to play a role in society not dissimilar to National Councils of Churches in other societies, that is, as simply one of many nonpolitical organizations in civil society.

Where Have the Prophets Gone?
An Update on Actors and Events

In April 1994, South Africa held its first nonracial elections, which propelled Nelson Mandela to the presidency as the head of the interim Government
of National Unity, overwhelmingly dominated by the African National Congress. It soon became clear that the ANC was grateful to those who had fought
so long and hard to see the birth of the new political dispensation. Moreover, it
was willing to show this gratitude by rewarding many longtime anti-apartheid
activists with positions of power. While many of the actors in the contextual
theology movement chose to remain in the theological realm, committed to
keeping a vigilant eye on the new government and ready to criticize it when
necessary, many of the other key players in the prophetic Christian movement
chose to accept the rewards offered by the ANC. Indeed, an overview of key
government positions can read like a veritable "who's who" of the radical Christian activists of the 1980s. This section provides a brief update on many of the
actors who contributed in a major way to the story told in this book.

Those who chose to forego political careers include Albert Nolan and Beyers Naudé. Nolan has continued his work at the Institute for Contextual Theology, as one of its main theologians and as the editor of its monthly magazine,
Challenge. Naudé (one-time General Secretary of the SACC) has also continued
to be actively involved in the contextual theology movement, as head of a theological think tank called the Ecumenical Advice Bureau, whose offices are located in the same building as the ICT. Naudé was joined in this endeavor by
Wolfram Kistner, the former director of the SACC's Division of Justice and
Reconciliation.

Those who chose to enter the realm of politics include Frank Chikane,
Smangaliso Mkhatshwa, and Allan Boesak. Several political institutions were
put in place in the run-up to the 1994 elections, one of which was the Independent Electoral Commission (IEC). The role of the IEC was to ensure the
integrity of the elections, by ascertaining whether the various political parties
and their supporters, as well as the armed forces, adhered to an established Electoral Code of Conduct, and by disciplining them when they did not. To en-
hance public trust in the independence and impartiality of the IEC, only individuals of high moral stature were chosen as commissioners.[156] The IEC was
the organization primarily responsible for conducting the elections, through
promoting conditions conducive to free and fair elections, and by having ultimate responsibility for certifying the results. Frank Chikane was chosen as one
of the eleven South African Commissioners, a testament to the respect he had
earned across South African society. Chikane left his post as General Secretary
of the SACC and was replaced by Brigalia Bam, one of his Deputy General

Secretaries. After a brief stint as a fellow in the Research Institute for Christianity in South Africa (RICSA) at the University of Cape Town, Chikane was propelled onto the national political scene in November 1995 as policy and administration advisor to Vice-President Thabo Mbeki. In 1997, Chikane was given the title of Director General of Mbeki's office. One of Chikane's major tasks in that position has included determining the reallocation of Reconstruction and Development Programme (RDP) functions, as well as overseeing the restructuring of social security services.[157] In October 1997, Chikane made an unsuccessful bid for the chairmanship of the ANC in Gauteng province, a position he lost to Mathole Motshekga.

Smangaliso Mkhatshwa, former General Secretary of both the SACBC and the ICT, became a member of Parliament, representing the ANC. This touched off a debate in Catholic circles which eventually reached the level of the Vatican, since the church prohibits clergy from being involved in party politics. Eventually, however, the Vatican sanctioned Mkhatshwa's position as an MP. Mkhatshwa then took up a position in the GNU's cabinet as Deputy Minister of Education.

Allan Boesak has not fared as well as either Chikane or Mkhatshwa in his role as politician, despite tremendous ANC support. Boesak was selected as the ANC leader in the Western Cape, in the hope that he would help the ANC capture the majority of the Colored vote in that region in the 1994 election. However, the ANC did not win a majority of the votes in the Western Cape, and many held Boesak responsible for the loss, for failing to bridge the gap between Africans (numerically strong within the ANC and a primary source of ANC support) and Coloreds. Despite the loss of this province, in which the city of Cape Town is located, the ANC was still willing to reward Boesak for years of service in the anti-apartheid movement (both as a clergyman who spearheaded the international church effort to declare apartheid a heresy, as leader of the World Alliance of Reformed Churches, and through his activities in the UDF), and nominated him for the prestigious post of ambassador to the United Nations in Geneva.[158] However, the situation soon turned negative for Boesak, who became embroiled in several scandals, forcing his withdrawal from the ambassadorial nomination.[159] Boesak then moved to the United States, where he became a lecturer at the American Baptist Seminary in Berkeley, California. However, South Africa's Office of Serious Economic Offences continued to investigate Boesak, eventually charging him, as director of the Foundation for Peace and Justice (FPJ), with the misappropriation of several million Rand of donor funds. In March 1997, Boesak returned to South Africa to face fraud allegations and to prepare for his criminal trial. He was charged with twenty-one counts of theft and fraud, to which he pled not guilty. At the time of this writing, Boesak's trial is underway. Boesak's role in mobilizing resistance against apartheid was immense, and his oratory was almost unrivaled. But, as one opinion editorial stated, he soon became a symbol of what many South Africans fear, the anti-apartheid hero who falls victim to the temptations of the post-apartheid era.[160]

While neither Archbishop Desmond Tutu nor theologian and academic Charles Villa-Vicencio became involved in party politics, both received national prominence in the post-election period through their roles on the Truth and Reconciliation Commission (TRC). This body was created to investigate past human rights abuses carried out by groups across the political spectrum, grant amnesty to perpetrators of those abuses, recommend reparations to apartheid's victims, and compile a comprehensive report on gross violations of human rights which occurred in South Africa between 1960 and 1994. The TRC has set off a national debate in South Africa concerning the granting of amnesty versus prosecuting perpetrators of crimes against humanity; it has touched South Africans to the core, resulting in an emotional and psychological national soul-searching. During the period of public hearings, the TRC received almost daily media coverage. Tutu and Villa-Vicencio played invaluable roles in this emotion-charged attempt to foster national healing—Tutu as chairman of the seventeen-member Commission, and Villa-Vicencio as the Commission's Director of Research.

In the post-apartheid era, many of the previously unsolved acts of repression against both the SACC and SACBC have finally been solved. Included in these once mysterious acts are the bombings of Khotso and Khanya Houses, the respective headquarters of the SACC and SACBC, and the poisoning of Frank Chikane. South Africans are beginning to learn the truth about these and other human rights violations, in part due to the work of the Truth and Reconciliation Commission. When Khotso House was bombed in August 1988, the Minister of Law and Order, Adriaan Vlok, stated that the building had most likely been damaged by the ANC because it had been used by guerrillas for storing and manufacturing explosives. On October 21, 1996, in testimony before the Truth and Reconciliation Commission, General Johann van der Merwe, former Commissioner of Police, admitted that he had ordered the bombing and claimed that it had been approved by Minister Vlok. Moreover, he testified, he believed that Vlok had gone to South African president P. W. Botha for final approval.[161] Besides bombing SACC headquarters, security police kept leading figures of the SACC under constant surveillance. In June 1995, former security policeman Paul Erasmus disclosed that the near-fatal poisoning of Frank Chikane had been carried out by security police stationed at John Vorster Square in Johannesburg. Chikane was a target of particular venom among security police, Erasmus said, because "the South African Council of Churches was the evil empire, and, like the UDF and COSATU, it had to be eliminated."[162] The SACBC was also the target of anti-liberation movement repression, for example, in the October 1988 arson attack on Khanya House. In

May 1990, a member of a far-right wing militant group, Barend Hendric Strydom, was sentenced to death on eight charges of murder. During the trial, he claimed responsibility for the attack on Khanya House.

Conclusion

"The political dimension of our faith varies according to the requirements of each different context," remarked Archbishop Tutu in a 1993 interview.[163] When South Africa's political context changed in February 1990, the SACC and SACBC underwent something akin to an "identity crisis." The spiral of church/state conflict collapsed once the state chose—at least publicly—to negotiate with its former enemies, thereby removing the need for the confrontational approach taken by many civil society organizations, including the SACC and SACBC. While both organizations continued their commitment to promoting social change, each now had to assess the most appropriate methods for doing so. As a result, theologians in South Africa had to search for ways to interpret the changing political context for their constituency, and to provide guidelines for actions. The "universe of religious discourse" changed in South Africa, with concepts such as "prophetic mediation" being discussed for the first time. Radical Christians insisted that this was simply a new form of contextual theology, and cautioned against churches withdrawing from political life by retreating to the sanctuary. As the political context further changed (marked by decreasing repression) and entered new phases (marked by negotiations and elections), so too did the theological interpretation of it. Prior to the 1994 national election, contextual theology took the form of "prophetic mediation" (although some theologians maintained a wary attitude towards mediation), while in the post-election period, contextual theological ideas have collectively come to be known as a "theology of reconstruction," with primary emphasis on nation-building, fostering a human rights culture, and economic justice.

The role that both organizations, but especially the SACC, had played as the church of resistance disappeared in a remarkably short period. This was not only a result of the changing political and religious contexts but also a consequence of institutional shrinkage, both financially and in terms of personnel (which was itself a result of the new political context of the opening of civil society). During the 1980s, the SACC was home to people who could not express their views in other venues. The SACC, in a sense, was providing hospitality to these people who were, metaphorically speaking, homeless. The only space that existed where some form of resistance could take place was within religious organizations, and people willingly came from outside the church to occupy this space. In the process, these religious organizations were turned into an intense site of the struggle and church leaders were forced to exercise a political role. After 1990, their houses were returned to them, and they went back home. Many people chose to serve the liberation process outside of the churches, and joined other political organizations. The radicalizing thrust of the SACC began to disappear. The money soon followed. During the 1980s, the SACC was virtually the only organization in which money for the liberation process could legally enter the country. With political freedom, money meant for overtly political purposes went to overtly political organizations. Activities the SACC had been expected to perform a few short years earlier were now being performed quite openly by unbanned organizations. Charismatic leadership was no longer centrally located in church structures.

What will happen to the alternative church? South Africa experienced a transition that was peaceful beyond the imaginations of many political analysts and South African activists. As noted above, some Christians have expressed concern over the waning of the prophetic voice in South Africa. They have cautioned the churches against becoming so caught up in the spirit of reconciliation that they ignore the signs of the times, which indicate that the poor and the marginalized are far from doing well. Peter Walshe epitomizes this warning with the following observation and questions:

> Good intentions and beneficence are not enough. Apartheid has left a terrible legacy and history will inevitably generate new class, ethnic and sexist tensions. In this context there are troubling questions. Will a searching, self-critical but prophetic voice be able to reassert itself in the difficult decades that lie ahead? Will a growing minority of Christians renew their social analysis, break out of ideological straight-jackets and again challenge both their churches and the state to recognize that 'reconciliation is measured by the development of the poor?'[164]

There is no shortage of issues that church organizations might take up: the economic impact of structural adjustment programs, especially on women and children; environmental destruction which has thus far accompanied economic development around the world; domestic violence, which is alarmingly high in South Africa; and AIDS—to name but a few. In the future, more likely than not, the churches will have to be reminded of their responsibility by those who are again located outside church structures. Whether churches will again re-emerge as a dominant force fighting social injustice, or whether the intersection of the institutional and prophetic church during the 1980s was an aberration, remains to be seen.

A Note on Primary Sources

MANY OF THE sources used in writing this book included documents, correspondence, speeches, and other material from archives located in South Africa. The archives of three organizations were particularly useful: the Institute for Contextual Theology in Johannesburg, the South African Council of Churches, also in Johannesburg, and the Southern African Catholic Bishops' Conference in Pretoria. Archival material includes official publications of these organizations; documents not necessarily written by individuals directly associated with these organizations, and therefore not always official publications; and documents written by individuals working for these organizations which were never published. Unpublished documents are identified as photocopied. All primary sources (both published and unpublished) are followed in the notes by abbreviations in parentheses which indicate the archive where the document was located, and which serve as a guide for locating the source in the bibliography.

The key to the archives is as follows:

BCA—SACBC Archives
CCA—SACC Archives
CTA—ICT Archives
Connor—Personal archives of Bernard Connor, O.P. As a former member of the SACBC Theological Advisory Commission (TAC), Connor's personal archives pertain to the TAC. Therefore, documents from this archive have been listed with other SACBC archives.
OPD—Other Primary Documents. A small number of documents are located in places other than the three archives listed above.

In addition, several interviews were conducted in South Africa with theologians, religious leaders, and lay Christians representing both "official" and opposition thinking within Christian organizations in South Africa. A list of interviewees and dates is included in the bibliography. In the notes, interviews are identified by date and interviewee.

Notes

Preface

1. For an explanation of this "curious neglect," see Christian Smith, ed., *Disruptive Religion: The Force of Faith in Social Movement Activism* (New York: Routledge Press, 1996).

2. See, for example, Mark Orkin, ed., *Sanctions against Apartheid* (New York: St. Martin's Press, 1989), and Joseph Hanlon, ed., *South Africa: The Sanctions Report* (London: James Curry, 1990).

3. See for example, Michael McFaul, "The Demise of World Revolutionary Process: Soviet-Angolan Relations under Gorbachev," *Journal of Southern African Studies* 16, no. 1 (March 1990): 165–189.

4. Of the few examples that exist, two excellent analyses include Peter Walshe, "Prophetic Christianity and the Liberation Movement," *Journal of Modern African Studies* 29, no. 1 (1991): 27–60, and Peter Walshe, *Prophetic Christianity and the Liberation Movement in South Africa* (Pietermaritzburg: Cluster Publications, 1995).

5. See, for example, the various essays in Shaun Johnson, ed., *South Africa: No Turning Back* (London: MacMillan, 1988), and Robert M. Price, *The Apartheid State in Crisis: Political Transformation in South Africa, 1975–1990* (New York: Oxford University Press, 1991).

6. Especially, Daniel H. Levine, *Religion and Politics in Latin America: The Catholic Church in Venezuela and Colombia* (Princeton: Princeton University Press, 1981); Brian Smith, *The Church and Politics in Chile: Challenges to Modern Catholicism* (Princeton: Princeton University Press, 1982); Daniel H. Levine, *Popular Voices in Latin American Catholicism* (Princeton: Princeton University Press, 1992); Daniel H. Levine, ed., *Religion and Political Conflict in Latin America* (Chapel Hill: University of North Carolina Press, 1986); Scott Mainwaring and Alexander Wilde, eds., *The Progressive Church in Latin America* (Notre Dame, Ind.: University of Notre Dame Press, 1989); and Scott Mainwaring, *The Catholic Church and Politics in Brazil: 1916–1985* (Stanford, Calif.: Stanford University Press, 1986).

7. The most sophisticated theoretical treatments of the changing relations between churches and the South African state in the 1980s come from theologian Charles Villa-Vicencio, especially in his studies *Trapped in Apartheid: A Socio-Theological History of the English-Speaking Churches* (Maryknoll, N.Y.: Orbis Books, 1988) and *Civil Disobedience and Beyond: Law, Resistance, and Religion in South Africa* (Grand Rapids, Mich.: Eerdmans, 1990). Other studies which broadly address several themes in the field of religion and politics have likewise been contributed by theologians, including John W. de Gruchy's *The Church Struggle in South Africa* (Grand Rapids, Mich.: Eerdmans, 1979), Christine Lienemann-Perrin and Wolfgang Lienemann, eds., *Political Legitimacy in South Africa* (Heidelberg, FRG: Protestant Institute for Interdisciplinary Research, 1988), Zolile Mbali, *The Churches and Racism: A Black South African Perspective* (London: SCM Press, 1987), and David Chidester, *Shots in the Streets: Violence and Religion in South Africa* (Boston: Beacon Press, 1991).

Of the few academic accounts by a political scientist of the interaction of a church organization with the South African state, two are Peter Walshe's *Church versus State in South Africa: The Case of the Christian Institute* (Maryknoll, N.Y.: Orbis Books, 1983) and *Prophetic Christianity and the Liberation Movement in South Africa*. From the perspective of sociology, an excellent treatment of the interaction of religion and politics in South Africa is Jean

Comaroff, *Body of Power, Spirit of Resistance: The Culture and History of a South African People* (Chicago: University of Chicago Press, 1985).

8. See Levine, *Religion and Politics in Latin America* and *Popular Voices in Latin American Catholicism*, respectively.

9. See Brian Smith, *The Church and Politics in Chile.*

10. Mainwaring and Wilde, *The Progressive Church in Latin America*, p. 10.

11. Ibid., pp. 12–14.

12. Mainwaring, *The Catholic Church and Politics in Brazil*, p. 17.

13. See, for example, Daryl M. Balia, *Christian Resistance to Apartheid* (Johannesburg: Skotaville Publishers, 1989); Mbali, *The Churches and Racism;* de Gruchy, *The Church Struggle in South Africa;* James Cochrane, *Servants of Power: The Role of the English-Speaking Churches, 1903–1930* (Johannesburg: Ravan Press, 1987); Marjorie Hope and James Young, *The South African Churches in a Revolutionary Situation* (Maryknoll, N.Y.: Orbis Books, 1983); Villa-Vicencio, *Trapped in Apartheid;* and Walshe, *Church versus State in South Africa.*

14. See, for example, Garth Abraham, *The Catholic Church and Apartheid* (Johannesburg: Ravan Press, 1989); Bernard Spong and Cedric Mayson, *Come Celebrate! Twenty-Five Years of the South African Council of Churches* (Johannesburg: SACC, 1993); Noel Benedict Peters, *South Africa: A Catholic Perspective* (Fresno, Calif.: Pioneer Publishing Co., 1991); and Andrew Prior, *Catholics in Apartheid Society* (Cape Town: David Philip, 1982).

15. See, for example, Allan Boesak, *Farewell to Innocence: A Socio-Ethical Study on Black Theology and Power* (Maryknoll, N.Y.: Orbis Books, 1976); John W. de Gruchy and Charles Villa-Vicencio, eds., *Apartheid Is a Heresy* (Grand Rapids, Mich.: Eerdmans, 1983); Louise Kretzschmar, *The Voice of Black Theology in South Africa* (Johannesburg: Ravan Press, 1986); Albert Nolan, *God in South Africa: The Challenge of the Gospel* (Grand Rapids, Mich.: Eerdmans, 1988); Desmond Tutu, *Crying in the Wilderness* (Great Britain: Mowbray, 1986); and Itumeleng J. Mosala and Buti Thlagale, eds., *The Unquestionable Right to Be Free: Essays in Black Theology* (Johannesburg: Skotaville Publishers, 1986).

16. See, for example, SACBC Theological Advisory Commission, *The Things That Make for Peace* (Pretoria: SACBC, 1985); Rachel Tingle, *Revolution or Reconciliation? The Struggle in the Church in South Africa* (London: Christian Studies Centre, 1992); Charles Villa-Vicencio, ed., *Theology and Violence: The South African Debate* (Johannesburg: Skotaville Publishers, 1987); and Walter Wink, *Jesus' Third Way: The Relevance of Nonviolence in South Africa Today* (Johannesburg: SACC, 1987).

17. Especially good are Villa-Vicencio, *Civil Disobedience and Beyond*, and Walshe, "Prophetic Christianity and the Liberation Movement."

18. Frank Chikane, *No Life of My Own: An Autobiography* (London: Catholic Institute for International Relations, 1988); Wolfram Kistner, *Outside the Camp: A Collection of Writings* (Johannesburg: SACC, 1988); Charles Villa-Vicencio and John W. de Gruchy, eds., *Resistance and Hope: South African Essays in Honor of Beyers Naudé*, (Cape Town: David Philip, 1985); and Mothobi Mutloatse and John Webster, eds., *Hope and Suffering: Sermons and Speeches of The Right Reverend Desmond Mpilo Tutu* (Grand Rapids, Mich.: Eerdmans, 1984).

1. Politics, Ideas, and Institutions

1. World Council of Churches, "Text of the Lusaka Statement," in *The Churches' Search for Justice and Peace in Southern Africa: Report on Meeting in Lusaka, Zambia, 4–8 May, 1987* (Geneva: WCC Program to Combat Racism, 1987), pp. 28–29 (CCA).

2. This "consent-based" definition of legitimacy is essentially a Weberian one. Max Weber presented his understanding of legitimacy most explicitly in *Economy and Society,* and

his discussion of the concept has laid the foundation for much of the modern social science literature on legitimacy. It has spawned the growth of the "belief" or "subjectivist" theory of legitimacy among social scientists, which equates legitimacy with the conviction on the part of those ruled that they should accept and obey authorities. Legitimacy for Weber is relational, as it involves a relationship between the rulers and the ruled and is based on the perception or belief by the ruled that the authorities have the right to demand obedience. For Weber, legitimacy consists of voluntary submission to domination as a result of a "genuine acceptance" of a given power order. He created a typology consisting of three "types of legitimate domination," which he defined as "voluntary submission to power systems in whose validity the subject believes." In his typology, voluntary compliance, or obedience, is given on one of three bases: on the belief of the legality of patterns of rules and in the right of the authorities established under such rules to issue commands—which he called *legal authority;* on the respect for "the sanctity of immemorial traditions" and of the status of those ruling under them—which he called *traditional authority;* and on devotion to charisma, defined as "the specific and exceptional sanctity, heroism or exemplary character of an individual person"—which he called *charismatic authority.* Max Weber, in Guenther Roth and Claus Wittich, eds., *Economy and Society* (New York: Bedminster Press, 1968), pp. 212–245.

A more recent definition of legitimacy, which draws on Weber, is provided by Juan Linz in *The Breakdown of Democratic Regimes: Crisis, Breakdown, and Reequilibration* (Baltimore, Md.: Johns Hopkins University Press, 1978). Linz provides perhaps the most basic definition of legitimacy: "a legitimate government is one considered to be the least evil of the forms of government" (p. 18). For Linz then, as for Weber, legitimacy is based on the perceptions of the ruled, who consent to orders by voluntarily complying with them. He says, "no government can survive without the belief on the part of a substantial number of citizens. . . . " (p. 16). One significant contribution by Linz, which is relevant to the South African case, is the argument that there are degrees of legitimacy. He states, "Gains and losses of support for governments, leaders, parties, and policies in a democracy are likely to fluctuate rapidly while the belief in the legitimacy of the system persists." However, Linz argues, when all political actors of a regime have lost support, the regime itself is likely to suffer a loss of legitimacy. As chapter 2 makes clear, this is exactly what occurred over a long period of time in South Africa. The loss of legitimacy suffered by particular parties eventually evolved into a lack of legitimacy of the government and finally of the state.

3. One of the questions facing citizens of an illegitimate regime is whether they will obey its laws or resist, and some argue that there can be no duty to obey an illegitimate regime, but rather there is an obligation to resist and defend oneself against the state. Wolfgang Lienemann, untitled unpublished paper prepared for the Conference on the Legitimacy of the South African Government, Harare, Zimbabwe, September 1989, p. 8, photocopy (CCA).

4. Voluntary cooperation with the rules of a state creates legitimate authority, and the acceptance of this authority is demonstrated by acting in the manner prescribed by the law. Lack of consent thus runs the risk of evolving into acts of civil disobedience as increasing numbers of people defy laws and bypass, ignore, or boycott state institutions. It is possible to have the appearance of "consent," through low levels of civil disobedience, without actually having a legitimate government. Obedience to a law may be seen as providing support to a system which overall is morally good, but might also be given solely because of fear of the consequences. As one South African academic states, "it is hardly plausible to deduce from the fact that most South African blacks are law-abiding citizens that this signifies their having tacitly consented to the whole set of institutions and laws which comprise the South African state." Mervyn Frost, "On the Question of the Legitimacy or Illegitimacy of the South African State," unpublished paper prepared for the Conference on the Legitimacy of the South African Government, Harare, Zimbabwe, September 1989, p. 2, photocopy (CCA).

5. This legal criterion was the primary focus of Edwin Cameron's paper delivered at the CALS conference, which addressed the question of why many South Africans continued over decades to obey the laws of the regime. Cameron argued, "is it possible to deny that they obey not because the law by its power and authority creates standards against which they regard it as appropriate to measure their own and others' conduct, but rather because they fear that disobedience will bring on them penalties which are too harsh for their lives to sustain?" Edwin Cameron, "Illegitimacy and Disobedience," unpublished paper prepared for the CALS/ICT Seminar on the Legitimacy of Governments, 1987, p. 15, photocopy (CCA).

This criterion is clearly related to both Weber's and Linz's definition of legitimacy, as it rests on the issue of voluntary obedience, which is the basis of Weber's definition. From the South African perspective, the state is legitimate if it is governed on the basis of noncoercive rule of law. When the government begins to rule by coercion, it loses its authority and thus its legitimacy. In other words, those who are ruled no longer obey the laws of the government. Juan Linz discusses the relationship between authority and obedience thus: "the legitimacy of a democratic regime rests on the belief in the right of those legally elevated to authority to issue certain types of commands, to expect obedience, and to enforce them, if necessary, by the use of force." Linz, *Breakdown of Democratic Regimes*, p. 17.

6. In other words, if power is exercised outside of the realm of law, it is no longer authority, and power holders are no longer legitimate. When social institutions, including governments, begin to rely on overtly coercive methods to influence behavior, they no longer have power allied to authority and so become illegitimate.

7. This criterion was the result of theological contributions to the legitimacy debate in South Africa. Of all the criteria established by South African lawyers, academics, and theologians, this one is least related to the Weberian understanding of legitimacy. It was, however, seen as a valid criterion inside South Africa, even by social scientists, and it was given a fair amount of attention in the final report of the international conference held in Harare in 1989.

8. Wolfgang Lienemann, second untitled unpublished paper prepared for the Conference on the Legitimacy of the South African Government, Harare, September 1989, p. 2, photocopy (CCA).

9. Frost, "On the Question of Illegitimacy," pp. 4–5.

10. It is important, however, to remember the distinction between the SACC, *as an organization*, and the churches which comprise the SACC membership. Several authors have argued that although the SACC never cooperated with the apartheid state, the "English-speaking" churches as a whole at times failed in their criticism, and were much more moderate and cautious than the socio-political context warranted. For examples of this argument, see especially Cochrane, *Servants of Power*, and Villa-Vicencio, *Trapped in Apartheid*.

11. Villa-Vicencio, *Civil Disobedience and Beyond*.

12. Johann Baptist Metz, *Faith in History and Society: Towards a Practical Fundamental Theology* (London: Burns and Oates, 1980), pp. 88ff., quoted in Villa-Vicencio, *Civil Disobedience and Beyond*, p. 184.

13. Walshe, *Church versus State in South Africa*, p. 62.

14. Peter Walshe, "The Evolution of Liberation Theology in South Africa," *Journal of Law and Religion* 5, no. 2 (1987): 303.

15. de Gruchy, *The Church Struggle in South Africa*, pp. 128–131.

16. World Council of Churches, "Text of the Lusaka Statement," in *The Churches' Search for Justice and Peace in Southern Africa*, pp. 28–29 (CCA).

17. In particular, the rise of the "progressive church" in Latin America has been the focus of much analysis, with attention centering on two major questions: the nature and

causes of change within the Catholic Church and the relationship of religious changes to politics. For studies which focus on the rise of the progressive church, see especially Mainwaring and Wilde, *The Progressive Church in Latin America;* Levine, *Popular Voices in Latin American Catholicism, Religion and Political Conflict in Latin America,* and *Religion and Politics in Latin America;* and Phillip Berryman, *The Religious Roots of Rebellion: Christians in Central American Revolutions* (Maryknoll, N.Y.: Orbis Books, 1984).

18. There is an abundance of research outside of the field of religion and politics, and especially in the field of international political economy, using ideas as explanatory variables. For examples of this literature see John Odell, *U.S. International Monetary Policy: Markets, Power, and Ideas as Sources of Change* (Princeton, N.J.: Princeton University Press, 1982); Eric Foner, *Politics and Ideology in the Age of the Civil War* (Oxford: Oxford University Press, 1980); Anthony King, "Ideas, Institutions and Policies of Governments: A Comparative Analysis, Parts I and II," *British Journal of Political Science* 2, no. 3 (July 1973); Anthony King, "Ideas, Institutions and Policies of Governments: A Comparative Analysis, Part III," *British Journal of Political Science* 3, no. 4 (October 1973); Louis Hartz, *The Liberal Tradition in America* (New York: Harcourt, 1955); Peter Hall, ed., *The Political Power of Economic Ideas: Keynesianism across Nations* (Princeton: Princeton University Press, 1989); Peter Hall, *Governing the Economy* (Oxford: Oxford University Press, 1986); Judith Goldstein, "The Impact of Ideas on Trade Policy: The Origins of the U.S. Agricultural and Manufacturing Policies," *International Organization* 43 (Winter 1989); Emmanuel Adler, *The Power of Ideology: The Quest for Technological Autonomy in Argentina and Brazil* (Berkeley: University of California Press, 1987); and Max Weber, *The Protestant Ethic and the Spirit of Capitalism,* trans. Talcott Parsons (New York: Charles Scribner's Sons, 1958).

19. Two important contributors to this theoretical argument include Kathryn Sikkink, *Ideas and Institutions: Developmentalism in Brazil and Argentina* (Ithaca, N.Y.: Cornell University Press, 1991), and Judith Goldstein, "Ideas, Institutions, and American Trade Policy," *International Organization* 42, no. 1 (Winter 1988): 179–217. In her study of the emergence of developmentalism in Brazil and Argentina, Sikkink argues that it is impossible to explain this change without understanding the impact of ideas, and that a broad-based ideological shift about development had a profound impact on the economic policies adopted by Latin American government. Policy changes in these two countries depended on how relevant actors perceived the social and economic setting and structured the kinds of options available. However, she argues, new ideas do not enter an ideological vacuum, but are instead inserted into a political space already occupied by historically formed ideologies. In other words, new ideas are competing with, and often challenge, an existing universe of discourse. For Sikkink, the degree to which new ideas replace an existing discourse is dependent upon the existing ideological conditions, the manner in which the new ideas were introduced, and the institutional support for the new ideas. Linked to this is the fact that the same set of ideas can be interpreted quite differently. These last two issues, that of different levels of institutional support as well as different interpretations of new ideas, will prove to be important in explaining different outcomes in the SACC and the SACBC. Goldstein, in her study of American trade policy, contributes to this line of argument through her analysis of the political influence of the content of any idea, arguing that there are competing interpretations of optimal policies in any given environment, and the ascendance of one policy idea rather than another has important policy ramifications. For her, ideas are "critical independent variables that explain why different [policies] arise in different historical periods" (pp. 183 and 192, note 6).

20. In her study of the women's rights movement in France, Jane Jenson argues that the movement was not successful until the universe of political discourse changed. My argument about new religious discourses draws from Jenson's theoretical analysis of this move-

ment. Jane Jenson, "Changing Discourse, Changing Agendas: Political Rights and Reproductive Policies in France," in Mary Fainsod Katzenstein, and Carol McClurg Mueller, eds.,
*The Women's Movements of the U.S. and Western Europe: Consciousness, Political Opportunity,
and Public Policy* (Philadelphia: Temple University Press, 1987), pp. 64–88.

    21. See especially Levine, *Popular Voices in Latin American Catholicism, Religion and
Politics in Latin America,* and *Religion and Political Conflict in Latin America;* and Mainwaring, *The Catholic Church and Politics in Brazil.* For non–Latin American studies on the
role of religious ideas, see Karen E. Fields, *Revival and Rebellion in Colonial Central Africa*
(Princeton: Princeton University Press, 1985), and Comaroff, *Body of Power, Spirit of Resistance.*

    22. W. E. Hewitt, *Base Christian Communities and Social Change in Brazil* (Lincoln:
University of Nebraska Press, 1991), p. 13.

    23. Levine, *Religion and Politics in Latin America,* p. 35.

    24. Levine, *Popular Voices in Latin American Catholicism,* p. 35.

    25. Levine, *Religion and Politics in Latin America,* p. 36, and *Religion and Political
Conflict in Latin America,* pp. 8–9.

    26. Levine, *Religion and Politics in Latin America,* p. 37.

    27. Ibid., p. 36.

    28. Daniel H. Levine, "Religion, Society, and Politics: States of the Art," *Latin Ameri-
can Research Review* 16 (1981): 196.

    29. Even before the Medellín meeting, another important event occurred in the devel-
opment of a new discourse in Latin America. In March 1967, Pope Paul VI, successor to
John XXIII, published the encyclical *Populorum Progressio (On the Progress of Peoples),* which
took a stronger stance on social issues than any earlier encyclical. This document had a tremendous impact on the development of a new religious discourse in Latin America and was
quoted extensively both at Medellín and later. In formulating a new theology specific to the
Latin American context, theologians drew on two particular aspects of the encyclical. The
document attacked the abuses of the international economic system in strong language, so
that by the time of Medellín, the issue of the moral validity of the established economic and
political system was within the scope of religious discourse. Bishops at Medellín could now
fuse social science thinking on "dependency" with new Church teachings on the need for
moral and structural change. Perhaps the most important issue in the encyclical for the bishops at Medellín was its statement on violence. While strongly discouraging violent revolution,
it left open the possibility that a revolutionary uprising may be justified in a situation of
"manifest, long-standing tyranny which would do great damage to fundamental personal
rights and dangerous harm to the common good." Pope Paul VI, *Populorum Progressio,* in
Joseph Gremillion, ed., *The Gospel of Peace and Justice: Catholic Social Teaching since Pope John*
(Maryknoll, N.Y.: Orbis Books, 1967), p. 396, quoted in Christian Smith, *The Emergence of
Liberation Theology: Radical Religion and Social Movement Theory* (Chicago: University of
Chicago Press, 1991), p. 126. See also Paul E. Sigmund, *Liberation Theology at the Crossroads:
Democracy or Revolution?* (New York: Oxford University Press, 1990), pp. 25–27, on *Popu-
lorum Progressio.*

    30. Levine, *Religion and Political Conflict in Latin America,* pp. 10–11.

    31. Mainwaring and Wilde, *The Progressive Church in Latin America,* pp. 8–9.

    32. Levine, *Religion and Politics in Latin America,* p. 39.

    33. Levine, *Religion and Political Conflict in Latin America,* p. 11.

    34. Besides the specific works on liberation theology cited here, for further analyses see
Ricardo Antoncich, *Christians in the Face of Injustice: A Latin American Reading of Catholic
Social Teaching* (Maryknoll, N.Y.: Orbis Books, 1987); Phillip Berryman, *Liberation Theology*
(New York: Pantheon, 1987); Deane W. Ferm, *Third World Liberation Theologies* (Maryknoll,
N.Y.: Orbis Books, 1986); Arthur McGovern, *Liberation Theology and Its Critics* (Maryknoll,

N.Y.: Orbis Books, 1989); and Richard Rubenstein and John Roth, eds., *The Politics of Latin American Liberation Theology* (Washington, D.C.: Washington Institute Press, 1988).

35. Juan Luis Segundo, *The Liberation of Theology* (Maryknoll, N.Y.: Orbis Books, 1976), p. 8.

36. Gustavo Gutierrez, *A Theology of Liberation* (Maryknoll, N.Y.: Orbis Books, 1973), pp. 267–268.

37. Levine, *Popular Voices in Latin American Catholicism,* p. 17.

38. For example, Berryman, *Religious Roots of Rebellion,* discusses in one paragraph the growth of liberation theology in Protestant churches, especially through ISAL (Iglesia y Sociedad en América Latina or Church and Society in Latin America), which served as a network for Protestants articulating this theology. He states that "Protestants who became radicalized in a process similar to that described above tended to find themselves isolated from their parent churches and would gravitate to ecumenical circles" (p. 32). Dodson and Nuzzi-O'Shaughnessy spend somewhat more pages discussing the growth of a Protestant context-specific theology. They state that the renewal in the Catholic Church was a catalyst for the Protestants. Michael Dodson and Laura Nuzzi-O'Shaughnessy, *Nicaragua's Other Revolution: Religious Faith and Political Struggle* (Chapel Hill: University of North Carolina Press, 1990), p. 97. The progressive Protestant mission evolved in Latin America through three conferences of CELA (Conferencia Evangelica Latinoamerica or Latin American Evangelical Conference). Finally, Christian Smith states that ISAL's leader, Richard Shaull, created a Protestant "Theology of Revolution," which represented an intellectual school that "after 1968 propelled an organized body of Protestant theologians—soon joined by Catholic theologians—into the leadership of the liberation theology movement." In addition, Smith states that "it would be wrong to overestimate ISAL's influence on liberation theology. Still, ISAL contributed to a foundation on which insurgent consciousness was later built, and produced a group of radical theologians who helped increase organizational strength." Christian Smith, *Emergence of Liberation Theology,* pp. 116–117.

39. In her study of the emergence of developmentalism in Brazil and Argentina, Sikkink states, "I suggest that the organizational infrastructure, the operating procedures, and the accumulation of intellectual talent in an insulated portion of the bureaucracy are the principal differences between the institutional structure in Brazil and Argentina, and that they help explain differences in the implementation of developmentalist policy." Sikkink, *Ideas and Institutions,* p. 27.

40. G. John Ikenberry, "Conclusion: An Institutional Approach to American Foreign Economic Policy," *International Organization* 42, no. 1 (Winter 1988): 242.

41. As Mainwaring and Wilde state, "in the emergence of the progressive church in Latin America, the political dimension was particularly important. . . . The church's efforts at religious reform in the period were given concrete content by the political context of the region as a whole and of different national settings." Mainwaring and Wilde, *The Progressive Church in Latin America,* p. 12.

42. The basic ideology guiding the repressive states of Latin America was the doctrine of national security, according to which there was no distinction between war and peace—all times were war times. National security was no longer confined to the defense of borders, but now required internal security to counteract new forms of aggression in the form of guerrilla warfare. So-called subversion and communism were to be combated, and this required a strong security apparatus. From the military's perspective the armed forces were above ideological, political, economic and social disputes and were therefore the most suitable interpreters of national goals. The traditional institutions of legislature, executive, and judicial powers became nothing more than administrative services for the real power, that of the military. These were not old-style personal dictatorships; rather, they represented systematic

control of the state by armed forces as institutions. The most important institution became the secret service, which assured the strength and primacy of national security at all times. This often required action against the behavior of citizens, who were always receptive to infiltration. All people were suspected of subversion. Under this system, any dissenting voices and denunciations of the regimes, including protests from the churches, were regarded as attacks on the nation itself. Roberto Calvo, "The Church and the Doctrine of National Security," *Journal of Interamerican Studies and World Affairs* 21, no. 1 (February 1979): 81. See also Jose Comblin, *The Church and the National Security State* (Maryknoll, N.Y.: Orbis Books, 1979), pp. 70–78; Berryman, *Liberation Theology,* p. 97; and Levine, *Religion and Politics in Latin America,* p. 50.

43. Brian Smith, "Churches and Human Rights in Latin America: Recent Trends in the Subcontinent," *Journal of Interamerican Studies and World Affairs* 21, no. 1 (February 1979): 89–91, and *The Church and Politics in Chile,* p. 312.

44. Penny Lernoux, *Cry of the People: The Struggle for Human Rights in Latin America—The Catholic Church in Conflict with U.S. Policy* (New York: Penguin Books, 1982), p. 466.

45. Ibid., p. 13.

46. Walshe, "Prophetic Christianity and the Liberation Movement," p. 56.

47. For further analysis of the conjuncture between religious and political change, see especially Levine, *Popular Voices in Latin American Catholicism,* chapter 2.

48. Studying the church as an organization is not new. Much research has been conducted using traditional institutional analysis in which change in institutions is seen as an attempt to defend interests and expand influence. In this approach, church change is best understood as an elite-generated strategy designed to counteract a variety of religious and secular pressures that threaten the influence of the established institutional interests. Church action is seen as a mechanism developed to maintain church hegemony over a population whose allegiance is threatened by new social, economic, and political situations. This is translated into the Latin American case by studying how the hierarchy instituted change as part of a calculated response to specific challenges, such as the rise of Protestantism or socialism. Additionally, the hierarchy appears to have moved to change in an effort to stem the erosion of its religious monopoly resulting from other dilemmas, such as the endemic lack of clergy and a low level of religiosity among the nominally Catholic masses. Hewitt, *Base Christian Communities,* pp. 19–20. In all of these studies, church action is seen as a calculated response to particular social and religious challenges. According to this model, organizational behavior is rationally administered and changes in organizational patterns are planned in order to improve the level of efficiency. Departures from "rationality" are seen as deriving from random mistakes or lack of complete information. Alvin W. Gouldner, "Organizational Analysis," in Robert K. Merton et al., eds., *Sociology Today: Problems and Prospects* (New York: Basic Books, 1959), pp. 404–405.

There are several problems with this approach, as Mainwaring has argued. First, those working from the traditional organizational approach fail to understand that different models of the church result in different conceptions of its interests; and they fail to distinguish between instrumental goals, such as increasing mass attendance, and more fundamental church objectives, such as saving souls. Which set of goals a church chooses to emphasize is dependent upon its particular model of the church. There are no objective interests which a church *must* pursue. Second, it is not easy to determine whether a particular strategy has resulted in increased church influence. Third, it is difficult to discern the most efficient strategy for promoting institutional interests, even in the most rational organizations. In organizations like a church, with a huge range of goals, "knowing" the best strategy becomes almost impossible. Mainwaring, *The Catholic Church and Politics in Brazil,* pp. 4–7.

49. James G. March and Johan P. Olsen, "The New Institutionalism: Organizational Factors in Political Life," *American Political Science Review* 78 (September 1984): 735 and 738–739.

50. Ikenberry, "Conclusion: An Institutional Approach," p. 223.

51. Walter W. Powell and Paul J. Dimaggio, eds., *The New Institutionalism in Organizational Analysis* (Chicago: University of Chicago Press, 1991), pp. 10–11.

52. This may well be a function of the fact that, as mentioned above, most of the research on why and how churches change has focused on Latin America, where the Catholic Church is the majority church.

53. See Brian Smith, *The Church and Politics in Chile.*

2. A Legacy of Protest and Challenge

1. Following common usage in South Africa through the 1980s, "black" in this chapter refers to all nonwhite groups, including Africans, Coloreds, and Indians. The term African refers only to indigenous South Africans. The term "black" was popularized by the black consciousness movement in the 1970s, which urged a solidarity of these groups in the struggle against a perceived common enemy: white racism and oppression. "Black" was not a racial identity but a class one. Blacks were "those who are by law or tradition politically, economically and socially discriminated against as a group in the South African society and identifying themselves as a unit in the struggle towards the realization of their aspirations." Mokgethi Motlhabi, *The Theory and Practice of Black Resistance to Apartheid: A Social-Ethical Analysis* (Johannesburg: Skotaville, 1984), p. 106. The term "black" is considered a more positive statement than "nonwhite," and this latter term is used here only as it was used in historical context.

2. These various analyses include: Peter Walshe, *The Rise of African Nationalism in South Africa* (London: Christopher Hurst and Co., 1979); André Odendaal, *Black Protest Politics in South Africa to 1912* (Totowa, N.J.: Barnes and Noble, 1984); Tom Lodge, *Black Politics in South Africa since 1945* (Johannesburg: Ravan Press, 1983); and T. R. H. Davenport, *South Africa: A Modern History* (South Africa: Southern Book Publishers, 1989).

These scholars explain South African political events from various perspectives. Walshe, for example, can be categorized as coming from a political culture perspective, while Lodge's explanation is primarily a class-based, Marxist one. As noted above, while these are excellent analyses, none of these authors touch upon the issue of legitimacy. Thus, while this chapter draws upon these works, especially for factual information, this secondary literature is interpreted in a new light.

3. The evidence for arguments on how protest movements viewed their relationship to the state is drawn largely from primary texts, especially the various speeches and documents of these movements. Thousands of primary documents, from political speeches, to flyers, to minutes of meetings, have been compiled in a four-volume work edited by Thomas Karis and Gwendolen M. Carter, *From Protest to Challenge: A Documentary History of African Politics in South Africa 1882–1964* (Stanford: Hoover Institution, 1973).

4. Villa-Vicencio, *Civil Disobedience and Beyond*, p. 61.

5. Joseph Bensman, "Max Weber's Concept of Legitimacy: An Evaluation," in Arthur J. Vidich and Ronald M. Glassman, eds., *Conflict and Control: Challenge to Legitimacy of Modern Governments* (Beverly Hills, Calif.: Sage Publications, 1979), p. 36.

6. The analysis begins in 1910 because that is when, for the first time, one government ruled all of the previously separate units. The pre-Union period is covered extensively by several scholars, including Davenport, *South Africa;* Leonard Thompson, *A History of South*

Africa (New Haven: Yale University Press, 1990); and Eric Walker, *A History of Southern Africa* (London: Longmans, Green, and Co., 1957). What is important to note here is that the Union of South Africa emerged as a result of a devastating civil war from 1899 to 1902 between British white South Africans, who had first arrived in South Africa in 1806, and Afrikaners, descendants of white settlers primarily from Holland in 1652. At the time of the civil war, known as the Boer War, the area which was to become the Union of South Africa consisted of two British colonies, Natal and the Cape Colony, and two Boer (Afrikaner) republics, the Orange Free State and the Transvaal. The period between the end of the Boer war and the creation of the Union (1902–1909) was one of reconstruction, during which British administrators rehabilitated Afrikaners who had lost almost everything, the gold-mining industry was revitalized, and the problems of railways and customs tariffs between the four colonies were solved. During this period, the movement towards political union also gathered momentum. For details on the Boer War and its political effects, see Thomas Pakenham, *The Boer War* (New York: Random House, 1994).

7. Walshe, *Rise of African Nationalism*, p. 20.

8. For example, in October 1908 the Transvaal Natives' Union sent a petition with over three thousand signatures to the National Convention demanding a common roll franchise throughout South Africa. Native Congresses were also held in the Orange River Colony, the Cape, the Transvaal, and Natal. At each meeting, representatives passed resolutions against the color bar clauses and the failure to extend a non-European franchise to the north. Ibid., pp. 20–21.

9. Early African politics was dominated by a new African elite which began to emerge throughout southern Africa, and which included teachers, religious ministers, farmers, craftsmen, clerks, and traders. Ibid., p. 2. The domination of protest politics by elites did not change until the 1950s, when the African National Congress (ANC) became a mass-based movement.

10. Odendaal, *Black Protest Politics*, p. 143.

11. Quoted by Walshe, who states that "The convention's resolutions were simply a plea for the retention and extension of the Cape tradition. Its method was a reliance on past Imperial responsibilities. Union was desirable and inevitable but its aim should be the welfare of all inhabitants. Colour bar clauses . . . were emphatically rejected and . . . the Cape vote was to be made unalterable." Walshe, *Rise of African Nationalism*, p. 21.

12. The political details are merely sketched here. For a full account of the events surrounding the formation of Union, see especially Walshe, *Rise of African Nationalism*, Odendaal, *Black Protest Politics*, Davenport, *South Africa*, and Walker, *History of Southern Africa*.

13. Odendaal, *Black Protest Politics*, p. 222.

14. Ibid., p. 168.

15. The first national executive committee of the SANNC clearly represented elite interests, and was composed of four ministers of religion, lawyers, an editor, a building contractor, a teacher and estate agent, an interpreter, and a Native Labour Agent, who recruited African mineworkers. Many had attended mission schools, and five had studied abroad. They played important roles in local political organizations, in the African press, and in church leadership. Francis Meli, *A History of the ANC: South Africa Belongs to Us* (London: James Curry, 1988), p. 34.

16. Walshe, *Rise of African Nationalism*, p. 34.

17. Ibid., p. 38.

18. Many discriminatory laws were passed immediately; however, it is beyond the scope of this chapter to describe them. For such detail, see especially Karis and Carter, *From Protest to Challenge*, Odendaal, *Black Protest Politics*, Davenport, *South Africa*, Walshe, *Rise of African*

Nationalism, and Meli, *History of the ANC.* A serious violation of rights, and one of the primary complaints of blacks, were the pass laws, which regulated the movement and residence of Africans. As one African political leader, D. D. T. Jabavu, stated, "if ever one race in the world did ever seek the most signal way to repress and humiliate another, human invention could not have done it more effectually than the system of Pass Laws. . . . This thing . . . is simply perpetuated martial law in peace time." D. D. T. Jabavu, "Native Unrest," paper read at Natal Missionary Conference, July 1920, in Karis and Carter, *From Protest to Challenge,* 1:121 (hereafter denoted as KCI, II, or III for volumes 1, 2, and 3, respectively, followed by the page number).

19. Meli, *History of the ANC,* p. 52.

20. The early days of African resistance politics were filled with appeals to the British Crown, the House of Commons, and the British people to uphold the British constitutional tradition of nonracialism. Having no voice in the discussions of the new constitutional model, Africans looked for some kind of reassurance and guarantee that their interests would not be ignored by Britain, which they regarded as the ultimate constitutional authority. In a petition to the House of Commons, for example, the delegation pleaded "that the status of the coloured people and natives will be lowered, and that an injustice will be done to those who are the majority of the people in British South Africa, who have in the past shown their unswerving loyalty to the Crown, their attachment to British institutions, their submission to the laws of the land, and their capacity for exercising full civil and political rights." W. P. Schreiner, A. Abdurahman, J. Tengo Jabavu, et al., "Petition to the House of Commons," July 1909, KCI: 56.

21. Walshe, *Rise of African Nationalism,* p. 37.

22. Ibid., p. 38.

23. Odendaal, *Black Protest Politics,* p. 154.

24. Meli, *History of the ANC,* p. 41.

25. Quoted in Lawrence T. Farley, *Plebiscites and Sovereignty: The Crisis of Political Illegitimacy* (Boulder, Colo.: Westview Press, 1986), p. 5.

26. Rev. Z. R. Mahabane, "The Exclusion of the Bantu," Address, 1921, KCI: 294.

27. Ibid., KCI: 296.

28. KCI: 149, 153.

29. KCII: 3–4.

30. KCII: 4.

31. The AAC directed their petitions to several levels. The Governor-General was asked to refuse to assent to the Cape franchise clause, King George and the Imperial Parliament were asked for "an expression of their opinion," the British High Commission Territories were alerted to the policies to which they would be subject should they be incorporated into the Union, and a deputation was sent to Cape Town to meet with the prime minister and present AAC views to the Bar of the House of Assembly. Walshe, *Rise of African Nationalism,* p. 122.

32. Ibid., p. 113.

33. KCII: 43. At this stage, black political protesters continued to accept the state as legitimate, choosing instead to concentrate on challenging individual policies. A case in point was the debate over participation in, versus the boycotting of, the newly created Native Representative Council. During the AAC, this Council had been outright rejected as a substitute for the franchise—that is, the Cape common voters role. Yet once the bills became laws, the AAC abandoned the option of a complete boycott. Instead it worked within these constitutional structures, accepting them as part of the machinery for representation, in the hopes of using the NRC and parliamentary representatives as platforms to continue their opposition

to racial discrimination. The ironic outcome was that Africans were now participating in the very segregated political institutions that had sparked the formation of the AAC in the first place.

34. Walshe, *Rise of African Nationalism,* p. 112.

35. Lodge, *Black Politics in South Africa,* p. 11.

36. Walshe, *Rise of African Nationalism,* p. 129.

37. Only white troops were permitted to join combat units, while Colored and African solders were confined to auxiliary services. South African forces participated in the reconquest of Ethiopia from the Italians in 1940–1941, seized Madagascar in 1942 in order to prevent a possible Japanese landing, and took part in North African campaigns against German and Italian forces in Egypt and Libya. The 6th South African Armored Division was sent to Italy as part of the American Fifth Army. In total, some 200,000 uniformed South Africans took part in the war, of whom close to 9,000 were killed. Davenport, *South Africa,* pp. 330–331.

38. The Committee on Africa, the War, and Peace Aims, *The Atlantic Charter and Africa from an American Standpoint* (New York: Phelps-Stokes Fund, 1942), p. 35.

39. As opposed to "equal rights for all civilized men" as in its 1923 Bill of Rights. See KCII: 89. Until the publication of *African Claims,* ANC leadership was prepared to accept a qualified franchise, as under the old Cape common voters role.

40. For the complete text of *African Claims,* see KCII: 209–223.

41. Walshe, *Rise of African Nationalism,* p. 274.

42. "Basic Policy of Congress Youth League," manifesto issued by the National Executive Committee of the ANC Youth League, 1948, KCII: 324.

43. KCII: 73.

44. Thompson, *History of South Africa,* p. 173.

45. Ibid., p. 189.

46. Ibid., p. 196.

47. KCIII: 7.

48. Davenport, *South Africa,* p. 362.

49. Motlhabi, *Theory and Practice of Black Resistance,* p. 13.

50. KCII: 103.

51. "Programme of Action," Statement of Policy adopted at the ANC Annual Conference, December 1949, KCII: 337–338.

52. The Campaign demanded the repeal of six "unjust laws," including the pass laws, which were being enforced with greater vigor after 1948; the Suppression of Communism Act; the Group Areas Act and the Stock Limitation and Bantu Authorities Acts; and the Separate Representation of Voters Act.

53. Villa-Vicencio, *Civil Disobedience and Beyond,* p. 49.

54. KCIII: 41.

55. The Charter was divided into ten points: the people shall govern; all national groups shall have equal rights; the people shall share in the country's wealth; the land shall be shared among those who work it; all shall be equal before the law; all shall enjoy equal human rights; there shall be work and security; the doors of learning and of culture shall be opened; there shall be houses, security and comfort; there shall be peace and friendship. "Freedom Charter," adopted by Congress of the People, June 1955, KCIII: 205–208.

56. Motlhabi, *Theory and Practice of Black Resistance,* p. 13.

57. KCIII: 295.

58. The act defined communism to mean not only Marxist-Leninism but also "any related form of that doctrine" which sought to establish the dictatorship of the proletariat, or any activity to bring about "any political, industrial, social or economic change within the Union by the promotion of disturbances or disorder." Any person who was suspected of

"furthering the aims of communism" could be banned. No reason had to be given for the banning and the victim had no legal means of challenging the order. It was later extended to include anyone who had ever professed communism and its operation was made retroactive. The concept of "statutory communism" became common in South African legal circles. Davenport, *South Africa,* pp. 368–369.

59. The General Law Amendment Act was further amended in 1961, 1962, 1963, 1964, 1966, 1968, 1969, 1972, 1973, 1974, and 1975. Each subsequent amendment further restricted the activities of persons and organizations. For details of each amendment, see Muriel Horrell, *Laws Affecting Race Relations in South Africa* (Johannesburg: South African Institute of Race Relations, 1978).

60. Motlhabi, *Theory and Practice of Black Resistance,* p. 31.

61. Thompson, *History of South Africa,* p. 199.

62. For example, influx control laws were tightened, and from the mid-1950s onward, no African could be in an urban area for more than seventy-two hours without special permission. Once in a city, Africans lived under very detailed regulations and were required to register at a labor bureau and report to it. Any African considered to be "idle and disorderly" could be ordered to leave an urban area immediately. In relation to the violation of due process rights, search and seizure were permitted without a warrant if it was believed that "internal security" was endangered—a decision that could be made by any police officer. On the violation of free speech, anyone whose words were meant to "incite to civil disobedience," or whose probable consequences were public violence, could be severely punished. Freedom of assembly was curtailed through the prohibition of public meetings of more than ten Africans unless specially permitted. Assemblies in private as well as public places were regulated. The rights of African laborers were also violated through the prohibition on African strikes and the reservation of jobs by race. For more detail concerning these human rights violations, see especially KCIII: 48–55.

63. Nelson Mandela, "In Our Lifetime," KCIII: 246.

64. Albert Lutuli, "The Road to Freedom Is via the Cross," statement issued in November 1952, KCII: 488.

65. Gail Gerhart, *Black Power in South Africa: The Evolution of an Ideology* (Berkeley: University of California Press, 1978), p. 94.

66. Mandela, "In Our Lifetime," KCIII: 246.

67. KCIII: 349.

68. The Pan Africanist Congress was formed in 1959 when a number of "Africanists" within the ANC became unhappy with its increasingly close ties with other non-African organizations, including SACPO and SAIC. They accused the ANC of compromising on African ideals and broke away to form a new organization. The PAC insisted that the liberation of Africans must come solely from Africans themselves, and thus embarked on a program of empowering Africans. For more detail, see Gerhart, *Black Power in South Africa.*

69. The specific demands of the campaign included the abolition of pass laws, a minimum salary of £35, and no victimization of leaders. KCIII: 571.

70. This account of Sharpeville and its aftermath is drawn primarily from KCIII: 330–339.

A second precipitating factor for the turn towards violence was the ANC's final, unsuccessful attempt to establish dialogue with the government. This came in the 1961 All-in African Conference, which called upon the government to convene a national convention with "sovereign powers." Such a convention was to represent "all people on a fully democratic basis . . . to lay the foundations of a new union, a non-racial democracy, belonging to all South Africans, and in line with the United Nations Charter. . . . " "A Statement by the Emergency Committee of the African National Congress," issued in April 1960, KCIII: 573. Any hope of initiating this interracial dialogue or a multiracial national convention was dashed, however, when Prime Minister Verwoerd declared that the government would "be as unyielding as a wall of granite."

71. Nelson Mandela, "Statement during the Rivonia Trial," April 1964, KCIII: 777.

72. Ibid., p. 781.

73. Ibid., p. 777.

74. KCIII: 675.

75. Mandela's court statements, October and November 1962, KCIII: 730.

76. For details on the BCM, see Motlhabi, *Theory and Practice of Black Resistance*, pp. 106–153, and Gerhart, *Black Power in South Africa*, pp. 257–299.

77. Steve Biko, *I Write What I Like*, ed. C. R. Aelred Stubbs (New York: Harper and Row, 1978), p. 49, quoted in Thompson, *History of South Africa*, p. 212.

78. In recognition that the BCM considered the state illegitimate, nine BCM leaders were put on trial in 1974 under the Terrorism Act for fomenting student unrest on black campuses, and for "conspiring to transform the state by unconstitutional, revolutionary and/or violent means." All were convicted and sent to prison. Davenport, *South Africa*, pp. 418–419.

79. For details concerning the exile period, see especially Lodge, *Black Politics in South Africa*, pp. 295–362.

80. KCIII: 646.

81. The accused were not tried under the common law of high treason because it would have placed a greater burden on the state to provide proof without a reasonable doubt. This would have required a preparatory examination, useful to the defense, as well as two witnesses to every overt act of treason. Rather, they were accused under a newly passed law, the Sabotage Act, which also carried the death penalty. Nevertheless, observers have described the trial, known as the Rivonia Trial, as a "classical case of high treason par excellence." In fact, in his final judgment, the judge himself agreed that the case had been essentially one of treason. KCIII: 677.

82. The ANC never formally and decisively declared the state illegitimate, and it would be interesting to examine why. The use of the term legitimacy actually came very late in the process of challenge (not until 1985 and the Kairos Document). It appears that the term was a product of the struggle rather than its driving force.

83. Walshe, "Prophetic Christianity and the Liberation Movement," p. 28.

3. Changing Political Context

1. Walshe, "Prophetic Christianity and the Liberation Movement," p. 36.

2. Jack Spence, "The Military in South African Politics," in Johnson, *South Africa: No Turning Back*, pp. 243–244.

3. Price, *Apartheid State in Crisis*, p. 85.

4. SACBC, "N.S.M.S. and the Church," undated, p. 3, photocopy (BCA).

5. The Council became a policy-formulating body involved in virtually all domestic and foreign matters—part of a "security establishment" in which decision making was centralized around a managerial committee system made up of top military and security personnel. In the 1980s, the SSC became a central decision-making forum in the government, probably more important than the cabinet. The permanent members of the SSC were the President, Minister of Defense, Minister of Foreign Affairs, and top military and police brass. Others, including the ministers of Law and Order, Defense, Foreign Affairs, Justice, Con-

stitutional Development and Planning, and Cooperation and Development, were invited in on an ad hoc basis. It became the core of six components of the "security establishment," the others being the SADF; the National Intelligence Service (NIS); the Security Police; the Department of Military Intelligence; and the South African Police (SAP). In addition to the SSC, other organizational infrastructures were developed, including both the National Security Management System (NSMS) and Joint Management Centers (JMCs). The NSMS was created to implement the policies developed by the SSC, in addition to providing it with technical and expert advice. The JMCs brought together military and police officers, state bureaucrats, and businessmen to coordinate security at local and regional levels and to serve as early warning systems to identify areas of potential unrest. Additionally, the JMCs coordinated the security police. John Brewer, "The Police in South African Politics," in Johnson, *South Africa: No Turning Back*, p. 274.

6. Price, *Apartheid State in Crisis*, p. 119.

7. Ibid., p. 125.

8. Yet another area of reform was "influx control," through which the state sought to limit and control the movement of Africans into urban, "white" areas. In the early 1980s, both the Job Reservation Act, which had legalized the color bar by reserving certain occupations for whites, and the Pass Laws, which required all Africans to carry and produce identity documents that listed their officially approved places of employment and residence, were abolished. However, these laws were subsequently replaced with others intended to control the movement of Africans under a policy of Orderly Urbanization, one goal being the removal of urban blacks to commuter townships.

9. Ann Seidman, *The Roots of Crisis in Southern Africa* (Trenton, N.J.: Africa World Press, 1985), p. 31.

10. Price, *Apartheid State in Crisis*, p. 144.

11. Ibid., p. 160.

12. As explained in chapter 2, the black consciousness movement of the 1970s was not an organization as much as an intellectual movement, although it certainly does qualify as a mass movement of black opposition. It did not have the organizational structure of the ANC, PAC, or UDF.

13. Anton Harbor, "United—In the Politics of Refusal," *Rand Daily Mail*, June 8, 1983 (OPD).

14. The state reacted swiftly and violently against these protests in an attempt to crush the UDF, but was not successful in doing so. The key to the UDF's resilience lay with its diffuse organization and its ability to mobilize at a grass-roots level. Because its membership had filtered to the level of "street committees," layer upon layer of leadership could be detained, only to be replaced by new leaders. Consequently, opposition to the government not only survived but continued to strengthen throughout the 1980s. Indeed, so decentralized and widespread was the movement, that stayaways could be called overnight as a result of the network of strong areas and of street and bloc committees. Within months after the formation of the UDF in 1983, the government attempted to cripple the activities of its members without actually banning them. This it did by outlawing public meetings as well as administrative meetings in an attempt to prevent them from functioning efficiently. By 1987, the government was attempting to break the UDF by removing national, regional, and local leadership from their community base through assassinations, imprisonment, and bannings. In addition, the police carried out repeated raids on its regional and national offices. Other attempts to crush the UDF included treason trials of its leadership to eliminate them from political life. By June 1988, 51 political trials involving 165 leading activists had taken place. A further 58 trials were in progress, involving 232 accused. In the face of each new repressive

tactic, the UDF succeeded in adapting its organization to work under more secretive conditions while still exploiting every available inch of legal space. Human Awareness Program, *Info. '89* (Johannesburg, 1989), section C16, p. 3 (OPD).

15. Price, *Apartheid State in Crisis,* p. 193.

16. Ibid., p. 253.

17. The SADF first became involved in internal security in October 1984, with the deployment of 7,000 troops on a "seal and search" operation (Operation Palmiet) in Sebokeng township. By the end of 1985, over 35,000 troops were on duty in the townships. At the same time, there was a huge increase in both the size and the number of the police. In addition, police manpower was supplemented by part-time forces, a volunteer Reserve Police Force (intended primarily to attract schoolchildren), and the Police Reserve consisting of ex-members of the SAP. Simultaneously, expenditure on the regular police force rose by 69 percent between the financial years of 1983–1984 and 1985–1986. In 1986 the SAP was given its own secret expenditure account. By the second state of emergency, special township or municipal police forces known as *kitskonstables* (instant police) were in place. By late 1987, there were over 9,000 of them, 4,000 of whom had been recruited after the 1986 state of emergency. Recruited from the unemployed, illiterates, and criminals, they quickly developed a reputation for extreme brutality and undiscipline in their attempts to reimpose township council rule. Brewer, "Police in South African Politics," pp. 259–260.

18. Ibid., pp. 269–271.

19. Price, *Apartheid State in Crisis,* p. 258.

20. Human Awareness Program, *Info. '89,* section C16, p. 3 (OPD).

21. Brewer, "Police in South African Politics," p. 273.

22. Human Awareness Program, *Info. '89,* section C4, p. 2 (OPD).

23. Price, *Apartheid State in Crisis,* p. 152.

24. Ibid., p. 257.

25. Margaret Nash, ed., *Your Kingdom Come.* Papers and Resolutions of the 1980 SACC National Conference (SACC, 1980), pp. 22–23 (CCA).

26. *Ecunews* (September 1981): 12 (CCA).

27. Nash, *Your Kingdom Come,* p. 6 (CCA).

28. South African Institute of Race Relations (SAIRR), *Race Relations Survey,* 1981, p. 34.

29. SACBC, *The Bishops Speak,* vol. 3, 1981–1985 (Pretoria: SACBC, 1989), p. 2 (BCA).

30. Specifically, the report stated that it was the "almost unanimous opinion of those to whom we spoke that the great majority of the people do not want the South African imposed constitution." Furthermore, in exposing gross violations of human rights carried out by the South African security forces in their quest to eliminate those sympathetic to SWAPO guerrillas, it claimed, "that detention and interrogation in any part of the country are accompanied by beating, torture, spare diet and solitary confinement is accepted as common knowledge." The report supplied detailed descriptions of torture by those who had experienced it firsthand. Finally, the report drew the anger of the government because it called for the implementation of UN Resolution 435, which called for a cease-fire, troop withdrawals, and UN supervised elections—a proposal the South African government categorically rejected. The SACBC concluded the report by stating that there was universal consensus (with South Africa the only dissenting voice) that South Africa had no right to be in Namibia, and by a call for prayer for the withdrawal of South Africa "from a situation of violence that appears totally unacceptable to us." SACBC, *Report on Namibia* (Pretoria: SACBC, 1982), pp. 17–20 (BCA).

31. Archbishop Denis E. Hurley, "The Catholic Church and Apartheid," *Africa Report* 28 (July/August 1983): 19.

32. *Ecunews* 2 (1982): 9 (CCA).

33. The SACBC never declared apartheid a heresy. This may be one reason that the state viewed the SACC as more "radical" than the SACBC. Possible reasons for the more cautious approach of the bishops are explored in chapter 6.

34. Charles Villa-Vicencio, "Southern Africa Today: A Consensus against Apartheid," *Journal of Theology for Southern Africa* 41 (December 1982): 85.

35. Jim Leatt, "The Church in Resistance Post 1976," revised research paper for a Conference on South Africa beyond Apartheid, Boston, January 1987, p. 7 (OPD).

36. *Ecunews* (August 1983): 2 (CCA).

37. It is interesting to note that while the SACBC was very outspoken in its rejection of the constitution, it never formally declared apartheid a heresy.

38. The bishops issued a pastoral letter, read in all Catholic parishes in September 1983, which set out reasons for rejecting the proposed constitution, asserting that it would not be a satisfactory step on the road to peace in South Africa, but would further entrench apartheid as well as put too much power in the hands of the president. SACBC Pastoral Letter, quoted in Catholic Institute for International Relations, *The Church and Apartheid* (London: CIIR, 1985), p. 5.

39. Hurley, address given on August 22, 1984, quoted in Trócaire, *South Africa Information Pack* (Dublin: Trócaire, undated) (BCA).

40. SACC National Conference Resolutions, 1983, Resolution 21, photocopy (CCA).

41. Ibid., Resolution 22.

42. Harbor, "United—In the Politics of Refusal" (OPD).

43. In February 1983, one month after the SACBC published its *Namibia Report,* Hurley stated in a press conference that he had heard that the South African–trained special police unit *Koevoet* (Crowbar) was committing atrocities against the local population in Namibia. Soon thereafter, he was informed that the Attorney General was investigating him for the statement under section 27B of the Police Act, which made it a crime to publish "untrue matter in relations to any action by the South African Police Force."

44. Margaret A. Novicki, "The Reverend Allan Boesak: An Interview," *Africa Report* 28 (July/August 1983): 7.

45. Wolfram Kistner, "Response to the Evaluation of the Activities of the SACC Division of Justice and Reconciliation in the Memorandum of the South African Police," SACC Submission to the Eloff Commission, undated, pp. 1–2, photocopy (CCA).

46. *Ecunews* (February 1983): 30 (CCA).

47. The government accepted the commission's recommendations and prepared to bring the SACC into the ambit of the Fund-Raising Act. In the end, however, the state dropped any further action against the SACC, which was not subject to the Fund-Raising Act. Since the commission's own auditors had admitted that any financial irregularities had long been cleared up, the only explanation for the government's response must be that it used the commission as the least damaging way to place a tighter control on the SACC; any action taken against the organization on solely political grounds would have been more difficult to accomplish, since it would have raised the issue of religious freedom.

48. Desmond Tutu, "The Divine Intention," presentation by Bishop D. Tutu, General Secretary of the South African Council of Churches to the Eloff Commission of Inquiry (Johannesburg: SACC, 1983), p. 5 (CCA).

49. Ibid., p. 29.

50. *ICT News* (December 1984): 5 (CTA).

51. *Ecunews* (February 1984): 10–11 (CCA).

52. Desmond Tutu, "The Blasphemy That Is Apartheid," *Africa Report* 28, no. 4 (July/August 1983): 6.

228 *Notes to Pages 58–60*

53. *Ecunews* (March 1984): 17 (CCA).

54. By year's end, the SACBC further antagonized the state by publishing its *Report on Police Conduct during Township Protests.* Again, the SACBC did not set out deliberately to intensify its conflict with the state, although this was certainly a consequence of the report. Rather, the SACBC was responding to the increasingly repressive situation in the townships. This report leveled allegations against the police, including the indiscriminate use of firearms resulting in the death of children, the reckless use of teargas, and rape. SAIRR, *Race Relations Survey,* 1984, p. 909.

55. Ibid., p. 57.

56. Including nine African languages, as well as Swedish, Dutch, and German.

57. White men conscripted were required to serve an initial two-year period of continuous service, followed by 720 days over the next twelve years, in six two-year cycles of 120 days in each cycle. Not more than ninety days could be served in one year. Interim goals of the ECC included broadening the definition of conscientious objection to include both selective and universal, and both secular and religious, grounds for objecting; alternative service to be established in both nonstate and state bodies; reducing the length of alternative service to the length of military service; and giving conscripts the choice of whether or not to serve in the townships or Namibia. End Conscription Campaign pamphlet, "What is the End Conscription Campaign?" 1985 (BCA).

58. The 1974 SACC National Conference passed a resolution supporting the right to conscientious objection, as did the 1977 SACBC Plenary Session. While the SACC actually supported the ECC earlier than the SACBC—through a conference resolution at its 1984 National Conference—the bishops appear to have embraced the issue more strongly, possibly because of their strong stance on the occupation of Namibia by South African forces. When the Defense Amendment Act was originally promulgated in 1983, Cardinal McCann protested to the Minister of Defense that it was inadequate because it made no provisions for objection based on the view that the war in Namibia was unjust. The Cardinal requested that the bill be amended to include the "so-called political objector," and added that if this was not done, the bishops would have no choice but to reject the bill as unjust. Nevertheless, the bill was enacted with none of the suggested SACBC amendments; as a result, at its 1985 Plenary Session meeting the SACBC formally supported the ECC. Archbishop Stephen Naidoo, "A Request to the SACBC to Support the Call to End Conscription," speech delivered to the 1985 SACBC Plenary Session, photocopy (BCA).

59. "What Others Say on Violence and non-Violence," *Crisis News* (April/May 1988): 1 (CTA).

60. The Bishops' Conference as a whole, however, never declared the war in Namibia unjust, even though it was pushed to do so by its own Justice and Peace Commission, as well as its own theologians. In its preliminary report on the justness of the Namibian war, the SACBC's Theological Advisory Committee (TAC) stated, "Since the South African occupation and rule of Namibia is clearly illegitimate, it had no right to declare and wage this war." This was only a draft of the TAC report. SACBC Justice and Peace Commission, "Proposal to the January Plenary Session RE: War in Namibia," 1988, appendix 2, photocopy (BCA); and Catholic Institute for International Relations, "Testimony of Archbishop Denis Hurley," in *Country and Conscience: South African Conscientious Objectors* (London: CIIR/Pax Christi, 1988), p. 19.

61. *Ecunews* (February 1984): 11 (CCA).

62. IMBISA (Inter-territorial Meeting of Bishops of Southern Africa) Plenary Assembly, "Report on the Situation in South Africa," Harare, September 1987, pp. 4–45, photocopy (BCA).

63. Margaret Nash, ed., *Women—A Power for Change*, SACC Conference Report, 1985, p. 57 (CCA).

64. Any organization or individual who publicly supported sanctions was liable for a ten-year prison sentence or R20,000 fine, or both. Naudé reiterated his stance, stating that "even if in advocating them (disinvestment and economic sanctions), I have to go to jail, I plead for them, and I'll take the consequences for the sake of the future of our land." Beyers Naudé, address given in November 1985 to the British Council of Churches, quoted in Trócaire, *South Africa Information Pack* (BCA).

65. Nash, *Women—A Power for Change*, p. 5 (CCA).

66. *Financial Mail*, July 5, 1985, p. 4 (OPD).

67. SACBC, *The Bishops Speak*, vol. 3, 1981–1985, p. 86 (BCA).

68. SACC, "A Theological Rationale and a Call to Prayer for an End to Unjust Rule," June 16 Memorial Service handout, 1986 (CCA).

69. *Ecunews* (June/July 1985): 17 (CCA).

70. *The Kairos Document: Challenge to the Church: A Theological Comment on the Political Crisis in South Africa*, rev. 2d ed. (Grand Rapids, Mich.: Eerdmans, 1985), p. 30.

71. Ibid., pp. 28–29.

72. *Ecunews* (March/April 1985): 2, 4 (CCA).

73. *ICT News* (March, 1986): 3 (CTA).

74. This intransigence was evidenced in part by the collapse of the Eminent Persons Group. In the midst of the political crisis of 1986, the Commonwealth countries sent an Eminent Persons Group (EPG) to mediate in an attempt to forestall economic sanctions against South Africa. The EPG also had extensive contacts with the regime and political leaders in the liberation movements, both in prison within South Africa and in exile. The government welcomed the initiative and even offered to meet the Eminent Persons, who included a former Australian prime minster and the former Nigerian head of state. While the EPG was in South Africa, the SADF attacked ANC installations in Zambia, Botswana, and Zimbabwe, though it had recently announced the decision to negotiate in the hopes of bringing peace. The raids, then, were proof that the South African state was not serious and instead intended to violently repress opposition. The EPG was "mortally wounded" and concluded that "while the Government claims to be ready to negotiate, it is in truth not yet prepared to negotiate fundamental change. . . . Its programme of reform does not end apartheid, but seeks to give it a less human face." The Commonwealth Group of Eminent Persons, *Mission to South Africa: The Commonwealth Report* (London: Penguin, 1986), pp. 132–133, and Balia, *Christian Resistance to Apartheid*, pp. 134–135.

75. SACBC, "Report on Extraordinary Plenary Session of the Southern African Catholic Bishops' Conference," April 29–May 1, 1986, pp. 5–6, photocopy (BCA).

76. Ibid., p. 10.

77. Ibid., p. 14.

78. SACBC, "Minutes of the 1989 Plenary Session," August 21–25, 1989, appendix 3, p. 3 (BCA).

79. Ibid., p. 11.

80. SACBC, "Minutes of the 1990 Plenary Session," January 24–30, 1990, p. 90 (BCA).

81. Leatt, "Church in Resistance Post 1976," p. 9 (OPD).

82. IMBISA, 1987, p. 5 (BCA).

83. SACBC, *The Bishops Speak*, vol. 4, 1986–1987 (Pretoria: SACBC, 1989), p. 8 (BCA).

84. Sr. Margaret Kelly, O.P., "The Catholic Church and Resistance to Apartheid," unpublished paper, November 1991, photocopy (BCA).

85. Hurley further drew the wrath of the state when in April 1986, in defiance of the

law, he and Mkhatshwa led a delegation to consult with the ANC leadership at their head-quarters in exile. In addition to the official talks, Hurley led the ANC in prayer at a memorial service. Through this meeting, the SACBC came closer than ever to supporting the liberation movement, agreeing with the ANC argument that "anybody not doing anything to oppose apartheid is in fact supporting it." In a joint communiqué, the bishops and ANC stated that apartheid could not be reformed and had to be completely abolished and replaced by a new system. Two months later, Mkhatshwa was redetained for a year.

86. *ICT News* (December 1986): 5 (CTA).

87. Frank Chikane was vice-president of the UDF Transvaal branch, Smangaliso Mkhatshwa served on the Northern Transvaal executive, and Allan Boesak and Beyers Naudé were patrons of the UDF. Many many others served on local and regional structures. Mkhatshwa is another interesting example to illustrate this point. He was detained repeatedly, not so much because of his role as General Secretary of the SACBC but because of his activities in the BCM as well as the UDF. Starting in 1976, he was detained several times, for periods ranging from six months to a year. He was also banned and restricted from 1977 and 1983. He was one of the first to be detained at the time of the declaration of a state of emergency in June 1986. He was detained for an entire year, during which time he was assaulted and tortured by the security police. He was finally charged with subversion for addressing an illegal gathering but was eventually acquitted of all charges. A mass held in 1984 to remember Mkhatshwa while in detention was attended by over three thousand worshipers and by the Security Police as well. *ICT News* (June 1988): 7, and *Ecunews* (February 1984): 20 (CTA).

88. Reverend Sol Jacob, ed., *Hope In Crisis,* 1986 SACC National Conference Report, p. 31 (CCA).

89. SACBC Commission for Justice and Reconciliation, "Use of Church Buildings and Facilities," 1986 Plenary Session Report, pp. 1–2, photocopy (BCA).

90. The SACBC never officially adopted the Lusaka Statement, and in fact had serious reservations about it. Possible reasons for this will be discussed in chapter 6.

91. The SACC's rejection of legitimacy *as a conference* was foreshadowed in 1986 when its Justice and Reconciliation division stated, "the authorities which claim to be the government have become the main force in spreading lawlessness, disruption and disorder in the South African state. . . . South Africa is therefore a state with a government that cannot claim legitimacy." Ibid., p. 88 (CCA).

92. World Council of Churches, "Text of the Lusaka Statement," in *The Churches' Search for Justice and Peace in Southern Africa,* pp. 28–29 (CCA).

93. Ibid.

94. Peter Storey, the former president, stated that he "could not vote for the implication that taking up arms is something in which one had no choice." Black delegates at the conference, however, voted unanimously against this sentiment.

95. Sol Jacob and Oswal Mtshali, eds., *Refugees and Exiles: Challenge to the Churches,* Report of the Nineteenth Annual National Conference of the South African Council of Churches (Johannesburg: SACC, 1987), p. 58 (CCA).

96. SACBC TAC, "Minutes of the Theological Advisory Commission Meeting," June 10–11, 1987 (Connor).

97. SACBC TAC, "Minutes of the Theological Advisory Commission Meeting," November 2–4, 1987, p. 2 (Connor).

98. SACBC, "Some Results of the Hammanskraal Consultation for Future Use," unpublished paper, March 1987, p. 1, photocopy (BCA).

99. Ibid., p. 4, emphasis in original.

100. SACBC TAC, "Minutes of the Theological Advisory Commission Meeting," March 23–24, 1988 (Connor).

101. SACBC TAC, "Minutes of the Theological Advisory Commission Meeting," June 6–7, 1988, emphasis in original (Connor).

102. SACBC TAC, "Discussion on Documents Presented to Board Meeting," May 1989 (Connor).

103. SACBC, "Draft Documents for SACBC Discussion on the Question of Legitimacy," Paper 2, p. 6, photocopy (BCA).

104. "Clergy Defy the Detainees Proclamations," *Crisis News* (April/May 1987): 1 (CTA).

105. *Internos* (April 1987): 9 (BCA).

106. Catholic Institute for International Relations, "New Nation—Gagged: Silencing the People's Paper" (London: CIIR, undated), p. 1 (BCA).

107. Frank Chikane, "The Church's Prophetic Witness against the Apartheid System in South Africa (25th February—8th April, 1988)," *SACC Booklet* (Johannesburg: SACC, 1988), pp. 2–4 and 33–36 (CCA).

108. Ibid., pp. 7–8.

109. SACC, *Senzenina [What have we done?]: The Day 300 Church Leaders, Clergy and Laity Marched on the South African Parliament* (Johannesburg: SACC, 1988), pp. 9–10 (CCA).

110. "Documentation: The Church-State Confrontation, Correspondence and Statements February–April 1988," *Journal of Theology for Southern Africa* 63 (June 1988): 73.

111. SACC, Letter from Rev. Chikane to P. W. Botha, March 18, 1988, in "Report of the Emergency Convocation of Churches in South Africa," May 30, 1988 (CCA).

112. "Documentation: The Church-State Confrontation, Correspondence and Statements February–April 1988," *Journal of Theology for Southern Africa* 63 (June 1988): 78–79.

113. Ibid., pp. 83–85.

114. Ibid., p. 87.

115. SAIRR, *Race Relations Survey*, 1988/1989, p. 718.

116. The one exception to this rule was that an "affected organization" could still receive funds from a foreign embassy inside South Africa. This presented a problem for the SACC, which does not, in principle, accept money directly from any government.

117. *Ecunews* (July 1988): 20 (CCA). The bill's final form was the Disclosure of Foreign Funding Act, which passed into legislation in March 1989. The stated objection of the act was to "regulate the disclosure of the receipt of money from outside the Republic or for certain organizations and persons; and to provide for matters connected therewith."

118. This bill did not have similar implications for the SACBC because it represented a church and not an "organization." It would have been virtually impossible for the state to declare the Catholic Church an "affected organization" or to ban it. It could, however, have banned individual Catholics, such as Archbishop Hurley, had it chosen to do so.

119. *Church Action in the South African Crisis*, The South African Council of Churches National Conference Report (Johannesburg: SACC, 1988), p. 185 (CCA).

120. Frank Chikane, "The Churches and the South African Crisis" (London: CIIR, 1988), p. 4, pamphlet (CCA). Shortly after the bill was promulgated, Kagiso Trust, a foundation for funding victims of apartheid and administered through the SACC, was declared a "reporting organization." The trust responded by refusing to provide any information to the state.

121. ICT, "Annual General Meeting Conference Report," 1989, p. 5 (CTA).

122. *Ecunews* (June 1988): 5 (CCA).

123. Chikane, "The Churches and the South African Crisis," p. 8 (CCA).

124. SACC, "The Standing for the Truth Campaign," 1988, pamphlet (CCA).

125. Ibid.

126. In June, the state promulgated an emergency regulation which made it "illegal to

incite members of the public to boycott or not to take part in an election of members of a local authority, or to commit any act whereby such an election is prevented, frustrated or impeded." SAIRR, *Race Relations Survey,* 1988/1989, p. 720.

127. Frank Chikane, "1988: A Turning Point for the Church in South Africa," June 27, 1988, opening address to the 1988 SACC National Conference, photocopy (CCA).

128. SACC, "The Church Charged with Subversion," October 1988, pamphlet (CCA).

129. *Ecunews* (August 1988): 1 (CCA).

130. Human Awareness Program, *Info. '89,* section C27, p. 3 (OPD).

131. SACBC, *After the Fire: The Attack on Khanya House* (Pretoria: SACBC, 1989), p. 1 (BCA).

132. The Campaign had multiple goals, from direct nonviolent action to force desegregation of social services such as hospitals, schools, and transportation, to setting up "a process through which people and organisations will gradually unban themselves." *Crisis News* (September 1989): 2 (CTA). In supporting the self-unbannings, the church leaders stated, "We believe that if their demand is not met they would be justified in ignoring the terms of their restriction orders and in asserting their right to move freely and to engage in peaceful political activity." ICT, "Negotiations, Defiance and the Church," pamphlet published by the ICT and the Standing for the Truth Campaign, September 1989, p. 10 (CTA).

133. Ibid., p. 12.

134. SAIRR, *Race Relations Survey,* 1989/1990, p. 290.

135. Villa-Vicencio, *Civil Disobedience and Beyond,* pp. ix–xi.

136. *Crisis News* (October 1989): 1 (CTA).

137. Villa-Vicencio, *Civil Disobedience and Beyond,* p. x.

138. This process was exemplified by the Catholic bishops' reaction to a Security Police search of a bishop's home and the seizure of documents, which they viewed as a violation of the bishop's personal rights and integrity. While a bishop's residence, they pointed out, does not legally enjoy diplomatic immunity, it is universal practice that it be treated with similar respect. Such personal attacks, the SACBC warned, would "precipitate a crisis of conscience for church leaders regarding the validity of such demands [turning over documents] and the morality of complying with them. We regard an action of this kind as an attack upon the church as a whole." *Ecunews* (April 1988): 24 (CCA).

139. Peter Storey, "Here We Stand: Submission to the Commission of Inquiry into the South African Council of Churches by The Rev. Peter John Storey, President of the SACC on 9th March, 1983" (Johannesburg: SACC, 1983), p. 47 (CCA).

140. Ibid., p. 48.

141. Ibid., p. 55.

142. Nash, *Women—A Power for Change,* p. 81 (CCA).

143. Storey, "Here We Stand," p. 61.

144. Charles Villa-Vicencio, "The Church: Discordant and Divided," *Africa Report* (July/August 1983): 15.

145. SACBC, "Minutes of the 1987 Plenary Session," January 27–28, 1987, p. 36 (BCA).

146. The SACBC was also much quicker to call for the lifting of sanctions—which it did in December 1991—than was the SACC. After the SACBC made the call, Chikane stated publicly that the SACC had concluded that the time was not yet ripe for their lifting; some positive changes had taken place, but these were not yet irreversible since no constituent assembly had yet been created, the apartheid legislative structures were still sovereign, and the basic structures of apartheid remained intact. Frank Chikane, "Review of our Sanctions and Disinvestment Strategies," speech given on April 17, 1991, photocopy (CCA).

147. *Natal Mercury,* September 22, 1986, p. 9 (OPD).

148. *Pretoria News,* March 2, 1983 (OPD).

149. SACBC, "What the Bishops Have Said So Far on the Question of Elections," 1988, photocopy (BCA).

150. The TAC stated that "an unjust law that tries to oblige us to commit a sin (e.g. a law that says after two children a woman must be sterilised) MUST be destroyed. But an unjust law that assigns different beaches to different race groups does not *have* to be disobeyed." SACBC TAC, "Civil Disobedience: Reflections of the TAC for SACBC Administrative Board," June 7, 1988, p. 1 (emphasis in original), photocopy (Connor).

151. Ibid., p. 2.

152. Albert Nolan, O.P., "Summary of Research on the Question of the Legitimacy of the Government," from the SACBC Plenary Session Study Day on the Legitimacy of the Government, 1987, p. 10, photocopy (CCA).

4. Changing Religious Context

1. See chapter 1 for more discussion of the ideas emanating from Vatican II and their impact on fostering a new self-identity for the worldwide Catholic Church. See also Christopher Hollis, *The Achievements of Vatican II* (New York: Hawthorn Books, 1967), and George P. Schner, ed., *The Church Renewed: The Documents of Vatican II Reconsidered* (Lanham, Md.: University Press of America, 1986).

2. Hollis, *Achievements of Vatican II*, p. 91. Moreover, *Pacem in Terris* treated the issue of equality, stating that "every civil authority must strive to promote the common good in the interest of all, without favouring any individual citizen or category of citizen." John W. de Gruchy, "Democracy and the Church," IDASA Occasional Paper No. 5, 1987, p. 4 (OPD).

3. Michael Stogre, "Commentary on the Pastoral Constitution on the Church in the Modern World: Gaudium et Spes," in Schner, *The Church Renewed*, p. 20. The church's commitment to working for social justice was further developed in the document's third chapter, "Economic and Social Life." It contained the recognition that world social, economic, and political structures, rather than affirming the dignity of the person, denied it. Thus, the document stated, the church—as the People of God—was duty-bound to transform these structures. It also maintained that Christians should work towards reforms, including land and work reforms, that would eliminate the roots of social conflict and disparity.

4. Ibid., pp. 27–29.

5. First, the document called for increased aid and commitment to the problems of developing countries, and secondly, it castigated the fundamental assumptions of the international economic system of liberal capitalism, which "considers profit as the key motive for economic progress, competition as the supreme law of economics, and private ownership of the means of production as an absolute right that has no limits and carries no corresponding social obligation." *Populorum Progressio*, quoted in Denis Hurley, "Catholic Social Teaching and Ideology," in Andrew Prior, ed., *Catholics in Apartheid Society* (Cape Town: David Philip, 1982), p. 37.

6. It stated that to solve economic problems it is necessary to take political actions, and that the church had to concern itself with political matters, such as the right of people to participate in decision making in society.

7. Hurley, "Catholic Social Teaching and Ideology," p. 35.

8. The term was used to refer to the overcoming of everything that restricts human freedom, especially the overcoming of sin that underlies and is embodied in evil structures in society. As such, the pope used the word to mean both economic and political liberation, although its meaning was not restricted to these spheres.

9. In that year the Bantu Laws Amendment Bill was promulgated with a separate

Church Clause attached, which represented a direct invasion of the freedom of worship in South Africa. The Church Clause stated that a minister could prevent blacks from attending religious services in white residential areas if they were deemed to be "causing a nuisance" to the residents there, or if it was considered undesirable to have large numbers of blacks in "white" churches. Moreover, all churches which admitted blacks to their functions would have to obtain express permission of the Minister of Native Affairs. Several Catholic bishops as well as leaders from other churches spoke out vehemently against the proposed bill. Despite their opposition, the Native Laws Amendment Bill, including the Church Clause, was passed in July 1957 by the House of Assembly. The Catholic Church responded by stating that it refused to accept the bill's provisions, no matter what the consequences. Two weeks after its passing, a letter was read in all Catholic churches which stated that there would be no restrictions on attendance at any Catholic church. For more details surrounding the bill and its clause, see Abraham, *The Catholic Church and Apartheid,* pp. 108–112.

10. SACBC, *The Bishops Speak,* vol. 1, 1952–1966 (Pretoria: SACBC, 1980), p. 14 (BCA).

11. Apartheid was declared a heresy, although the SACBC never declared the South African state a heresy.

12. SACBC, *The Bishops Speak,* vol. 1, 1952–1966, p. 38 (BCA).

13. Ibid., pp. 43–52.

14. SACBC, *The Bishops Speak,* vol. 2, 1967–1980 (Pretoria: SACBC, 1980), pp. 9–15 (BCA).

15. In a controversial January 1964 talk entitled "Apartheid: A Crisis of Conscience," Hurley demolished the arguments used to defend apartheid as Christian, declaring it morally unacceptable. The talk, the Hoernlé Memorial Lecture, was given on the occasion of his election to the presidency of the South African Institute of Race Relations. It was met with criticism by Archbishop Whelan, who, as director of publicity of the SACBC's administrative board, published an official response which was seen by many as a qualified acceptance by the SACBC of the government's apartheid policies. Hurley, along with other liberal members of the Conference, found the statement unacceptable, and a compromise position was struck in which the SACBC issued a statement reaffirming their official policy as stated in the 1952, 1957, and 1962 pastoral letters, and declaring that statements made by individual bishops were their own responsibility—not the policy of the Conference. This incident makes clear that although a growing number of bishops were willing to accept that the church had a role to play in criticizing apartheid, this sentiment was by no means embraced by all bishops. Abraham, *The Catholic Church and Apartheid,* p. 127.

16. An example of this cautious attitude—even reactionary by present standards—could be found in the 1957 statement, in which the bishops declared, "the condemnation of the principle of apartheid as something intrinsically evil does not imply that perfect equality can be established in South Africa by a stroke of the pen. There is nothing more obvious than the existence of profound differences between sections of our population which make immediate total integration impossible. People cannot share fully in the same political and economic institutions until culturally they have a great deal in common. All social change must be gradual if it is not to be disastrous. Nor is it unjust for a state to make provision in its laws and administration for the differences that do exist. A state must promote the well-being of all its citizens. If some require special protection it must be accorded. It would be unreasonable, therefore, to condemn indiscriminately all South Africa's differential legislation." *The Bishops Speak,* vol. 1, 1952–1966, p. 15 (BCA).

17. Throughout the 1970s, the bishops published many statements which showed an increasing concern with the plight of the poor and oppressed in South Africa. The statements can be found in the five-volume compilation, *The Bishops Speak,* which includes all SACBC statements issued between 1952 and 1990.

18. *The Bishops Speak,* vol. 2, 1967–1980, p. 45 (BCA).

19. For a more detailed overview of the Christian Institute and its role in the development of contextual theology, see Walshe, *Church versus State in South Africa,* and de Gruchy, *The Church Struggle in South Africa,* chapter 2.

20. In March 1960, sixty-nine Africans, mostly women, were shot—many in the back—and killed by members of the South African police during an anti-pass demonstration. Almost two hundred more were wounded. As part of the nationwide crackdown following the shooting, both the African National Congress and the Pan Africanist Congress were banned.

21. Although the report was critical of apartheid, it was hardly radical and was subject to diverging viewpoints among the various representatives. While the English-speaking churches found apartheid "unacceptable in principle," several white Dutch Reformed Churches found "separate development the only realistic" approach to race relations and refused to sign it, although the largest of these churches, the NGK, did sign. The document did, however, also make several bolder assertions, including the principle that the natural diversity among people should be sanctified within the church; believers should not be excluded from any church on grounds of race or color; there were no scriptural grounds for the prohibition of mixed marriages; wage structures were below the poverty line for millions; and blacks should have the right to participate in the government of their country. Peter Walshe, "Church versus State in South Africa: The Christian Institute and the Resurgence of African Nationalism," *Journal of Church and State* 19, no. 3 (Autumn 1977): 459.

22. de Gruchy and Villa-Vicencio, *Apartheid Is a Heresy,* p. xvi.

23. The Commission of Inquiry into Certain Organisations, better known as the Schlebusch-LeGrange Commission, was held to investigate the emerging radical theological movement in South Africa, which included not only the Christian Institute but its various associated black theological movements as well. The Commission met in secret. Members of the suspected organizations (including the Christian Institute, the South African Institute of Race Relations, the University Christian Movement [UCM], and the National Union of South African Students [NUSAS]) were summoned for interrogation without being informed of the charges against them, nor were they entitled to a lawyer, and it was a criminal offense to refuse to answer questions. Naudé and other Institute members refused to testify, stating that they would be willing to do so if the proceedings were subject to the normal rule of law. Those supporting radical theological ideas were condemned as working under foreign influences and were therefore "Communist-inspired." As a result of the Commission's final report in 1975, the Christian Institute was declared an "affected organization" and was then barred from receiving any foreign funds. Several staff members were also held without trial under the terrorism act. Catholic Institute for International Relations, "Address by Mr. Niall MacDermot, Secretary General of the International Commission of Jurists, Geneva, to the Annual General Meeting of the Catholic Institute for International Relations" (London: CIIR, June 1976), pp. 7–8 (BCA). For more detail on the Commission, see also Walshe, *Church versus State in South Africa.*

24. Boesak, *Farewell to Innocence,* p. 1.

25. I am indebted to Nancy Joy Jacobs for her analysis of the various phases of black theology in "Consciousness, Liberation, and Revolution: Black Theology in South Africa" (master's thesis, Los Angeles, University of California, 1987) (OPD).

26. For an excellent overview of the black consciousness movement and its ties with black theology, see Johannes Nicolaas Jacobus (Klippies) Kritzinger, "Black Theology—Challenge to Mission" (doctoral dissertation, Pretoria, University of South Africa, 1988) (CTA).

27. Ibid., p. 9.

28. Examples of this stress on black identity could be found frequently in *Pro Veritate;* for instance, "Black Consciousness . . . says to the black man, you are black and you are

beautiful. You are black and your blackness is something to be proud of. Reject the white man's image of yourself, accept the new image as revealed through Jesus Christ." Ernest Baartman, "Black Consciousness," *Pro Veritate* (March 1973): 6 (CCA).

29. Biko wrote, for example:

> In a country teeming with injustice and fanatically committed to the practice of oppression, intolerance and blatant cruelty because of racial bigotry; in a country where all black people are made to feel the unwanted stepchildren of a God whose presence they cannot feel; in a country where father and son, mother and daughter alike develop daily into neurotics through sheer inability to relate the present to the future because of a completely engulfing sense of destitution, the Church further adds to their insecurity by its inward-directed definition of the concept of sin and its encouragement of the "*mea culpa*" attitudes. (Biko, *I Write What I Like*, p. 56)

30. Simon Maimela, "Black Power and Black Theology in South Africa," *Scriptura* 12 (1984): 44.

31. For Boesak, liberation was a biblical imperative, and he supported this claim through a detailed exegetical overview of liberation themes in the Bible. He stated, "The gospel of Jesus Christ *is* the gospel of liberation. Again, liberation is not merely part of the gospel, nor merely 'one of the key words' of the gospel; it is the content and framework of the whole biblical message." Boesak, *Farewell to Innocence*, p. 17.

32. Ibid., p. 55.

33. Maimela, "Black Power and Black Theology," p. 48.

34. Jacobs, "Consciousness, Liberation, and Revolution," p. 61. (OPD).

35. Boesak, quoted in ibid., p. 65. As an interesting aside, Boesak represents an example of a theologian who was able to evolve his religious thinking to the point where race became almost nonexistent in his writings. In 1987, for example, Boesak declared: "It is a question of not really shifting from Black and Reformed [the title of his 1984 book] to Black and Christian, but from Black and Reformed to oppressed and Christian, because the oppression is suffered by Christians, and the oppression is sometimes perpetrated by Christians. And that is why Black and Reformed can no longer deal with what we have here today. So we talk about Theology for Justice." Boesak, quoted in Dwight N. Hopkins, *Black Theology USA and South Africa: Politics, Culture, and Liberation* (Maryknoll, N.Y.: Orbis Books, 1989), p. 104.

36. At the end of the second phase of black theology, another black theologian, Bonganjalo Goba, previews the major concern that theologians in the years to come would grapple with: the issue of making the church relevant. Goba's concern was how the institutional church could participate in the process of liberation, for he felt that black theological reflection was not enough if it was not accompanied by "critical social praxis." The practical implications of Goba's writings, that is, the imperative of churches to become concretely engaged in the process of liberation, would not be fully realized for several years to come, and not until intense debate on the issue had first taken place within both the SACC and the SACBC. Bonganjalo Goba, "Doing Theology in South Africa: A Black Christian Perspective," *Journal of Theology for Southern Africa* 31 (June 1980): 28.

37. This theological statement was issued as a result of a conference on Pseudo-Gospels. The conference itself was held under the auspices of the Theological Commission of the newly formed SACC, which came into existence in 1967. Theologians from both the SACC and the Christian Institute comprised the Commission, which examined the misrepresentation and obstruction of the gospel by those claiming that apartheid was biblically legitimated.

38. Text of "A Message to the People of South Africa," in Spong and Mayson, *Come Celebrate!* appendix, pp. 139–143.

39. Walshe, "Evolution of Liberation Theology," p. 303.

40. Spong and Mayson, *Come Celebrate!*, p. 143.

41. This issue will be discussed in detail in chapter 6.

42. Shortly after the resolution was passed, the government amended the Defence Act by providing for fines of several thousand dollars or ten years imprisonment for any one dissuading conscripts from doing military service.

43. Text of Conscientious Objection Resolution, in David G. Thomas, *Councils in the Ecumenical Movement: 1904–1975* (Johannesburg: SACC, 1979), appendix C, pp. 114–115.

44. Walshe, *Church versus State in South Africa*, p. 143.

45. SPOBA was formed in 1966 to draw attention to the failure of the SACBC to implement the decisions of Vatican II within the Catholic hierarchy, and to highlight the continuing segregation of Catholic schools, hospitals, seminaries, and convents. SPOBA was an early manifestation of black theology within the rank and file of the Catholic church. This manifestation became more assertive in the aftermath of the growing radicalization of the whole black community after 1976, and found its roots in the Catholic Church in the BPSG. Kritzinger, "Black Theology," pp. 66–69 (CTA).

46. Ibid., pp. 72–73.

47. The use of this term has not been uniformly supported in South Africa. Ideological tension developed between those theologians who remained loyal to the black consciousness brand of theology, and those who moved towards embracing the non-racialism of contextual theology. The Institute for Contextual Theology was formed in 1981, and in 1983 it established a task force on black theology. Tensions resulted in this body and in its sponsored conference, entitled "Black Theology Revisited." In the conference's official report, ICT's General Secretary, Frank Chikane, noted, "the division on the surface seems to be . . . the play between the class and race models in trying to understand the South African society. . . . " In 1985 an independent Black Theology Project was established, which grew out of the ICT task force and the 1983 conference. The organizational separation from the ICT stemmed from the fact that a number of the more militant black theologians rejected the term "contextual theology" and the approach which it suggests. These theologians believed that the use of the term revealed the class interests of "white and privileged theologians," and that those who identified their theology as contextual underestimated the racial component of oppression in South Africa. This group of theologians represented a resurgence of the black consciousness strand of theology in the 1980s, and rejected an alliance with whites in the struggle. Kritzinger, "Black Theology," pp. 76 and 83 (CTA).

Moreover, contextual theologians do not often like to label themselves as theologians, because by their definition of contextual theology as a theology by the people and for the people, religious reflection—and the production of new ideas—can be done by all people who reflect on their situations from the perspective of the gospel. Theological innovation is no longer the sole purview of professional, highly trained people.

48. One person in whom this meshing is especially obvious is the radical Catholic priest and theologian Buti Tlhagale. More than most, Tlhagale's writings embody the continuity between race and class analyses. Steeped in black theology, he has never been entirely comfortable with being characterized as a contextual theologian. In his theological reflections, however, he draws heavily on Marxism and incorporates both race and class in his analysis of South African society. Tlhagale is particularly interested in creating a theology of labor, and continues to refer to the racial issue in acknowledgment that South African capitalism was built primarily on the back of black labor. His analysis is traditionally Marxist with Christian overtones: "Labour in the service of capital runs contrary to the Christian understanding of justice." Although Tlhagale still stresses the racial element in his analysis, this becomes subservient to the class issue. He critiques the early black consciousness movement for its failure

to take up economic issues and for its total emphasis on race; rather, he calls for an allegiance to the working-class struggle above any ethnic or racial solidarity. Again, his conclusion melds Marxism with Christianity: "*A revolutionary consciousness is bound to see the two as inextricably intertwined*. Our theological reflection also shows this unity to be a key emphasis of Christian liberation." Buti Tlhagale, "Towards a Black Theology of Labour," in Villa-Vicencio and de Gruchy, *Resistance and Hope,* pp. 132–133, emphasis in original. See also Mothobi Mutloatse, "Tlhagale Completes Sensitive Review on Black Consciousness," *Ecunews* 9 (October 1983): 30–31 (CCA).

Even though contextual theology in the 1980s tended to be concerned with class oppression, there appears to have been an ideological split within the circle of contextual theologians between those who embraced Marxism and those who were critical of any theological borrowing of Marx. While some contextual theologians went out of their way to distance themselves from Marxism, others such as Tlhagale borrowed heavily on Marx for their social analysis. Albert Nolan rejected Marxist analysis and went to some length to distance his ideas from those that drew on Marx. He points out that even though Christians might be critical of capitalism, this does not necessarily make them Marxist. Moreover, just because contextual or liberation theologians happen to come to the same conclusion as Marx, one should not assume they are therefore Marxists. Nolan concludes, "There is nothing to be afraid of here. There is no borrowing or dependence or accommodation or communist infiltration and manipulation." Albert Nolan and Richard Broderick, *To Nourish Our Faith: Theology of Liberation for Southern Africa,* Proceedings from the 1986 Catholic Theological Winter School in Southern Africa (compiled by the Southern African Order of Preachers, 1987), lecture 6, pp. 62–68 (BCA).

49. Contextual theologians use the word "revolution" in a very specific way, meaning a radical change in the basic structures in society—as opposed to the word "reform," which implies a mere adaptation of the structures to the changing circumstances. The type of revolution envisioned by these theologians and church leaders is nonviolent, effected through pressure brought to bear upon the state. Nolan, *God in South Africa,* p. 173.

50. Goba, "Doing Theology in South Africa," p. 28.

51. Steering committee members included Beyers Naudé, Bonganjalo Goba, Simon Maimela, Cedric Mayson (former editor of *Pro Veritate*), and Charles Villa-Vicencio, among others. Jacobs, "Consciousness, Liberation, and Revolution," p. 71. Allan Boesak also played an instrumental role in the launching of the ICT, through several discussions between him and theologians in EATWOT, the Ecumenical Association of Third World Theologians, an organization dedicated to the development and dissemination of Third World liberation theology.

52. ICT Constitution, 1981 (CTA).

53. ICT Annual Report, 1983, p. 1 (CTA). The Institute tried to bring about these goals through a specific method, which included: (a) doing theology explicitly and consciously from within the context of real life in South Africa; (b) starting from the fundamentally political character of life in South Africa; (c) taking fully into account the various forms of oppression that exist in South Africa, namely racial oppression, class oppression, and gender oppression; and (d) starting from the actual experience of the oppressed themselves. ICT brochure, "What is Contextual Theology?", undated, p. 10 (CTA).

54. "What is Contextual Theology?", pp. 4–6 (CTA).

55. Ibid., p. 1.

56. John W. de Gruchy, "Theologies in Conflict: The South African Debate," in Villa-Vicencio and de Gruchy, *Resistance and Hope,* p. 86.

57. Frank Chikane, "Doing Theology in a Situation of Conflict," in ibid., p. 199.

58. The principal characteristic of a prophetic message, according to theologian Albert

Nolan, is that it is not timeless; rather it is a message that is meant for a particular time, and the prophetic paradigm is consequently: "the time has come, the day is near." Nolan, *God in South Africa*, p. 14.

59. Nolan and Broderick, *To Nourish Our Faith*, p. 38 (BCA).

60. Albert Nolan, "The Option for the Poor in South Africa," in Villa-Vicencio and de Gruchy, *Resistance and Hope*, p. 190. Elsewhere (Nolan and Broderick, *To Nourish Our Faith*, pp. 48–49), Nolan is very critical of both the Vatican's as well as the SACBC's interpretation of the "option for the poor," specifically for their qualification that this option is "preferential" rather than "exclusive." Nolan insists that when the "option for the poor" is viewed as an option for the content of the gospel (which is the correct interpretation according to Nolan) rather than the option for the people who are poor (the incorrect interpretation), this becomes a moral judgment about which cause is right and just and which cause is wrong and sinful. For Nolan, the question is not *to whom* the gospel will be preached, but *what* will be preached to everyone, rich or poor. This option can never be preferential; it must be exclusive. As Nolan states, "We do not simply prefer justice to injustice; we do not opt for justice in a non-exclusive manner." Nolan's point is that the Vatican, and at times the SACBC, have interpreted the option for the poor as an option for people who are poor. This becomes a choice about the people to whom to preach the gospel, give pastoral care, give assistance, and so forth. This is clearly a preference (thus a "preferential option for the poor); however, it cannot be exclusive, for the church as a whole cannot exclude people from assistance, pastoral care, etc. . . . It is this interpretation of which Nolan is so disdainful, namely, one that allows some people to claim that they have taken an option for the poor and yet maintain that they will not take sides in the conflict.

61. Tlhagale, "Towards a Black Theology of Labour," p. 126.

62. Nolan and Broderick, *To Nourish Our Faith*, p. 53 (BCA).

63. Chikane, "Doing Theology in a Situation of Conflict," p. 99; Nolan and Broderick, *To Nourish Our Faith*, p. 27 (BCA); and Nolan, *God in South Africa*, p. 28.

64. Nolan and Broderick, *To Nourish Our Faith*, pp. 24 and 28 (BCA). Nolan also refers to this methodology as "See-Judge-Act." By this he means that theology begins with questions and practical experiences of life in a socio-historical context (SEE). It then proceeds to a judgment, assessment, evaluation, or reflection upon those questions, from the perspective of the Bible and church teachings (JUDGE). Finally, conclusions are drawn about what Christians should or should not do (ACT).

65. Chikane, "Doing Theology in a Situation of Conflict," p. 100.

66. Nolan, *God in South Africa*, p. 199.

67. Chikane, "Doing Theology in a Situation of Conflict," p. 102.

68. Ibid., pp. 100–101.

5. Contextual Theology and the Spiral of Involvement

1. A heresy, according to Boesak's definition, is "not merely the expression of a false idea, but the use of the Word of God in such a way that it becomes divisive and separates human beings from God and each other . . . [it is] an expression of the Word in service of some other interest than the love of and communion with Jesus Christ." de Gruchy and Villa-Vicencio, *Apartheid Is a Heresy*, p. xii.

2. The issue of theological justification of apartheid was especially sensitive to Boesak, since this support was given by his own Reformed tradition. He felt challenged to confront his own church (or at least the white branch of it) for its initial suggestion to the government to establish apartheid, and its continued justification of the policy.

3. Allan Boesak, "The Declaration of Apartheid as a Heresy," The First Campbell Sermon, Cambridge, United Kingdom, 1984, pp. 4–5, photocopy (CCA).

4. Charles Villa-Vicencio, "Introduction," in Allan Boesak and Charles Villa-Vicencio, eds., *A Call for an End to Unjust Rule* (Edinburgh: Saint Andrew Press, 1986), p. 16.

5. As discussed in the next chapter, until 1991 the regional councils, while affiliated with the SACC, still acted independently and could often disagree with that body.

6. Text of "A Theological Rationale and a Call to Prayer for an End to Unjust Rule," in Boesak and Villa-Vicencio, *A Call for an End to Unjust Rule*, p. 26.

7. Ibid., p. 29.

8. Villa-Vicencio viewed the Theological Rationale as nothing less than a paradigm shift in contextual theology, for it represented a move from praying *for* a government that had already been condemned as failing to bring about the will of God, to praying *against* that government. Charles Villa-Vicencio, "Some Refused to Pray: The Moral Impasse of the English-speaking Churches," in Boesak and Villa-Vicencio, *A Call for an End to Unjust Rule*, p. 59.

9. The Kairos Document was signed by just over 150 theologians and clergy from twenty-two Christian denominations in South Africa. Exactly who did and did not support the document will be discussed in further detail in a later part of this chapter.

10. Albert Nolan, perhaps not entirely objectively (he was intimately tied to the writing of the document), goes so far as to say that "The Kairos Document is not only a milestone in the history of theology in South Africa, it is not only a milestone in modern development of liberation theology, but it is also a milestone in the whole history of Christian theology." Nolan and Broderick, *To Nourish Our Faith*, p. 78 (BCA). Whether this claim is exaggerated or not, the Kairos Document is permeated with the major tenets of contextual theology listed above.

11. This is stated in the document, beginning with its title: *The Kairos Document: Challenge to the Church: A Theological Comment on the Political Crisis in South Africa.*

12. Bonganjalo Goba, "The Kairos Document and Its Implications for Liberation in South Africa," *Journal of Law and Religion* 5, no. 2 (1987): 313.

13. A *Kairos* is a time of opportunity, demanding a response; it is a favorable time when God issues a challenge to decisive action. In South Africa, it was a moment of truth not only for apartheid but also for the church. It was a time fraught with new possibilities, but also a potentially dangerous time; for if it was ignored, the loss for both the church and the people of South Africa would be immeasurable. There is a sense of urgency and conviction in the document, because "there come times when the situation is so grave, so fraught with radical consequences, that fence-sitting is no longer possible. One must be for or against." Robert McAfee Brown, *Kairos: Three Prophetic Challenges to the Church* (Grand Rapids, Mich.: Eerdmans, 1990), p. 9.

14. *Kairos Document*, p. 3.

15. Leatt, "Church in Resistance Post 1976," p. 12 (OPD).

16. *Kairos Document*, pp. 9–10.

17. Ibid., p. 11.

18. Ibid., p. 22.

19. Ibid., p. 22, emphasis in original.

20. Ibid., p. 15.

21. The consultation brought together church leaders from Southern Africa (including thirty-seven from South Africa), Tropical Africa, Western Europe, North America, and Australia, as well as representatives from the WCC, the World Alliance of Reformed Churches, the Lutheran World Federation, and the All Africa Council of Churches. Both the ANC and PAC sent representatives with the status of observers.

22. Text of Harare Declaration of December 6, 1985, in *ICT News* (March 1986): 3 (CTA).

23. Ibid.

24. SACC, "Statement on WCC/SACC Meeting, 4–6 December, 1985," photocopy (CCA). This is a separate statement from the official, much shorter "Harare Declaration," issued at the same time.

25. Ibid.

26. World Council of Churches, "Text of the Lusaka Statement," in *The Churches' Search for Justice and Peace in Southern Africa,* pp. 28–29 (CCA).

27. Ibid.

28. The violence question, specifically the issue of the structural violence of the state, was taken up by the SACC in its 1974 resolution on conscientious objection. As noted in chapter 4, its preamble states, "[t]he Republic of South Africa is at present a fundamentally unjust and discriminatory society and this injustice and discrimination constitute the primary institutionalised violence which has provoked the counter violence of the terrorists or freedom fighters." The resolution further states, "it is hypocritical to deplore the violence of terrorists or freedom fighters while we ourselves prepare to defend our society with its primary, institutionalized violence by means of yet more violence." For the first time, the apartheid regime was considered so unjust as to have forfeited the right to be defended by its citizens, and Christians were asked to examine in good conscience whether they could believe that a war to defend the oppressive structures of apartheid could ever be called just. Text of Conscientious Objection Resolution, in Thomas, *Councils in the Ecumenical Movement,* appendix C, pp. 114–115.

The SACBC as a Conference did not respond officially to the SACC's resolution. However, Cardinal McCann, the archbishop of Cape Town, issued a personal response. He stated that while he agreed with the gravity with which the SACC viewed the present situation, he could not agree that it "justifies the wholesale withdrawal of young men from military service for the defence of our country." He furthermore felt that even though the defense of an unjust and discriminatory society was precluded under the "just war" tradition, South Africans might still have the duty to defend its borders because such defense can be for reasons not only of maintaining injustice, but also for "the right of a controlled and non-chaotic change." SACBC, *The Bishops Speak,* vol. 2, 1967–1980, pp. 76–77 (BCA).

The bishops' own statement on conscientious objection, issued in 1977, did not take as radical a stance against the state as that of the SACC. The statement attempted to portray both sides of the debate: "On the one side the conviction has grown in a significant sector of the oppressed majority that only violence will bring liberation. On the other, the minority in power sees itself threatened by indiscriminate violence supported by international Communism." It thereby refused to point the finger at the structural violence of the state, as the SACC was willing to do three years earlier. SACBC, *The Bishops Speak,* vol. 2, 1967–1980, p. 47 (BCA).

29. Boesak, *Farewell to Innocence,* p. 70, emphasis added.

30. SACC, "Background paper for the discussion of the problem of a 'just revolution,'" in "Proceedings from the SACC Consultation on Combating Racism," February 1980, appendix 6, photocopy (CCA).

31. The basis for the workshop was the 1987 book, edited by Charles Villa-Vicencio, entitled *Theology and Violence: the South African Debate.* Contributors to the book include Allan Boesak, Desmond Tutu, Buti Tlhagale, John de Gruchy, Albert Nolan, Charles Villa-Vicencio, and Frank Chikane, as well as several other contextual theologians.

32. *ICT News* (December 1987): 4 (CTA).

33. Charles Villa-Vicencio, "Introduction," in Villa-Vicencio, *Theology and Violence,* pp. 2–5.

34. Buti Tlhagale, "Christian Soldiers," in ibid., p. 83.

35. Villa-Vicencio, "Introduction," in ibid., pp. 7–8.

36. "SACC Press Release on the Theology and Violence Workshop," November 30, 1987, photocopy (CCA).

37. Frank Chikane, "Where the Debate Ends," in Villa-Vicencio, *Theology and Violence,* pp. 301–309.

38. Frank Chikane, "Kairos Which Way?" Talk given by Chikane on January 18, 1988, photocopy (CCA).

39. Although the SACC reflected upon and stated its theology various times throughout the 1980s, it did so most explicitly at the time of the Eloff Commission. This event is therefore analyzed here as an example of the SACC's refinement of its own theological understanding. It is not my intention to imply that this was the only occasion that such refinement took place within the SACC during the 1980s.

40. In their memorandum submitted to the commission, the South African Police stated, "The Council has degenerated into a political pressure group with a political Gospel that is supported by a political theology which is involved in a variety of political actions." Kistner, "Response to the Evaluation of the Activities of the SACC Division of Justice and Reconciliation in the Memorandum of the South African Police Submitted to the Eloff Commission," p. 12, photocopy (CCA).

41. Bosch stated, "The S.A. Council of Churches, if I interpret it correctly, would subscribe to the conviction that ROM. 13:1–7 in no sense excludes the possibility of the church challenging and even rebuking the state for social evils in the body politic." David J. Bosch, "Submission to the Eloff Commission," February 1983, p. 12, photocopy (CCA).

42. Kistner, "Response to the Evaluation," p. 26 (CCA).

43. Desmond Tutu, "The Divine Intention," p. 3 (CCA).

44. Ibid., p. 26.

45. During the latter half of the 1980s, the Dependents' Conference was the largest of the SACC's programs. Its goal was to minister to the needs of political prisoners, detainees, banned persons, and their dependents. Carrying out this goal included provision of legal aid for those accused of terrorism, and grants to families of exiles. From 1987 to 1990, the Dependents' Conference had an average yearly expenditure of R5 million.

This raises the point that if one is interested in determining whether the SACC and SACBC were working under the influence of contextual theology, one might look at the type of activities they funded. Rachel Tingle has determined that from 1987 to 1990, a full 83 percent of SACC funds went towards supporting "Justice and Society" activities (although Tingle used these statistics to severely critique the SACC). Tingle, *Revolution or Reconciliation?* p. 174.

In addition to the Dependents' Conference described above, during the 1980s the SACC General Secretary controlled a discretionary fund called the Asingeni Fund. Originally created to provide assistance to those who had been affected by the 1976 uprisings, in the 1980s it was used for such activities as helping with funeral expenses and providing legal expenses for political trials and other assistance to the victims of apartheid.

Additionally, both the SACC and SACBC were the recipients of European Community money to assist the victims of apartheid. In 1985 the EC foreign ministers initiated the Special Community Programme of Assistance for the Victims of Apartheid (VOA). In addition to the SACC and SACBC, a third organization was created to receive VOA money. The Kagiso Trust was established, and trustees included Naudé, Boesak, Chikane, Tutu, Mkhatshwa, and Hurley, along with representatives of secular organizations. EC grants were used to defend those arrested under state of emergency regulations and conscientious objectors, and to support education projects designed to bring about fundamental change in society, as well as several UDF-affiliated anti-apartheid organizations. See Tingle, *Revolution or Reconciliation?*, pp. 181–191. An examination of the types of activities and groups funded by the SACC and SACBC (and the Kagiso Trust, which was closely affiliated with both organizations) makes clear that these organizations were indeed interpreting their Christian mission as taking sides, by working with the poor and those working for the removal of apartheid structures.

46. IMBISA (Inter-territorial Meeting of Bishops of Southern Africa) Plenary Assembly, "The Prophetic Mission of the Church," 1983, p. 1, photocopy (BCA).

47. Ibid., p. 9.

48. Ibid., p. 5.

49. Nolan and Broderick, *To Nourish Our Faith*, p. 89 (BCA). The workshop's afternoon sessions were devoted to developing methods of "doing" theology in the South African context. While several methods were discussed, each had one common element: they adhered to the hermeneutic circle, which was translated in the methodology of "See-Judge-Act." Workshop participants learned to start from the reality of their everyday lives, to look at that reality in the light of faith, and to try and change their situation through taking action. That this methodology associated with contextual theology did not remain within the confines of workshops, but was increasingly given credence by the SACBC itself, was evidenced in a cartoon-strip booklet produced by the Justice and Peace Commission entitled "Negotiation for a Just South Africa." The introduction explains that it is designed to help Catholics "look at the issue of negotiations and see what is happening. After that the Bishop's Pastoral letter on '*Rerum Novarum* and Negotiations' can be read to judge what is happening. After that comes Action." SACBC Justice and Peace Commission, "Negotiating for a Just South Africa," undated, photocopy (BCA).

50. While the SACBC adopted the Charter in 1987, the SACC adopted it in 1980.

51. SACBC TAC, "Freedom Charter," December 1987, p. 1, photocopy (Connor).

52. This silence is somewhat surprising, given that as early as 1957 the bishops had declared apartheid "intrinsically evil," which is tantamount to declaring it a heresy.

53. It is unclear why Gaybba entered the debate five years after the initial declaration. According to Gaybba, for an idea or concept such as apartheid to be heretical, it must be a belief that conflicts with the gospel, as that gospel is understood by a church. Moreover, that belief must nevertheless claim to be Christian, and this conviction must be "pertinaciously adhered to." Brian Gaybba, "The Characteristics of Heresy and the Defence of Apartheid as Christian," 1987, photocopy (CCA).

54. SACBC TAC, "Minutes of the Theological Advisory Commission Meeting," March 11–12, 1987 (Connor).

55. SACBC TAC, "Minutes of the Theological Advisory Commission Meeting," November 2–4, 1987 (Connor).

56. In a 1987 paper entitled "The Gospel and Apartheid," the TAC stated that when one considered the appalling effects that enforced separation had on the lives of millions of people, its evil character was clear. The paper concluded with a very strong stance that "any position taken by Christians that would justify it or argue for its compatibility with Christian beliefs or values is heresy. This statement is being made in utter seriousness and with the full realization of its implications: namely that anyone who pertinaciously maintains that apartheid is compatible with Christian belief is guilty of heresy and is no longer in communion with the Catholic Church." SACBC TAC, "The Gospel and Apartheid," November 1987, p. 13, photocopy (Connor).

57. *Ecunews* (June/July 1985): 7 (CCA), and *Ecunews* (May 1985): 4 (CCA).

58. Boesak and Villa-Vicencio, *A Call for an End to Unjust Rule*, appendix, p. 175.

59. This issue will be further addressed in the following chapter.

60. Boesak and Villa-Vicencio, *A Call for an End to Unjust Rule*, p. 164. Again, however,

the situation is more complex than it first appears. While this statement is clearly not as radical as calling for "the removal of the tyrannical structures of oppression and the present rulers of the country," individual bishops were much more outspoken. Archbishop Hurley, for example—in his capacity as leader of the SACBC—did support the Call to Prayer for an End to Unjust Rule. *Ecunews* (June/July 1985): 7 (CCA).

61. Tutu stated, "I am in agreement with the basic thrust of that document," although he felt that it had unfairly dismissed the "so-called white church leadership" and might thus alienate some who were supportive of the Kairos Document's basic ideas. Moreover, Tutu subsequently supported the National Initiative for Reconciliation (NIR), a separate church effort in September 1985, mostly associated with evangelical Christians, which demanded the very "reforms" that the Kairos Document rejected. The NIR argued for a "Third Way Theology" which, in contrast to contextual theology, held that the best way to bring about reconciliation was to remain neutral and not take sides with the liberation movements. It was this "Third Way" that the Kairos document deplored. Walter Schwarz, "Moment of Truth Arrives," *London Guardian,* October 18, 1985 (CTA).

Tutu had his greatest disagreeement over the Kairos Document's conceptualization of reconciliation. The Kairos Document stated that there can be no reconciliation between justice and injustice, good and evil; rather, there can only be a taking of sides. On this issue, Tutu stated, "I think the Kairos document's discussion of reconciliation is not fair to the biblical position. One must never forget that when one talks about reconciliation one is not talking about positions but about people. Reconciliation is a very personal thing." Allister Sparks, "Both Sides in South Africa Invoke Christianity," *Washington Post,* October 2, 1985 (CTA). Sparks felt that the Kairos Document was to the left of both Tutu and Boesak, both of whom he characterized as "relatively moderate and restraining."

62. This was not unique to the Catholic Church. The document was not signed by the heads of the Catholic, Anglican, Presbyterian, Congregational, or Methodist Churches of South Africa. Apparently these leaders were not asked to sign, since the Kairos Document was in fact a critique of these churches. While some leaders, most notably Archbishop Hurley, would most likely have signed the document, others probably would not have. Nevertheless, none of these Churches publicly denounced it, although several had denounced the Call to Prayer for an End to Unjust Rule a mere four months earlier. Several, like the SACBC, in fact publicly supported the main thrust of the Kairos argument. Hurley is quoted as "having hailed the document as a blueprint for future Christian action." *ICT News* (March 1986): 7 (CTA).

63. SACBC, *The Bishops Speak,* vol. 3, 1981–1985, pp. 103–107 (BCA).

64. Within the TAC, however, there was no clear consensus on the Kairos Document. Brian Gaybba, a TAC member, although writing as an individual and not as a representative of that body, severely criticized it. He argued that not only did it lack a strong theological base ("it is hard to find any clear theological theme or themes forming the backbone of the document," Gaybba wrote), but also its social analysis of the South African situation was seriously faulty. Brian Gaybba, "The Kairos Document: A Response," undated (est. 1985), pp. 1–2, photocopy (BCA). Other Catholic theologians disagreed with Gaybba. In April 1986, by request of the bishops, the TAC wrote a "Pastoral Reflection on Certain Issues Raised by the Kairos Document." The TAC agreed with many of the tenets of the document, including its ideas on reconciliation and violence. On reconciliation, the Pastoral Reflection stated that it "is not possible without a genuine repentance of evil. In South Africa there can be no reconciliation as long as apartheid prevails and justice is undermined." On the issue of violence and neutrality, the Reflection read:

We cannot adopt a position of neutrality towards the parties involved in violent conflict by regarding both sides as necessarily wrong. . . . We have to distinguish between two kinds of physical violence: that of the state, and the counter-violence of the oppressed. . . . These two cannot be placed on the same moral footing; for the violence of the oppressed is essentially a reaction to the violence of the state. . . . For this reason we cannot adopt a neutral stance to the present conflict.

SACBC TAC, "Pastoral Reflection on Certain Issues Raised by the Kairos Document," April 1986, p. 5, photocopy (Connor).

65. During the conference, SACC General Secretary Naudé delivered one of the main addresses. He made clear reference to many of the ideas emanating from contextual theology. Naudé stated that the responsibility and role of Christian churches was to strive for justice and liberation, and to take a position of solidarity with the poor and oppressed. Beyers Naudé, "South Africa: The Current Situation and the Challenge Facing the Churches in Their Search for Justice and Peace," Report to the Lusaka Conference, 1987, p. 5, photocopy (CCA).

66. SACBC TAC, "Report of Activities," January–December, 1987 (Connor).

67. *ICT News* (December 1988/January 1989): 9 (CTA).

68. SACC, *Senzenina [What have we done?]*, p. 10 (CCA).

69. Frank Chikane, "Opening Address to the Convocation of Churches in South Africa: 30–31 May, 1988," p. 3, photocopy (CCA). The Convocation's final statement reaffirmed several key tenets of contextual theology:

We dare not be overcome by impotence, nor is confession of sin sufficient. We are called to repentance, relocating ourselves on the side of those who suffer most—in resistance, action, intercession and compassionate solidarity. . . . We are obliged to regard the suffering, victimisation and oppression of the people of God as a violation of the Body of Christ. . . . Called to proclaim and witness to truth in living, and even by dying, we now commit ourselves with solemn resolve in prayer and action to end unjust rule in our country and to see the advent of the democratic society of justice and peace.

"Statement of the Convocation of Christians Meeting in Johannesburg on 30–31 May 1988," photocopy (CCA).

70. "ICT Annual General Meeting Conference Report," 1989, pp. 6–7 (CTA).

71. *SACBC Justice and Peace News* (August 1989): 12 (BCA).

72. In 1993, during his last year in that position, Chikane said, "I still regard the black theology debate as the most important theological debate ever to have taken place in South Africa." Spong and Mayson, *Come Celebrate!*, p. 113.

73. Chikane's political activities in the UDF were a direct outgrowth of his theology. "I have always been involved in prophetic ministry, so when the need to be involved in the UDF confronted me, the conflict was between the tradition of the church and the responsibility of the UDF. The question for me was could I theologize outside the struggle of the people or not? And so the activities of the UDF are an integral and necessary part of my theology. I do not see that one can meaningfully theologize about the gospel of the poor without being with them in their struggle." Chikane, quoted in Jacobs, "Consciousness, Liberation, and Revolution," pp. 90–91 (OPD).

74. ICT Annual Report, 1985, p. 1 (CTA).

6. The Institutional Context of Political Debates

1. SACC, "South African Council of Churches: Ecumenical Co-operation for South Africa Today," undated pamphlet (CCA). The SACBC became a full member of the SACC in 1995.

2. SACC Constitution, June 1991, pp. 6–7, photocopy (CCA).

3. A smaller General Purposes Committee of six or seven members meets more frequently, however.

4. Prior to a 1991 revision of the SACC's constitution, these regional councils were merely affiliated with, and not branches of, the SACC. Since 1991, people working for regional councils have been regular employees of the SACC's headquarters in Johannesburg. Regional councils also elect representatives to the SACC's NEC. Although the SACBC steadfastly refused to alter its status as an observer member of the SACC throughout the entire period under discussion here, during the phase of regional affiliation (as opposed to branch status) with the Council, several Catholic dioceses joined regional councils as full members and remain so to date.

5. During interviews with various religious leaders in South Africa, interviewees repeatedly responded to my inquiry regarding differences between the SACBC and the SACC with the following question: "Do you mean the SACC in terms of its member churches, or do you mean Khotso House?"—a reference to the staff working at the SACC headquarters in Johannesburg. Khotso is an African word for peace.

6. Other divisions included: Mission and Evangelism; Youth Ministries; Home and Family Life; Inter-Church Aid; Hunger and Relief; Refugee Ministries; African Bursary Fund; Dependents' Conference; Communications; Finance; and Administration. In 1991, in the face of a new political context, the SACC revised its constitution and restructured its organization. The number of divisions was severely reduced, with several being subsumed under the General Secretariat. The number of staff was likewise cut back. "SACC Restructures: Sacrifices, Agony and Ecstasy," *Ecunews* (December 1991): 7 (CCA).

7. Author's interview with Frank Chikane, July 16, 1993.

8. Thomas, *Councils in the Ecumenical Movement,* p. 62.

9. On rare occasions, select individuals were able to speak for both sides—as was the case with Desmond Tutu, who in many ways was the premier spokesperson for the alternative church and yet was also the Anglican archbishop of Cape Town. Author's interviews with Charles Villa-Vicencio, March 23 and June 23, 1993.

10. SACBC, "The Southern African Catholic Bishops' Conference," undated pamphlet (BCA).

11. Commissions have included the Justice and Peace Commission; the Commission for Christian Service; the Commission for Seminaries; the Commission for Priests, Deacons, and Religious; the Commission for Christian Education and Worship; the Commission for Ecumenism and Interreligious Affairs; the Commission for Mission, Immigrants, and Refugees; the Commission for the Laity; the Commission for Social Communications; the Finance Commission; the Commission of Church and Work; and the Theological Advisory Commission.

12. From 1981 to 1987, the Justice and Peace Commission was named Justice and Reconciliation, in an effort to be in line with the SACC's division of the same name. However, in 1987 it reverted to the international name of Justice and Peace, which is used by other such commissions around the world.

13. All of the scholars listed in this section draw on the distinction between "church" and "sect" developed by Ernst Troeltsch, *The Social Teaching of the Christian Churches,* vol. I, trans. Olive Wyon (New York: Macmillan, 1931), pp. 331–343, and refined by Max Weber in "The Protestant Sects and the Spirit of Capitalism," in H. H. Gerth and C. W. Mills, eds. *From Max Weber: Essays in Sociology* (New York: Oxford University Press, 1946), pp. 302–322.

14. Mainwaring, *The Catholic Church and Politics in Brazil,* p. 9.

15. Ibid., pp. 2–3.

16. Eric O. Hanson, *The Catholic Church in World Politics* (Princeton: Princeton University Press, 1987), p. 120, emphasis added.

17. Levine, *Religion and Political Conflict in Latin America,* p. 347.

18. Author's interview with Archbishop Wilfred Napier, July 15, 1993.

19. Villa-Vicencio interview, March 23, 1993. Smangaliso Mkhatshwa, former General Secretary of the SACBC, agrees, arguing that the fact that the SACBC looks first to the Vatican for theological guidance impeded its ability to adopt and consolidate the ideas emanating from the Institute for Contextual Theology. Author's interview with Smangaliso Mkhatshwa, June 8, 1993.

20. Author's interview with Bernard Connor, O.P., March 31, 1993.

21. Villa-Vicencio interview, March 23, 1993. Boff, a Franciscan priest and well-known Latin American liberation theologian, was summoned to Rome in 1985 by conservative Cardinal Joseph Ratzinger of the Vatican's Congregation for the Doctrine of the Faith. Several aspects of Boff's theological writings were condemned, and he was ordered to withdraw from public life. Boff retreated to a Franciscan monastery, until his "penitential silence" was lifted several months later. On June 26, 1992, however, Boff announced that he was resigning from the Franciscan order but would continue working as a Catholic layman, vowing to continue fighting with the poor against their poverty and for their liberation.

22. John W. de Gruchy, James Cochrane, and Robin Petersen, "Towards a Practical Theology of Social Transformation," paper presented at a Workshop on Practical Theology at the Federal Theological Seminary, February 10–12, 1988, p. 16, photocopy (CTA).

23. Connor interview, March 31, 1993.

24. Author's interview with Brother Jude Pieterse, June 10, 1993.

25. In accordance with the SACC constitution, churches with up to 60,000 members are allowed to send two delegates to the National Conference; those with a membership between 60,000 and 100,000 are allowed three delegates; those with membership between 100,000 and 200,000 are allowed four delegates; and for every additional 100,000 members above the figure of 200,000, churches are allowed one delegate, up to a maximum of eight representatives. SACC Constitution, June 1991, pp. 7–8, photocopy (CCA).

26. Author's interview with Bernard Spong, May 7, 1993.

27. Author's interview with Albert Nolan, June 17, 1993. As Eric Hanson notes, displaying this sense of unity not only is important to the bishops of the Southern African region, but is a characteristic of the Catholic Church as a whole: "Catholic bishops perceive their loyalty to institutional unity as an integral part of their religious faith. Just as they take their faith seriously, they take their institution seriously. . . . Devotion to public unity also comes from genuine feelings of episcopal collegiality." Hanson, *The Catholic Church in World Politics,* pp. 120–121.

28. "Archbishop Hurley Spoke for All," *Southern Cross,* October 1983, cited in *Ecunews* (October 1983): 26 (OPD).

29. Kevin Neuhouser, "The Radicalization of the Brazilian Catholic Church in Comparative Perspective," *American Sociological Review* 54 (April 1989): 238.

30. Exactly how much consultation can take place in the Bishops' Conference is illustrated by the following example. In March 1986, the SACBC held an extraordinary plenary session on the political crisis in South Africa. Prior to the session, the Justice and Peace Commission decided they would ask the bishops to call for the withdrawal of the SADF from the townships. In preparation for this discussion, the Commission asked its Sub-Committee on Peace and War to determine Catholic sentiment on the matter. Stephen Lowry, Secretary of the Sub-Committee, sent the following letter: "I am intending to travel throughout the country to discover how the various groups would respond to this. I am hoping to meet with lay organisations, religious congregations, schools, welfare organisations, Justice and Reconciliation groups, parish and pastoral Councils, Bishops, priests, etc. . . . " It is unlikely that any similar resolution put before delegates at the SACC National Conference would have

undergone a comparable consultative process. Letter from Stephen Lowry, Secretary of the War and Peace Sub-Committee of the SACBC Justice and Peace Commission, March 1986, photocopy (BCA).

31. Author's interview with Sr. Margaret Kelly, O.P., May 10, 1993.

32. SACBC, "Some Results of the Hammanskraal Consultation for Future Use," unpublished paper, March 1987, p. 1, photocopy (BCA).

33. SACBC Justice and Reconciliation Commission, "The Namibian Conflict," presentation to the 1984 SACBC Plenary Session, p. 1, photocopy (BCA).

34. Kelly interview, May 10, 1993. There are several possible reasons why the bishops never declared the war unjust, and the full answer will probably never be known. It is possible that the bishops were truly concerned for those who might be affected by such a declaration, such as Catholic conscripts in the SADF, who would then be morally obligated to seek conscientious objector status with its resulting penalties. It is also possible that conservative bishops within the SACBC repeatedly blocked such a declaration, so that the bishops as a whole were never able to produce a consensus statement.

35. *Info SA* 3, no. 1 (February 1988): 5 (BCA).

36. SACBC TAC, "Minutes of the Theological Advisory Commission Meeting," March 15–16, 1990, p. 1 (Connor).

37. Connor interview, March 31, 1993.

38. SACC Constitution, June 1991, p. 18, photocopy (CCA).

39. SACBC, "The Southern African Catholic Bishops' Conference," p. 3 (BCA).

40. Hurley's own unwillingness to commit himself without first consulting others occurred on several occasions in the 1980s. In 1982, shortly after the bishops' Namibia Report was published, Hurley was asked what the report meant for those seeking conscientious objector status. While expressing his concern, Hurley said that he could "not commit the whole bishops' conference by giving a definite answer at a public meeting of that nature." In addition, when asked whether the Catholic Church viewed the war in Namibia as unjust, Hurley replied, "In answering that question I'd have to distinguish between speaking as an individual church leader in our church and the whole leadership of the church speaking authoritatively." Catholic Institute for International Relations, *Country and Conscience*, p. 19.

41. Storey, "Here We Stand," p. 68 (CCA).

42. Bernard Connor, in addition to being a member of the TAC, was also a longtime editor of the Catholic newspaper, *The Southern Cross*. In 1993 Connor stated that whereas he received an average of two press releases per week from the SACC, he received at most a press release once a month from the SACBC. He explains this difference by the freedom possessed by the SACC's General Secretary, who does not need to consult with the member churches before issuing a statement. In contrast, Connor says, "the SACBC President is the only person authorized to make a statement, and he cannot do that twice a week. He's got all sorts of other things to do, and doesn't want to take a position that has not been collectively decided on by all the bishops." Connor interview, March 31, 1993.

The difference between this approach and that of the SACC is highlighted by the SACC's personnel director, who says, "The SACC has to react quickly. The General Secretary cannot call a meeting every time a statement is put out. The statement goes out by the General Secretary who has the job of interpreting the feeling of the Council." Author's interview with Pam Barnes, May 17, 1993. The SACBC's president does not have a similar interpretive authority.

43. Hennie Serfontein, "Chikane New SACC General Secretary," *African Challenge* (August 1987): 8 (OPD).

44. Tlhagale makes the point that Chikane's ties with the UDF contributed to the SACC's reputation of "the ANC at prayer." In contrast, although Smangaliso Mkhatshwa

was a longtime member of the ANC, the SACBC never acquired a similar reputation. Author's interview with Buti Tlhagale, June 14, 1993.

45. Kelly interview, May 10, 1993.

46. Ibid.

47. This was *not* the case in Zimbabwe, where in the late 1970s a controversial relationship between the Zimbabwe (at that time Rhodesian) Justice and Peace Commission and the bishops arose. The Commission, unhappy with the caution of the Zimbabwe bishops, took to publishing their own more radical statements. The SACBC Justice and Peace Commission made a deliberate decision not to follow the route of the Zimbabwe Catholic Church. Margaret Kelly sums up the reasons for this: "If the Justice and Peace Commission went to parish and diocesan groups and told them, 'the bishops are saying X, but we are saying Y,' it would be a disaster" (Kelly interview). Therefore, at the time of its formation, the SACBC Justice and Peace Commission declared, "It is essential for the credibility of the Church in this country that the Commission be seen as an integral part of the Conference and not at odds with it as was often the case in Rhodesia. Good communication between bishops and Commission at both diocesan and national level is of prime importance in order to maintain mutual trust and the optimum climate for dialogue." SACBC Department of Justice and Reconciliation, "Memorandum Motivating the Need for a Justice and Peace Commission of the SACBC," presentation to the 1981 SACBC Plenary Session, p. 5, photocopy (BCA).

48. Nolan interview, March 4, 1993.

49. In effect, Hurley did personally declare the war unjust. This occurred in the 1986 hearing of conscientious objector Philip Wilkinson, at which Archbishop Hurley testified. When asked point-blank whether he considered the activities of the SADF, both inside and outside South Africa, as constituting an unjust war, Hurley replied, "Yes, personally I think that we are in a situation of an unjust war, promoted by the SADF as the armed-force of the South African Government against the oppressed people of South Africa." Hurley's testimony at the trial highlights how, as an individual, he was ahead of the bishops' conference as a whole on justice issues. At the trial Hurley said, "Personally I think that we have to move in the direction of speaking much more clearly about the injustice of the situation in South Africa and its support by the South African Defence Force, as we have done in regard to Namibia, but we haven't done so yet as a body." Catholic Institute for International Relations, "Testimony of Archbishop Denis Hurley," in *Country and Conscience*, p. 19.

50. Tlhagale interview, June 14, 1993.

51. Spong interview, May 7, 1993. One such is Catholic priest Albert Nolan, who, in a presentation to the SACBC's 1990 Plenary Session, acknowledged that although it did not quite fit this category, "the ICT is in a position that has similarities with the numerous critical theologians in the Church today who are sometimes spoken of as Catholic dissidents." SACBC, "Minutes of the 1990 Plenary Session," August 6–10, 1990, p. 84 (BCA).

52. Villa-Vicencio interview, March 23, 1993.

53. Chikane interview, July 16, 1995.

54. Villa-Vicencio interview, March 23, 1993.

55. The Eloff Commission Report, quoted in Margaret Nash, "The SACC: Part of or Alienated from the Church?" *South African Outlook* 114, no. 1357 (July 1984): 123.

56. Villa-Vicencio interview, June 23, 1993.

57. Villa-Vicencio interview, March 23, 1993. It should be pointed out, however, that throughout the 1980s, many member churches *did* pass resolutions that represented the stance taken at the National Conference. These included resolutions denouncing the homelands system and forced relocations; supporting various acts of civil disobedience, including officiating at mixed marriage weddings; calling for conscientious objection; and endorsing the Harare and Lusaka statements.

58. Napier interview, July 15, 1993.

59. SACBC TAC, "Should the SACBC Become a Full Member of the SACC?" study document, undated (est. 1992), p. 1, photocopy (Connor). This is yet another example of the bishops rejecting a TAC recommendation. In 1991, after listing the pros and cons of full membership, the TAC concluded that it could find no theological objection to the SACBC joining the SACC as a full member. Again, in 1992, the TAC weighed the drawbacks and benefits of three possible options: a complete rejection of the idea of full membership; an upgraded interim arrangement (which would be a transitional phase, consisting of a newly formed joint consultative body which would constantly explore new forms of cooperation and prepare joint projects with the goal of gradual consolidation); and full membership. The TAC fully supported the third option. This mirrored a similar conclusion taken almost twenty years previously. In 1974 a joint working group recommended that the SACBC become a full member and asked both organizations to come to a decision in the next year. The bishops did not adopt these recommendations for several years.

60. In some ways, the SACBC benefited from the type of relationship that existed between the two, because it allowed the bishops to work closely together on campaigns of the SACBC's choice, while absolving them from any responsibility for the actions and statements of the SACC.

61. Napier interview, July 15, 1993. An example of contradictory messages to overseas partners occurred in 1991 with the decision of the SACBC to call for the lifting of international sanctions; at the same time the SACC was arguing that sanctions were necessary precisely because the changes that had occurred thus far were not irreversible, and in order to force the South African state to agree to a constituent assembly. One week after the SACBC issued its call, Frank Chikane publicly stated that the SACC had concluded that the time was not yet ripe for the lifting of sanctions. In response, Archbishop Napier said, "I am not sure if the statement by the SACC expresses the views of its member churches. But if it does, then it is unfortunate, there could be a problem." "Catholics Explain Sanctions Stance," *New Nation*, December 13–19, 1991 (BCA).

62. This change in the racial composition of the SACC occurred quite rapidly. In 1970, of the sixteen members of the NEC, ten were white and six were black. This ratio was reversed the following year, with the 1971 NEC consisting of ten blacks and six whites. For this reason, the SACC was classified by the state as a black organization the following year. Spong interview, May 7, 1993. Moreover, blacks began increasingly to move into senior positions in the SACC. By the end of 1975, seven of the twelve full-time divisional directors were black. Thomas, *Councils in the Ecumenical Movement*, p. 64.

63. With his election to the post of General Secretary, Tutu challenged white Christians on their convictions with speeches such as the following, given four months after assuming his new position:

> What did you do about the Steve Biko situation? Are you satisfied with the Magistrate's inquest verdict? If not, what have you done? Many people, many black people have been detained just like that for months on end and then released without charges being preferred against them. Do you seriously believe that Mr. Kruger [the Minister of Law and Order] would let them go free if he had enough evidence to convict them? His police have had time enough to build up their cases against them. He bans people without disclosing the evidence which led him to take such a decision. . . . What have you done, what are you doing about this? Or are you among those who say when somebody gets into trouble with the Security Branch that there couldn't be smoke without fire? I think that if the Archbishop of Cape Town [who was not Tutu at the time] were to be taken in, that would be the verdict of most white people.

Desmond Tutu, "The WCC, the SACC and All That," talk given by Tutu on November 23, 1978, p. 8, photocopy (CCA).

64. Tlhagale interview, June 14, 1993.

65. In 1974 the Conference adopted the now-famous "Hammanskraal Resolution" supporting conscientious objection, and in 1975, the Executive Committee unanimously accepted a "Statement on Race Relations" (submitted to the National Conference a month earlier, but not discussed due to time constraints), which officially supported the black consciousness movement. Thomas, *Councils in the Ecumenical Movement*, pp. 69–70.

66. "Text of the Black Confessing Church Statement," in *SACC Justice and Reconciliation News* (July 1980): 13 (CCA).

67. These included the creation of several African Independent Churches that have become full members of the SACC, such as the African Catholic Church, the National Baptist Church, and the Bantu Methodist Church. Thomas, *Councils in the Ecumenical Movement*, p. 65. In mid-1988, the racial breakdown of the Christian population of South Africa was estimated as: Africans—68 percent, Whites—20 percent, Coloreds—12 percent, and Indians—0.004 percent. Seventy-eight percent of the religious population of South Africa is Christian. The total membership of churches belonging to the SACC is estimated between ten and twelve million. The membership of the Catholic Church, which represents only 9 percent of the total South African population, is close to three million. *Ecunews* (October/November, 1990): 5 (CCA), and Human Awareness Program, *Info. '89* (Johannesburg 1989): section C26, p. 1 (OPD).

68. As recently as 1975, however, only three of thirty bishops were black and roughly one priest in ten was black. Aware of the disproportional representation of whites in leadership positions, the bishops adopted their "Declaration of Commitment on Social Justice and Race Relations within the Church," whose set of twenty-one commitments was partially aimed at improving this situation. Commitment number seven, for example, read: "To do all in our power to speed up the promotion of Black persons to responsible functions and high positions in the Church, to encourage them to accept such functions and responsibilities, so that the multi-cultural nature of the Church in South Africa may be clearly recognised, and to provide the training necessary for this purpose." SACBC, *The Bishops Speak,* vol. 2, 1967–1980, p. 43 (BCA).

Despite progress, over twenty years later the Catholic Church, in terms of priests and bishops, is still composed of a majority of whites. Albert Nolan gives an example of this situation. In the Northern Transvaal region of South Africa, Nolan says, almost all Catholic priests are whites, many of whom are Irish. In the Lutheran Church in that same region, every single bishop and priest is black. There are several reasons for this shortage of local priests, Nolan believes, including the requirement of celibacy and the higher educational requirements for the Catholic priesthood in comparison to other denominations. Nolan interview, June 17, 1993.

69. This tension dates back at least to 1971, when a group of radical black Catholics, including three priests (Smangaliso Mkhatshwa among them), loudly interrupted the SACBC's plenary session, carrying protest signs which read, "Must we tolerate white bosses in the Church as well?" That same year five Catholic priests, again including Mkhatshwa, published a controversial document entitled "The Black Priests' Manifesto." In it, they pointed out that almost all positions of power, influence, and responsibility in the Church had been monopolized by whites, while African clergy were treated as "glorified altar boys." Ken Jubber, "The Roman Catholic Church and Apartheid," *Journal of Theology for Southern Africa* 15 (June 1976): 29, and Smangaliso Mkhatshwa, "Black Priests Manifesto Revisited," *Challenge* (August 1991): 22 (CTA).

70. "Pope Horrifies Priests," *Internos* (August/September 1984): 4, 8 (BCA).

71. "Should Pope John Paul II Have Agreed to Meet the P.M.?" *Ecunews* (September/October 1984): 18–20 (CCA).

72. "Study document by the Justice and Peace Commission on the Pros and Cons of a Papal Visit," 1987, photocopy (BCA).

73. The Vatican's explanation of why South Africa was dropped from the initial itinerary did not make mention of advice from the SACBC. A Vatican official stated that the pope had decided not to visit South Africa because he "was outraged at what he sees as the persecution of South Africa's black citizens. He is horrified at the prospect of being escorted and protected by Botha's brutal police." *Internos* (August 1987): 7 (BCA).

74. Nolan interview, June 17, 1993.

75. The SACBC's General Secretary, Smangaliso Mkhatshwa, *was* detained and tortured. However, Mkhatshwa was not a bishop and thus, as discussed above, had little influence on the policy outcomes of the SACBC.

76. Napier interview, July 15, 1993.

77. Tlhagale interview, June 14, 1993.

78. For example, the elections of the 1993 National Conference produced an NEC in which the President, Senior Vice-President, Vice-President, General Secretary, and Deputy General Secretary were all blacks, three of whom were women. In contrast, in 1993, the SACBC had a black President (Napier), but a white Vice-President, General Secretary, and Deputy General Secretary.

Peter Storey, who was president of the SACC during the Eloff Commission of Inquiry, told the Commission that the representative nature of the SACC was sometimes difficult for whites to accept. Storey said, "The Council is the only body in South Africa where black and white Christians are wrestling with South African realities in a forum which is generally representative of our black/white population ratio. . . . In the SACC whites have had to learn to be a minority, and in this sense the SACC is a prototype of the future South Africa. The experience can be a traumatic one for those who have succumbed to the 'white majority complex' whereby we automatically assume that we will have the last and deciding word on everything in this land. . . . The SACC is able to hear and articulate an authentic black voice which whites desperately need to be exposed to, no matter how uncomfortable it may be. Speaking as a white person, I must say that it came as a surprise to me to hear significant numbers of blacks saying that no matter how high the price in suffering for themselves and their people, they would welcome far more harsh economic pressure on South Africa." Storey, "Here We Stand," pp. 58–59 (CCA).

This last comment by Storey gives some indication of why the SACBC's statement on economic sanctions was so much less radical than the SACC's.

79. Tlhagale interview, June 14, 1993.

80. Mkhatshwa interview, June 8, 1993.

81. These include the Church of the Province of South Africa, the Evangelical Lutheran Church in Southern Africa, the Evangelical Presbyterian Church in South Africa, the Methodist Church of Southern Africa, the Moravian Church in South Africa, the Presbyterian Church of Africa, the Presbyterian Church of Southern Africa, the Reformed Presbyterian Church in Southern Africa, and the United Congregational Church of Southern Africa. Ans J. van der Bent, *Handbook Member Churches of the World Council of Churches* (Geneva: WCC, 1985), pp. 55–61.

82. The debate resulted in the declaration that "any form of segregation based on race, color or ethnic origin is contrary to the gospel and is incompatible with the Christian doctrine of man with the nature of the church of Christ." Baldwin Sjollema, "The Initial Challenge," in Pauline Webb, ed., *A Long Struggle: The Involvement of the World Council of Churches in South Africa* (Geneva: WCC, 1994), p. 2.

83. At its 1961 New Delhi assembly, for example, the WCC stated:

> The church is called to strive actively for racial justice. Christians should not be tied to any one way of action but should make creative use of various means—conciliation, litigation, legislation, mediation, protest, economic sanctions and non-violent action— including cooperation with secular groups working toward the same ends. . . . The churches should identify themselves with the oppressed race.

Through such statements, the WCC expressed early contextual theology ideas long before any South African religious institution. In a meeting in Zambia in 1964, WCC General Secretary W. A. Visser 't Hooft argued that armed violence to force an end to the apartheid regime could not be entirely ruled out, and in 1966, the WCC underlined the need for the churches to see racism as a result of political and economic structures of society. Sjollema, "The Initial Challenge," p. 5.

84. Ibid., pp. 9–11.

85. Baldwin Sjollema, "Eloquent Action," in Webb, *A Long Struggle,* p. 13.

86. Several criteria were established for the grants: they were to be used for humanitarian activities; they were to be given to groups that "combat racism" and not to welfare organizations eligible for aid from other WCC departments; they were to focus "on raising the level of awareness and on strengthening the organizational capabilities of the racially oppressed people"; priority was to be given to southern Africa because of the "overt and intensive nature of white racism" there, and they were to be "made without control over the manner in which they were spent." This last was a very controversial stipulation, giving rise to the charge that even *if* the money was intended for humanitarian purposes, there would be no control over whether it was used to buy arms. Richard E. Sincere, Jr., *The Politics of Sentiment: Churches and Foreign Investment in South Africa* (Washington, D.C.: Ethics and Public Policy Center, 1984), p. 20.

87. In the first ten years of its existence, the PCR gave substantial grants to three movements: the South West African People's Organization (SWAPO), which received almost $700,000 during that time; the ANC, which received close to $300,000; and the PAC, which received $162,000. In addition, smaller grants were made to the ANC's Lutuli Memorial Foundation, which received $32,500. In total, during those first ten years, almost 40 percent of PCR funds went directly to anti-apartheid organizations. Sincere, *Politics of Sentiment,* pp. 21–22.

88. de Gruchy, *The Church Struggle in South Africa,* pp. 128–131.

89. Sincere, *Politics of Sentiment,* p. 22. The response by the state was even angrier, with Prime Minister John Vorster accusing the WCC of being communist-infiltrated and providing terrorist organizations with funds for buying arms.

90. "Violence, Non-Violence, and Civil Conflict," Statement by the WCC Central Committee, 1973, quoted in Charles Villa-Vicencio, "The Church and Violence," in Webb, *A Long Struggle,* p. 109.

91. Thomas, *Councils in the Ecumenical Movement,* p. 78.

92. Sjollema, "Eloquent Action," pp. 19–20. Close to a thousand corporations were targeted for pressure.

The 1972 resolution read as follows:

> *The World Council of Churches,* in accordance with its own commitment to combat racism, considering that the effect of foreign investments in Southern Africa is to strengthen the white minority regimes in their oppression of the majority of the peoples of this region, and implementing the policy as commended by the Uppsala Assembly (1968) that investments in "institutions that perpetuate racism" should be terminated:

(a) *instructs* its Finance Committee and its Director of Finance
   (i) to sell forthwith existing holdings and to make no investments after this
   date in corporations which, according to information available to the Finance
   Committee and the Director of Finance, are directly involved in investment
   in or trade with any of the following countries; South Africa, Namibia, Zimbabwe, Angola, Mozambique and Guinea Bissau; and
   (ii) to deposit none of its funds in banks which maintain direct banking operations in those countries.
(b) *urges* all member churches, Christian agencies, and individual Christians outside
Southern Africa to use all their influence including stockholder action and disinvestment to press corporations to withdraw investments from and cease trading with
these countries.

John Rees, "Investment in Southern Africa: The Stand of the World Council of Churches
towards South Africa and the Reaction from South Africa," *South African Institute of International Affairs* 5, no. 3 (1973): 36–37.

93. Leon Sullivan, an American Baptist minister and civil-rights activist, formulated
a code of conduct for U.S. firms in South Africa. Like the Sullivan Principles, the SACC
Code called for, among other things, nonsegregation of races in all eating, comfort, and work
facilities; equal and fair employment practices for all employees; equal pay at market rates for
all employees doing equal or comparable work; training programs to prepare blacks in substantial numbers for supervisory, administrative, clerical, and technical jobs; an increase in
blacks in management and supervisory positions; and refusal to use migrant labor unless housing was provided for spouses. The SACC code went further than the Sullivan Principles by
also calling for such things as an immediate recognition of existing trade unions; a voluntary
self-tax on gross corporate profits, to be contributed to black education; and the refusal to
invest in or assist projects connected with arms manufacture. David Thomas, *Investment in
South Africa*, Report Submitted by the Division of Justice and Reconciliation to the SACC
National Conference, Hammanskraal, July 26–28, 1977 (Johannesburg: SACC, 1977), p. 31
(CCA).

94. On several highly-publicized foreign trips, Tutu called for diplomatic, political, and
economic pressures on South Africa. Tutu's stance created tension between himself and several SACC member churches, many of whom distanced themselves from his statements. The
SACC Executive Committee along with a group of member church leaders issued a statement
in the aftermath of Tutu's pronouncements on sanctions which affirmed his right as General
Secretary of the SACC to express his convictions on political developments in South Africa,
while at the same time recognizing that there were many within their constituency who held
a very different view of sanctions.

95. Barbara Rogers, *Race: No Peace without Justice: Churches Confront the Mounting Racism of the 1980s* (Geneva: WCC, 1980), appendix 2, "Working Group Reports," p. 112.

96. The question that one might ask is why the WCC was so radical at such an early
time. The answer, as in the case of the SACC, lies in the composition of the Council. The
shift in the WCC's position at Uppsala in 1968 reflected the changing makeup of its constituency. Whereas in 1948 (the year the WCC was founded), 42 of the 147 member churches
were from the Third World, twenty years later that number had increased to 103 out of 253.
Forty-one of these were from newly independent African countries. These churches pushed
the WCC to take notice of the suffering of Christians involved in the liberation struggle in
Southern Africa. Sjollema, "The Initial Challenge," p. 11.

97. Nolan interview, March 4, 1993.

98. "Academic Honours for Albert," *ICT News* (December 1990): 21 (CTA).

99. SAIRR, *Race Relations Survey,* 1987/1988, p. 237.

100. Ibid. Additionally, Napier accused Mees of being selective in his warning not to become involved in politics. Responding at a press conference to Mees's report that the pope wished the bishops to remain in dialogue with the South African government, Napier said, "by any standard this would seem to imply that we should be speaking to political leaders. If that's not telling us to be involved in politics, I don't know what is." *Internos* (February 1987): 16 (BCA).

101. The issue of racial discrimination has long been a topic for Catholic social teaching—being addressed, for instance, in both *Gaudium et Spes* and *Populorum Progressio*—and it was upon these teachings that the popes drew in their analyses of apartheid.

102. *Ecunews* (September/October 1984): 20 (CCA).

103. "The Popes on Apartheid," *Internos* (December 1987): 21 (BCA).

104. SAIRR, *Race Relations Survey,* 1988/1989, p. 723.

105. Ibid., 1989/1990, p. 298.

106. SAIRR, *Race Relations Survey,* 1985, p. 574.

107. Mkhatshwa interview, June 8, 1993.

108. Hanson, *The Catholic Church in World Politics,* p. 6.

109. Berryman, *Liberation Theology,* p. 109.

110. Levine, *Religion and Political Conflict in Latin America,* p. 238.

111. Ian Linden, *Back to Basics: Revisiting Catholic Social Teaching* (London: CIIR, 1994), p. 15. Eric Hanson believes that Ratzinger is Pope John Paul II's "single most important appointment." Ratzinger, according to Hanson, articulates the concern of those who would challenge the power of the national episcopal conferences and condemn the "heresies" of progressive theologians. Hanson, *The Catholic Church in World Politics,* pp. 91–92.

112. Tlhagale interview, June 14, 1993.

113. Chikane interview, July 16, 1993.

114. Tingle, *Revolution or Reconciliation?,* p. 257.

115. From 1986 to 1990, the largest donor nations were Denmark (with 16.6 percent of total donations), Germany (14 percent), Norway (12.4 percent), the Netherlands (11.6 percent), Sweden (11.3 percent), the U.K., (8.8 percent), and the U.S. (5.1 percent). Additionally, the WCC donated almost 7 percent of the total.

116. Joseph Wing, "Address to the 1982 SACC National Conference," reprinted in *Ecunews* (July 1982): 16–20 (CCA).

117. Author's interview with Ian Linden, July 1994.

118. Mkhatshwa interview, June 8, 1993.

119. The theology of the WCC was often equated with Marxism. This line of thought was promoted by people like Ernest Lefever, founding president of a conservative U.S. religious think tank, the Ethics and Public Policy Center, and foreign policy advisor to Ronald Reagan during his 1980 presidential campaign. Lefever said of the WCC, "The WCC has gradually moved from its original, largely Western concept of political responsibility to a more radical ideology. By 1975 it had embraced the concept and practice of 'liberation theology,' whose diagnosis and prescriptions bear a striking resemblance to those of the most powerful secular utopianism of our time, Marxism. The positions of this 'revolutionary' theology on Third World and other issues have often been indistinguishable from those expressed in Moscow and Havana." Lefever, quoted in Rogers, *Race: No Peace without Justice,* p. 8.

120. The association of the WCC with South African–based theological developments extended beyond the SACC. During the LeGrange-Schlebusch Commission's investigation of black theology, the commissioners found that "It is clear that this theology is under the influence of Communist ideology." Moreover, the final report asserted, "it is not far-fetched to seek the theological roots of Black Theology in the World Council of Churches

propaganda as well." Manas Buthelezi, "Black Theology and the LeGrange-Schlebusch Commission," *Pro Veritate* 13, no. 6 (October 1975): 4–5 (CCA).

121. Sjollema, "Eloquent Action," p. 29. Increasingly, information is being uncovered about the South African government's efforts to infiltrate churches, both domestically and internationally, in order to fight the WCC and especially its PCR. One of the first studies to reveal the government's attempts to subvert churches, as well as its connections with extreme right-wing movements in several countries of Europe and the United States, was Derrick Knight's *Beyond the Pale: The Christian Political Fringe* (London: Kogan Page, 1980).

122. Rogers, *Race: No Peace without Justice*, appendix 2, "Working Group Reports," p. 105. The government was further angered when a WCC-sponsored Eminent Church Persons' Group (ECPG)—which was formed in 1987 to lobby Western governments and Japan to implement full and compulsory sanctions as the last remaining nonviolent means of ending apartheid—denounced in its final report the "confused and hypocritical attitude to the use of violence in South Africa, one which amounted to a double standard; as well as an exaggeration of the reputed radicalism (the 'communist bogey') of groups opposed to apartheid, which in actuality expressed an ideological fear for the future of free market capitalism in south Africa." James Mutambirwa, *South Africa: The Sanctions Mission Report of the Eminent Church Persons' Group* (Geneva: WCC, 1989), p. 119.

123. Hanson points out that Vatican support of the West against communism predates Pope John Paul II. During the Cold War, Hanson says, Pope Pius XII (1939–1958) articulated a strong anticommunist position, "which made the papacy the ideological leader of the Western forces." Hanson, *The Catholic Church in World Politics*, p. 9.

124. Napier interview, July 15, 1993.

125. Mkhatshwa interview, June 8, 1993.

126. Author's interview with Cedric Mayson, May 28, 1993.

127. Villa-Vicencio interview, March 23, 1993.

7. South Africa in the 1990s

1. Mainwaring and Wilde, in *Progressive Church in Latin America*, show that in several Latin American countries, a retrenchment or muting of progressive Catholicism resulted both from changes in the religious context, with liberation theology coming under increasing attack from the Vatican and CELAM, and from changes in the political context, with increasing democratization in various countries. The church experienced a sense of crisis— the unity between progressives and moderates, based on common opposition to repressive governments, eroded in the new political context. The resulting tensions came to a head at CELAM's Third General Meeting, held in Puebla, Mexico, in 1979, which has been described as "a tie between progressives and neo-conservatives that had been engaged in an intramural struggle over the preceding years" (p. 30).

2. Ibid., p. 26.

3. James Mutambirwa, "Update on South Africa," PCR press release, March 1990, p. 1, photocopy (CCA).

This speech came in the aftermath of the virtual reemergence of the ANC as a de facto organization—an emergence which was greatly facilitated by the Mass Democratic Movement, of which church leaders and activist Christians were highly supportive. The factors which influenced de Klerk's decision to travel down this road, and with such haste, are numerous. They include the realization that the ANC was indeed emerging as a potent political force; a power struggle between the National Party and its rival in white politics, the Conservative party; and the hope of easing international sanctions and a vote-catching improvement in the economy. Patrick Laurence, "De Klerk's Rubicon," *Africa Report* (March/April 1990): 14–16. For an in-depth analysis of the convergence of political factors leading to the events of 1990, see especially Martin J. Murray, *The Revolution Deferred: The Painful Birth of Post-Apartheid South Africa* (New York: Verso, 1994).

4. Mutambirwa, "Update on South Africa," p. 2. Chikane's statement on conditions for negotiations refers to the "Declaration of the Organization of African Unity's (OAU) Ad hoc Committee on Southern Africa on the Question of South Africa," made in Harare in August 1989, which contained the principles and preconditions that the South African government had to meet for creating a climate conducive to negotiations. The Declaration was later adopted, with amendments, by the Commonwealth, the Non-aligned Movement, and the United Nations. The UN, borrowing from the OAU Declaration, laid down the "universally accepted objectives of the struggle" in its General Assembly Declaration on South Africa in December 1989. These objectives included that South Africa should become a united, nonracial and democratic state; all its people should enjoy common and equal citizenship; all its people should have the right to participate in government on the basis of universal, equal suffrage, under a nonracial voters' roll, and by secret ballot; all would have the right to form and join any political party of their choice; all should enjoy universally recognized human rights, protected under an entrenched Bill of Rights; South Africans should enjoy legality under the law with an independent and nonracial judiciary; and a just economic order should be created. *Ecunews* (January/February 1990): 13, 19 (CCA).

Chikane, along with other church leaders, as well as other civil society organizations, was arguing that although de Klerk had indeed opened the door towards addressing the obstacles in the way of negotiations, he had at the same time excluded several key aspects of the demands made under the Harare Declaration. The demands included the release of *all* political prisoners (de Klerk had excluded prisoners sentenced for "murder, terrorism, sabotage, or arson," who constituted the vast majority of what was generally considered a political prisoner); the return of all exiles (de Klerk offered safe return only to those who had not "committed crimes" in South Africa); the termination of the state of emergency and the repeal of all legislation which circumscribed political activity; the cessation of all political trials and political executions; and the removal of troops from townships. Until such conditions were met, the SACC was not prepared to unconditionally congratulate de Klerk. Frank Chikane, "Report of the General Secretary to the National Executive Committee of the SACC, 20–21 February, 1990," pp. 1–2, photocopy (CCA).

5. While preliminary "talks about talks" were ongoing, they were symbolized primarily by two meetings which took place in the first half of 1990: the Groote Schuur meeting and the Pretoria meeting. The Groote Schuur meeting took place between the government and the ANC in May. The bulk of this meeting was devoted to discussing the preconditions for negotiations as outlined in the Harare Declaration, removing the obstacles which stood in the path of negotiations, and the violence in the country. The Pretoria meeting took place a few months later and produced the Pretoria Minute, in which the ANC suspended the armed struggle.

6. These included: that South Africa should become a united democratic nonracial state; all its people should enjoy common and equal citizenship and nationality; a universal suffrage under a common voters' roll; an entrenched Bill of Rights; and a just economic order. John Lamola, "The Role of Religious Leaders in Peacemaking and Social Change in Africa: The Case of South Africa," unpublished paper, 1993, photocopy (CCA).

7. These preconditions included those listed in the Harare Declaration, as presented by Chikane to the SACC National Executive Committee (see note 4 above).

8. Murray, *Revolution Deferred*, p. 180.

9. Ibid., p. 181.

10. The ANC argued for a 66.6 percent requirement, no veto by the Senate, and a time limit of several months. The NP insisted on a 75 percent requirement, the possibility of a veto by any group, and no set time frame, although a period of five to ten years was mentioned. "SACC Analysis: CODESA 2 Negotiations," SACC press release, May 25, 1992, photocopy (CCA).

11. In the end, CODESA's negotiating parties held two sittings: CODESA 1, on December 20–21, 1991, and CODESA 2, on May 15–16, 1992.

12. Murray, *Revolution Deferred*, p. 183.

13. Ibid., p. 184.

14. The transitional executive council (TEC) can be thought of as a "super Cabinet," which was intended to function as a parallel cabinet operating alongside existing structures. The main functions of the TEC included providing the parties at the negotiating forum the opportunity to participate in the governance of South Africa, facilitating the formation of a national peace-keeping force, and monitoring the various armies which would have to become integrated. Ibid., p. 190.

15. Ibid., pp. 186–187.

16. Ibid., p. 190.

17. The GNU was to consist of two houses: a 400-member national assembly elected by proportional representation, with half the representatives from national party lists and the other half from regional lists; and a senate composed of ten members from each of the nine provinces, elected by the provincial legislatures. A twenty-seven-member cabinet would consist of ministers from all parties winning more than 5 percent of the popular vote. When seated as the constituent assembly, prevailing decisions would require a two-thirds majority of the 400-member parliament. Ibid., p. 192.

18. Walshe explains the principle behind the double strategy as follows: "If the transitional period could be prolonged through protracted negotiations, the Afrikaner National Party might well be able to retain a disproportionate share of power by thwarting the ANC's capacity to consolidate its majority support. Simultaneously, the de Klerk government expected to build a coalition with 'homeland' leaders and other ethnically-based organizations. . . . For this strategy to be successful, continued intra-black violence would be helpful." Walshe, *Prophetic Christianity and the Liberation Movement in South Africa*, p. 134.

19. *Ecunews* (March 1993): 2 (CCA).

20. Murray, *Revolution Deferred*, p. 186.

21. Lamola, "Role of Religious Leaders," p. 12 (CCA).

22. Ibid., pp. 2–3.

23. Frank Chikane, "Come Holy Spirit, Renew the Whole Creation—Update on the Crisis in South Africa," speech given by Chikane, August 27, 1991, photocopy (CCA).

24. Walshe, *Prophetic Christianity*, p. 147.

25. Angus MacSwan (Reuters Online: Clarinews@clarinet.com), "Tutu Appeals for Peace, Hails New South Africa," in (clari.world.africa.south_africa), April 24, 1994 (OPD).

26. Murray, *Revolution Deferred*, p. 209.

27. Boesak, Chikane, and Tutu then outlined for de Klerk the steps they thought the government should immediately take. These steps closely mirrored those listed in the OAU's Harare Declaration, including lifting the state of emergency; lifting the restrictions on people imposed in terms of emergency regulations and the Internal Security Act; releasing all people detained without trial; lifting the bans on political organization; releasing all political prisoners; reprieving all those sentenced to death and declaring a moratorium on the death penalty; allowing exiles to return home; repealing the "pillars of apartheid" (i.e., the Population Registration Act, and the Group Areas Act, the Land Act); repealing laws which allowed the

government to restrict political activity; and embarking on negotiations with liberation movements. *Bishopscourt Update* (October 25, 1989) (CCA).

28. Saki Macozoma, "The Church and Negotiations," paper read at the Standing for the Truth Campaign Workshop, March 7, 1990, p. 10, photocopy (CCA).

29. Speaking for the SACC, Saki Macozoma offered the following list of activities for church involvement in the negotiation process: to inform the church constituency about the nature of negotiations, and what they are meant to achieve; to engage in action that would ensure that, when negotiations did begin, all parties would remain at the negotiation table; to engage in action that would create a disincentive for all parties, but especially strong parties, to renege on agreements; to ensure that the aim of negotiations is the creation of a just society; to assist in the creation of a political culture that accepts conflict resolution through dialogue and negotiations; and to monitor developments with regard to negotiations, and decide where pressure should be applied. Ibid., pp. 10–11.

The SACBC offered its ideas on the role of the Catholic Church in negotiations in a 1991 pastoral letter. In response to the question "Can we as members of the Church do anything to help [the negotiations]?" the letter answers, "Certainly we can. We can influence public opinion in the right direction. In regard to negotiations we can help to promote a Christian outlook among the members of our Church, among our friends and neighbours. . . . A very important aim should be the fostering of a spirit of tolerance between people who hold different political opinions." SACBC, "Pastoral Letter On the Occasion of the Centenary of the First Papal Encyclical on Social Justice—*Rerum Novarum*—and Its Implications for Negotiations in South Africa" (Pretoria, 1991), pp. 5–6 (BCA).

30. Lamola, "Role of Religious Leaders," p. 12 (CCA).

31. In the early 1990s, a new format for meeting was created by church leaders, known as the Church Leaders Meeting. This was an ad hoc gathering of heads of churches, some of which were not members of the SACC. These leaders met frequently in times of crisis, such as after the Boipatong massacre. Meetings were facilitated by the SACC and chaired by the president of the SACC. This ad hoc organization included a broader representation of South African Christians than that of the SACC, since leaders from churches which had traditionally rejected the SACC were often invited to join the group on occasions when they could play an important role in mediating a particular crisis. An example of one such leader was Johan Heyns of the NGK (the largest white Dutch Reformed Church). Ibid., p. 2.

32. Frank Chikane, "Report of the General Secretary to the National Executive Committee," February 1992, p. 2, photocopy (CCA).

33. *Challenge* (September 1992): 3 (CTA).

34. Examples of such proposals included: a speedy installation of an interim government; joint control of security forces; the apprehension by the police of all perpetrators of violence; an international monitoring force; disclosure of all past covert operations, at least to select church leaders; the disbanding of all special military formations, such as battalion 32 and Koevoet, which had been used in Angola and Namibia and deployed in South African townships; and the suspension of government officials and security personnel implicated, even on a prima facie basis, in acts of violence. Lamola, "Role of Religious Leaders," p. 16 (CCA).

35. In a letter addressed to de Klerk dated July 28, 1992, the church leaders stated that, although each party had a moral obligation to try and break the deadlock, "a unique responsibility rests with the Government in power because there are some things only Government can do." Frank Chikane, "Report of the General Secretary to the National Executive Committee of the SACC," August 25, 1992, appendix A, photocopy (CCA).

In this letter, the leaders made the following proposals to de Klerk: that he announce unequivocally on television that the constitution would be written by a body elected on the basis of universal suffrage, and that the elections for a constitution-making body would take place within a time frame determined only by the reasonable requirement of proper organization across the country.

In a letter sent two days later, the church leaders urged the government to take the initiative in ending the escalating violence through the immediate fencing and strong police presence at hostels which were identified as potential flashpoints; taking demonstrable action against members of the security forces who may have been implicated in alleged covert operations; and the restriction to barracks and disarming of Battalions 31, 32, and Koevoet. Ibid., appendix B.

36. SACC National Conference Resolutions, 1992, Resolution 2, photocopy (CCA).

37. *Bishopscourt Update* (December 1990) (CCA).

38. *Ecunews* (December 1991): 5 (CCA).

39. Church leaders met with de Klerk in March 1990 after the so-called "seven-day war" in Pietermaritzburg; in August 1990 following the outbreak and spread of the violence into the Transvaal; in October 1991 following the July 1991 revelations of the complicity of the security forces; and in May 1992, at which point de Klerk was presented with a memorandum which proposed ways to end the violence. *Ecunews* (March 1993): 2 (CCA).

40. *Bishopscourt Update* (October 15, 1991): 2 (CCA).

41. *Ecunews* (March 1993): 2–3 (CCA).

42. The genesis of the National Peace Accord was a conference called by de Klerk but rejected by his rivals. In April 1991, de Klerk called for a conference to be held the following month to deal with the issue of violence. The conference was rejected by the ANC, COSATU, AZAPO, and the PAC as a propaganda stunt meant to bolster de Klerk's image before a planned trip abroad. At the same time, leaders of the business community expressed their concern about the endemic violence to the SACC, and requested the SACC's assistance in facilitating a possible end to it. A four-person delegation from the SACC and the business community then met with de Klerk, in the hope of persuading him to either cancel or redefine his conference, or to agree to let others convene it. While they were unsuccessful in this mission (and de Klerk's conference was attended mainly by those who supported the apartheid regime before February 2, 1990), this core group eventually evolved into a convening committee for the National Peace Accord. *Ecunews* (December 1991): 4 (CCA).

At the end of its first meeting, held on June 4, 1991, the group, which became known as the joint facilitating committee, issued a statement that its self-designated task would be to bring together political leaders "to deal with the violence and intimidation problems in South Africa." However, the committee stated, it would "act merely as a low-profile catalyst to bring leadership together in order for the latter to discuss the solutions to the common enemy of all South Africans, vis-à-vis violence-related problems." At a one-day meeting held on June 22, three key tasks were identified: the establishment of codes of conduct for political organizations and security forces; the facilitation of socioeconomic development and reconstruction; and the setting up of enforcement mechanisms, such as local and regional peace secretariats. SAIRR, *Race Relations Survey,* 1991/1992, pp. 99–100.

43. Walshe, *Prophetic Christianity,* p. 147.

44. Ibid.

45. Ibid., p. 150. Other representatives included the General Secretaries of both the SACC and SACBC, and representatives of the ANC, the SACP, and the PAC.

46. World Council of Churches, *From Cottesloe to Cape Town: Challenges for the Church in a Post-Apartheid South Africa* (Geneva: WCC Program to Combat Racism, 1991), p. 104.

47. Frank Chikane, "General Secretary's Report to the 25th National Conference," July 5–9, 1993, p. 8, photocopy (CCA).

48. Task forces dealt with the provision of housing, education, health care, and employment. SAIRR, *Race Relations Survey,* 1989/1990, p. 290.

49. The National Coordination Committee was comprised of seven representatives from the SACC, three from the SACBC, five from the WCRP, two each from the ANC, the PAC, and AZAPO, and two co-opted members. Frank Chikane, "General Secretary's Report to the 23rd National Conference of the SACC," June 24–28, 1991, p. 11, photocopy (CCA).

50. Sr. Margaret Kelly, O.P., "South Africa in Transition and the Role of the Catholic Church 1989–1993," unpublished paper, 1993, p. 5, photocopy (BCA).

51. The NCCR was dissolved after much criticism, including reports of fraud involving R300,000; an inability to reconcile a masterlist of returnees; and a criminal investigation. As a result, the SACC Executive Committee decided in November 1992 to phase out the program. Chikane, "General Secretary's Report to the 25th National Conference," July 5–9, 1993, p. 15, photocopy (CCA).

52. SACC National Conference Resolutions, 1992, Resolution 1, photocopy (CCA).

53. Frank Chikane, "Update on the Crisis in South Africa," speech given by Chikane, August 27, 1991, p. 6, photocopy (CCA).

54. SACC National Executive Committee Report, May 26–27, 1992, appendix 4, "Conclusions of the Implementation Committee of the Emergency Summit on Violence Dealing with the Resolution on International Monitoring," May 7, 1992, photocopy (CCA).

55. Some remnants of the church/state conflict still existed in the early 1990s. For example, in the homeland of Bobphutatswana, Roman Catholic bishop Kevin Dowling, along with other church leaders and EMPSA monitors, was repeatedly harassed by police, as homeland president Lucas Mangope tried to maintain power (Mangope also boycotted the CODESA talks and allied himself to the IFP, the Ciskei homeland, and the right-wing Conservative Party). Walshe, *Prophetic Christianity*, p. 152.

56. *Internos* (July–August 1990): 9 (BCA). In the aftermath of the February 1990 unbannings, many expected church leaders to become directly involved in politics. Leaders such as Tutu and Chikane were named as being among those likely to seek greater political influence and participation. These leaders, however, made their views on the role of the church clear: the church was to act as a facilitator, allowing South Africans to voice their own ideas and ideals. Tutu, for example, spelled out his position during questioning by journalists on what role he envisaged for himself, by claiming that he did not aspire to become involved in government, as a cabinet minister, for example; he stated, "People could very well ask certain church leaders to represent them. But, for myself, I have to say I would hope I would not be put in that position." *Bishopscourt Update* (October 9, 1989) (CCA).

Many of those church leaders who had actively adopted the role of overt political actors thus went to great lengths to state that they were not going to enter into negotiations with the government, but would rather facilitate the creation of a climate conducive to negotiations. They felt that the so-called "Muzorewa Option" (named after the part played by Bishop Muzorewa in the then Rhodesian political transition) was inappropriate, as opposed to helping South Africans speak for themselves through now legal political parties and organizations. *Ecunews* (December 1989): 8 (CCA).

57. "The Church in the Middle?" *Ecunews* (December 1991): 10 (CCA).

58. Lamola, "Role of Religious Leaders," p. 4 (CCA).

59. *Internos* (July–August 1990): 8 (BCA).

60. Smangaliso Mkhatshwa, "The Role of Contextual Theology in a Changing South Africa," *Journal of Theology for Southern Africa* 72 (September 1990): 3.

61. Ibid., p. 4.

62. ICT, "The Release of Nelson Mandela: Reading the Signs of Our Times," pamphlet, March 1990, p. 12 (CTA).

63. ICT, "Kairos for the Church in South Africa," unpublished paper, 1990, p. 4, photocopy (CTA).

64. ICT, "Report on the 1990 Annual General Meeting" (July 16–19, 1990), p. 7 (CTA).

65. Ibid.

66. *Ecunews* (December 1991): 16 (CCA).

67. *Ecunews* (November 1992): 13 (CCA).

68. *Bishopscourt Update* (February 28, 1990) (CCA).

69. *Bishopscourt Update* (June 19, 1992) (CCA).

70. Charles Villa-Vicencio, "The Irreversibility of Change," unpublished, undated speech (est. 1991), photocopy (CCA).

71. *Challenge* (February 1993): 20–21 (CTA).

72. John Lamola, "Mediation Plus Prophecy Equals Facilitation," unpublished paper, 1992, photocopy (CCA).

73. Sr. Margaret Kelly, O.P., "South Africa in Transition," p. 6, photocopy (BCA).

74. Lamola, "Mediation Plus Prophecy" (CCA).

75. Ibid.

76. *Ecunews* (November 1992): 11 (CCA).

77. Albert Nolan, O.P., "The Role of the Church in the Struggle for Negotiations and Democracy," transcript of speech delivered at the ICT's Emergency Conference on the Current Situation, August 17–21, 1992, photocopy (CTA).

78. *Challenge* (February 1992): 16 (CTA).

79. Ibid., p. 17.

80. James Cochrane, "The South African Church in the Present Context: A Balance of Forces," unpublished speech delivered at the ICT's Emergency Conference on the Current Situation, August 17–21, 1992, photocopy (CTA).

81. Charles Villa-Vicencio, *A Theology of Reconstruction: Nation Building and Human Rights* (New York: Cambridge University Press, 1992), p. 23.

82. Ibid., p. 20.

83. Charles Villa-Vicencio, "The Kingdom of God and People's Democracy," *Journal of Theology for Southern Africa* 74 (March 1991): 3.

84. ICT, "Minutes of an ICT Consultation: A New Kairos—What Is at Stake for the People of South Africa?" October 28–31, 1990, photocopy (CTA).

85. Naudé, cited in Walshe, *Prophetic Christianity,* pp. 144–145.

86. SACC, "Standing for the Truth," pamphlet, 1991, p. 22 (CCA).

87. ICT, "Report on the 1992 Annual General Meeting" (September 14–18, 1992), p. 13 (CTA).

88. ICT, "Report on the 1990 Annual General Meeting" (July 16–19, 1990), pp. 14–15 (CTA).

89. The conference actually originated with F. W. de Klerk, who, in a Christmas message broadcast in December 1989, invited church leaders to discuss with him the role of churches in the changing South Africa. Several conservative churches accepted his offer immediately, but the invitation was rejected by the SACC, which stated that if churches were going to have a meaningful joint discussion with the state president, they needed to meet alone first to address several serious issues which had left them deeply divided in the aftermath of the 1960 Cottesloe Conference. Moreover, the SACC argued, it was not the role of the state president to prescribe to churches what their role should be nor was it his role to convene such a conference. Churches should first address issues raised at Cottesloe and the intervening decades in order to determine if there even existed enough common ground for a united Christian witness. De Klerk subsequently withdrew his invitation to the churches to meet with him, and the envisioned conference of religious organizations was held at Rustenburg. SAIRR, *Race Relations Survey,* 1989/1990, pp. 288–289, and *Ecunews* (October/November 1989): 3, 7 (CCA).

Walshe highlights another possible reason for the SACC's rejection of de Klerk's offer: "From the regime's viewpoint, a meeting of church leaders so broad as to produce an amorphous outcome would have been a public relations bonanza—consolidating de Klerk's image as a peace maker and legitimating his government's efforts in the negotiating process." Walshe, *Prophetic Christianity,* p. 139.

90. Delegates included leaders from denominations that had held long-standing suspicions of contextual theology and had supported the regime's attempts to reform apartheid in the 1980s, including the Apostolic Faith Mission Church, evangelicals, and several African Independent Churches. Also represented was the white Dutch Reformed Church, NGK, which had long justified the system of apartheid on biblical grounds, along with ecumenical organizations such as the ICT and SACC, which had condemned the very same system theologically. Ibid., p. 140.

91. The act of confession began when one of the invited speakers, Professor Willie Jonker (a member of the NGK, but not one of its official delegation), diverged from his prepared speech to declare: I confess before you and before the Lord, not only my own sin and guilt, and my personal responsibility for the political, social, economical and structural wrongs that have been done to many of you, and the results which you and our whole country are still suffering from, but *vicariously* I dare also to do that in the name of the DRC of which I am a member, and for the Afrikaans people as a whole." Louw Alberts and Frank Chikane, eds., *The Road to Rustenburg* (Cape Town: Struik Christian Books, 1991), p. 87, emphasis in original.

Archbishop Tutu responded by going to the podium and accepting Jonker's confession, adding "my Church has to confess too. My Church has to confess its racism. I have to confess as a black person. How many times have I treated others in my own community as if they were less than the children of God? What is my share in our common sin?" Ibid., p. 102.

92. These victims confessed: "Those of us who are victims of apartheid acknowledge our own contribution to the failure of the church. . . . We acknowledge that many of us have responded with timidity and fear, failing to challenge our oppression. . . . Some of us have become willing instruments of the repressive State machinery. Others have reacted to oppression with a desire for revenge. Many of us who have achieved privilege have exploited others. . . . With a broken and contrite spirit we ask the forgiveness of God and of our fellow South Africans. . . . " Ibid., pp. 277–279.

93. Cochrane, "The South African Church in the Present Context," photocopy (CTA).

94. Ibid.

95. *Challenge* (February 1992): 16 (CTA).

96. Cochrane stated before the Rustenburg Conference took place that "The theologies and policies of those who enter into the consultation on the basis of repentance for past support for, or indifference to, the history of oppression and impoverishment of black South Africans, must be assumed to be substantially the same as before. New initiatives on their part, such as this consultation, are evidence not of profound theological and policy shifts, but of the shift of the political and economic ground under their feet. The burden of proof must be upon them, and the conditions for establishing their integrity and sincerity must be clear and radical." Cochrane, "The South African Church in the Present Context," photocopy (CTA).

97. Ibid.

98. Beyers Naudé, "After Admission—What Next?" *Cross Times* (February 1991): viii (OPD).

99. *ICT News* (December 1990): 3 (CTA).

100. A brief review of Cottesloe reminds the reader that, in response to the threat by the Anglican archbishop of Cape Town to withdraw his church's membership unless the

WCC expelled the DRC for its continued support of apartheid after Sharpeville, the WCC called its member churches in South Africa to a consultation at Cottesloe in December 1960. The consultation resulted in the government's forcing the DRC to withdraw from the WCC, and subsequently from the SACC. In fact, no WCC official had visited South Africa since the outcry which had followed the establishment of the PCR, with its grants to the ANC and the PAC in 1970. At the time, South African prime minister Vorster threatened to act against any South African churches which did not resign from the WCC. When the SACC and the WCC tried to meet to discuss the grants, the government insisted that the meeting be held at the Jan Smuts Airport, thus denying the WCC General Secretary entry to South Africa. World Council of Churches, *From Cottesloe to Cape Town,* p. 7.

101. The "Cape Town Consultation's Proposals for Action" was divided into nine sections, covering the following areas: strengthening the inner life of the church; ecumenical action; violence; reconciliation in church and nation; sanctions; economic justice and restitution; women and youth; AIDS; and poverty and development. For a detailed description of these proposals, see ibid., pp. 103–108.

102. Walshe, *Prophetic Christianity,* p. 143.

103. This was, of course, not a new issue facing the contextual theology movement, as identified in chapter 6. However, for the first time, ecumenical organizations were publicly acknowledging this serious problem.

104. Chikane, "Report of the General Secretary to the National Executive Committee of the SACC," February 1992, p. 4, photocopy (CCA).

105. Ibid.

106. Nolan, O.P., "The Role of the Church," photocopy (CTA).

107. Nolan argued, "What happens when the church gives support to one kind of project and doesn't give support to another is that the church is legitimizing one way of acting and delegitimizing the other. I think that is our biggest role." Ibid.

108. Themba Dladla, ed., *Kairos '95: At the Threshold of Jubilee—A Conference Report* (Johannesburg: ICT, 1996), p. 7 (CTA).

109. Ibid., p. 12.

110. Ibid., p. 14.

111. Ibid., p. 15.

112. Villa-Vicencio, *Theology of Reconstruction,* p. 6. The theme of the SACC's 1991 National Conference was, in fact, "From Egypt to the Wilderness: The Ecstasy and the Agony."

113. During the post-exilic period, the Israelites received their "constitution," and during their transitional period, South Africans should be thinking about their laws. The story of the Golden Calf contained a warning to South Africans not to follow the example of Israelites, who, instead of spending their time consolidating their gains or reconstructing, engaged in the worship of money and materialistic things. Finally, the journey through the desert was characterized by power struggles and leadership struggles. Again, South Africans should heed the implicit warnings, Naudé said. ICT, "Minutes of the 1990 Annual General Meeting," July 16–19, 1990, pp. 15–16 (CTA).

114. *Challenge* (February 1993): 25 (CTA). The ICT also took up the post-exilic theme, using the symbolism of the release from Babylonian captivity. This release was the sign of hope and a challenge to the people to rebuild the nation of Israel—a struggle which would be long and hard with many obstacles and failures, as well as successes. Similarly, the ICT argued, the release of Mandela was the victory of one struggle which opened the door to a new one. While the release was filled with promise, it also spelled out the need for a long and arduous struggle to bring about the structures necessary for a nonracial and democratic society. ICT, "The Release of Nelson Mandela," pp. 11–12 (CTA).

115. *Challenge* (February 1993): 25 (CTA).

116. Charles Villa-Vicencio, "The Kingdom of God and People's Democracy," pp. 7–9.

117. Villa-Vicencio, *Theology of Reconstruction*, p. 8.

118. Ibid., p. 15.

119. Ibid., p. 274.

120. Ibid., p. 31.

121. First-generation rights are also known as civil and political rights; second-generation rights are economic, social, and cultural rights; third-generation rights are known as solidarity or development rights.

122. Ibid., pp. 239–240.

123. Frank Chikane, "The State of the Nation: From Kairos to . . . Jubilee," in Dladla, *Kairos '95,* p. 21 (CTA).

124. Ibid., pp. 27–28.

125. Dladla, *Kairos '95,* p. 88.

126. SACC, "Toward a Code of Investment for South Africa: An Ethical Challenge," unpublished paper, February 1992, photocopy (CCA).

127. Lamola, "Role of Religious Leaders," pp. 20–22 (CCA).

128. *Ukukhanya* (Daily Publication of the 25th SACC National Conference) 2 (July 5, 1993): 1 (CCA).

129. SACBC, "A Call to Build a New South Africa," Pastoral Letter of the Southern African Catholic Bishops' Conference (January 1992), p. 5 (BCA).

130. Some of the actions called for in the Declaration included an examination by churches of their land ownership policies, and a commitment to return expropriated land; the reviewing of private church school policies in an effort to making them more accessible to underprivileged; for churches to make available financial and human resources for reconstruction; the need for churches to work for a new economic order; and working for the eradication of poverty and hunger. Alberts and Chikane, *Road to Rustenburg,* pp. 284–285.

131. SACC National Conference Resolutions, 1991, photocopy (CCA).

132. The full title of the pastoral letter was "Pastoral Letter on the Occasion of the Centenary of the First Papal Encyclical on Social Justice—*Rerum Novarum*—and Its Implications for Negotiations in South Africa." As its title implies, it was written to commemorate the centennial anniversary of the first papal encyclical on social justice, *Rerum Novarum,* issued by Pope Leo XIII on May 15, 1991, which marks the beginning of Catholic Social Justice teachings.

133. "The Declaration issued by the Rustenburg Conference has led us with considerable pain to examine our own history. . . . So in welcoming this Declaration, we recognise that its message applies to our church as a corporate body. We must admit with sorrow that although as a church we have often spoken out against the sin of apartheid we are not innocent of all complicity in supporting or going along with it. So we ask forgiveness from all those, both within the church and beyond, who have suffered from our actions, blindness and negligence in the past." SACBC, "Pastoral Letter on the Occasion of the Centenary of the First Papal Encyclical on Social Justice—*Rerum Novarum*—and Its Implications for Negotiations in South Africa," pp. 2–3 (BCA).

134. Ibid., p. 3.

135. *Internos* (July–August 1990): 9 (BCA).

136. The Catholic bishops made their stance most explicit in their 1986 Pastoral Letter on Economic Pressure for Justice. In it they pronounced that "economic pressure" was a morally justifiable means of forcing an end to apartheid. The bishops never recommended any specific pressures, claiming that they did not possess the competency to make such political judgments. In contrast, the SACC's National Conference in 1986 called for comprehensive economic sanctions against the apartheid regime.

137. Frank Chikane, "General Secretary's Report to the 22nd National Conference," June 25–29, 1990, p. 7, photocopy (CCA).

138. Montshiwa Moroke, "Repeal of Acts 'Not Irreversible,'" *Star,* June 26, 1991 (OPD).

139. Chikane, "Come Holy Spirit," p. 7, photocopy (CCA).

140. *Ukukhanya* 4 (July 7, 1993): 1 (CCA).

141. Frank Chikane, "General Secretary's Report to the 25th National Conference," July 5–9, 1993, appendix 1, photocopy (CCA).

142. SACC National Conference Resolutions, 1993, Resolution 2, photocopy (CCA).

143. SACBC, "Discussion Booklet on Negotiations," February 1990, p. 4 (BCA).

144. Sr. Margaret Kelly, O.P. "The Catholic Church and Resistance to Apartheid," p. 6, photocopy (BCA), and "Catholics Explain Sanctions Stance," *New Nation* (December 13–19, 1991) (BCA).

145. Frank Chikane, "25 Years of a Costly Struggle: A Vision for the Future," Opening Address to the 25th National Conference, July 5, 1993, photocopy (CCA).

146. Chikane, "General Secretary's Report to the 25th National Conference," July 5–9, 1993, p. 28, photocopy (CCA).

147. Ibid., p. 29.

148. World Council of Churches, *From Cottesloe to Cape Town,* p. 94.

149. Ibid., p. 95.

150. The loss of SACC funding was mirrored around the world. Much of the loss occurred because the SACC no longer received financial support from European and American NGOs. Many of these NGOs had been conduits of funds allocated to them by their governments, and these NGOs then allocated the funds to the SACC. With the political changes in South Africa, however, overseas governments began to deal directly with the new South African government. Thus, not only did South African NGOs suffer financial loss, so too did their European and American partners.

151. Frank Chikane, "Report of the General Secretary to the National Executive Committee of the SACC," November 24–25, 1992, appendix 17, p. 4, photocopy (CCA).

152. In his report to the SACC's National Executive Committee in March 1991, Frank Chikane highlighted the various ways in which these cuts affected his organization: first, they had caused enormous pain for those who awaited the final verdict on their futures; second, they had demoralized those who would not be losing their jobs; third, they severely affected the performance of staff; fourth, they forced a redirection of energy from the outward-looking ministry of the Council to inward-looking concerns; and fifth, they had paralyzed the General Secretariat. Frank Chikane, "Report of the General Secretary to the National Executive Committee of the SACC," March 12–13, 1991, pp. 2–3, photocopy (CCA).

153. Villa-Vicencio interview, June 23, 1993.

154. Frank Chikane, "Report of the General Secretary to the National Executive Committee of the SACC," August 25, 1992, Annexure D, "WCC Policy on South Africa," photocopy (CCA).

155. Villa-Vicencio interview, June 23, 1993.

156. The IEC was composed of eleven South African citizens chosen by the TEC and formally appointed by the state president. These individuals were expected to be "impartial, respected and suitably qualified men and women who do not have a high political profile." In addition, five nonvoting observers from the international community were also commissioned to serve on the IEC. The five persons chosen came from Canada, Denmark, Eritrea, the United States, and Zimbabwe.

157. "New South Africa Fails Its Pensioners," *Weekly Mail and Guardian* (http://wn.-

apc.org/wmail/issues/), August 30, 1996, and "Mbeki Gears Up," *Weekly Mail and Guardian,* March 20, 1997 (OPD).

158. Some political commentators in South Africa argued that Boesak received the ambassadorial nomination not only as a reward for services rendered, but also as a way of sidelining Boesak, who had proven to be a political liability to the ANC in his failure to draw significant Colored support in the election.

159. The various scandals revolved around foreign funds received by Boesak's Foundation for Peace and Justice (FPJ), which never reached donors for whom the funds were intended. Included in these funds were substantial amounts of money received from Danchurch Aid (a Danish charity), the Coca-Cola Foundation, and singer Paul Simon. In addition to these disappearing funds, Boesak's FPJ was also caught up in another scandal, which involved a complicated fraudulent $40 million bank loan from Indonesia in 1992, at a time when Boesak and his foundation, along with the ANC and the SACC, were publicly still supporting economic sanctions against South Africa.

160. "Editorial: The Velcro Priest," *Weekly Mail and Guardian* (http://wn.apc.-org/wmail/issues/), December 6, 1995 (OPD).

161. Suzanne Daley, "Former South Africa Police Chief Admits Role in Terrorizing Blacks," *New York Times,* October 22, 1996, pp. A1 and A16 (OPD).

162. "Targets Bopabe, Chikane, Dalling, 702's Robbie," *Weekly Mail and Guardian* (http://wn.apc.org/wmail/issues/), June 23, 1995 (OPD).

163. *Challenge* (February 1993): 6 (CTA).

164. Walshe, *Prophetic Christianity,* pp. 158–159.

Bibliography

Books and Articles

Abraham, Garth. *The Catholic Church and Apartheid*. Johannesburg: Ravan Press, 1989.

Adler, Emmanuel. *The Power of Ideology: The Quest for Technological Autonomy in Argentina and Brazil*. Berkeley: University of California Press, 1987.

Alberts, Louw, and Frank Chikane, eds. *The Road to Rustenburg*. Cape Town: Struik Christian Books, 1991.

Antoncich, Ricardo. *Christians in the Face of Injustice: A Latin American Reading of Catholic Social Teaching*. Maryknoll, N.Y.: Orbis Books, 1987.

Balia, Daryl M. *Christian Resistance to Apartheid*. Johannesburg: Skotaville Publishers, 1989.

Bensman, Joseph. "Max Weber's Concept of Legitimacy: An Evaluation." In *Conflict and Control: Challenge to Legitimacy of Modern Governments*, ed. Arthur J. Vidich and Ronald M. Glassman, 17–48. Beverly Hills, Calif.: Sage Publications, 1979.

Berryman, Phillip. *Liberation Theology*. New York: Pantheon, 1987.

———. *The Religious Roots of Rebellion: Christians in Central American Revolutions*. Maryknoll, N.Y.: Orbis Books, 1984.

Biko, Steve. *I Write What I Like*. Ed. C. R. Aelred Stubbs. New York: Harper and Row, 1978.

Boesak, Allan. *Farewell to Innocence: A Socio-Ethical Study on Black Theology and Power*. Maryknoll, N.Y.: Orbis Books, 1977.

Boesak, Allan, and Charles Villa-Vicencio, eds. *A Call for an End to Unjust Rule*. Edinburgh: Saint Andrew Press, 1986.

Brewer, John. "The Police in South African Politics." In *South Africa: No Turning Back*, ed. Shaun Johnson, 258–279. Great Britain: David Davies Memorial Institute of International Studies, 1989.

Brown, Robert McAfee. *Kairos: Three Prophetic Challenges to the Church*. Grand Rapids, Mich.: Eerdmans, 1990.

Calvo, Roberto. "The Church and the Doctrine of National Security." *Journal of Interamerican Studies and World Affairs* 21, no. 1 (February 1979): 69–88.

Catholic Institute for International Relations. *The Church and Apartheid*. London: CIIR, 1985.

———. *Country and Conscience: South African Conscientious Objectors*. London: CIIR/ Pax Christi, 1988.

Chidester, David. *Shots in the Streets: Violence and Religion in South Africa*. Boston: Beacon Press, 1991.

Chikane, Frank. "Doing Theology in a Situation of Conflict." In *Resistance and Hope: South African Essays in Honor of Beyers Naudé*, ed. Charles Villa-Vicencio, 98–102. Cape Town: David Philip, 1985.

———. *No Life of My Own: An Autobiography*. London: Catholic Institute for International Relations, 1988.

————. "Where the Debate Ends." In *Theology and Violence: The South African Debate,* ed. Charles Villa-Vicencio, 301–309. Johannesburg: Skotaville, 1987.

Cochrane, James. *Servants of Power: The Role of the English-Speaking Churches, 1903–1930.* Johannesburg: Ravan Press, 1987.

Comaroff, Jean. *Body of Power, Spirit of Resistance: The Culture and History of a South African People.* Chicago: University of Chicago Press, 1985.

Comblin, Jose. *The Church and the National Security State.* Maryknoll, N.Y.: Orbis Books, 1979.

The Committee on Africa, the War, and Peace Aims. *The Atlantic Charter and Africa from an American Standpoint.* New York: Phelps-Stokes Fund, 1942.

The Commonwealth Group of Eminent Persons. *Mission to South Africa: The Commonwealth Report.* London: Penguin, 1986.

Davenport, T. R. H. *South Africa: A Modern History.* South Africa: Southern Book Publishers, 1989.

de Gruchy, John W. *The Church Struggle in South Africa.* Grand Rapids, Mich.: Eerdmans, 1979.

————. "Theologies in Conflict: The South African Debate." In *Resistance and Hope: South African Essays in Honor of Beyers Naudé,* ed. Charles Villa-Vicencio and John W. de Gruchy, 85–97. Cape Town: David Philip, 1985.

de Gruchy, John W., and Charles Villa-Vicencio, eds. *Apartheid Is a Heresy.* Grand Rapids, Mich.: Eerdmans, 1983.

"Documentation: The Church-State Confrontation, Correspondence and Statements, February–April 1988." *Journal of Theology for Southern Africa* 63 (June 1988): 68–87.

Dodson, Michael, and Laura Nuzzi-O'Shaughnessy. *Nicaragua's Other Revolution: Religious Faith and Political Struggle.* Chapel Hill: University of North Carolina Press, 1990.

Farley, Lawrence T. *Plebiscites and Sovereignty: The Crisis of Political Illegitimacy.* Boulder, Colo.: Westview Press, 1986.

Ferm, Deane W. *Third World Liberation Theologies.* Maryknoll, N.Y.: Orbis Books, 1986.

Fields, Karen E. *Revival and Rebellion in Colonial Central Africa.* Princeton: Princeton University Press, 1985.

Foner, Eric. *Politics and Ideology in the Age of the Civil War.* Oxford: Oxford University Press, 1980.

Gerhart, Gail. *Black Power in South Africa: The Evolution of an Ideology.* Berkeley: University of California Press, 1979.

Goba, Bonganjalo. "Doing Theology in South Africa: A Black Christian Perspective." *Journal of Theology for Southern Africa* 31 (June 1980): 23–35.

————. "The Kairos Document and Its Implications for Liberation in South Africa." *Journal of Law and Religion* 5, no. 2 (1987): 313–325.

Goldstein, Judith. "Ideas, Institutions, and American Trade Policy." *International Organization* 42, no. 1 (Winter 1988): 179–217.

————. "The Impact of Ideas on Trade Policy: The Origins of the U.S. Agricultural and Manufacturing Policies." *International Organization* 43, no. 1 (Winter 1989): 31–71.

Gouldner, Alvin W. "Organizational Analysis." In *Sociology Today: Problems and Prospects,* ed. Robert K. Merton et al., 400–420. New York: Basic Books, 1959.

Gremillion, Joseph, ed. *The Gospel of Peace and Justice: Catholic Social Teaching since Pope John.* Maryknoll, N.Y.: Orbis Books, 1967.

Gutierrez, Gustavo. *A Theology of Liberation.* Maryknoll, N.Y.: Orbis Books, 1973.

Hall, Peter. *Governing the Economy.* Oxford: Oxford University Press, 1986.

———, ed. *The Political Power of Economic Ideas: Keynesianism across Nations.* Princeton: Princeton University Press, 1989.

Hanlon, Joseph, ed. *South Africa: The Sanctions Report.* London: James Curry, 1990.

Hanson, Eric O. *The Catholic Church in World Politics.* Princeton: Princeton University Press, 1987.

Hartz, Louis. *The Liberal Tradition in America.* New York: Harcourt, 1955.

Hebblethwaite, Peter. "Changing Vatican Policies 1965–1985: Peter's Primacy and the Reality of Local Churches." In *World Catholicism in Transition,* ed. Thomas M. Gannon, S.J., 36–53. New York: MacMillan, 1988.

Hewitt, W. E. *Base Christian Communities and Social Change in Brazil.* Lincoln: University of Nebraska Press, 1991.

Hollis, Christopher. *The Achievements of Vatican II.* New York: Hawthorn Books, 1967.

Hope, Marjorie, and James Young. *The South African Churches in a Revolutionary Situation.* Maryknoll, N.Y.: Orbis Books, 1983.

Hopkins, Dwight N. *Black Theology USA and South Africa: Politics, Culture, and Liberation.* Maryknoll, N.Y.: Orbis Books, 1989.

Horrell, Muriel. *Laws Affecting Race Relations in South Africa.* Johannesburg: South African Institute of Race Relations, 1978.

Hurley, Denis E. "The Catholic Church and Apartheid." *Africa Report* 28 (July/August 1983): 17–20.

———. "Catholic Social Teaching and Ideology." In *Catholics in Apartheid Society,* ed. Andrew Prior, 22–44. Cape Town: David Philip, 1982.

Ikenberry, G. John. "Conclusion: An Institutional Approach to American Foreign Economic Policy." *International Organization* 42, no. 1 (Winter 1988): 219–243.

Jenson, Jane. "Changing Discourse, Changing Agendas: Political Rights and Reproductive Policies in France." In *The Women's Movements of the United States and Western Europe: Consciousness, Political Opportunity, and Public Policy,* ed. Mary Fainsod Katzenstein and Carol McClurg Mueller, 64–88. Philadelphia: Temple University Press, 1987.

Johnson, Shaun, ed. *South Africa: No Turning Back.* London: MacMillan, 1988.

Jubber, Ken. "The Roman Catholic Church and Apartheid." *Journal of Theology for Southern Africa* 15 (June 1976): 25–38.

The Kairos Document: Challenge to the Church: A Theological Comment on the Political Crisis in South Africa. Rev. 2d ed. Grand Rapids, Mich.: Eerdmans, 1985.

Karis, Thomas and Gwendolen M. Carter, eds. *From Protest to Challenge: A Documentary History of African Politics in South Africa, 1882–1964.* Vols. 1–4. Stanford: Hoover Institution, 1973.

Katzenstein, Mary Fainsod, and Carol McClurg Mueller, eds. *The Women's Movements of the United States and Western Europe: Consciousness, Political Opportunity, and Public Policy.* Philadelphia: Temple University Press, 1987.

King, Anthony. "Ideas, Institutions and Policies of Governments: A Comparative Analysis, Parts I and II." *British Journal of Political Science* 2, no. 3 (July 1973): 291–313.

———. "Ideas, Institutions and Policies of Governments: A Comparative Analysis, Part III." *British Journal of Political Science* 2, no. 4 (October 1973): 409–423.

Kistner, Wolfram. *Outside the Camp: A Collection of Writings.* Johannesburg: SACC, 1988.

Knight, Derrick. *Beyond the Pale: The Christian Political Fringe.* London: Kogan Page, 1980.

Kretzschmar, Louise. *The Voice of Black Theology in South Africa.* Johannesburg: Ravan Press, 1986.

Laurence, Patrick. "De Klerk's Rubicon." *Africa Report* (March/April 1990): 14–16.

Lernoux, Penny. *Cry of the People: The Struggle for Human Rights in Latin America— the Catholic Church in Conflict with U.S. Policy.* New York: Penguin Books, 1982.

Levine, Daniel H. *Popular Voices in Latin American Catholicism.* Princeton: Princeton University Press, 1992.

———. *Religion and Politics in Latin America: The Catholic Church in Venezuela and Colombia.* Princeton: Princeton University Press, 1981.

———. "Religion, Society, and Politics: States of the Art." *Latin American Research Review* 16 (1981): 185–199.

———, ed. *Religion and Political Conflict in Latin America.* Chapel Hill: University of North Carolina Press, 1986.

Lienemann-Perrin, Christine, and Wolfgang Lienemann, eds. *Political Legitimacy in South Africa.* Heidelberg, FRG: Protestant Institute for Interdisciplinary Research, 1988.

Linden, Ian. *Back to Basics: Revisiting Catholic Social Teaching.* London: CIIR, 1994.

Linz, Juan. *The Breakdown of Democratic Regimes: Crisis, Breakdown, and Reequilibration.* Baltimore: Johns Hopkins University Press, 1978.

Lodge, Tom. *Black Politics in South Africa since 1945.* Johannesburg: Ravan Press, 1983.

Maimela, Simon. "Black Power and Black Theology in South Africa." *Scriptura* 12 (1984): 40–53.

Mainwaring, Scott. *The Catholic Church and Politics in Brazil: 1916–1985.* Stanford, Calif.: Stanford University Press, 1986.

Mainwaring, Scott, and Alexander Wilde, eds. *The Progressive Church in Latin America.* Notre Dame, Ind.: University of Notre Dame Press, 1989.

March, James G., and Johan P. Olsen. "The New Institutionalism: Organizational Factors in Political Life." *The American Political Science Review* 78 (September 1984): 734–749.

Mbali, Zolile. *The Churches and Racism: A Black South African Perspective.* London: SCM Press, 1987.

McFaul, Michael. "The Demise of World Revolutionary Process: Soviet-Angolan Relations under Gorbachev." *Journal of Southern African Studies* 16, no. 1 (March 1990): 165–189.

McGovern, Arthur. *Liberation Theology and Its Critics.* Maryknoll, N.Y.: Orbis Books, 1989.

Meli, Francis. *A History of the ANC: South Africa Belongs to Us.* London: James Curry, 1988.

Metz, Johann Baptist. *Faith in History and Society: Towards a Practical Fundamental Theology.* London: Burns and Oates, 1980.

Mkhatshwa, Smangaliso. "The Role of Contextual Theology in a Changing South Africa." *Journal of Theology for Southern Africa* 72 (September 1990): 3–8.

Mosala, Itumeleng J., and Buti Thlagale, eds. *The Unquestionable Right to Be Free: Essays in Black Theology.* Johannesburg: Skotaville Publishers, 1986.

Motlhabi, Mokgethi. *The Theory and Practice of Black Resistance to Apartheid: A Socio-Ethical Analysis.* Johannesburg: Skotaville Publishers, 1984.

Murray, Martin J. *The Revolution Deferred: The Painful Birth of Post-Apartheid South Africa.* New York: Verso, 1994.

Mutambirwa, James. *South Africa: The Sanctions Mission Report of the Eminent Church Persons' Group.* Geneva: WCC, 1989.

Mutloatse, Mothobi, and John Webster, eds. *Hope and Suffering: Sermons and Speeches of The Right Reverend Desmond Mpilo Tutu.* Grand Rapids, Mich.: Eerdmans, 1984.

Nash, Margaret. "The SACC: Part of or Alienated from the Church?" *South African Outlook* 114, no. 1357 (July 1984): 122–124.

Neuhouser, Kevin. "The Radicalization of the Brazilian Catholic Church in Comparative Perspective." *American Sociological Review* 54 (April 1989): 233–244.

Nolan, Albert. *God in South Africa: The Challenge of the Gospel.* Grand Rapids, Mich.: Eerdmans, 1988.

———. "The Option for the Poor in South Africa." In *Resistance and Hope: South African Essays in Honor of Beyers Naudé,* ed. Charles Villa-Vicencio and John W. de Gruchy, 189–198. Cape Town: David Philip, 1985.

Novicki, Margaret A. "The Reverend Allan Boesak: An Interview." *Africa Report* 28 (July/August 1983): 7–12.

Odell, John. *U.S. International Monetary Policy: Markets, Power, and Ideas as Sources of Change.* Princeton: Princeton University Press, 1982.

Odendaal, André. *Black Protest Politics in South Africa to 1912.* Totowa, N.J.: Barnes and Noble, 1984.

Orkin, Mark, ed. *Sanctions Against Apartheid.* New York: St. Martin's Press, 1989.

Pakenham, Thomas. *The Boer War.* New York: Random House, 1994.

Peters, Noel Benedict. *South Africa: A Catholic Perspective.* Fresno, Calif.: Pioneer Publishing Co., 1991.

Pope Paul VI. "*Populorum Progressio.*" In *The Gospel of Peace and Justice: Catholic Social Teaching Since Pope John,* ed. Joseph Gremillion, 389–415. Maryknoll, N.Y.: Orbis Books, 1967.

Powell, Walter W., and Paul J. Dimaggio, eds. *The New Institutionalism in Organizational Analysis.* Chicago: University of Chicago Press, 1991.

Price, Robert M. *The Apartheid State in Crisis: Political Transformation in South Africa, 1975–1990.* New York: Oxford University Press, 1991.

Prior, Andrew. *Catholics in Apartheid Society.* Cape Town: David Philip, 1982.

Rees, John. "Investment in Southern Africa: The Stand of the World Council of Churches towards South Africa and the Reaction from South Africa." *South African Institute of International Affairs* 5, no. 3 (1973): 32–38.

Rogers, Barbara. *Race: No Peace without Justice: Churches Confront the Mounting Racism of the 1980s.* Geneva: WCC, 1980.

Rubenstein, Richard, and John Roth, eds. *The Politics of Latin American Liberation Theology.* Washington, D.C.: Washington Institute Press, 1988.

Schner, George P., ed. *The Church Renewed: The Documents of Vatican II Reconsidered.* Lanham, Md.: University Press of America, 1986.

Segundo, Juan Luis. *The Liberation of Theology.* Maryknoll, N.Y.: Orbis Books, 1976.

Seidman, Ann. *The Roots of Crisis in Southern Africa.* Trenton, N.J.: Africa World Press, 1985.

Sigmund, Paul E. *Liberation Theology at the Crossroads: Democracy or Revolution?* New York: Oxford University Press, 1990.

Sikkink, Kathryn. *Ideas and Institutions: Developmentalism in Brazil and Argentina.* Ithaca, N.Y.: Cornell University Press, 1991.

Sincere, Richard E., Jr. *The Politics of Sentiment: Churches and Foreign Investment in South Africa.* Washington, D.C.: Ethics and Public Policy Center, 1984.

Sjollema, Baldwin. "Eloquent Action." In *A Long Struggle: The Involvement of the World Council of Churches in South Africa,* ed. Pauline Webb, 12–44. Geneva: WCC, 1994.

———. "The Initial Challenge." In *A Long Struggle: The Involvement of the World Council of Churches in South Africa,* ed. Pauline Webb, 1–11. Geneva: WCC, 1994.

Smith, Brian. "Churches and Human Rights in Latin America: Recent Trends in the Subcontinent." *Journal of Interamerican Studies and World Affairs* 21, no. 1 (February 1979): 89–128.

———. *The Church and Politics in Chile: Challenges to Modern Catholicism.* Princeton: Princeton University Press, 1982.

Smith, Christian. *The Emergence of Liberation Theology: Radical Religion and Social Movement Theory.* Chicago: University of Chicago Press, 1991.

———, ed. *Disruptive Religion: The Force of Faith in Social Movement Activism.* New York: Routledge Press, 1996.

South African Institute of Race Relations. *Race Relations Survey.* Johannesburg: SAIRR, 1981.

———. *Race Relations Survey.* Johannesburg: SAIRR, 1984.

———. *Race Relations Survey.* Johannesburg: SAIRR, 1985.

———. *Race Relations Survey.* Johannesburg: SAIRR, 1987/1988.

———. *Race Relations Survey.* Johannesburg: SAIRR, 1988/1989.

———. *Race Relations Survey.* Johannesburg: SAIRR, 1989/1990.

———. *Race Relations Survey.* Johannesburg: SAIRR, 1991/1992.

Spence, Jack. "The Military in South African Politics." In *South Africa: No Turning Back,* ed. Shaun Johnson, 240–257. Great Britain: David Davies Memorial Institute of International Studies, 1989.

Spong, Bernard, and Cedric Mayson. *Come Celebrate! Twenty-Five Years of the South African Council of Churches.* Johannesburg: SACC, 1993.

Stogre, Michael. "Commentary on the Pastoral Constitution on the Church in the Modern World: *Gaudium et Spes.*" In *The Church Renewed: The Documents of Vatican II Reconsidered,* ed. George P. Schner, 19–36. Lanham, Md.: University Press of America, 1986.

"A Theological Rationale and a Call to Prayer for the End to Unjust Rule." In *A Call for an End to Unjust Rule,* ed. Allan Boesak and Charles Villa-Vicencio, 25–29. Edinburgh: Saint Andrew Press, 1986.

Thomas, David G. *Councils in the Ecumenical Movement: 1904–1975.* Johannesburg: SACC, 1979.

Thompson, Leonard. *A History of South Africa.* New Haven: Yale University Press, 1990.

Tingle, Rachel. *Revolution or Reconciliation? The Struggle in the Church in South Africa.* London: Christian Studies Centre, 1992.

Tlhagale, Buti. "Christian Soldiers." In *Theology and Violence: The South African Debate,* ed. Charles Villa-Vicencio, 79–88. Johannesburg: Skotaville, 1987.

———. "Towards a Black Theology of Labour." In *Resistance and Hope: South African Essays in Honor of Beyers Naudé,* ed. Charles Villa-Vicencio and John W. de Gruchy, 126–134. Cape Town: David Philip, 1985.

Troeltsch, Ernst. *The Social Teaching of the Christian Churches.* Vol. 1. Trans. Olive Wyon. New York: MacMillan, 1931.

Tutu, Desmond. "The Blasphemy that is Apartheid." *Africa Report* 28 (July/August 1983): 4–6.

———. *Crying in the Wilderness.* Great Britain: Mowbray, 1986.

van der Bent, Ans J. *Handbook Member Churches of the World Council of Churches.* Geneva: WCC, 1985.

Vidich, Arthur J., and Ronald M. Glassman, eds. *Conflict and Control: Challenge to Legitimacy of Modern Governments.* Beverly Hills, Calif.: Sage Publications, 1979.

Villa-Vicencio, Charles. "The Church and Violence." In *A Long Struggle: The Involvement of the World Council of Churches in South Africa,* ed. Pauline Webb, 102–115. Geneva: WCC, 1994.

———. "The Church: Discordant and Divided." *Africa Report* (July/August 1983): 13–19.

———. *Civil Disobedience and Beyond: Law, Resistance, and Religion in South Africa.* Grand Rapids, Mich.: Eerdmans, 1990.

———. "Introduction." In *A Call for an End to Unjust Rule,* ed. Allan Boesak and Charles Villa-Vicencio, 15–22. Edinburgh: Saint Andrew Press, 1986.

———. "Introduction." In *Theology and Violence: The South African Debate,* ed. Charles Villa-Vicencio, 1–10. Johannesburg: Skotaville, 1987.

———. "The Kingdom of God and People's Democracy." *Journal of Theology for Southern Africa* 74 (March 1991): 3–13.

———. "Some Refused to Pray: The Moral Impasse of the English-Speaking Churches." In *A Call for an End to Unjust Rule,* ed. Allan Boesak and Charles Villa-Vicencio, 43–59. Edinburgh: Saint Andrew Press, 1986.

———. "Southern Africa Today: A Consensus Against Apartheid." *Journal of Theology for Southern Africa* 41 (December 1982).

———. *A Theology of Reconstruction: Nation-Building and Human Rights.* New York: Cambridge University Press, 1992.

———. *Trapped in Apartheid: A Socio-Theological History of the English-Speaking Churches.* Maryknoll, N.Y.: Orbis Books, 1988.

———, ed. *Theology and Violence: The South African Debate.* Johannesburg: Skotaville Publishers, 1987.

Villa-Vicencio, Charles, and John W. de Gruchy, eds. *Resistance and Hope: South African Essays in Honor of Beyers Naudé.* Cape Town: David Philip, 1985.

Walker, Eric A. *A History of Southern Africa.* London: Longmans, Green and Co., 1957.

Walshe, Peter. *Church versus State in South Africa: The Case of the Christian Institute.* Maryknoll, N.Y.: Orbis Books, 1983.

———. "Church versus State in South Africa: The Christian Institute and the Resurgence of African Nationalism." *Journal of Church and State* 19, no. 3 (Autumn 1977): 457–479.

———. "The Evolution of Liberation Theology in South Africa." *Journal of Law and Religion* 5, no. 2 (1987): 299–311.

———. "Prophetic Christianity and the Liberation Movement." *Journal of Modern African Studies* 29, no. 1 (1991): 27–60.

———. *Prophetic Christianity and the Liberation Movement in South Africa.* Pietermaritzburg: Cluster Publications, 1995.

———. *The Rise of African Nationalism in South Africa*. London: Christopher Hurst and Co., 1979.

Weber, Max. *Economy and Society,* ed. Guenther Roth and Claus Wittich. New York: Bedminster Press, 1968.

———. *The Protestant Ethic and the Spirit of Capitalism*. Trans. Talcott Parsons. New York: Charles Scribner's Sons, 1958.

———. "The Protestant Sects and the Spirit of Capitalism." In *From Max Weber: Essays in Sociology,* ed. H. H. Gerth and C. W. Mills. New York: Oxford University Press, 1946.

Wink, Walter. *Jesus' Third Way: The Relevance of Nonviolence in South Africa Today.* Johannesburg: SACC, 1987.

World Council of Churches. *From Cottesloe to Cape Town: Challenges for the Church in a Post-Apartheid South Africa*. Geneva: WCC Program to Combat Racism, 1991.

Primary Documents

SACBC Documents and Documents found in the Archives of the SACBC (noted as BCA)

Catholic Institute for International Relations. "Address by Mr. Niall MacDermot, Secretary General of the International Commission of Jurists, Geneva, to the Annual General Meeting of the Catholic Institute for International Relations." London: CIIR, June 1976. (BCA).

Catholic Institute for International Relations. "New Nation—Gagged: Silencing the People's Paper." London: CIIR, undated. (BCA).

"Catholics Explain Sanctions Stance." *New Nation* (December 13–19, 1991). (BCA).

End Conscription Campaign. "What is the End Conscription Campaign?" Pamphlet. 1985. (BCA).

Gaybba, Brian. "The Kairos Document: A Response." Unpublished paper. Undated (est. 1985). (BCA).

IMBISA (Inter-territorial Meeting of Bishops of Southern Africa). "The Prophetic Mission of the Church." IMBISA Plenary Assembly Report. 1983. (BCA).

IMBISA (Inter-territorial Meeting of Bishops of Southern Africa). "Report on the Situation in South Africa." Report to the IMBISA Plenary Assembly. 1987. (BCA).

Info SA 3, no. 1 (February 1988).

Internos (February 1987).

Internos (April 1987).

Internos (August 1987).

Internos (July–August 1990).

Kelly, O.P., Sr. Margaret. "The Catholic Church and Resistance to Apartheid." Unpublished paper. 1991. (BCA).

———. "South Africa in Transition and the Role of the Catholic Church 1989–1993. Unpublished paper. 1993. (BCA).

Lowry, Stephen. Letter written by Lowry, Secretary of the War and Peace Sub-committee of the SACBC Justice and Peace Commission. 1986. (BCA).

Naidoo, Archbishop Stephen. "A Request to the SACBC to Support the Call to End Conscription." Speech delivered to the 1985 SACBC Plenary Session. (BCA).

Nolan, Albert, and Richard Broderick. *To Nourish Our Faith: Theology of Liberation for*

Southern Africa. Proceedings from the 1986 Catholic Theological Winter School in Southern Africa. Compiled by the Southern African Order of Preachers. 1987.

"Pope Horrifies Priests." *Internos* (August/September 1984).

"The Popes on Apartheid." *Internos* (December 1987).

SACBC. *After the Fire: The Attack on Khanya House*. Pretoria: SACBC, 1989.

SACBC. *The Bishops Speak, 1952–1966*. Vol. 1. Pretoria: SACBC, 1980.

SACBC. *The Bishops Speak, 1967–1980*. Vol. 2. Pretoria: SACBC, 1980.

SACBC. *The Bishops Speak, 1981–1985*. Vol. 3. Pretoria: SACBC, 1989.

SACBC. *The Bishops Speak, 1986–1987*. Vol. 4. Pretoria: SACBC, 1989.

SACBC. "A Call to Build a New South Africa." Pastoral Letter of the Southern African Catholic Bishops' Conference. January 1992. (BCA).

SACBC Commission for Justice and Reconciliation. "Use of Church Buildings and Facilities." 1986 Plenary Session Report. (BCA).

SACBC Department of Justice and Reconcilation. "Memorandum Motivating the Need for a Justice and Peace Commission of the SACBC." Presentation to the 1981 SACBC Plenary Session. (BCA).

SACBC. "Discussion Booklet on Negotiations." February 1990.

SACBC. "Draft Documents for SACBC Discussion on the Question of Legitimacy," Paper 2. (BCA).

SACBC Justice and Peace Commission. "Negotiating for a Just South Africa." Undated paper. (BCA).

SACBC Justice and Peace Commission. "Proposal to the January Plenary Session RE: War in Namibia." Appendix 2. 1988. (BCA).

SACBC Justice and Peace News (August 1989).

SACBC Justice and Reconciliation Commission. "The Namibian Conflict." Presentation to the 1984 SACBC Plenary Session. (BCA).

SACBC. "Minutes of the 1987 Plenary Session." January 27–28. (BCA).

SACBC. "Minutes of the 1989 Plenary Session." August 21–25. (BCA).

SACBC. "Minutes of the 1990 Plenary Session." January 24–30. (BCA).

SACBC. "Minutes of the 1990 Plenary Session." August 6–10. (BCA).

SACBC. "N.S.M.S. and the Church." Unpublished paper. Undated. (BCA).

SACBC. "Pastoral Letter on the Occasion of the Centenary of the First Papal Encyclical on Social Justice—*Rerum Novarum*—and Its Implications for Negotiations in South Africa." Pretoria: SACBC, 1991. (BCA).

SACBC. "Report on the Extraordinary Plenary Session of the Southern African Catholic Bishops' Conference." April 29–May 1, 1986. (BCA).

SACBC. *Report on Namibia*. Pretoria: SACBC, 1982.

SACBC. "Some Results of the Hammanskraal Consultation for Future Use." Unpublished paper. March 1987. (BCA).

SACBC. "The Southern African Catholic Bishops' Conference." Undated pamphlet.

SACBC Theological Advisory Commission (TAC). "Civil Disobedience: Reflections of the TAC for SACBC Administrative Board." Unpublished paper. June 1988. (Connor).

SACBC TAC. "Discussion on Documents Presented to the Administrative Board Meeting." May 1989. (Connor).

SACBC TAC. "Freedom Charter." December 1987. (Connor).

SACBC TAC. "The Gospel and Apartheid." Unpublished paper. November 1987. (Connor).

278 *Bibliography*

SACBC TAC. "Minutes of the Theological Advisory Commission Meeting." March 11–12, 1987. (Connor).
SACBC TAC. "Minutes of the Theological Advisory Commission Meeting." June 10–11, 1987. (Connor).
SACBC TAC. "Minutes of the Theological Advisory Commission Meeting." November 2–4, 1987. (Connor).
SACBC TAC. "Minutes of the Theological Advisory Commission Meeting." March 23–24, 1988. (Connor).
SACBC TAC. "Minutes of the Theological Advisory Commission Meeting." June 6–7, 1988. (Connor).
SACBC TAC. "Minutes of the Theological Advisory Commission Meeting." March 15–16, 1990. (Connor).
SACBC TAC. "Pastoral Reflection on Certain Issues Raised by the Kairos Document." Unpublished paper. April 1986. (Connor).
SACBC TAC. "Report of Activities." January–December 1987. (Connor).
SACBC TAC. "Should the SACBC Become a Full Member of the SACC?" Unpublished study document. Undated (est. 1992). (Connor).
SACBC TAC. *The Things That Make for Peace.* Pretoria: SACBC, 1985.
SACBC. "What the Bishops Have Said So Far on the Question of Elections." Unpublished paper. 1988. (BCA).
"Study Document by the Justice and Peace Commission on the Pros and Cons of a Papal Visit." 1987. (BCA).
Trócaire. *South Africa Information Pack.* Dublin: Trócaire, undated. (BCA).

SACC Documents and Documents found in the Archives of the SACC (noted as CCA)

Baartman, Ernest. "Black Consciousness." *Pro Veritate* (March 1973). (CCA).
Bishopscourt Update (October 9, 1989). (CCA).
Bishopscourt Update (October 25, 1989). (CCA).
Bishopscourt Update (February 28, 1990). (CCA).
Bishopscourt Update (December 1990). (CCA).
Bishopscourt Update (October 15, 1991). (CCA).
Bishopscourt Update (June 19, 1992). (CCA).
Boesak, Allan. "The Declaration of Apartheid as a Heresy." The First Campbell Sermon, Cambridge, United Kingdom. 1984. (CCA).
Bosch, David J. "Submission to the Eloff Commission." February 1983. (CCA).
Buthelezi, Manas. "Black Theology and the Le-Grange-Schlebusch Commission." *Pro Veritate* 13 (October 1975). (CCA).
Cameron, Edwin. "Illegitimacy and Disobedience." Unpublished paper prepared for the CALS/ICT Seminar on The Legitimacy of Governments. 1987. (CCA).
Chikane, Frank. "The Churches and the South African Crisis." Pamphlet. London: CIIR, 1988.
———. "The Church's Prophetic Witness against the Apartheid System in South Africa (25th February–8th April, 1988)." *SACC Booklet.* Johannesburg: SACC, 1988. (CCA).
———. "Come Holy Spirit, Renew the Whole Creation—Update on the Crisis in South Africa." Speech given by Chikane. August 27, 1991. (CCA).

———. "General Secretary's Report to the 22nd National Conference." June 25–29, 1990. (CCA).

———. "General Secretary's Report to the 23rd National Conference." June 24–28, 1991. (CCA).

———. "General Secretary's Report to the 25th National Conference." July 5–9, 1993. (CCA).

———. "Kairos Which Way?" Talk given by Chikane. January 18, 1988. (CCA).

———. "Opening Address to the Convocation of Churches in South Africa." Address given by Chikane. May 30, 1988. (CCA).

———. "Report of the General Secretary to the National Executive Committee of the SACC." February 20–21, 1990. (CCA).

———. "Report of the General Secretary to the National Executive Committee of the SACC." March 12–13, 1991. (CCA).

———. "Report of the General Secretary to the National Executive Committee of the SACC." February 1992. (CCA).

———. "Report of the General Secretary to the National Executive Committee of the SACC." August 25, 1992. (CCA).

———. "Report of the General Secretary to the National Executive Committee of the SACC." November 24–25, 1992. (CCA).

———. "Review of our Sanctions and Disinvestment Strategies." Talk given by Chikane. April 17, 1991. (CCA).

———. "Update on the Crisis in South Africa." Speech given by Chikane. August 27, 1991. (CCA).

———. "1988: A Turning Point for the Church in South Africa." Opening address to the 1988 SACC National Conference. June 27, 1988. (CCA).

———. "25 Years of a Costly Struggle: A Vision for the Future." Opening address to the 25th National Conference. July 5, 1993.

Church Action in the South African Crisis. The South African Council of Churches National Conference Report. Johannesburg: SACC, 1988.

Ecunews (September 1981).

Ecunews 2 (1982).

Ecunews (February 1983).

Ecunews (August 1983).

Ecunews (October 1983).

Ecunews (February 1984).

Ecunews (March 1984).

Ecunews (September/October 1984).

Ecunews (March/April 1985).

Ecunews (May 1985).

Ecunews (June/July 1985).

Ecunews (April 1988).

Ecunews (June 1988).

Ecunews (July 1988).

Ecunews (August 1988).

Ecunews (October/November 1989).

Ecunews (December 1989).

Ecunews (January/February 1990).

Ecunews (October/November 1990).

Ecunews (December 1991).

Ecunews (November 1992).

Ecunews (March 1993).

Frost, Mervyn. "On the Question of the Legitimacy or Illegitimacy of the South African State." Unpublished paper prepared for the Conference on the Legitimacy of the South African State, Harare, Zimbabwe. September 1989. (CCA).

Gaybba, Brian. "The Characteristics of Heresy and the Defence of Apartheid as Christian." 1987. (CCA).

Jacob, Sol, ed. *Hope in Crisis.* SACC National Conference Report. Johannesburg: SACC, 1986.

Jacob, Sol, and Oswal Mtshali, eds. *Refugees and Exiles: Challenge to the Churches.* Report of the Nineteenth Annual National Conference of the South African Council of Churches. Johannesburg: SACC, 1987.

Kistner, Wolfram. "Response to the Evaluation of the Activities of the SACC Division of Justice and Reconciliation in the Memorandum of the South African Police Submitted to the Eloff Commission." SACC Submission to the Eloff Commission. Undated (est. 1982). (CCA).

Lamola, John. "Mediation Plus Prophecy Equals Facilitation." Unpublished paper. 1992. (CCA).

———. "The Role of Religious Leaders in Peacemaking and Social Change in Africa: The Case of South Africa." Unpublished paper. 1993. (CCA).

Lienemann, Wolfgang. Two untitled papers prepared for the Conference on the Legitimacy of the South African State, Harare, Zimbabwe. September 1989. (CCA).

Macozoma, Saki. "The Church and Negotiations." Paper read at the Standing for the Truth Campaign Workshop. March 7, 1990. (CCA).

Mutambirwa, James. "Update on South Africa." PCR press release. March 1990. (CCA).

Mutloatse, Mothobi. "Tlhagale Completes Sensitive Review on Black Consciousness." *Ecunews* (October 1983).

Nash, Margaret, ed. *Women—A Power for Change.* SACC National Conference Report. Johannesburg: SACC, 1985.

———. *Your Kingdom Come:* Papers and Resolutions of the 1980 SACC National Conference. Johannesburg: SACC, 1980.

Naudé, Beyers. "South Africa: The Current Situation and the Challenge Facing the Churches in Their Search for Justice and Peace." Report to the Lusaka Conference. 1987. (CCA).

Nolan, Albert. "Summary of Research on the Question of Legitimacy of the Government." Summary paper for the SACBC Plenary Session Study Day on the Legitimacy of the Government. 1987. (CCA).

"SACC Analysis: CODESA 2 Negotiations." SACC press release. May 25, 1992. (CCA).

SACC. "The Church Charged with Subversion." Pamphlet. October 1988.

SACC Constitution. June 1991. (CCA).

SACC. National Conference Resolutions. 1983. (CCA).

SACC. National Conference Resolutions. 1991. (CCA).

SACC. National Conference Resolutions. 1992. (CCA).

SACC. National Conference Resolutions. 1993. (CCA).

SACC National Executive Committee Report, May 26–27, 1992, appendix 4. "Conclusions of the Implementation Committee of the Emergency Summit on Violence Dealing with the Resolution on International Monitoring." May 7, 1992. (CCA).

"SACC Press Release on the Theology and Violence Workshop." November 30, 1987. (CCA).

SACC. "Proceedings from the SACC Consultation on Combating Racism." Unpublished conference proceedings. February 1980. (CCA).

SACC. "Report of the Emergency Convocation of Churches in South Africa." Unpublished paper. May 30, 1988. (CCA).

"SACC Restructures: Sacrifices, Agony and Ecstasy." *Ecunews* (December 1991).

SACC. *Senzenina [What have we done?]: The Day 300 Church Leaders, Clergy and Laity Marched on the South African Parliament.* Johannesburg: SACC, 1988. (CCA).

SACC. "South African Council of Churches: Ecumenical Co-operation for South Africa Today." Pamphlet. Johannesburg: SACC, undated.

SACC. "Standing for the Truth." Pamphlet. 1991.

SACC. "The Standing for the Truth Campaign." Pamphlet. 1988.

SACC. "Statement of a Consultation on the Legitimacy of the South African Government." Statement from the September 1989 Conference on Legitimacy. Harare, Zimbabwe. 1989. (CCA).

SACC. "Statement on WCC/SACC Meeting, 4–6 December." 1985. (CCA).

SACC. "A Theological Rationale and a Call to Prayer for the End to Unjust Rule." June 16 Memorial Service handout. 1986. (CCA).

SACC. "Toward a Code of Investment for South Africa: An Ethical Challenge." Unpublished paper. February 1992. (CCA).

"Should Pope John Paul II have Agreed to Meet the P.M?" *Ecunews* (September/October 1984).

"Statement of the Convocation of Christians Meeting in Johannesburg on 30–31 May 1988." Press Statement. 1988. (CCA).

Storey, Peter. "Here We Stand: Submission to the Commission of Inquiry into the South African Council of Churches by the Rev. Peter John Storey, President of the SACC on 9th March, 1983." *SACC Booklet.* Johannesburg: SACC, 1983. (CCA).

"Text of Black Confessing Church Statement." *SACC Justice and Reconciliation News* (July 1980). (CCA).

Thomas, David. *Investment in South Africa.* Report Submitted by the Division of Justice and Reconciliation to the SACC National Conference. Johannesburg: SACC, 1977. (CCA).

Tutu, Desmond. "The Divine Intention." Presentation by Bishop D. Tutu, General Secretary of the SACC to the Eloff Commission of Inquiry. Johannesburg: SACC, 1983. (CCA).

———. "The WCC, The SACC, and All That." Talk given by Tutu. November 23, 1978. (CCA).

Ukukhanya (Daily Publication of the 25th SACC National Conference). July 1993. (CCA).

Villa-Vicencio, Charles. "The Irreversibility of Change." Unpublished speech. Undated (est. 1991). (CCA).

Wing, Joseph. "Address to the 1982 SACC National Conference." *Ecunews* (July 1982): 16–20.

World Council of Churches. *The Churches' Search for Justice and Peace in Southern*

Africa: Report on Meeting in Lusaka, Zambia, 4–8 May, 1987. WCC Booklet. Geneva: WCC Program to Combat Racism, 1987. (CCA).

ICT Documents and Documents found in the Archives of the ICT (noted as CTA)

"Academic Honours for Albert." *ICT News* (December 1990).
Challenge (February 1992).
Challenge (September 1992).
Challenge (February 1993).
Chikane, Frank. "The State of the Nation: From Kairos to . . . Jubilee," *in Kairos '95: At the Threshold of Jubilee—A Conference Report*, ed. Themba Dladla. Johannesburg: ICT, 1996.
"Clergy Defy the Detainees Proclamations." *Crisis News* (April/May 1987). (CTA).
Cochrane, James. "The South African Church in the Present Context: A Balance of Forces." Unpublished speech delivered at the ICT's Emergency Conference on the Current Situation. August 17–21, 1992. (CTA).
Crisis News (September 1989). (CTA).
Crisis News (October 1989). (CTA).
de Gruchy, John W., James Cochrane, and Robin Petersen. "Towards a Practical Theology of Social Transformation." Paper presented at a Workshop on Practical Theology at the Federal Theological Seminary. February 10–12, 1988. (CTA).
Dladla, Themba, ed. *Kairos '95: At the Threshold of Jubilee—A Conference Report*. Johannesburg: ICT, 1996.
"ICT Annual General Meeting Conference Report." 1989. (CTA).
ICT Annual Report. 1983. (CTA).
ICT Annual Report. 1985. (CTA).
ICT Constitution. 1981. (CTA).
ICT. "Kairos for the Church in South Africa." Unpublished paper. 1990. (CTA).
ICT. "Minutes of an ICT Consultation: A New Kairos—What Is at Stake for the People of South Africa?" October 28–31, 1990. (CTA).
ICT. "Minutes of the 1990 Annual General Meeting." July 16–19, 1990.
ICT. "Negotiations, Defiance and the Church." Pamphlet published by the ICT and the Standing for the Truth Campaign. September 1989. (CTA).
ICT News (December 1984).
ICT News (December 1986).
ICT News (March 1986).
ICT News (December 1987).
ICT News (June 1988).
ICT News (December 1988/January 1989).
ICT News (December 1990).
ICT. "The Release of Nelson Mandela: Reading the Signs of Our Times." Pamphlet. March 1990. (CTA).
ICT. "Report on the 1990 Annual General Meeting." July 16–19, 1990. (CTA).
ICT. "Report on the 1992 Annual General Meeting." September 14–18, 1992. (CTA).
ICT. "What is Contextual Theology?" Brochure. Undated. (CTA).
Kritzinger, Johannes Nicolaas Jacobus. "Black Theology—Challenge to Mission." Doctoral dissertation, Pretoria, University of South Africa, 1988. (CTA).
Mkhatshwa, Smangaliso. "Black Priests Manifesto Revisited." *Challenge* (August 1991).

Nolan, Albert, O.P. "The Role of the Church in the Struggle for Negotiations and Democracy." Transcript of speech delivered at the ICT's Emergency Conference on the Current Situation. August 17–21, 1992. (CTA).

Schwarz, Walter. "Moment of Truth Arrives." *London Guardian* (October 18, 1985). (CTA).

Sparks, Allister. "Both Sides in South Africa Invoke Christianity." *Washington Post* (October 2, 1985). (CTA).

"What Others Say on Violence and Non-Violence." *Crisis News* (April/May 1988). (CTA).

Other Primary Documents

"Archbishop Hurley Spoke for All." *Southern Cross* (October 1983).

Daley, Suzanne. "Former South Africa Chief Admits Role in Terrorizing Blacks. *New York Times* (October 22, 1996).

de Gruchy, John W. "Democracy and the Church." IDASA Occasional Paper no. 5 (1987).

"Editorial: The Velcro Priest." *Weekly Mail and Guardian* (http://wn.apc.org/wmail/issues/). December 6, 1995.

Financial Mail (July 5, 1985).

Harbor, Anton. "United—In the Politics of Refusal." *Rand Daily Mail* (June 8, 1983).

Human Awareness Program. *Info '89*. Johannesburg: HAP, 1989.

Jacobs, Nancy Joy. "Consciousness, Liberation, and Revolution: Black Theology in South Africa." Master's thesis, Los Angeles, University of California, 1987.

Leatt, Jim. "The Church in Resistance Post 1976." Research paper for a Conference on South Africa beyond Apartheid. Boston. January 1987.

MacSwan, Angus (Reuters Online: Clarinews @ clarinet.com). "Tutu Appeals for Peace, Hails New South Africa." In (clari.world.africa.south_africa). April 24, 1994.

"Mbeki Gears Up." *Weekly Mail and Guardian* (http://wn.apc.org/wmail/issues/). March 20, 1997.

Moroke, Montshiwa. "Repeal of Acts 'Not Irreversible.'" *The Star* (June 26, 1991).

The Natal Mercury (September 22, 1986), p. 9.

Naudé, Beyers. "After Admission—What Next?" *Cross Times* (February 1991).

"New South Africa Fails Its Pensioners." *Weekly Mail and Guardian* (http://wn.apc.org/wmail/issues/). August 30, 1996.

The Pretoria News (March 2, 1983).

Serfontein, Hennie. "Chikane New SACC General Secretary." *The African Challenge* (August 1987).

"Targets Bopabe, Chikane, Dalling, 702's Robbie." *Weekly Mail and Guardian* (http://wn.apc.org/wmail/issues/). June 23, 1995.

Author's Interviews

Aitken, Marylynn. Former Secretary, Justice and Peace Commission, SACBC. Johannesburg, June 8, 1993.

Barnes, Pam. Personnel Director, SACC. Johannesburg, May 17, 1993.

Broderick, M.S.C., Richard. Johannesburg, June 9, 1993.

Chikane, Frank. General Secretary, SACC. Johannesburg, July 16, 1993.

Cochrane, James. University of Natal, Department of Religious Studies. Pietermaritzburg, July 13, 1993.

Connor, O.P., Bernard. Former Secretary, SACBC Theological Advisory Commission. Cape Town, March 31, 1993.

Duncan, Sheena. Former Vice-President, SACC. Johannesburg, July 30, 1993.

Gaybba, Brian. Rhodes University, Department of Religious Studies. Grahamstown, June 30, 1993.

Hurley, O.M.I., Denis. Former Archbishop of Durban; former President, SACBC. Durban, July 14, 1993.

Kearney, Paddy. Director, Diakonia. Durban, July 14, 1993.

Kekana, Khotso. Institute for Contextual Theology. Johannesburg, March 12, 1993.

Kelly, O.P., Margaret. Secretary, Justice and Peace Commission, SACBC. Pretoria, May 10, 1993.

Kistner, Wolfram. Ecumenical Advice Bureau; Former Secretary, Division of Justice and Reconciliation, SACC. Johannesburg, April 28, 1993.

Lamola, John. Secretary, Division of Justice and Reconciliation, SACC. Johannesburg, July 19, 1993.

Linden, Ian. General Secretary, Catholic Institute for International Relations. Notre Dame, Indiana, July 1992.

———. Written interview, July 15, 1994.

Mayson, Cedric. SACC. Johannesburg, May 28, 1993.

Mkhatshwa, Smangaliso. General Secretary, Institute for Contextual Theology; former General Secretary, SACBC. Johannesburg, June 8, 1993.

Napier, Wilfred. Archbishop of Durban; former President, SACBC. Durban, July 15, 1993.

Nolan, O.P., Albert. Institute for Contextual Theology. Johannesburg, March 4, 1993.

———. Johannesburg, March 12, 1993.

———. Johannesburg, June 17, 1993.

Naudé, Beyers. Ecumenical Advice Bureau; former General Secretary, SACC. Johannesburg, April 5, 1993.

Pieterse, Jude. General Secretary, SACBC. Pretoria, June 10, 1993.

Spong, Bernard. Communications Division, SACC. Johannesburg, May 7, 1993.

Tlhagale, Buti. Johannesburg, June 14, 1993.

Van Rensburg, Basil. Guguletu, Cape Town, June 25, 1993.

Villa-Vicencio, Charles. University of Cape Town, Department of Religious Studies. Cape Town, March 23, 1993.

———. Cape Town, June 23, 1993.

Index

About the Author

Tristan Anne Borer is Assistant Professor of Government at Connecticut College and the author of a number of articles on South Africa.